Sexuality and the Unnatural in Colonial Latin America

Sexuality and the Unnatural in Colonial Latin America

Edited by

Zeb Tortorici

UNIVERSITY OF CALIFORNIA PRESS

University of California Press, one of the most distinguished university presses in the United States, enriches lives around the world by advancing scholarship in the humanities, social sciences, and natural sciences. Its activities are supported by the UC Press Foundation and by philanthropic contributions from individuals and institutions. For more information, visit www.ucpress.edu.

University of California Press
Oakland, California

Library of Congress Cataloging-in-Publication Data

Names: Tortorici, Zeb, 1978– editor.
Title: Sexuality and the unnatural in colonial Latin America / edited by Zeb Tortorici.
Description: Oakland, California : University of California Press, [2016] | Includes bibliographical references and index.
Identifiers: LCCN 2015037516 | ISBN 978-0-520-28814-0 (cloth : alk. paper) | ISBN 978-0-520-28815-7 (pbk. : alk. paper) | ISBN 978-0-520-96318-4 (ebook)
Subjects: LCSH: Sex—Latin America—History. | Sex and law—Latin America—History. | Sex—Latin America—Religious aspects—History. | Sex crimes—Latin America—History. | Latin Americans—Sexual behavior—History.
Classification: LCC HQ18.L29 S497 2016 | DDC 306.7098—dc23
LC record available at http://lccn.loc.gov/2015037516

Manufactured in the United States of America

25 24 23 22 21 20 19 18 17 16
10 9 8 7 6 5 4 3 2 1

In keeping with a commitment to support environmentally responsible and sustainable printing practices, UC Press has printed this book on Natures Natural, a fiber that contains 30% post-consumer waste and meets the minimum requirements of ANSI/NISO Z39.48-1992 (R 1997) *(Permanence of Paper)*.

To María Elena Martínez, whose work has pushed the boundaries of queer historical scholarship in radical and imaginative ways.

CONTENTS

FOREWORD

Asunción Lavrin

Zeb Tortorici's request of a foreword for this volume led me to delve into my own "archeological" memory as a historian. Although most of the time I am reluctant to engage in that exercise, I have to confess that in this instance it has proven more interesting than I anticipated. It has brought up dusted personal memories and engaged me in assessing my own generation's contribution to the shaping of a field of studies that is flourishing today.

In the early 1980s, historians of colonial Latin America tentatively began to write on topics of sexual behavior, and in 1989 I published my own anthology, *Sexuality and Marriage in Colonial Latin America,* the first English-language edited collection dedicated to the topic. Not long ago, Zeb told me that this anthology, along with the work of Pete Sigal, served as inspiration for him to enter the field of sexuality in colonial Latin America and expand it—as *Sexuality and the Unnatural in Colonial Latin America* certainly does. Whether or not my own volume had an equally stimulating effect on others is not for me to judge; as I remember, I was not planning to do more than open a dialogue. When I called on colleagues to help put together that volume, I did not see myself as a revolutionary person in the field of gender and sexuality, but simply as someone who wished to extend the field of women's studies in ways that historians in other fields were already doing and to respond to some of the questions posed by research materials with which I was acquainted. It was important for me to link the concepts in the title—*sexuality* and *marriage*—and make clearer their existential bond. First there was sexuality: marriage came after that. It was not a revolutionary concept. Rather, it reflected the reality that others and I were finding in the colonial archives.

At the time, addressing the issue implicit in the title demanded a collective effort. Although in Mexico and other places in Latin America researchers were addressing the challenges of sexual behavior, the field was growing slowly and there were simply not enough studies to guide anyone. I was happy to work with a team of equally interested colleagues for whom the adventure into the field of sexuality was just as new and exciting as it was for me.

Certain assumptions in the type of historical inquiry that developed in the 1970s begged a second look when it came to sexuality and marriage. By the 1980s, analysis of the racial and age profiles of duly-wedded partners to arrive at marriage patterns was the main preoccupation of social and quantitative historians. I thought someone needed to point out that sex in colonial Latin America was not only part of marriage, but it took place outside of marriage as well. In other words, marriage was simply the key consequence of sexuality in a society that used the legal and religious bonding of men and women to legitimize social aspirations and gendered hierarchies and to comply with religious obligations that blessed the oft-unspoken yet obligatory carnal union. Where was the "flesh," the passion and desire, that I found registered in the historical archives? How might we explain the high patterns of out-of-wedlock births discovered by quantitative historians? Since wedded sex was not the only expression of human sexuality, why could we not approach sex outside of wedlock as a legitimate expression of behavior? Once we posed those questions, the gate of curiosity was opened wide, not only for me and my collaborators, but for future generations of scholars in what eventually became a "field" of history.

At the time, however, although all of us had heard and read about bestiality, sodomy, masturbation, and incest, few had had the courage to write about such topics. Would such scholarship be "publishable" in traditionally respected and peer-reviewed journals? If the study of "women" as a subject was still facing some displeased grunts from well-known editors, imagine what response an article discussing anal sex or coitus interruptus would have elicited from editorial boards! Even today some readers express distaste for the "disgusting" or "unnatural" activities of people who lived several centuries ago, located outside prescribed forms of sexual expression.

Thus, as beginners in the game we edged slightly away from such topics and remained within the space of "lust" and its consequences but still somewhat shy of the "beyond." Yet once one poses questions about the "sins" and "crimes" exposed by ecclesiastical tribunals, inquisitorial judges, and civil courts, there can be no return to pious and bland acceptance of marriage as the only venue for sexual engagement. All that was needed was a green light, a signal that, indeed, we should look beyond the values dictated by arbiters of human behavior in the past, be they twentieth-century historians or colonial theologians and jurists. *Sexuality and Marriage* gave many that green light to enter into more challenging territories, and I am glad it performed that role.

It is satisfying to state that in the last two decades historians of sexuality have made great strides in seeking answers relevant to our times. The new generation coming to maturity in the early twenty-first century is now in charge of ensuring that this field remains open and continues to widen. No longer will the history of patterns of marriage define the only "sexual" behavior of people in the past, though there is historiographical merit in such studies as well. I see the new trends in the history of sexuality helping us to learn more about intimacy and affection or love (as well as their ties to violence or coercion), in whatever forms they took. The history of emotions is coming of age and taking us to frontiers and landscapes that are quite different from the more aseptic studies that simply quantified marriage, concubinage, and illegitimate births. In other words, we are seeing a fuller rendition of life at both microhistorical and macrohistorical levels.

The degrees of knowledge about intimacy and sexuality achieved by current studies are possible only because of records that lingered on them, provided by precisely those who were supposed to hide them from public view. Who knows to what other purpose historical actors intended archival documents and their narratives to be put? The Mexican Inquisition files detailing the late-sixteenth-century torrid love affair of chaplain Father Plata and Sor Agustina of the Conceptionist convent in Mexico City, for example, were, when I came upon them, completely worn out by use, with many pages out of place—a fact that suggests nineteenth-century readers were fascinated too by the libidinous details of the past. Colonial inquisitors, theologians, and jurists were also connoisseurs of human sexuality! Now we share some of their privileged knowledge. Sexuality studies today are a positive reaffirmation that no matter how hard civil laws and religious tenets tried to repress sexual behavior, men and women managed to express themselves as they saw fit and natural to themselves, even though their behavior was at times contradictory and laced with guilt.

As a historian, I expect that the study of accepted male-female sexuality as acknowledged by secular and ecclesiastical canons in the past will also be enriched by the study of what was regarded as deviant, perverse, or unnatural. Neither "natural" nor "unnatural" has an unshakable definition, after all. Reaching that conclusion, however, is the result of learning more about what we do as historians. The people that we encounter in the archives are real actors who experienced intimacy. We are reading into what was a reality in the past, paying attention to what people did, not just what they said. If such an endeavor challenges the assumptions of the authorities, canons, and even us historians, so be it. Such a wealth of human ambiguity exists under the rigid categorizations; disregarding it would only impoverish our visions of the past. This means we must acknowledge the existence of "low," popular understandings of sexuality vis-à-vis "high," institutional ones, of private and personal perceptions that face and interact with public ones. We are acknowledging that intimacy—when revealed—rewards us with a fuller view of human behavior and promotes a more satisfying view of all of us, then and now.

I can see many possibilities in the development of the new history of sexuality that go beyond the more modest parameters historians set several decades ago. We now have a broad spectrum of behaviors to study and analyze: pre- and post-conquest peoples of all social and ethnic groups speak to us as full protagonists of colonial Latin American history. The new history of sexuality is not narrowly defined by sexual behavior, however. It embraces symbolic as well as real expressions of human bonding; it connects the secular with the religious, the juridical with the artistic, and the mundane with the philosophical. It leads us to reexamine other topics that are taking shape in colonial history, such as the cultural meanings of masculinity and femininity, shame and honor, the gendered symbols of power in public and private scenarios, and others that seemed unimaginable only a few decades ago. We are no longer buckling under the pressure of prescribed straightforward sexuality or accepting the social and theological rejection of so-called unnatural acts and relationships in all their nuance. If in previous centuries some people discharged their own inhibitions and prejudices on the activities of others, we no longer can afford to do so. Returning to my own views and experience, I see that we have dropped much of our academic and personal uncertainty about the reception of research on sexuality of all orientations within the discipline of history. This volume suggests that we can now go well beyond past configurations of religious and legal sources and, in the process, open up to topics that appeared threatening decades ago. This is a welcome change.

ACKNOWLEDGMENTS

The works of so many scholars in the field of gender and sexuality in colonial Latin America have been inspirational, and I wish to thank those who first drew me into the field: Louise M. Burkhart, Israel Burshatin, John F. Chuchiak, Martha Few, Serge Gruzinski, David Higgs, Jacqueline Holler, Nora Jaffary, Asunción Lavrin, Sonya Lipsett-Rivera, María Elena Martínez, Luiz Mott, Martin Nesvig, Lee Penyak, Matthew Restall, Barry D. Sell, Pete Sigal, Lisa Sousa, Ann Twinam, and Ronaldo Vainfas, among many others. The contributors to this volume have been a constant encouragement to me, and it has been a pleasure to work with them. I'd also like to thank those scholars with whom I have discussed and debated the contours of sodomy and desire across time and place, especially Leah DeVun, Héctor Domínguez-Ruvalcaba, Veronica de Jesus Gomes, Nathan Ha, Jonathan Ned Katz, Jolie Olcott, Saeyoung Park, Hiram Pérez, Yarí Pérez Marín, Helmut Puff, Jens Rhydström, Matthew Sommer, Laura Stokes, and Danielle Terrazas Williams.

Like most anthologies, this project was many years in the making. Throughout the entire process I was immersed in conversations with Daniel Marshall and Kevin P. Murphy about our "Queering Archives" project, which has very much influenced my approach to thinking about bodies, desires, and colonial archives here and elsewhere. I always look forward to our ongoing (and quite possibly never ending!) Skype conversations.

I am especially grateful to Kate Marshall, acquisitions editor at the University of California Press, who has been immensely supportive of this project since I first mentioned it to her. Without her help and the help of the wonderful UC Press staff— Stacy Eisenstark, Zuha Khan, Ryan Furtkamp, and Rose Vekony—this book never would have seen the light of day. I also extend my gratitude to two anonymous readers for UC Press, whose generous feedback and suggestions were invaluable to me and to the book's contributors. All authors are appreciative of good editorial advice, and Anne Canright's nuanced editing of the book manuscript has strengthened each of the chapters of this anthology. Any final errors in the book are, of course, those of the authors. Claudia Smelser at UC Press designed the beautiful cover of this book based on a manuscript that I first saw at the Lilly Library at Indiana University, where I held the Everett Helm Visiting Fellowship in the summer of 2015. I am grateful to the Lilly Library for permission to use this image, and especially to Nile Arena, David Frasier, and Kristin Leaman for their help navigating the library's manuscripts and special collections. Finally, I sincerely thank Roger Gathman for his careful editorial comments and suggestions on the introduction.

Participation in the NYU Humanities Initiative in 2013–14 gave me the precious time to make progress on this book. I am truly thankful to director Jane Tylus, Gwynneth C. Malin, and my former Fellows—especially Ademide Adelusi-Adeluyi, Dwai Banerjee, J. DeLeon, Dania Hueckmann, Thomas Looser, Eduardo Matos Martin, Ara Merjian, Andrew Romig, Cara Shousterman, and Delia Solomons—for such a phenomenal, productive, and fun year. I am also grateful to the NYU Center for the Humanities for a Grant-in-Aid that supported this book.

Numerous friends and interlocutors from UCLA, Tulane University, Stanford University, and New York University have made researching, writing, and teaching the history of sexuality over the years an absolute pleasure. For their willingness to engage my scholarship, extraordinary thanks go to Gabriela Basterra, Bryan Cameron, Ben Cowan, Robin Derby, Gigi Dopico-Black, Jim D. Fernández, Xóchitl Flores, Frederico Freitas, Helaine Gawlica, Gabriel Giorgi, Rebecca Goetz, Jonathan Gómez Núñez, Robinson Herrera, Cristel Jusino Díaz, Karen Krahulik, Jo Labanyi, Jill Lane, Francisco Marguch, Enmanuel Martínez, Osdany Morales, Alejandro Moreno Jashés, Rocío Pichon Rivière, Paul Ramírez, Rubén Ríos-Ávila, Dylon Robbins, Danielle Roper, Teo Ruiz, Abel Sierra Madero, Diana Taylor, Marvin J. Taylor, Kevin Terraciano, Laura Torres, Irina Troconis, Dana Velasco Murillo, Emmanuel Velayos, Leif Weatherby, Mir Yarfitz, Ari Zighelboim, and many others. I was lucky to have had Marcelo Carosi, Pilar Espitia, Tess Rankin, and Laura Vargas in "Queer Colonial Latin America," my first graduate seminar at New York University in the fall of 2012. Their generous and provocative conversations shaped the directions that this book eventually took.

Finally, much of this project was written, compiled, translated, and revised in the company (and homes!) of Erik Fritz, Osvaldo Gómez, Gela Frutis Huesca, Scott Lucas, Yuki and Reiko Maeda, David Sada, Elza Wang, Jonathan Yaffe, my parents, Roberta and Liberato Tortorici, and my sister and brother-in-law, Lisa and Adam Hohnbaum. I am, of course, eternally grateful to Su Anne Takeda (and her family). I thank everyone for their immense encouragement and support over the years.

Introduction

Unnatural Bodies, Desires, and Devotions

Zeb Tortorici

In the 1595 edition of Alonso López de Hinojosos's *Summa y recopilación de cirugía, con un arte para sangrar, y examen de barberos*—one of the earliest medical treatises to be published in New Spain (the first edition was from 1578)—the author devotes a lengthy section to various gynecological and obstetrical issues having to do with the female body. The ninth book in the treatise, "On the Difficulty of Childbirth" *(De la dificultad del parto)*, which is divided into thirteen chapters, focuses on such topics as why some women cannot conceive, the signs of pregnancy, the fragile formation of the fetus within the womb, and various remedies for uterine and menstrual problems. Notions of Nature and sexuality are, perhaps unsurprisingly, central to López de Hinojosos's explication of the proper and improper functioning of the human body in both sickness and health, all of which brings up a problem: to what extent can the human body, according to López de Hinojosos—or according to other medics, theologians, judges, and officials in the early modern and modern Iberian Atlantic world—deviate from Nature? How might the fetus stray from the "natural" course of intrauterine physiological development, and how might such alterations be brought on by Nature itself? How does López de Hinojosos invoke notions of Nature and the unnatural in ways that both confirm and challenge other manifestations of "Nature" and the "unnatural" that were espoused by the author's contemporaries in the realms of science, medicine, law, and religion?

Chapter four of the ninth book, "How the Seeds Are Fomented, and How the Child Is Nourished in Its Mother's Womb" *(Como se formentan las simientes, y se alimenta el niño en el vientre de su madre)*, concerns the formation and development of the fetus and the deviations that can occur in this process. Beginning with

1

conception, López de Hinojosos informs his readers that after sex, the seeds of the man and the woman are united inside the womb, and that six days after "fomentation," the milky admixture covers the *télica*—a weblike tissue that, according to the author, "is the first membrane that nature *[naturaleza]* ordered for many things: the first so that these seeds do not become separated, because from every tiny bit of these seeds will raise a child, or a monster."[1] In this way, López de Hinojosos poses the question of what accounts for the differences between humanity and monstrosity, and in particular, what role Nature plays in the differentiation.

What the authors in *Sexuality and the Unnatural in Colonial Latin America* are generally concerned with is the matrix of assumptions and questions posed not just in the example I have chosen from López de Hinojosos, but by the entire intellectual and conceptual order of the early modern and modern Iberian Atlantic world: How does Nature come to order the body, and how does the body come to order (or disorder) the ontological boundaries of Nature? How were Nature and its range of possible counterparts—the "unnatural" and that which theologians and judges deemed "against nature" *(contra natura)*—inextricably interconnected and wrapped up in all of the complex and often contradictory significations of the other? What distinguished a "child" from a "monster," and what ways could one read the human body as evidence to articulate and enunciate such differentiations?

López de Hinojosos, to an extent, is also trying to answer these questions, and in so doing merges Nature, the body, sex, and gender in multiple ways. Shortly after introducing the categorical differences between the *niño* and the *monstruo*—the child and the monster—in the course of fetal development, he describes how, during the first weeks of pregnancy, organs of the fetus begin to take shape, develop, and interact with one another. He writes that customarily

> the liver sends veins and nutritive blood to the heart and to the brain, and the brain sends nerves to the liver and to the heart, and the heart sends spirited blood to the rest of the members, and in that way each one communicates its virtue to the other, and the child comes to be formed, and if after thirty days it has sufficient heat and the other necessary dispositions, God instills the soul, and it is a man; and if it lacks a degree of heat, a woman comes out and [she is] manly who speaks like a man *[muger y hombruda que abla como hombre]*, and has the conditions of a man, and if there is a lack of heat, this passes at sixty days; and if at the time of animation [of the soul] a degree of heat rises, a man is made, and it is a womanly man, that speaks like a woman *[y es hombre amarionado, que habla como muger]*.[2]

This passage demonstrates how, for the author, Nature can construe its Other—the ambiguous and "unnatural"—by a mere change of the settings of degrees of heat within the womb, and by failing to properly differentiate the cold and wet nature of women from the hot and dry nature of men. Here, López de Hinojosos employs the vocabulary of the theories of bodily humors espoused by Aristotle and Galen to explain the *muger hombrudo* ("manly woman") or the *hombre amarionado* ("womanly man") in terms of lack or excess of heat inside the womb. Yet as Jonathan Goldberg has demonstrated, while such terms remain partly untranslatable between the medieval and early modern contexts and the Spanish lexicon of today, they are nonetheless inextricable from notions of deviant and unnatural sexuality.[3] The early modern Hispanic categories of cross-gendered behavior and illegible bodies that López de Hinojosos discusses here intimate sodomitical sexual desires, illicit gendered presentation, and, at the extreme, even hermaphroditism.

Here, we witness how López de Hinojosos's medical knowledge of the bodily humors and their possible mixtures, which allow for dry cold manly women and moist hot womanly men, purposefully affixes itself to notions of monstrosity and to unnatural sexes, bodies, and desires. Nature and the unnatural intimately commingle, in a process that strips these categories of their assumed oppositional values. As the passage above demonstrates, Nature can simultaneously order and disorder, create and pervert, reproduce and thwart reproduction. López de Hinojosos carries this paradox into his language at this point: the organs and physiologies of human reproduction, such as the umbilical cord that carries nutrients, the developmental interaction between the fetus and the mother, the moment of conception, and the subsequent development of the fetus all amount to an *artificio admirable*, or an "admirable artifice" of Nature itself. In López de Hinojosos's understanding of things, Nature is an *artifice*—cunning, clever, and occasionally insincere and deceptive, insofar as that which is natural gives rise to that which is unnatural, using Nature's materials and sustained by Nature's processes. In this way, Nature holds its authority but undermines its conceptual definition, showing itself to be both artful and deceitful. This logical paradox is not idiosyncratic with López de Hinojosos: for innumerable medieval and early modern theologians, jurists, and medical experts, Nature's deceit came to be grafted onto the ways that bodies were read, interpreted, and imagined in their varied states of lust and unbridled passion. López de Hinojosos's text is merely clearer than many others in showing us the elasticity of the concept of Nature, which nonetheless maintains its sovereignty, just as it did in the Iberian Atlantic legal and theological spheres.

Indeed, when studying the Spanish regulation of "unnatural" sexual practices, we are confronted by terms that are the work of a long institutionalized chain of reasoning that goes back to the early Church Fathers like Saint Augustine and medieval theologians like Thomas Aquinas. As early as the fifth century, Saint Augustine influentially deemed unnatural and sinful those sexual acts that did not take place in a "vessel fit for procreation."[4] Regarding sodomy, bestiality, masturbation, and unnatural sexual positions between men and women—all "vices against nature" included in the category of *luxuria* (lust)—Aquinas in his thirteenth-century *Summa Theologica* wrote: "Just as the order of right reason is from man, so the order of nature is from God himself. And so in sins against nature, in which the very order of nature is violated, an injury is done to God himself, the orderer of nature."[5] Since, as Asunción Lavrin notes, voluntary pollution "contravened the Church's view that seminal emission must be carried into the female vagina *(intra vas naturale)* for the purpose of procreation," masturbation, sodomy, and bestiality, all forms of voluntary pollution, must be sins defined by the Church's view of what was and what wasn't in accordance with Nature and "natural" desire.[6]

Ultimately, Lavrin observes, "all sexual activity approved by the Church had one avowed and legitimate purpose: the perpetuation of the human species."[7] Nature, in this view, is an eminently teleological structure within which proper sexual desire was not the desire for the sexual act itself but, instead, the desire for the ideal result of that act: procreation. In this way the "sins against nature," which were delineated in social terms as contravening the institutions of marriage and the family, were then elaborated ontologically as the perversion of the true purpose of sexuality, procreation. Yet this casuistic reasoning involved inherent contradictions, as a close examination of López de Hinojosos's text shows. Nature can sometimes operate outside of the teleological structure that supposedly defines it, creating on its own the bodies and desires that, at least in the view of the Catholic Church, could impede the impetus to reproduce among humans and other animals.[8] Acts such as masturbation, sodomy, and bestiality, which did not have procreative aims, still used Nature's materials and processes. Thus the "unnatural" as a category was formed out of this inflection of Nature, allowing these things to be labeled and demonized by the Church and punished by ecclesiastical and secular authorities throughout the medieval and early modern European world.

In this way, in both medieval and early modern Europe at the onset of the sixteenth century, theologians and jurists could with good conscience obsessively invoke the notions of "Nature" and the "unnatural" to mark out difference on the bodies of others. The theologians, jurists, doctors, and natural philosophers of colonial Latin America, as the chapters in this volume attest, were no exceptions to this rule. For that reason, it is essential to examine the genealogy of the term *contra natura* ("against nature"), which was frequently employed in criminal and Inquisition cases from early modern Spain, Portugal, and their respective overseas colonies. The term *contra natura*, as several chapters in this anthology show, was alive and well in the legal lexicon up through the nineteenth century, leaving its mark on the legal codes of the new nations forged from the Spanish and Portuguese colonies' struggle for independence. The framers of these new laws often based their legal reasoning on colonial, early modern, and even medieval codes. As Lorraine Daston and Fernando Vidal note, "The derivatives of the Latin *natura* in modern European languages have notoriously long and rich definitions, and their common Latin root itself derives many of its connotations from the Greek *physis*, which has its own convoluted semantic history."[9] In tracing the polysemic nature of *natura* in the legal, religious, and popular spheres, we gain a better sense of those rich and convoluted definitions.

The mere fact that the Spanish word *natura* ("nature") in the medieval, early modern, and modern contexts had so many definitions attests to its complexity, which can be seen, specifically, in the way it applied simultaneously to the exteriority and interiority of the human body. In the sixteenth century, European priests and missionaries arrived in the Americas carrying a notion of Nature with a long genealogy, and with rich definitions stemming from a common Latin root, *natura*. Logically, this also entailed a priori understandings of the unnatural, in part stemming from "natural law," which had been defined by Aquinas as a set of fundamental principles *(prima praecepta)* granted by God and understood by all "rational creatures."[10] The Europeans sought to impose upon the indigenous inhabitants of what eventually came to be the Spanish and Portuguese viceroyalties, demarcated in theory by the 1494 Treaty of Tordesillas, a code that, on the one hand, defined Nature as originating outside of the human being and, on the other, defined nature as that which was interior to the human self. Nature—both *natura* and *naturaleza*—was itself complex, imprecisely defined, and riddled with subtleties, as can be seen by the mere fact that it was something both exterior and interior to all living beings.

Natura was also fixed onto the body, as the frequent use of the term *vaso natural* ("natural vessel")—regularly used to denote the vagina in medical and theological treatises, criminal cases, and Inquisition documents of the early modern Iberian world—shows. Similarly, the anus, in this semantic system, is put in opposition to the *vaso natural*. The rectum of a man or a woman was referred to as the *vaso contra natura*—the "vessel contrary to nature." The phrase *pecado contra natura* ("sin against nature") is in the same family as these terms. The possibility of procreation is what determines the logic of *natura* and its derivatives in both anatomy and jurisprudence. Yet it is not only *natura* but also its derivatives that signify the body in both its normal state and its excesses—much like the bodies López de Hinojosos described in the sixteenth century. Such is the case with *naturaleza*, for instance. The 1726 version of the *Diccionario de la lengua castellana* defines *naturaleza* primarily as "the essence and natural being of any thing," and secondarily in relation to the geography and physical environment of a given place.[11] However, along with these abstractions, *naturaleza* also incorporates both animals and procreative sexuality within its definition. One of the latter definitions of *naturaleza*, for example, refers specifically to the "temperament of the qualities in the physical body of an animal: in this sense it is said that one is of a dry nature, a cold nature, etc."[12] The *Diccionario* also notes that *naturaleza* may be used in reference to genitals, especially those of women.

The coupling of nature and sexuality comes out in a variety of phrases. *Alterarse la naturaleza*—to alter one's nature—refers to the physiological changes that came about when a man felt sexually excited. In yet another twist of the term, the opposite of an *hijo legítimo*—a legitimate child—is an *hijo natural*, a child born out of

Overlapping meanings

wedlock.[13] As these diverse meanings attest, within the family of uses of *naturaleza* and its cognates, we find not a central signifier, but rather a term that seems to bifurcate at every turn, and to lend itself both to the essence of things and to a moral order among things, creating an overlap that reaches deep into the colonial mindset. And so it comes about that Nature touches on all beings and objects, the physical environment, the temperament of animals, the genitals of males and of females, and procreative sexuality, without gathering these disparate ideas under one central conceptual category. One of the primary goals of this book, therefore, is to disentangle and unravel the convoluted definitions and connotations of Nature and the unnatural that traverse the European side of the discourses of colonial Latin America and the wider Iberian Atlantic world. Together, these essays recast Iberian Atlantic cultural history through the prism of "sins against nature," showing that the colonial perspective often relied on the unnatural as a fundamental category of difference.

As we have seen in my observations on López de Hinojosos's sixteenth-century discussion of procreative sexuality, with its attendant aspects of conception, pregnancy, and childbirth, the concepts of the natural and unnatural are bound together in a complex configuration that are not always defined in opposition to one another. Nature and the unnatural assume different relations to one another at different moments. While one might facilely assume that the category of the unnatural was simply derived from the negation of the natural, this is misleading. In an important study on sodomy in Reformation Germany and Switzerland, Helmut Puff writes that it would be difficult to "render precisely what magistrates and officials imagined as nature's 'other' when they employed *contra naturam* in its vernacular variants. As a phrase, the concept 'against nature' invoked the supreme authority of God in order to justify the harshest of responses to an act deemed criminal."[14] We might pose this same dilemma for the early modern Iberian Atlantic world, as *natura, naturaleza*, and their "others" were imbued with multiple, overlapping, and occasionally contradictory meanings by medics, scholars, jurists, judges, priests, and theologians.

What, then, was Nature's "other" in the context of colonial Latin America and the wider Iberian Atlantic world? Nature, in all of its convoluted definitions, is of central concern to the chapters of this book, but even more so is the *un*-natural potential inhering in the imbrication of bodies, desires, and devotions in the views of secular and ecclesiastical authorities. In their explorations of the "sins against nature," most historians of the early modern Iberian Atlantic world have tended to privilege same-sex sexual acts (with a primary focus on male-male intimacies or male "homosexuality"), thereby obscuring the multiplicity of desires found under this rubric and their ambiguities. This anthology therefore seeks to open up the category of the unnatural by exploring a wider variety of nonprocreative corporeal acts that approximated the unnatural, without necessarily being officially designated as such. The chapters of this anthology deal both with those acts that were technically considered to be unnatural heresies and crimes against nature—masturbation, sodomy, bestiality, and unnatural sexual positions—and with crimes that bordered on the unnatural, such as incest, solicitation in the confessional, sex with the Devil, abortion and infanticide, erotic desecration of holy images, and suicide.

The first chapter, "Archival Narratives of Clerical Sodomy and Suicide from Eighteenth-Century Cartagena" by Nicole von Germeten, interrogates the conceptual framework of the natural/unnatural very consciously in the tradition of Natalie Zemon Davis and other practitioners of microhistory. Focusing on the region of New Granada, von Germeten looks at the case of an eighteenth-century Mercedarian friar, Esteban Sobrino, whose eventual suicide in the prison of the Inquisition was closely tied to the circulation of rumors about his solicitation of sexual favors from women and men in the confessional. During the course of his trial, Sobrino confessed to having touched six young boys, bringing them to orgasm; yet he swore that his acts stemmed from affection and a "sincere and honest love" rather than from lust, impure thoughts, or malice. In analyzing the priest's confession, von Germeten shows how the priest's defense operated at numerous points along the natural-unnatural spectrum, for "with his words he tried to render these acts natural, innocent, and harmless for both himself and the boys." Through her analysis of the archival record, von Germeten shows how, following Sobrino's suicide in 1779, inquisitors and clergymen colluded to protect the local church's reputation partly by construing a rhetorical narrative that minimized the severity of Sobrino's "unnatural" desires and sexual acts, which spanned a broad panorama from lustful acts with women to sodomitical acts with men. This exploration of a case shows how often the natural and the unnatural, the orthodox and the heterodox, and the criminal and the heretical overlapped.

From von Germeten's sophisticated reading of inquisitorial archival narratives we move, in the chapters by Nora Jaffary and Jacqueline Holler, to the topic of eroticized religiosity and acts of desecration among nuns, beatas, and laywomen in colonial Mexico. Jaffary's chapter also engages microhistory, delving into the fascinating eighteenth-century Inquisition case of a poor young woman in Mexico City, María Getrudis Arévalo, to reveal how devotion, desecration, religious doubt, and unnatural desires converged. Arévalo, perhaps not unlike others in the Iberian Atlantic world, was riddled with doubt about the existence of God and the validity of miracles, and began to take vengeance on God, Jesus, the Virgin Mary, the saints, and the Church in a symbolically and corporeally charged fashion. Arévalo engaged in escalating acts of desecration, such as taking communion immediately after having sex, inserting the rosary or the Eucharist into her "suspicious part" (parte sospechosa) and her "filthy vessel" (vaso inmundo), and applying religious engravings to "the most indecent parts of her body." Interestingly, as

Jaffary shows, Mexican inquisitors appear *not* to have been overly concerned with such corporeal forms of sacramental desecration, a finding that has been echoed by recent scholars who work on the intersections of heresy and sexuality. Jaffary's focus on inquisitorial disinterest forces us to question whether the reading and interpretation of female sexuality in the colonial period through the lens of transgression is anachronistic. This chapter ultimately complicates our understandings of the Holy Office of the Mexican Inquisition, demonstrating that inquisitors did not view all that was "against nature"—in this instance, masturbation and eroticized religiosity—as threatening, disruptive, or subversive. Jaffary's contribution can also be seen as an extension of her scholarship on false mysticism *(alumbradismo),* medicalized sexuality, eroticized devotional practices, abortion and infanticide, and monstrous childbirths—all of which does much to advance our knowledge of the conceptual and practical boundaries of Nature and the unnatural in colonial Mexico.[15]

Holler, in turn, examines a fascinating corpus of Mexican Inquisition cases in which the Devil, through the phenomenon of the demonic pact *(pacto con demonio),* became an ideal "lover" for some women. Many of the cases culminate in explicit sexual interactions between the women and their diabolical consort. Holler demonstrates that both the women *and inquisitors* viewed sex with the Devil as commonplace, expressive of female desire (and other emotions such as melancholia), and governed by the gendered norms of colonial society. Here, the binary of Nature and the unnatural was employed in surprising and unexpected ways at both popular and learned levels of colonial society, framing a narrative in which the Devil figures as a handsome, young, and virile lover. Here we can see one of the unexpected twists of the ideology of the natural: demonic copulation was framed by many of the women who initiated demonic pacts as being potentially procreative, which would align it with Nature. At the same time, Holler shows that "unnatural demonic lust provided essential proof of the workings of the sacred and the demonic in everyday life." Demonic sex was therefore at the same time completely radical and entirely mundane. Affective and physical encounters with the Devil temporarily allowed these women—through an assimilation of the natural, the unnatural, and the supernatural—to enact heterosexual coupling more perfectly than they could have with their unsatisfactory lovers and husbands.

The final chapter in part 1, coauthored by Ronaldo Vainfas and me, moves us from colonial Spanish America to the early modern Lusophone world. "Female Homoeroticism, Heresy, and the Holy Office in Colonial Brazil" is based largely on previous archival research and writings by Vainfas, yet he and I worked closely together to reframe the chapter and consider the connections between female sodomy, perceptions of heresy, and the unnatural for this anthology. In doing so, we offer some brief yet revealing comparisons between the punishment of female sodomy in colonial Brazil and in colonial New Spain. As Chad Black's essay in this volume (chapter 6) also attests, archival records on female sodomy in colonial Latin America are exceedingly rare. Yet our essay expounds on Vainfas's previous research on a fascinating corpus of documentation in which Heitor Furtado de Mendonça, the Portuguese inquisitorial visitor in northeastern Brazil between 1591 and 1595, recorded a total of twenty-nine female suspects of sodomy through denunciations and self-denunciations. Only a few of those denunciations turned into prosecutions, yet the details that they offer around female same-sex intimacies in early colonial Brazil are illuminating and provocative. This essay also highlights the semantic differences between "formal heresy" and "material heresy," conceding that from a strictly theological point of view, sodomy was *not* a form of heresy. But Vainfas assembles evidence for his assertion that, in practice, sodomy in Brazil was popularly associated with heresy by priests, inquisitors, and laypersons alike. Sodomites, in essence, were "treated *as if they were heretics.*" While sodomy in itself was not evidence of sacrilege, there always existed the possibility that those who displayed the signs of sodomy would also, under questioning, reveal signs of sacrilege.

Like all scholarly texts, *Sexuality and the Unnatural in Colonial Latin America* is a product of a particular historical and political moment, especially with respect to the burgeoning historiography on gender and sexuality in colonial contexts and the rapidly growing interdisciplinary field of queer studies in conjunction with a decidedly politicized interest in generating scholarship that is linked to the broader arena of LGBTQ social movements in Latin America. This is of course not to say that the impetus for this anthology arose from the recent recognition of same-sex unions in Mexico City, Argentina, Brazil, and Uruguay; rather, the support of LGBTQ rights in the present is, for many scholars, inextricable from the scholarship that they themselves produce on nonheteronormative practices and desires in Latin America's colonial past. This explicit linking of colonial history and queer politics is clearly (and admirably, if all too rarely) undertaken by some scholars of gender and sexuality in colonial Latin America. The scholar who has perhaps done this most successfully is the Brazilian anthropologist and activist Luiz Mott, author of several works on sodomy and "homosexuality" in early modern Portugal and colonial Brazil that have served as inspiration for myself and for many of the authors included in this anthology. Mott is a well-known anthropologist and historian of colonial Brazil and early modern Portugal at the Universidade Federal da Bahia in Salvador, Brazil, and founder (in 1980) of the Grupo Gay da Bahia (GGB), the oldest and largest organization for the defense of LGBT rights in Brazil.[16] Mott unabashedly and explicitly links scholarship and politics in ways that make more meaningful connections between past and present than does much of the historiography of sexuality in early modern and colonial contexts. As one walks through the main center of the GGB, for example, the past-present connection is unmistakably stated on a marble plaque that proclaims: INQUISIÇÃO NUNCA MAIS! 1593*GGB*1993 (fig. 1)—marking on the one hand the period when Father Heitor

FIGURE 1. Marble plaque in the headquarters of the Grupo Gay da Bahia in Salvador, Brazil. Photo courtesy of Luiz Mott.

Furtado de Mendonça oversaw the first Portuguese inquisitorial visitation to Brazil (1591–93 in Bahia and 1593–95 in Pernambuco) and, on the other, the quincentennial, in 1993, of the Inquisition's persecution of sodomites. Mott's unequivocal assertion of INQUISITION NEVER AGAIN! has become a motto and rallying cry for LGBT activism and the Grupo Gay da Bahia. This iconic slogan highlights the intimate ties between archival research on sexuality, historiography, social activism, and LGBT rights discourse. In speaking of "homoeroticism," "homosexuality," and "gay" and "lesbian" subjects in the colonial past, Mott (and several other scholars) are being consciously, and perhaps provocatively, anachronistic. In doing so, they invite us to think about the repressions of the past in terms of the present, and vice versa. In an effort to make more intimate the connection between scholarship and activism, I have decided to donate my portion of the royalties from this book to the Grupo Gay da Bahia and other LGBT rights organizations in Latin America.

As the reader will already have noted, this anthology is divided into two parts, focusing respectively on unnatural heresies and unnatural crimes. The two things were not, in fact, absolutely divided, especially given the implicit jurisdictional overlap and popular confusion between sexual sins, heresies, and crimes throughout the Iberian Atlantic world. The division does, however, have roots in everyday practice and law in the early modern Iberian world. The chapters in part 1 of the book—"Unnatural Heresies"—deal primarily, though not exclusively, with cases that ecclesiastical and inquisitorial courts tried in Spain, Portugal, colonial Brazil, and the viceroyalties of New Spain and New Granada. In contrast, the authors of the chapters in part 2—"Unnatural Crimes"—largely select their evidence from secular court cases, from the viceroyalties of Rio de la Plata, Peru, New Granada, and New Spain. Here, the question of jurisdiction is crucial, even though it has occasionally been oversimplified by some scholars who, neglecting the archives of secular municipal courts, have been led astray by the assumption that sodomy cases were always the province of the Inquisition, independent of place. While it is true that the sodomy cases in early modern Portugal and its colonies were tried in ecclesiastical courts and by the Portuguese Inquisition, early modern Spain and its American colonies offer a more complex jurisdictional picture.

In New Spain, for example, the Holy Office by and large did *not* have jurisdiction over the *pecado nefando,* or "nefarious sin" of sodomy, or over the other "sins against nature." This limited jurisdiction contrasts with much of the early modern Iberian world, including the Spanish cities and municipalities of Valencia, Barcelona, Zaragoza, and Palma de Mallorca, as well as Portugal and its overseas colonies of Brazil and Goa, where both sodomy and bestiality technically fell under the jurisdiction of the Inquisition.[17] Between 1540 and 1700, the tribunals of the Inquisition in Spain prosecuted 380 cases of sodomy in Valencia, 791 in Zaragoza, and 433 in Barcelona.[18] Between 1587 and 1794, the Portuguese Inquisition tried some 400 individuals for sodomy, about 30 of whom were executed for their crimes.[19] In Castilian Spain, Ferdinand the Catholic placed sodomy under the jurisdiction of the Inquisition in 1505, but he subsequently revoked that decree and in 1509 placed it under the purview of the secular authorities.[20] As a consequence, in Castile, Granada, and Seville, secular rather than ecclesiastical authorities prosecuted sodomy. Secular courts in Madrid were responsible for the deaths of over one hundred sodomites from the 1580s to the 1650s. In Palermo, Sicily, which was then under Spanish dominion, between 1567 and 1640 at least eighty-three men were publicly executed for "homosexuality."[21] Due to the fact that the Indies had been incorporated into the Crown of Castile in the sixteenth century, the Castilian legal system and its administrative and judicial bureaucracies were transposed to those territories.

Despite recent assertions by one historian that "over the course of the colonial period, both secular and ecclesiastical authorities held jurisdiction over sodomy cases in the tribunals of New Spain," in reality, the law was clear: the Mexican Inquisition was allowed to prosecute cases of sodomy *only* when some overt heresy (like solicitation in the confessional), heretical propositions (like asserting that "sodomy is not a sin"), or a priest were involved.[22] The tribunal of the Inquisition in Mexico was even warned in 1580 that Rome, despite the Aragonese precedent, would never allow sodomy to be tried in Mexican ecclesiastical courts.[23] Priests were an exception to this rule: those accused of sodomy were tried in ecclesiastical courts even when they were careful not to commit any heresy. My own research shows that the Mexican Inquisition acknowledged that it did not have jurisdiction over unnatural sexual acts per se, but that such acts were sometimes (though not always) coupled with heretical statements.[24] This partially refutes Jorge

Bracamonte Allaín's claims that the colonial period was characterized by a pro-
longed jurisdictional dispute between the church and the state over the control of
"deviant" practices like sodomy, bestiality, prostitution, and incest.[25]

The fact that sodomy fell under various jurisdictions in the whole of the Spanish
empire did create some confusion in New Spain. It wasn't uncommon for laypersons and even ecclesiastical authorities, at times, to incorrectly treat the crime as a
religious one to be denounced to and prosecuted by the Holy Office. Sometimes
improper imprisonment by ecclesiastical authorities led to heated debates about the
nature of the crime and the Inquisition's jurisdiction over it. A 1691 sodomy Inquisition case from Mérida, Mexico, against Juan Ramírez, a *mulato* man, and Andrés
Chan, an indigenous man, for example, gave rise to an extended debate among
ecclesiastical officials as to whether or not sodomy fell under the jurisdiction of the
Church.[26] Some asserted that sodomy was in fact *mixti fori*—a crime that could be
punished by either a secular or an ecclesiastical court, depending on which commenced action first. The inquisitor don Nicolás de Salazar finally decided that this
case of sodomy did not meet the conditions that would make it fall under the Inquisition's jurisdiction in New Spain: it had neither occurred in the confessional nor
been accompanied by heretical statements. Accordingly, he ordered the prisoners to
be handed over to secular authorities for trial (though no records of this criminal
case have been located in the archives).[27] In theory, priests and inquisitors in New
Spain were to ignore complaints of sodomy inasmuch as they did not involve heresy, blasphemy, or another cleric. It was hard to eradicate the popular associations
between sodomy and heresy, however, and though such connections were theologically erroneous, they were common among laypersons and priests alike.

The reasons behind dividing this book into two parts—"Unnatural Heresies"
and "Unnatural Crimes"—reflect the competing jurisdictions where cases were
tried according to a standard in which Nature figured centrally in determining the
boundaries of heterodox bodies, desires, and devotions. Part 2 therefore focuses
on the treatment of cases of sodomy, bestiality, incest, and autoerotic exploration
by legal codes, local secular courts, and personal writings throughout colonial
Latin America. While most of the authors in part 2 employ criminal cases as their
data base, Martín Bowen Silva opens the section with an exceedingly rare historical document: the late-eighteenth-century unpublished writing of José Ignacio
Eyzaguirre, *Confesión generalísima,* discovered in Chile's national archive. The
author of the "General Confession" was a young member of the Chilean elite who
between 1799 and 1804 assiduously recorded a list of his sins in order to make
a complete general confession, thereby organizing and cataloguing his own experimentations with his body and with the bodies of others. Eyzaguirre's format
was determined by the Catholic practice of confessing one's innermost sins and
desires, which could simultaneously produce pleasure and shame; in this way he
created a fascinating record of personal sins and deeds that built upon his own

knowledge of the body. In defiance of the natural/unnatural binary, for Eyzaguirre it appears to have been both "normal" and "natural" for teenage students to engage in corporeal experimentation such as masturbation, touching other boys, and inserting one's fingers into one's own anus. If we were to go by official theological and legal discourse, all these acts would be "against nature" and even criminal. Bowen Silva's essay therefore points to a productive tension between values and meanings in the popular understandings and categorizations of the body and official discourse on the body. By choosing to model this record on the confession, Eyzaguirre appropriates a discursive form in which "natural" and "unnatural" desires figure largely; but, he never articulates them as such, and his testimony actually calls both categories into question in subtle ways.

While the historiography of sodomy and "homosexuality" in the Iberian Atlantic world has grown considerably in recent decades, historians have tended to privilege male sexuality in their researches, in part due to the greater availability of archival documentation. Chad Black's fascinating essay on two late-eighteenth-century cases of female sodomy from colonial Quito expands our understanding of female intimacies in colonial Spanish America and adds to the growing historiography on female same-sex sexuality in the Iberian Atlantic world.[28] In contrast to the Portuguese empire, very few cases of female sodomy have turned up in the Spanish American historical archives; thus, Black's chapter provides an important corrective to the near-exclusive focus on sodomy as a crime among men. He shows how two different pairs of women in Bourbon Quito came to be embroiled in the colonial criminal justice system for the unnatural (and largely invisible) crime of female sodomy, despite the absence of definitive proof that penetration had taken place. As sodomy was technically (and phallocentrically) defined through the act of penetration—with either a penis or an instrument—officials were more inclined to investigate men than women. Black's elucidation of these two cases shows how the authorities, in rare instances, dealt with women based on circumstantial evidence they believed demonstrated moral depravity and inversions of "natural" gendered behavior. Black argues that the central tension in these unique cases is between judicial interpretations of certain behaviors as "unnatural" and the defendants' own interpretations of them as customary and normal, including such things as publicly drinking alcohol, gambling, or sharing a bed with a member of the same sex. Despite the fact that courts acquitted all four women of the specific charge of sodomy, the women were nonetheless punished for such "excesses" as upending acceptable gender norms and marital obligations.

Fernanda Molina's essay provides a deep reading of debates about sodomy, gender identity, and the "juridical subject" (to use Foucault's term) in colonial Peru, providing us with an interesting counterpoint to the cases discussed in the previous chapters. Molina is less interested in the penalties meted out to male sodomites in the viceroyalty of Peru than in the way the testimony of the men who engaged in sex with other men shows how they construed their activity, always conscious of the dangers of being publicly exposed. Molina's analysis of the everyday lived realities of "sodomites" in colonial Peru deflates the notion that sodomy was understood in everyday life simply (or even primarily) as an act "against nature." Rather, the criminal and ecclesiastical cases she examines are enacted against a complex world of public male same-sex affection and occasional long-term cohabitation. Instead of framing sodomy as an act of immediate sexual satisfaction, Molina emphasizes the affective dynamic of many sodomitical relationships, finding ample evidence of public and private manifestations of "hugs, kisses, and amorous words" that were exchanged between men, which in many ways mimicked the courtship practices and sexual economies of women and men in colonial society. In the popular and legal spheres, these physical, verbal, and affective signs of sodomy deprivileged the moment of penetration as the defining characteristic of "sodomy." This essay ultimately challenges us to reconsider the affective and quotidian contexts through which sodomy was read and conceptualized at all levels of society.

The final two essays of this volume—on incest and bestiality, respectively—extend their analyses to topics that merit serious consideration because of the ways they rupture the natural/unnatural binary. The first of these topics, incest, has been discussed amply in the historiographical literature, but rarely with an eye toward the "unnatural" potential of the act. Bestiality, in contrast, has largely escaped the purview of historians of colonial Latin America, despite the fact that criminal, state, and municipal archives throughout Latin America hold hundreds (if not thousands) of archival documents attesting to the ubiquity of bestiality in the seventeenth, eighteenth, and nineteenth centuries, especially in rural communities. In the book's penultimate chapter, Lee M. Penyak shows that despite the fact that incest is almost always excluded from the classification "sin against nature" in the juridico-theological discourse, this stance was far from universally accepted in late-colonial Mexico. The 1817 *Diccionario de la lengua castellana*, for example, makes clear that incest—"a carnal sin committed by relatives within prohibited degrees"—occasionally received the designation "*contra natura*." Penyak traces the varied approaches taken by the authorities faced with accusations or confessions of incest in a corpus of seventy-four criminal and ecclesiastical incest trials from central Mexico. Authorities typically considered incest to be unacceptable only when committed by close relatives or when extreme violence was involved. But they generally considered incest acceptable when cousins sought to marry their social equals. Thus, the crime of incest approximated the unnatural only in cases of father-daughter or brother-sister relations. Even there, however, it only rarely received the official designation, being treated with relative latitude. In essence, the unnaturalness of incest could be mitigated by a variety of social factors, including degree of consanguinity, social class, race, age, and the presence or lack of coercion and violence, which made it distinct from such "sins against nature" as sodomy and bestiality. Penyak's scholarship here complements his previous and ongoing work on criminalized and "deviant" sexuality, homosexuality, and rape, showing that we must attempt to understand these crimes in conjunction with one another rather than in isolation.[29]

The volume concludes with an important essay on bestiality in late colonial and early national Mexico by Mexican historian Mílada Bazant. On the scale of the unnatural, theological discourse framed bestiality, perhaps even more so than sodomy or cannibalism, as the epitome of that which contravened "natural law." Yet surprisingly, there are few serious studies of the topic in the historiographical literature. In *Confronting Animal Abuse: Law, Criminology, and Human-Animal Relationships*, Piers Beirne opines that scholars often treat bestiality as a "disturbing form of sexual practice that invites hurried bewilderment rather than sustained intellectual inquiry."[30] This pattern is certainly seen in the historiography of colonial Latin America. That said, the crime itself was not uncommon, and as Bazant shows in her chapter, the largely adolescent male perpetrators of bestiality were multiethnic and came from all social backgrounds. Importantly, we see how lawyers, witnesses, and judges regularly employed colonial stereotypes and the tropes of indigenous "rusticity" and "simplicity" to make legal sense of the crime, in some cases going so far as to make excuses for the accused even when the suspect was not indigenous. Bazant's historical examination of bestiality ultimately expands our understanding of the religious, legal, and cultural implications of the "sins against nature," specifically in relation to the fluid human-animal boundary in the Iberian Atlantic world. This final chapter also serves as an important reminder to scholars and historians that even those sexual acts and desires that do not fit comfortably into contemporary political agendas (such as championing the history of homosexuality) are historically significant, especially when tracing the broader contours of the period's understanding of Nature.

In the late 1980s and '90s, scholars of colonial Latin America were greatly influenced by feminist theory, and some of the hallmark books from this time period focused on gender in everyday life and on policing female sexuality. Just slightly later, inspired by Foucault, queer theory, and the advent of gay and lesbian history in other regions of the world, historians of colonial Latin America began to research and write on such topics for early modern Spain and Portugal, New Spain, colonial Brazil, and eventually other regions of colonial Latin America. In order to reflect on their own contributions to the field, and on important shifts and developments since their earlier works were published, this anthology is bookended by a pair of incisive essays by two leading scholars in the field: a foreword by Asunción Lavrin and a coda by Pete Sigal. It has been nearly three decades since Lavrin published her fundamental anthology *Sexuality and Marriage in Colonial Latin America* in 1989, which brought scholars together (in English) for the first time to debate and publish their findings on topics that included witchcraft, confession, marriage, divorce, adultery, concubinage, childbirth, and illegitimacy. Similarly, it has been nearly fifteen years since Sigal published his anthology *Infamous Desire: Male Homosexuality in Colonial Latin America,* which became a landmark in the growing field of historical inquiry into the realm of gender, (homo)sexuality, and colonialism. The brief reflective essays by Lavrin and Sigal help to situate the chapters in this edited volume within the theoretical, methodological, and historiographical shifts in colonial Latin American studies on gender and sexuality.

This anthology does not claim to be a definitive account of sexuality and the unnatural in colonial Latin America, but rather a starting point that may encourage other researchers to pose comparable questions, debate, and explore those bodies and sexualities that might otherwise be relegated to the margins of historical inquiry. Although the essays in this volume are thematically, geographically, and chronologically diverse, not all topics that approximate the unnatural could be covered. The topic of corporeal ambiguity and hermaphroditism in the early modern Iberian world, so skillfully treated by François Soyer in his *Ambiguous Gender in Early Modern Spain and Portugal* and by María Elena Martínez in her recent "Archives, Bodies, and Imagination," for example, is one such underrepresented topic.[31] Given that the majority of the chapters focus on same-sex sexuality, this book is perhaps unavoidably reflective of the dominant current of historiography on sodomy and "homosexuality" in the Iberian Atlantic world. Yet the goal is not merely to fill in the missing gaps of the historiography of sexuality, but rather to take seriously (and sometimes dispute) the salience of the "unnatural" within the everyday lives and realities, administration of justice, and gendered performances in colonial Latin America. The collection weaves together historiographical debates, microhistorical case studies, and macrohistorical analyses to trace the meanings of sex and gender, Nature and the unnatural, in the early modern Iberian Atlantic world.

Ultimately, this anthology explores the diverse legal and theological ends to which the concept of "Nature" has been put in early modern Spain, Portugal, and their respective colonies throughout Latin America, showing how some salient binary distinctions—male and female, human and animal, private and public, and the like—have been mapped onto the natural/unnatural trope. If, as proposed by the Church and colonial authorities, human sexuality ultimately exists for the purpose of procreation, then Nature's "other" could be *any* disordered desire or corporeal act that posed a threat to the putatively natural order of things, including the institutions of marriage and the family, gendered and racial hierarchies, and colonialism itself. Collectively, these chapters propose that Nature was conceptually complicit in the creation and proliferation of "unnatural" bodies, desires, and devotions in early Latin America. Nature, in other words, could not be cleanly closed off on itself as a coherent category as long as it represented both *physis* and a putative moral order. As the chapters here show, the boundaries of the "natural" were contested by all segments of society. As Pete Sigal has aptly asserted, "One cannot understand the cultural, political, and social history of early Latin America without studying the ways in which sexual acts and desires were created, manipulated, and altered."[32] Indeed, this anthology does much to advance this project of historically tracing the contours of "Nature" and of "unnatural" sexual acts and desires. In so doing, it necessarily delineates the boundaries of those bodies, acts, and desires that theological discourse and legal treatises deemed "against nature." Such things as the sixteenth-century notion of the "manly woman" and the "womanly man," with their supposedly monstrous bodies and wayward gendered identities, were, according to Alonso López de Hinojosos, set in motion by Nature itself—and thus exemplified Nature's potential to devolve into its "other," but always in a way that simultaneously embodied both the natural and the unnatural. "Nature" *(naturaleza)*, "nature" *(natura)*, and the "unnatural" *(contra natura)* suffer a certain collapse under the weight of their own semantic internal contradictions, even as these categories continued to hold authority in the juridical and theological realms of colonial Latin America or the wider Iberian Atlantic world, from the past to the present.

NOTES

I am extremely grateful to Lee M. Penyak, Roger Gathman, Martin Nesvig, and anonymous readers for their valuable questions, comments, and suggestions. I am also thankful to Kate Marshall of the University of California Press for her support and enthusiasm for this project.

1. Alonso López de Hinojosos, *Summa y recopilación de cirugía, con un arte para sangrar, y examen de barberos* (Mexico City: 1595), 168v: "Es la primera tunica que ordeno naturaleza para muchas cosas: la vna para q[ue] no se apartasen estas simientes, por que de cada migajita destas simientes, se criaria vn niño, o vn monstruo." This edition of the treatise is housed at John Carter Brown Library, Brown University, Providence, R.I.; I am grateful to Yarí Pérez Marín for her help and generosity in bringing this reference to my attention.

2. Ibid., 169r: "El higado embia venas y sangre nutritiua al coraçon y al celebro, y el celebro embia neruios al higado y al coraçon, y el coraçon embia sangre spirituosa, a los de mas miembros, y asi cada vno comunica al otro su virtud, y se va formando el niño, y si a los treinta dias tiene calor bastante y las demas disposiciones necesarias, ynfunde Dios el anima, y es hombre; y si le falta vn grado de calor sale muger y hombruda que abla como hombre, y tiene condiciones de hombre, y si ay falta de calor, pasa a los sesenta dias; y si al tiempo del animar, sube vn grado de calor, se haze hombre, y es hombre amarionado, que habla como muger." Readers should note that the authors of this anthology have opted not to modernize Spanish orthography in order to preserve the original linguistic sense of the documents. Thus, in many cases when the Spanish appears to be in the first person (such as *solicito*), it is actually in the third person when read within the context of the archival document (modernized orthography would be *solicitó*, or "he solicited").

3. Jonathan Goldberg notes that *amarionado* is one of the complicated and largely untranslatable terms of the early modern Hispanic vocabulary: "The stumbling block is, of course, the word *amarionado*, the antecedent of modern Spanish *amaricado* and the related *marica* and *maricon*, slurs on homosexuality the equivalent of 'queer,' 'pansy,' and 'sissy.' The term does not mean a man who has

'become' a woman through castration or even necessarily through gender-crossing behavior." Jonathan Goldberg, *Sodometries: Renaissance Texts, Modern Sexualities* (Stanford: Stanford University Press, 1992), 285.

4. Judith C. Brown, *Immodest Acts: The Life of a Lesbian Nun in Renaissance Italy* (New York: Oxford University Press, 1986), 15.

5. Quoted in Mark Jordan, *The Invention of Sodomy in Christian Theology* (Chicago: University of Chicago Press, 1997), 146. See also Brown, *Immodest Acts, 7.*

6. Asunción Lavrin, "Sexuality in Colonial Mexico," in *Sexuality and Marriage in Colonial Latin America,* ed. Asunción Lavrin (Lincoln: University of Nebraska Press, 1989), 51.

7. Ibid.

8. For more human and animal sexuality in medieval theological discourse, see Leah DeVun, "Animal Appetites," *GLQ: A Journal of Gay and Lesbian Studies* 20, no. 4 (2014): 461–90.

9. Lorraine Daston and Fernando Vidal, eds., *The Moral Authority of Nature* (Chicago: University of Chicago Press, 2004), 4.

10. Quoted in Kenneth Mills and William B. Taylor, *Colonial Spanish America: A Documentary History* (Wilmington, Del.: SR Books, 1998), 55.

11. Real Academia, *Diccionario de la lengua castellana* (Madrid: Real Academia, 1726), 419.

12. Ibid.

13. Ann Twinam, *Public Lives, Private Secrets: Gender, Honor, Sexuality, and Illegitimacy in Colonial Spanish America* (Stanford: Stanford University Press, 1999).

14. Helmut Puff, "Nature on Trial: Acts 'Against Nature' in the Law Courts of Early Modern Germany and Switzerland," in Daston and Vidal (eds.), *Moral Authority of Nature,* 239.

15. Nora E. Jaffary, *False Mystics: Deviant Orthodoxy in Colonial Mexico* (Lincoln: University of Nebraska Press, 2004); Nora E. Jaffary, "Reconceiving Motherhood: Infanticide and Abortion in Colonial Mexico," *Journal of Family History* 37, no. 1 (2012): 3–22; and Nora E. Jaffary, "Monstrous Births and Creole Patriotism in Late Colonial Mexico," *The Americas* 68, no. 2 (2011): 179–207.

16. www.ggb.org.br/ggb-ingles.html.

17. See, for example, the following works on Spain: Rafael Carrasco, *Inquisición y represión sexual en Valencia. Historia de los sodomitas (1565–1785)* (Barcelona: Laertes S.A. de Ediciones, 1985); William E. Monter, "Sodomy: The Fateful Accident," in *History of Homosexuality in Europe and America,* ed. Wayne R. Dynes and Stephen Donaldson (New York: Routledge, 1992); and Mary Elizabeth Perry, "The 'Nefarious Sin' in Early Modern Seville," in *The Pursuit of Sodomy: Male Homosexuality in Renaissance and Enlightenment Europe,* ed. Kent Gerard and Gert Hekma (New York: Harrington Park Press, 1989).

18. Federico Garza Carvajal, *Butterflies Will Burn: Prosecuting Sodomites in Early Modern Spain and Mexico* (Austin: University of Texas Press, 2003), 71.

19. Merry E. Wiesner-Hanks, *Christianity and Sexuality in the Early Modern World: Regulating Desire, Reforming Practice* (New York: Taylor & Francis, 1999), 126.

20. Carrasco, *Inquisición y represión sexual en Valencia,* 11.

21. Monter, "Sodomy: The Fateful Accident," 296.

22. Garza Carvajal, *Butterflies Will Burn,* 71.

23. Monter, "Sodomy: The Fateful Accident," 287.

24. See Zeb Tortorici, *Sins against Nature: Sex and Archives in Colonial New Spain, 1530–1821* (Durham, N.C.: Duke University Press, forthcoming).

25. Jorge Bracamonte Allaín, "Los nefandos placeres de la carne: La iglesia y el estado frente a la sodomía en la Nueva España, 1721–1820," *Debate Feminista* 18 (1998): 393–415, on 393.

26. Archivo General de la Nación, Mexico [hereafter cited as AGN], Inquisición 498, exp. 16, fols. 160–85.

27. AGN, Inquisición 498, exp. 16, fol. 175.

28. For other work on female sodomy, see Ligia Bellini, *A coisa obscura. Mulher, sodomia e Inquisição no Brasil colonial* (Editora Brasiliense, 1989); Ursula Camba Ludlow, "Gregoria la Macho y su 'inclinación a las mujeres': Reflecciones en torno a la sexualidad marginal en Nueva España, 1796–1806," *Colonial Latin American Historical Review* 12, no. 4 (2003): 479–97; Jacqueline Holler, "'More Sins than the Queen of England': Marina de San Miguel before the Mexican Inquisition," in *Women in the Inquisition: Spain and the New World*, ed. Mary E. Giles (Baltimore: John Hopkins University Press, 1999); Stephanie Kirk, *Convent Life in Colonial Mexico: A Tale of Two Communities* (Gainesville: University Press of Florida, 2007); and Sherry Velasco, *Lesbians in Early Modern Spain* (Nashville: Vanderbilt University Press, 2011).

29. See, for example, Lee M. Penyak, "Midwives and Legal Medicine in México, 1740–1846," *Journal of Hispanic Higher Education* 1 (2002): 251–66; Lee M. Penyak, "Obstetrics and the Emergence of Women in Mexico's Medical Establishment," *The Americas* 60 (2003): 59–85; and Lee M. Penyak, "Temporary Transgressions, Unspeakable Acts: Male Sodomy in Late-Colonial Mexico, 1744–1843," *Colonial Latin American Historical Review* 17, no. 4 (2008): 329–59. For more on why sodomy and rape should be analyzed in conjunction with one another, see Zeb Tortorici, "Sexual Violence, Predatory Masculinity, and Medical Testimony in New Spain," *Osiris* 30, no. 1 (2015): 272–94.

30. Piers Beirne, *Confronting Animal Abuse: Law, Criminology, and Human-Animal Relationships* (Lanham, Md.: Rowman & Littlefield, 2009), 113.

31. François Soyer, *Ambiguous Gender in Early Modern Spain and Portugal* (Leiden: Brill, 2012); and María Elena Martínez, "Archives, Bodies, and Imagination: The Case of Juana Aguilar and Queer Approaches to History, Sexuality, and Politics," *Radical History Review* 120 (2014): 159–82.

32. Pete Sigal, "(Homo)Sexual Desire and Masculine Power in Colonial Latin America: Notes toward an Integrated Analysis," in *Infamous Desire: Male Homosexuality in Colonial Latin America*, ed. Pete Sigal (Chicago: University of Chicago Press, 2003), 3.

PART I

Unnatural Heresies

Archival Narratives of Clerical Sodomy and Suicide from Eighteenth-Century Cartagena

Nicole von Germeten

Close to midnight on November 14, 1779, a "tempestuous and dark night," a secret procession rapidly strode through the streets of Cartagena de Indias.[1] The swift and silent group included several officials of the Holy Office of the Cartagena Inquisition tribunal—the lone local official inquisitor, don Felix Villegas, as well as lower-ranking tribunal functionaries—accompanied by two black male servants. The menials were carrying a sheet-wrapped corpse from the secret prison cells of the tribunal to a separate building that housed penitents with longer sentences, known as the *casa de la penitencia* (penitence house).[2] The servants rapidly dug a hole in the corral of this *lugar profano* (profane place), trying not to wake up the family of the warden who lived there. But a crying baby disturbed the residents, and women, children, and servants quietly eavesdropped on the secret midnight burial—terrifying Villegas, who desperately wanted to conceal the tragic result of his botched inquisitorial investigation of the life of a cleric accused of sodomy and solicitation in the confessional. What most concerned Inquisitor Villegas was the public exposure of the events that led to this procession at such an untimely hour of the night (what Villegas called the "deshoras de la noche"). Villegas wanted to suppress the identity of the buried corpse to avoid scandal and spreading rumors of moral and structural weakness among the local clergy, whose status had declined dramatically since the seventeenth century. However, a few clerics and locals knew of the shameful profane burial, brought about by the multilayered unnatural acts of one fray Esteban Sobrino, a Mercedarian friar who committed suicide in his cell in the Holy Office prison. Sobrino acted out his fatal plan shortly after the inquisitor had announced his penitential sentence for the crime of solicitation in the confessional, among "many other enormous crimes."[3]

This chapter explores the competing and contradictory archival narratives created by Sobrino and his inquisitor. In particular, it includes a careful analysis of how both the accused and the accuser constructed the surviving documentation, as well as how they themselves were constructed within the documentation. Their motivations for telling their own particular stories are revealed in Villegas's manipulation of Sobrino to protect the local church's reputation and Sobrino's creation of a persona and rhetoric that made his desires and sexuality seem "natural," even though they spanned a broad panorama from heterosexual lust to possible "perfect" sodomy. This methodological approach, with its emphasis on the specifics of archival narratives, draws from both Natalie Zemon Davis's classic acknowledgment of the "fiction in the archives" and Kathryn Burns's more recent model of foregrounding the notaries who created documents.[4] Although Sobrino ended his story with his own death, therefore granting Villegas the last word as the survivor and chronicler of Sobrino's biography, as historians we do not need to accept how Villegas shaped his version of the friar's life and untimely end. As Zeb Tortorici writes, "Officials that record and investigate suicide play an important role in the construction of its social meanings."[5] This case demands an untangling of Villegas's constructed meanings, textual emphases that derive from his own need to justify his actions and protect the local church from further scandal, as well as a close look at Sobrino's own narrative. Only close textual analysis and a microhistorical approach can expose what each man said in order to achieve diverging ends. Sobrino tried desperately to present himself as a forgivable, redeemable, even appealing sinner, who operated well within "natural" excusable male sexual desires. In contrast, Villegas wanted to show, through repetitive epitaphs of disgust, that the suicide was lost in a mire of willful, conscious vice and had disgracefully earned a secret, profane burial to protect the honor of the Church.[6] These contradictory angles demonstrate the flexibility and expansiveness of interpretation possible for the spectrum of natural to "against nature" *(contra natura)* in the framing and understanding of sexual acts.

Although Villegas's efforts to shape the file involved more general aspects of colonial life, Tortorici rightly recommends that historians should not always try to link suicide to the broader effects of colonialism. My analysis of Sobrino will focus closely on this unique individual and his life circumstances as revealed in the documents generated by Villegas's inquisitorial investigations. However, Villegas certainly understood the role of local slaves as symbols to call on to define the unnatural, especially the practice of suicide.[7] Throughout the colonial era, African slaves and their descendants, both free and enslaved, and often racially mixed, numerically dominated this region. In 1684, 7,341 free people lived in Cartagena, with slaves adding at least another 25 percent to that number. In the wake of the destructive 1697 French invasion, Cartagena was virtually depopulated, but the city gradually recovered to 4,556 inhabitants by 1708. The city's population increased dramatically in the late eighteenth and early nineteenth centuries: a detailed census calculated 13,690 residents in 1777, and 17,600 by 1809. Racially mixed and enslaved women outnumbered other groups in the population. In 1777, nearly 20 percent of local residents were unmarried free women of color in charge of a small family group or renting out rooms in their houses, often to traveling men or male slaves.[8] These women and their children make up all of the witnesses in this case who alleged that Sobrino either attempted to or succeeded in seducing them. Within the surviving documents, neither Sobrino nor Villegas offered any revealing commentary on the inherently colonial fact that all the targets of Sobrino's natural and unnatural sexual desires were nonwhite colonized subjects. The friar did frame all of his erotic and affectionate leanings as natural, thus implying that he viewed male and female slaves and free people of color as attractive potential sexual partners.[9]

The first tribunal of the Holy Office of the Inquisition came to New Spain in 1572, less than a century after the Catholic monarchs Ferdinand and Isabel founded this court in their Spanish dominions in an effort to stamp out what they viewed as heretical backsliding, most particularly the continued secret practice of Judaism by recent converts. Inquisitors over the course of the seventeenth and eighteenth centuries investigated what Martin Nesvig has called "sin-crimes": bigamy, heretical statements, blasphemy, solicitation in the confessional, various clerical sins, sorcery, and witchcraft.[10] Thanks to their investigations, historians can find thousands of pages of tribunal records in the Spanish national archives in Madrid documenting dozens of criminal, financial, clerical, and jurisdictional disputes. In the absence of notarial records or more complete criminal files, the documents drawn up in Inquisition trials, according to Richard Greenleaf, "provide an overview of colonial life not available from other sources. The way in which social institutions react to the rebel, the nonconformist . . . yields all manner of data."[11] Although Greenleaf made these comments decades ago, they remain relevant to this particular case, which offers complex and competing narratives of natural and unnatural acts.

Zeb Tortorici has shown that in colonial New Spain, especially in the eighteenth century, there was a "degree of tolerance for members of the clergy accused of sodomy or sexual acts with other males."[12] Inquisitors took an interest in Sobrino's sexual misconduct only after decades of hearing rumors of him soliciting women in the confessional and engaging in other generally unsuitable behaviors. In fact, according to Tortorici, the Cartagena and other American tribunals had "no official power over charges of sodomy or improper intercourse, unless they involved heresy," despite the fact that "the concepts of unnatural sexuality, heresy, sin, and criminality were often intermixed and overlapped in the minds of the inquisitors, secular authorities, and laypersons."[13] In general, Tortorici's evidence shows that the Holy Office hoped to conceal reported acts of clerical sodomy, even if they were well documented, numerous, and enduring. Priests received discreet private penances or just moved to another parish. Often, inquisitors did not even bother to

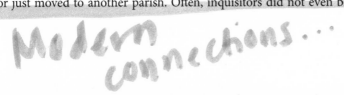

investigate the allegations. Late-eighteenth-century convicted sodomites, even lay-men, rarely endured execution, though public punishment was more frequent.[14]

As a friar, Sobrino would have enjoyed this discretion and lenient, protective attitude if he had not chosen to kill himself. Villegas wished to protect the honor and reputation of the local church by hiding or deescalating the gossip about Sobrino's acts to the degree possible. But Sobrino's choice to commit suicide could have become very public and in turn led to questioning about why the friar was imprisoned, thus revealing clerical secrets that Villegas hoped to remove from public circulation. For this reason, Villegas, panicked about Sobrino's burial, had to act quickly in a way that he thought would protect the Church's reputation from further criticism. In the moment, he decided that a secret nighttime secular burial would best serve the Cartagena Church's needs. He shaped the file to justify his decision, especially through repeated diatribes regarding Sobrino's irredeemable sinfulness, supported of course by the act of suicide and the testimonies of others who had experienced the friar's sexual talk and physical contact. Villegas con-structed Sobrino as the ultimate sinner, one unlikely to feel true repentance and reform.

Before returning to the documents' narratives, it is worth noting that the Carta-gena tribunal of the Holy Office had long suffered from local dissatisfaction and criticisms, and indeed had virtually disappeared after two foreign invasions since the late seventeenth century. The inquisitors arrived in 1610 and immediately began to investigate love magic and shamanistic practices. From the beginning, however, other crown institutions frequently challenged the inquisitors' decisions. The local elite had little difficulty in evading the inquisitors' sentences by calling on their own social status and ties to the colonial church, military, and governing authorities. This tribunal had jurisdiction over cases originating in a broad swath of the circum-Caribbean, including territories in the modern nations of Panama, Cuba, and Venezuela, but even within Cartagena itself, residents manipulated the inquisitors for their own personal and political ends. Outside the city, some colo-nial subjects openly mocked the tribunal and criticized it for corruption and inef-fectiveness.[15]

Cartagena had not yet recovered from a violent church/state conflict in the 1680s known as the *cessatio a divinis* that stopped local church services, when the French, led by baron de Pointis, sacked the city in 1697.[16] The Inquisition judges fled the city, so the attackers looted their building and possessions.[17] The facilities never recovered completely. In 1706, inquisitors complained that they had no funds; in their view they had been abandoned, because no ships had come from Spain in a decade. The court was moved to a private home for a time in the early 1700s, but an English naval attack led by Admiral Vernon destroyed it again in 1741; the building was not rebuilt until 1766. In the eighteenth century, the Carta-gena tribunal concentrated on censorship of Enlightenment ideas. The tribunal's decline is most obviously manifested in this case by the lone presence of one inquisitorial presiding judge, Villegas. In contrast, in the seventeenth century a more active Cartagena Holy Office necessitated two inquisitors. Adding to a sense of weakness and decline in the local church was the fact that twelve years before Sobrino's suicide, the eight Jesuits living in the city had acted on banishment orders received directly from Spain and left from the port with little or no objection from residents.[18] It is clear that in the eighteenth century, military and crown bureaucrats played a more vibrant role in Cartagena social, political, and economic life than did Catholic institutions.

Villegas carefully shaped the written records of his investigation into Sobrino's alleged crimes, which have survived as a 125-folio case file in Spain's national archive, the Archivo Histórico Nacional in Madrid. The file contains two intertwined and appended investigations: one of the sexual crimes and heresies Sobrino allegedly committed during his lifetime and the other dealing with Villegas's attempt to exculpate himself and the Holy Office from any blame for the suicide and to present his decision to carry out a secret burial as an appropriate response in a crisis. This case exists because Sobrino's desires and acts were viewed in his time as unnatural, vicious, and irreligious. Therefore, throughout the written record, Villegas strove to highlight the sinful, irredeemable, impenitent nature of the subject of his investigations, "a rhetoric replete with gestures of revulsion."[19] Villegas censured the friar's character and immoral life, and the Inquisition procedures and punishment ended in Sobrino's death, so the inquisitor created a narrative with Sobrino in the role of the antagonist.[20] Historical analysis requires recognition that document creators mold situations for their own ends. In this case, Villegas highlighted Sobrino's sinfulness to take the blame for the suicide off himself as well as to distract his superiors within the Holy Office bureaucracy from the possible misstep of the nighttime unconsecrated burial.

Sobrino, in contrast, felt very different pressures in how he narrated his autobiography to the inquisitor and other clerical investigators. Thus, the persona he created differs from the one created by his persecutors. This fact is especially important given the controversial and unproven nature of some of the accusations against him. His confessional narrative weaves together natural and unnatural desires, but he chose to end the story by taking his own life, a choice that provided fodder for further stories of his sin and unnaturalness. Perhaps he viewed suicide as the only possible response to the unwinnable clash between his self-presentation and his prosecution and ultimate penitential sentence, although it silenced any further contributions he might provide to shape his own story.

Sobrino's biography survives only through the medium of his Holy Office case file. When he killed himself, he was around fifty-eight years old, a weak, thin, pale, wrinkled old man, according to Villegas's biased description, which certainly sought to highlight the physical toll of a vicious life. A Cartagena local of old

Christian and Spanish heritage, Sobrino received his education from the Jesuits and took the habit of Nuestra Señora de la Merced at age twenty-two. He was assigned to small remote parishes in Panama shortly afterward, in response to rumors of a scandal with a Cartagena woman. Gossip about sinful sexual acts pursued Sobrino for the rest of his life. For almost four decades, fears of scandal, scribal recordings of hostile testimonies, and his own presentation of his personal archival narratives shaped his desires and sexual acts. Although Villegas and hostile witnesses tell a story of Sobrino's sinfulness and unnatural sexuality, the friar maintained for much of the investigation that he did not commit any serious sexual improprieties nor did he envision his desires as unnatural. He felt sexual attraction to—or as he viewed it, affection for—both males and females, and his sexual identity moved across the broad spectrum of natural to unnatural, defying eighteenth-century attempts to categorize sexuality and gender.[21]

The Holy Office and his Mercedarian superiors began to seriously investigate Sobrino's misconduct when he was in his late thirties. These investigations began with complaints from a woman he confessed in rural Panama as well as statements made by men who knew his reputation. The Holy Office file that Villegas compiled in 1780 incorporated copies of these early investigations. In 1760, a young enslaved woman claimed Sobrino tried to seduce her in the confessional by putting his hand under her skirt and saying that "he did this with many other women in other places." She rejected his advances, and he gave her absolution.[22] Sobrino also had a reputation for speaking inappropriately in his young adulthood. Two witnesses mentioned that in Panama he was known to make salacious jokes, such as his statement that the local women were "como vacas huyan del toro del día, y por la noche iban" (like cows that flee from the bull in the daytime, and at night they pursue them).[23] This joke used a reference to animals to comment on the hypocrisy of female sexuality, with Sobrino voicing his understanding of natural desires and behavior. In effect, his summation of male/female interaction in his place of residence was that it was bestial, and that even beasts (that is, the "cows" and the "bull") give in to their natural inclinations. Male sex drive, especially when it targeted women, often fits into a narrative of "natural," with the concept of "Nature" acting as "God's intermediary and [to] defend the order enshrined in His creation," but subject to certain rules and behavior standards.[24] Sobrino showed with his comments about animals and women that he understood nature's rules, although with his own whimsical, crude humor.

These inconclusive investigations of Sobrino's inappropriate behavior in the confessional led to his return to the Mercedarian convent in Cartagena but no further punishment. The Holy Office scribe did not record Sobrino's responses to the accusations originating in Panama until 1779, during his investigation for accusations of sodomy. Therefore, the documents saved in this file present a range of his sexual desires and choices over the course of nearly two decades. In the midst of his later interrogation, Sobrino offered a mix of reactions to his Panamanian solicitation accusations. First, he denied that he confessed anyone in the specified locale. Then he admitted that he did solicit women at that time, but only due to the uncontrolled passions of youth, explaining that "at that time the deponent did not live or think with the order that corresponds to his profession and state, in terms of honesty and other things, because as the youth that he was at that time, he let himself be dragged along by his passions" *(en aquel tiempo no vivía ni pensaba el declarante con el arreglo que correspondía a su profesión y estado en materia de honestidad como en otras cosas, pues como mozo que era entonces, se dejaba arrastrar de sus pasiones).*[25] In this self-characterization, Sobrino presented himself as subject to very natural, normal, young, male sexual needs, and implied that later he learned more self-control. The idea of "Nature" as an intermediary between God and humans allows for male sexual desire, which may or may not conform to social rules. Understanding and learning from his mistakes clearly supported Sobrino's self-construction as a repentant Christian.

Later in his confessions, Sobrino denied having any affairs or scandals with women in Panama. He spent more time, as did many of the witnesses, discussing more general aspects of his character that he hoped would explain or justify his reputation for inappropriate jokes, such as the line about women acting like cows chased by bulls. Repeatedly, Sobrino used phrases such as the following to describe how he spoke to women in the confessional: "as a youth with a comic and jocose disposition, I said some obscene and malicious words to them" *(como mozo y del genio tan alegre y jocoso, le diría algunas palabras obscenas o de malicia).* And even during confession, "in a joking, mirthful way, as was my disposition, I said some words to them that sound offensive or facetious or obscene, but not for solicitation" *(por modo de chacota o jocosidad por ser genio en mi le diría algunas palabras malsonantes o jocosas o obscenas al oírlas pero no con tal solicitación).* He admitted that he had been warned and reprimanded for "his buffooneries and obscenities and his occasional offensive expressions" *(sus bufonadas y dichos obscenos y tal vez unas expresiones de mal sonido)* and that he now understood the seriousness and respect with which he should treat the sacrament of confession.[26] Sobrino tried, through these repentant statements, to offer Villegas a contrite, sympathetic persona, one that fit within an acceptable, natural range of behavior. Sobrino probably believed that Villegas might excuse his weak character, especially if the friar demonstrated analytical self-awareness and a penitent attitude. The Mercedarian created a false persona, one that fit into the realm of the natural, to diminish the seriousness of his unnatural desires.

Sobrino's creation of this particular persona extended far beyond the tribunal and into nearly all of his social connections. Several witnesses, from his Mercedarian peers to a black female servant who had known him since infancy, also defined him as having a "simple, jocular disposition" *(genio sencillo y jocoso)* or stated that "he has an affable and easygoing nature, saying whatever comes to his imagination, without reflecting on it . . . he has been heard to say indecent words and expressions on occasion, but always in mockery or jest, not maliciously . . . [given] his joking and thoughtless character" *(es de genio jocoso y fácil en decir cuanto le viera a la imaginación, sin reflexionarlo . . . le ha oído palabras y expresiones poco honestas en algunas ocasiones pero siempre por modo de trisca y pasa tiempo no malicia . . . [given] su genio chancero y poco reflexivo).* The elderly free black woman who raised Sobrino offered the most sympathetic characterization, testifying that his "character is very good natured, calm and peaceful, naturally simple and funny, and that he is not unruly, wayward, or quarrelsome" *(carácter es de muy bien genio, sosegado, y pacífico, y naturalmente sencillo, y jocoso, y que no es díscolo, inquieto, y pendenciero).*[27] Sobrino may have created and promoted this joker character throughout his lifetime specifically to hide, excuse, diminish, or disguise what he knew were his unnatural sexual desires and actions. While this character was not highly honorable and even veered into disrespectfulness, vice, and sin, it was also not unnatural or uncorrectable.

Sobrino textually foregrounded this persona at every possible opportunity during the investigations. He argued throughout the case for Villegas's mercy, and reminded Villegas of the remorse the friar felt for (as he viewed it) his well-known character flaws and his private and perhaps even nonscandalous sins:

> I am no angel, but the worst in the world. I do not deserve the state I have. If God was not merciful to me, I would already be lost and like a beast, but he recognizes the weakness of his children, and consoles them. . . . [I] certainly [have] the bad habit of saying jokes, absurdities, obscene words, and playing dishonest games. . . . I am in a terrible predicament, but I have not indulged in *borrascas,* gambling, drinking parties, concubinage, nor have I been imprisoned, or fallen down in the street, or been caught out at night and brought to justice in my convent. My name is not proclaimed in songs, in the plazas, *pulperías,* or fandangos, nor on the beaches at night. . . . I am not scandalous, nor crazy, nor lacking reason . . . but I have cheerful and lively temperament.[28]

Seeking pity, Sobrino stressed here that all of his shortcomings were natural, pardonable, improvable, and, most important for Villegas, concealable. He was a joker and a sinner, but his desires were not *contra natura*—a fact that made his shortcomings more redeemable in his own eyes. Through these lines, Villegas could view himself (Sobrino hoped) as operating in the model of the divine forgiver, and no one would know any better. The friar presented his sins as relatively discreet.

As he aged and settled back into his hometown, Sobrino continued to employ his joking, purposefully obscene persona in the confessional, according to statements made by two Cartagena women. While these allegations suggest that Sobrino committed the serious infraction of solicitation in the confessional, which was well within the Holy Office's purview, they actually bolstered Sobrino's self-presentation as having natural (forgivable, understandable) sexual desires. His reputation for obscene talk, which he said did not confirm sexual acts, could explain some of these testimonies. An enslaved woman said that Sobrino told her numerous times that she was a "beautiful young black girl and she should not waste herself on a low-class man like a *sambo,* but should seek someone more decent, a *señor* with money." She also claimed that he smelled her skirts lasciviously and gave her generous gifts, soliciting her with his words, although he did not carry through on his "sordid words" *(palabras torpezas).* She said he even offered to buy her freedom and asked her why she didn't love him.[29] Another thirty-year-old Cartagena slave provided a great deal of detail regarding Sobrino's improper confessional conversations. During confession she said she intended to marry and he asked whom. She said she planned to marry a black man; in response, the padre recommended that she not make love with black men. She claimed that he continued this line of questioning by asking her if, since she was not married, she had had affairs with priests. When she said no, he asked if she would were a priest to fall in love with her, arguing that she should sin with white men, not black men. His discussion became more explicit: "he then asked her if she had a good ass and if she protected it" *(el entonces le pregunto si tenia buen culito que se lo guardase).*[30] Later she added more detail, saying Sobrino asked "if the black man had a very big one and if it hurt very much, so that she bled" *(si el negro lo tenia muy grande que si le dolia mucho, y que si echaba sangre)* (underlined in the original). He also asked more generally if she went out in the street, and she claimed that she presented herself as very virtuous, although he insisted that he wanted to be her lover. He then absolved her. She decided not to return to confess with him again because she believed this had not been an effective confession.

Analyzing these statements independently from Sobrino's defensive reaction to them, it appears that he used the confessional as a place to indulge his sexual fantasies toward both black men and black women and even attempted to carry them out. According to colonial confessional manuals, priests were expected to ask explicit questions to encourage male and female parishioners to reveal their sex-related sins. In the early seventeenth century, Alonso de Sandoval provided his fellow Cartagena Jesuits with a script to probe slaves' sexual desires, fantasies, and actions. Sandoval also viewed African sexuality as unnatural, since he pointed out that Africans had been known, since the time of St. Augustine, to have long-term same-sex relationships and practice transvestism: "Some of the histories of Ethiopian nations boast that men do not need women to be good husbands. The Jesuit fathers found many blacks called *chibandos* in the kingdom of Angola. These are great sorcerers, men who dress as women and shave themselves. They sit as if they were women and are very insulted if they are called men. They have husbands like other women and practice the sin that offends the very ears to hear it."[31] Educated in the local *colegio de la compañía,* Sobrino was a direct heir to this tradition. Given the accusations that Sobrino tried to seduce his young black male confessees, his alleged interest in black male and female genitalia clearly goes beyond even the most sexually explicit line of questioning permissible in the confessional. At this moment, although Sobrino asked for graphic details about men, he was in the process of questioning and even perhaps trying to seduce a woman, demonstrating how his sexual desires for men and women—in other words, his unnatural and natural desires and persona—blended and coexisted as he sat in the confessional. The questions themselves might have titillated him, until the confessional and the act of confession itself connected in his mind with sexual arousal.[32]

Of course, in his statements Sobrino did not openly acknowledge his complex desires, but framed his response to these accusations according to a self-protective defensive strategy. He denied or minimized most of the claims these women made, saying that he had only solicited women as a young man when his passions controlled him—again stressing that his desires were natural, part of a man's maturing process. He specified that he did not commit such acts with women as a mature man and blamed the accusations on his jocose, crude sense of humor. He admitted to saying some of the statements alleged by the women because he had an incautious and unreflective nature that led him to not give proper respect to the setting of the confessional. Sobrino said that he knew he often made rude and improper, even obscene, jokes, but he did not touch the women whatsoever or solicit them. In fact, he pointed out that the physical structure of the confessional prevented him from touching them. He also argued that many of these women's accusations disguised acceptable conversation in confession and that only their crude minds could have invented some of the more explicit alleged comments. He claimed that he believed that it was within the realm of appropriate priestly duties for him to ask if they were married, and to advise them to marry a more elite man if possible. He presented this as a proper way to offer them succor and consolation. Furthermore, he pointed out that in their testimonies the women sometimes contradicted themselves and could not be trusted. He observed that all the women who accused him were lost (in a moral sense) and worldly low-class women, possibly seeking some kind of vengeance.[33]

These accusations became known to Sobrino's Mercedarian superiors in the mid-1770s and led to them confining him to his convent. However, they permitted him to continue to confess men and boys within the semiprivacy of his cell. This new arrangement seems to have contributed to Sobrino indulging in the facet of his sexuality that his peers viewed as *un*natural: his desire for affection and physical contact with young men and boys. After denying the gravity of his interactions with women, in June 1779 Sobrino presented the inquisitor with a written confession regarding illicit touching *(tocamientos)* with a few, maybe two, boys, which he claimed he did only due to his fragility and not maliciousness. Again avoiding the language of the unnatural, Sobrino initially discussed the encounters in terms of temptation, lust, and desire with confusing statements regarding his confessional associations with these boys: "I have had several unchaste *tocamientos* committed with one or another [body] part, these have been . . . with servants. . . . It is certain that I confessed them before the obscene lusts, but after that I left and I did not see them, nor do I really know their names or who they are. . . . I did it all without reflection as a fragile man with nothing good about him, as God knows, not with malice against God, but only through evil propensities."[34] As a friar since his youth, educated by Jesuits, clearly Sobrino spoke Villegas's confessional language. He chose to dissimulate and give contradictory statements regarding how the sexual acts intersected with the confessional, as this was the most serious crime. He interjected self-analysis and his own version of his morality while presenting his acts very vaguely.

Unfortunately for him, other Mercedarians testified and provided more confirming evidence that Sobrino had committed sodomy with boys he confessed. As the investigation continued, three of Sobrino's fellow friars noted that he only confessed men and boys because he worked out of his cell. Several scandals developed involving six boys ranging between the approximate ages of eight and fourteen. The friars reported that when they passed by Sobrino's cell, they noted he had his arm around or was touching the buttocks *(trasero)* of some of the young boys in there to confess. Another report said they had seen him in impure acts with his *calzones caídos*—his pants dropped.[35] According to reports, one boy fled the cell because he said Sobrino did not give him the promised reward or payment "after taking it in the backside" *(después de habérselo metido por el trasero)*. The boy told this to a group of friars and the neighbors, so it became a topic of public gossip and eventually an archival narrative.[36] All of these acts placed Sobrino's sexuality squarely in the realm of the unnatural, despite the defendant's effort to frame himself as a more natural, redeemable sinner caught up in the past in the passions of youth or, more recently, in cravings for affection and love.

In an *audiencia* with Inquisitor Villegas less than three weeks before his suicide, Sobrino did not deny these new accusations. He admitted to touching six young boys but, continuing his strategy of self-analysis during his own confession, said he did it without malice or evil thoughts. Even when he touched their genitals and they both ejaculated, he said that he had no impure or immodest intentions, in hopes of satisfying inquisitorial interest in thoughts and intent. Instead he said he touched them affectionately with a sincere and honest love, not lustfully. With his words he tried to render these acts natural, innocent, and harmless for both himself and the boys. He claimed he never committed "perfect sodomy" and stated that he felt remorse afterward, thereby reframing himself as a normal or natural repentant Christian. His words emphasize the emotions he felt during these acts, assuming that this penitential approach would lessen his sinfulness in the eyes of the inquisitor who hoped to reconcile him within the Church. As the time of his final sentencing approached, Sobrino became more desperate, saying that the boys came to his cell without him specifically asking them to, that he was tempted by the devil and in the grip of passion. Almost as an aside, he mentioned that, under the pretense of Christian instruction, he visited the home of a young black girl whom he also touched for libidinous purposes.[37]

In response to Sobrino's confessions and the other friars' supporting evidence, Villegas sentenced Sobrino to a penance that could be completed in a semiprivate way, in line with the defendant's request. This sentence also might protect the Church from any further public scandal. Sobrino was banished from the diocese of Cartagena and its surrounding areas for ten years and sentenced to confinement in the Mercedarian convent in Panama. There he would always hold the lowest position among the friars, last in line in every procession and lowest in the hierarchy in any ceremony. He had to do serious penances regularly, sometimes at the hands of his fellow friars. He also had to make a general confession, examining the sins of his entire life. However, Villegas ruled that Sobrino should remain in the Cartagena Holy Office prison for the present, given that the war in progress made traveling difficult.[38] Sobrino thus continued living in the prison cell after his sentence. On the day of his death, two servants brought in his breakfast and saw nothing wrong with him.[39] When they returned to his cell for his next meal around 1 P.M., the *alcalde* and a slave found him hanging from the bars on his window, attached by his rope belt. He was wearing only his undergarments and a rosary around his neck. Upon discovery of the body, the servants quickly called their superiors within the local tribunal, who in turn called on various other ecclesiastical and secular authorities, including the bishop and the *protomedicato*. The medical official determined that, given the cold temperature of his body, Sobrino had died four hours before.

Sobrino died from the intense compression of his trachea, according to the protomedicato. The authorities were convinced that it was a motivated and intentional suicide, given the protomedicato's hypothesis that Esteban had climbed into the window and pushed his feet with intense and deliberate violence in order to squeeze his trachea with his thin, soft belt.[40] Villegas noted that this was a common method for killing oneself in Cartagena; indeed, a prisoner in the royal jail had recently managed it wearing shackles. An African slave had hung himself in the same manner in the tribunal's cells over 150 years previously, and the inquisitors had buried his body in their gardens, greatly fearing any further self-destructive acts.[41]

Villegas emphasized the sinfulness of suicide in his introductory remarks to this case file, presenting it as an unnatural, vicious death. Suicide was an offense against both God and Nature, because Nature advocated self-preservation and only God could decide one's fate.[42] To support this understanding of suicide and to distance it from natural practices common among Europeans, Villegas blamed the unchristian local Africans for the spread of this irreligious behavior: "It is believed that the blacks from Africa brought and established this so inhuman and execrable vice here, because they are the ones that most commonly practice it, or through errors the adults absorb it, or through their natural force, or because their masters care less about instructing them in the Catholic religion than in serving them" *(Se cree haber traído y radicado aquí este tan inhumano y excrerable vicio los negros de África, que son los que más comúnmente incurren en el, o por error en que vienen imbuidos los adultos, o por su fuerte natural, o porque los amos cuidan menos de instruirlos en la religión católica que en servirse de ellos).*[43] Although he framed it in an assessment of successful or unsuccessful Christianization, following in the footsteps of Alonso de Sandoval's seventeenth-century criticisms of the lack of Christianity in the Cartagena slave experience, Villegas highlighted racial difference to support his understanding of suicide as unnatural and even bestial or inhuman *(inhumano).*

In Cuba, Spanish secular and religious authorities, planters, and visitors also stressed a strong African tendency toward suicide, even specifying how certain ethnicities especially embraced this option.[44] Observers explained this propensity by noting that the Africans who killed themselves came from ethnicities that had a strong (although misguided) sense of honor, pride, and bravery, although of course these were not the motivating factors Villegas highlighted in Sobrino's case. Like Sobrino, African slaves in Cuba did kill themselves while imprisoned or after suffering humiliating punishments. Cubans also understood suicide as proof that slaves' masters had not Christianized them, because it seemed that Africans believed that committing suicide would release their souls to return to their homelands. In line with Villegas's opinions expressed in the quote above, in Cuba Spaniards believed that Christianization would end the practice of suicide among slaves, because it would teach them to leave their fate in God's hands. Both Villegas and these Cuban commentators distanced their religious traditions and even colonial conditions from the practice of suicide. Villegas included Sobrino and his unnatural sinfulness in that distancing from Christian civilization in his statements that implicitly connected the Mercedarian to the allegedly African tendency toward suicidal acts observed in Cartagena.

By not treating Sobrino's body with full Christian funereal pomp, Villegas implied that the friar should be grouped with Africans and criminals, people noted for their suicidal proclivities. The friars of Sobrino's order were especially sensitive to this dishonor to a cleric, an elite man of European ancestry. After Sobrino's burial in the *casa de la penitencia,* his Mercedarian superior further agitated Villegas by complaining that Sobrino should have had a church burial, supporting his claims with anecdotes about two suicidal clerics in Lima who had received this honor.[45] Leniency in burying suicides was not unknown in other parts of Spanish America: Tortorici gives an example of a suicidal friar in seven-teenth-century New Mexico, also imprisoned by the Holy Office, who received an ecclesiastical burial.[46] The authorities always used surviving clues to shape a narra-tive that would either condemn a suicide to a non-Christian burial or even dese-cration of his or her corpse, or, on the contrary, they might find clues that helped them interpret the suicide as repentant or unable to rationally control their acts and thus permit them burial within the Church. Priests in early modern Europe and Spanish America who committed suicide in fact often had the privilege of receiving a sacred burial, and probably many more clerical suicides were never documented as such to preserve the socially appropriate façade of clerical honor and reputation.[47] Their superiors might decide that priests who committed suicide should receive quiet, discreet, nighttime burials with no bells but still enjoy eternal rest in sacred ground.

Clerical suicides also did not fall under the jurisdiction of secular courts that might desecrate the posthumous bodies of the departed. Villegas emphasized that he had actually shown Sobrino's corpse some respect, because, as he noted, gener-ally Cartagena suicides were buried in the trash heaps or on the beaches.[48] Accord-ing even less respect to the physical body of a suicide, in nineteenth-century Cuba masters burned their slaves' bodies to convince other slaves that they would not return to Africa if they killed themselves.[49] If suicides' bodies in Cartagena, pos-sibly often African bodies, were treated as trash, it seems that the horrific treat-ment of corpses narrated in the early 1600s by Alonso de Sandoval, who described slaves' bodies left uncovered on patios, behind doors, and in the streets, had not improved in the intervening 160 years.[50] Whatever his sins, Sobrino's fellow Mer-cedarians did not appreciate the association, however indirect, of a member of their order with the desecration of a devalued, low-caste and low-status body.

Villegas felt he had acted to protect clerical honor, and he shaped this case file to justify that he made the right decision in secretly burying Sobrino at night in profane ground. The inquisitor valued secrecy to, in his view, protect the fragile reputation of some branches of the Catholic Church in Cartagena. He noted that the local Mercedarians did not have the corporate strength to endure being "pub-licly defamed" *(públicamente infamado)* because their "poor convent" was "almost deserted" and "made up of very few religious, some dehabilitated by illness and age, and the rest very young" *(se compone de pocos religiosos, unos inhábiles por enfermos y ancianos, y otros los mas muy jóvenes)*.[51] As the lone inquisitor in Carta-gena, Villegas viewed himself as a protector of the weak local church, threatened by Sobrino's sins. Villegas claimed he found the suicide and the rush of decisions he had to make in its aftermath, in rapid consultations with other clerics in atten-dance, almost unendurable. At the end of the night, Villegas said he was disturbed and mentally exhausted from lack of sleep, as a way to lessen the blame for what may have been a bad decision. He complained that he and his colleagues barely survived the night and endured "inconceivable embarrassment due to this horrific event."[52]

To further justify his decision and to highlight how he hoped he made the right choice, Villegas expressed the panic he felt during his search for an appropriate burial location. His desire to maintain secrecy competed with the hot damp climate that forced him to make rushed decisions. First Villegas suggested burial within the jail itself, which would have eased the pressures and his fears of the midnight walk through the streets, but the noise of tearing up the floors promised to draw the attention of neighbors. Despite his worries, it seems that he made the right decision according to the demands of the climate and in line with centuries of tradition for burying suicides. Expediency in burial and time of burial were important concerns in the tropical areas of Spanish America, even those significantly cooler than Cartagena. Late-eighteenth- and early-nineteenth-century reformers believed it was more healthful for bodies in transit to avoid contact with the public and the direct rays of the sun. They therefore chose early morning or the evening (not midnight) as appropriate times to transport corpses to their burial, using quieter streets.[53] Throughout early modern Europe, in cities as diverse as Amsterdam, Stockholm, London, and Leipzig, both common practice and law codes demanded a quiet, nonceremonial, nonreligious night burial for suicides, although in Protestant countries, at least in theory, the consecrated or unconsecrated status of cemeteries did not matter.[54] Not long after Sobrino's death, Bourbon reformers sought to secularize all Spanish American burials.[55]

Beyond these specific concerns about Sobrino's burial, Villegas had to formulate a character for the friar that stressed a willful, willing, clear-headed desire to die, unmitigated by melancholy, insanity, or thoughts of repentance. Sobrino was incorrigible, unemendable; not just suspect, but an actual heretic.[56] Otherwise there was a chance that he should have received burial within the Church and that Villegas made a bad decision. From the first pages of the case, Villegas presented Sobrino as a man "ravaged by vice, an inveterate faker, acting on his uncontrollable passions."[57] These three negative characteristics (sin, dishonesty, and irrational, inappropriate emotions and lusts) position Sobrino as acting against all of the cherished values of this society and its ideas of honor. He also acted sickly, but again the inquisitor said that that was all faked and that he had tricked them, according to a doctor who judged him as relatively healthy. Villegas sensed the false persona Sobrino created but emphasized his constant dishonorable dissimulation, not his joviality. He summed up Sobrino's character as so impenitent, abandoned, and irreligious that those who knew of his acts viewed his confessed unstoppable incontinence as unbelievable for a man his age.[58] Again there is an insinuation that the Holy Office can excuse "natural" sexual indiscretions in young men, but that older men act unnaturally if they have not moderated their sexuality. Villegas emphasized sin to portray Sobrino as unsympathetic and irredeemable, in order to prove that his burial was appropriate. The sole local inquisitor and the other tribunal functionaries also wanted to prove that Sobrino gave no external signs of considering suicide, to take the blame off themselves.

Villegas's investigation of Sobrino's suicide concentrated on documenting the friar's mental state leading up to his death, the rumors that may have been circulating about the death, and justification for the decision to bury him in profane ground. For all three goals, it is clear from the specific questions asked that the tribunal wished to protect its own reputation and prevent further investigation into the case by superiors. In regard to rumors of the secret burial, witnesses reported that those who lived in the *casa de la penitencia* believed the midnight burial was for the body of a *loco* who had been incarcerated in the Hospital de San Juan de Dios.[59] A *presbítero* said that it was "publicly known in the city that in the hospital there was a man that professed many blasphemies and propositions against our holy faith" *(había sido publico en la ciudad que en el hospital había un hombre que profecía muchas blasfemias y proposiciones contra nuestra santa fe).* Commonly people attributed suicide to insanity and irreligiousness, or at least that is how they presented it to the authorities. However, in this case, Villegas created his archival narrative to protect the local church, so this witness's words seem almost too convenient. The witness contends popular ignorance of Sobrino's suicide and burial, but support for the secret, profane burial of a nameless, penniless, insane blasphemer.

All witnesses, including a doctor, confirmed that Sobrino had shown no indications of dementia, rage, desperation, or any kind of dissatisfaction with the inquisitor and his sentence. On the contrary, he generally had a happy, reasonable, calm disposition. At the same time, he seemed to be penitent and suffering for his sins and prayed regularly, according to statements made by witnesses working within the jail. If Sobrino killed himself while in a sane state, legal traditions held him more accountable for the sin.[60] Historians argue that the era from the late seventeenth century to around the precise time of Sobrino's suicide actually encompass a time of growth in *non compos mentis* judgments that allowed suicides burial in sacred ground, especially noblemen who customarily received funereal honors. Very gradually suicide became not a crime or a sin, but a manifestation of mental illness.[61]

At only one moment did Sobrino's jailers notice any agitation. The prison warden and the slave who served the friar said that on the first day he spent in the cell he refused to eat until supper, but instead Sobrino said he would spend the entire day crying. This was the only sign he gave of any emotional distress. A woman incarcerated in the next cell claimed to have heard no cries or shouts, even on the day of his death. The inquisitor admitted denying Sobrino's request for a better cell, but this was not directly linked to his suicide. In a hybridized understanding of suicide, the witnesses from inside the jail noted Sobrino's short-lived melancholy (a valid medical explanation dating back at least to the 1600s) but were also led to consider psychological states such as dementia.[62] In contrast, Villegas adopted a religious or moralizing tone as he sought to package the investigations in a way that would gain his superiors' approval. While the jailers who saw Sobrino daily noted no signs of desperation, Villegas characterized the friar in this way, emphasizing that he had indulged himself in one of the gravest sins, an act that was "cruel, barbaric, and inspired by the devil."[63] In his introduction to the case, Villegas did not return to the witnesses' construction of Sobrino as penitent, because of course this went against the overall argument and the themes he wished to push with this case file and archival narrative.

By committing suicide, Sobrino created an ending for his active role in narrating his own life, surrendering that task to Villegas. Once he received his sentence, Sobrino must have known that the constant reiteration, by himself and others, of his joker or buffoon persona had failed to disguise his serious sins. Sentenced to a formal penance, he could no longer pretend that his acts were lighthearted fun or youthful high jinx. This realization struck at the root of his identity, perhaps causing him to face himself as man with unnatural desires, even if he could explain his emotions and actions as falling within the natural end of the spectrum. No defendant would want to present their own desires as being "against nature," but after sentencing, how could a false persona survive?[64] Sobrino now had to suffer officially sanctioned humiliation, as a prisoner of the Holy Office or as a permanently low ranking friar among his former peers. The Mercedarian most likely viewed his demotion and loss of freedom and power as unendurable, especially since he seemed to thrive on sexual and other kinds of power over his social inferiors. He may have even pondered the guidelines relating to suicides laid out by Alfonso X's *Siete partidas,* an important founding document in the Spanish legal tradition. Explaining this choice in the religious and judicial framework of the time, it makes sense that Sobrino viewed his death as necessary for two reasons: (1) despair caused by an accusation of a serious crime and the shame of guilt and fear of punishments and (2) the fact that he was a "rich, distinguished, or powerful" person who had lost "honor . . . which he formerly possessed."[65] Sobrino was used to controlling his own life and imposing his will on others. If his penance threatened that way of life and the persona he had created as a young man, with continued manifestation of personal power, he ended it.

Sobrino's suicide threatened the secrecy of Villegas's investigation into his alleged unnatural desires and proclivities for sodomy, so this fatal, decisive act actually had great power to spark fear and panic in the local inquisitor by publicly illuminating the many weak points in the local clergy. Sobrino effectively asserted his personal will and historical agency by killing himself, sowing chaos and possible scandal in Cartagena.[66] Unlike so many other inquisitorial investigations, in this case physical and corporeal evidence remained; as Craig Koslofsky observes in a study of suicide in Saxony, "the body of each suicide raised potentially divisive

questions of ritual form and administrative authority. Conflicts erupted because the body of the suicide remained a powerful and ambiguous sign."[67]
Cartagena had experienced internecine political conflicts and factionalism for centuries, but at this moment the Catholic Church was in a weaker state than ever. Villegas's duty, as the sole presiding inquisitor, was to assert and defend the ebbing Holy Office tribunal. Inquisitors, in practice, actually did not have that much experience dealing with bodies. They preferred cerebral theological debate that left behind only carefully filed and preserved written documents. Only by disposing of Sobrino's body in utter darkness and silence did Villegas believe that he could return clerical sexuality to the shadows of the convent, the confessional, and the hidden pages of the Holy Office archives. But, in the process, both men created archival narratives revealing their secrets, confounding the un/natural nature of desire in the very process.

NOTES

1. Archivo Histórico Nacional, Madrid, Inquisición 1669, *Proceso de fe de Fray Esteban Sobrino,* bloque 1, hoja 1.

2. Ibid., cuaderno 2, hoja 2.

3. Ibid., bloque 1, hoja 1. For origins of the Holy Office *casas de la penitencia* and the difficulties in enforcing incarceration, see Henry Charles Lea, *A History of the Inquisition of Spain,* vol. 3 (London, 1908), 154–56.

4. Natalie Zemon Davis, *Fiction in the Archives: Pardon Tales and Their Tellers in Sixteenth-Century France* (Stanford: Stanford University Press, 1987); Kathryn Burns, *Into the Archive: Writing and Power in Colonial Peru* (Durham, N.C.: Duke University Press, 2010).

5. Zeb Tortorici, "Reading the (Dead) Body: Histories of Suicide in New Spain," in *Death and Dying in Colonial Spanish America,* ed. Martina Will de Chaparro and Miruna Achim (Tucson: University of Arizon Press, 2011), 54.

6. These two sides fit very well with cases cited in Helmut Puff, "Nature on Trial: Acts "Against Nature" in the Law Courts of Early Modern Germany and Switzerland," in *The Moral Authority of Nature,* ed. Lorraine Daston and Fernando Vidal (Chicago: University of Chicago Press, 2004), 232–53.

7. See ibid., 248, and the mention of "Christianity's outsiders as proselytizers for the cause of the 'unnatural.'"

8. All population figures are from Adolfo Meisel Roca and María Aguilera Díaz, "Cartagena de Indias en 1777: Un análisis demográfico," *Boletín cultural y bibliográfico* 34, no. 45 (1997). This essay has also been published as *Tres siglos de la historia demográfica de Cartagena de Indias* (Bogotá: Banco de la República, 2009). See also Linda L. Greenow, *Family, Household, and Home: A Micro-Geographic Analysis of Cartagena (New Granada) in 1777* (Syracuse: Syracuse University, Geography Department, 1976), 7, 25–26, 29–30.

9. Tortorici, "Reading the (Dead) Body," 76–77.

10. See Martin Nesvig, *Ideology and Inquisition: The World of the Censors in Early Mexico* (New Haven, Conn.: Yale University Press, 2009), 6–9, 20–47, 168–73. The best overview of the Cartagena tribunal is Fermina Álvarez Alonso, *La Inquisición en Cartagena de Indias durante el siglo XVII* (Madrid: Fundación Universitaria Española, 1999). The other essential source for Cartagena is Anna María Splendiani, José Enrique Sánchez Bohórquez, and Emma Cecilia Luque de Salazar's *Cinquenta años de*

Inquisición en el tribunal de Cartagena de Indias, 1610–1660, vols. 1–4 (Bogotá: Centro Editorial Javeriano, 1997). Another good summary of inquisitorial practice, including in Cartagena, is Diana Luz Ceballos Gómez, *Hechicería, brujería e Inquisición en el nuevo reino de Granada. Un duelo de imaginarios* (Bogotá: Editorial Universidad Nacional, 1994), esp. 115–24.

11. Richard Greenleaf, *The Mexican Inquisition of the Sixteenth Century* (Albuquerque: University of New Mexico Press, 1969), 1.

12. Zeb Joseph Tortorici, "*Contra Natura:* Sin, Crime, and 'Unnatural' Sexuality in Colonial Mexico, 1530–1821," Ph.D. diss., University of California, Los Angeles, 2010, 89.

13. Ibid., 322.

14. Ibid., 202–7, 222–23, 225, and 228–29.

15. Nicole von Germeten, *Violent Delights, Violent Ends: Sex, Race, and Honor in Colonial Cartagena de Indias* (Albuquerque: University of New Mexico Press, 2013), chaps. 6 and 7.

16. For the history of the notorious scandals and conflicts involving Bishop Piedrola and Cartagena's convents in the 1680s, see José Manuel Groot, *Historia eclesiástica y civil de Nueva Granada*, tomo 1 (Bogotá, 1889), 385–97; and Henry Charles Lea, *The Inquisition in the Spanish Dependencies: Sicily—Naples—Sardinia—Milan—the Canaries—Mexico—Peru—New Granada* (New York: Macmillan, 1908), 491–97.

17. Lea, *Inquisition in the Spanish Dependencies*, 467–68, 499.

18. Charles Fleener, "The Expulsion of the Jesuits from the Viceroyalty of New Granada, 1767," Ph.D. diss., University of Florida, 1969.

19. Puff, "Nature on Trial," 243.

20. Davis, *Fiction in the Archives*, 2–3.

21. Cristian Berco and Stephanie Fink Debacker, "Queerness, Syphilis, and Enlightenment in Eighteenth Century Madrid," *Revista canadiense de estudios hispánicos* 35, no. 1 (2010): 31–48.

22. *Proceso de fe de Fray Esteban Sobrino*, bloque 2, hoja 5.

23. Ibid., bloque 1, hoja 73.

24. Puff, "Nature on Trial," 232–33, 239.

25. *Proceso de fe de Fray Esteban Sobrino*, bloque 1, hoja 25.

26. Ibid., bloque 1, hojas 32, 73–74.

27. Ibid., bloque 1, hojas 46, 49, 51–52.

28. Ibid., bloque 1, hoja 36.

29. Ibid., bloque 2, hojas 9, 12.

30. Ibid., bloque 2, hojas 13–14.

31. Alonso de Sandoval, *Treatise on Slavery: Selections from "De instauranda Aethiopum salute,"* ed. and trans. Nicole von Germeten (Indianapolis: Hackett, 2008), 153–55.

32. Tortorici, "*Contra Natura*," 210–11, 213, 218–19.

33. *Proceso de Fe de Fray Esteban Sobrino*, bloque 2, hojas 38–44.

34. Ibid., bloque 2, hojas 31–32.

35. Ibid., bloque 2, hoja 53.

36. Ibid., bloque 2, hoja 57.

37. Ibid., bloque 2, hojas 75–79.

38. Ibid., bloque 2, hojas 82–83.

39. Ibid., bloque 1, cuaderno 2, hoja 4. Unfortunately, the document cuts off his last words, which began with "a dios amiguito, todo lo cual. . . ." In this final way, we are reminded that these files present only a very limited window into Sobrino's experiences, especially given Villegas's obvious desire to manipulate the data for his own ends.

40. Ibid., bloque 1, cuaderno 2, hojas 9–12.

41. Paula de Eguiluz masterfully manipulated these fears. See Germeten, *Violent Delights, Violent Ends*, chap. 6.

42. Paul S. Seaver, "Suicide and the Vicar General in London: A Mystery Solved?" in *From Sin to Insanity: Suicide in Early Modern Europe*, ed. Jeffrey R. Watt (Ithaca, N.Y.: Cornell University Press, 2004), 29.

43. *Proceso de Fe de Fray Esteban Sobrino*, bloque 1, hoja 7.

44. Louis A. Pérez Jr., *To Die in Cuba: Suicide and Society* (Durham: University of North Carolina Press, 2005), 35–47.

45. *Proceso de fe de Fray Esteban Sobrino*, bloque 4, hojas 1–2.

46. Tortorici, "Reading the (Dead) Body," 53–54.

47. Ibid., 65–66; George Minois, *History of Suicide: Voluntary Death in Western Culture*, trans. Lydia G. Cochrane (Baltimore: Johns Hopkins University Press, 1999), 142–47.

48. *Proceso de Fe de Fray Esteban Sobrino*, bloque 1, hoja 8.

49. Pérez, *To Die in Cuba*, 43.

50. Sandoval, *Treatise on Slavery*, 58–59.

51. *Proceso de Fe de Fray Esteban Sobrino*, bloque 1, hoja 4.

52. Ibid., bloque 1, hoja 1.

53. See Adam Warren, *Medicine and Politics in Colonial Peru: Population Growth and the Bourbon Reforms* (Pittsburgh: University of Pittsburgh Press, 2010), 164–66.

54. Machiel Bosman, "The Judicial Treatment of Suicide in Amsterdam," in Watt (ed.), *From Sin to Insanity*, 18–20. See also (in the same volume) Seaver, "Suicide and the Vicar General," 31, 46; Craig M. Koslofsky, "Controlling the Body of the Suicide in Saxony," 52, 60; and Arne Jansson, "Suicidal Murders in Stockholm," 92.

55. Pamela Voekel, *Alone before God: the Religious Origins of Modernity in Mexico* (Durham, N.C.: Duke University Press, 2002), 106–22.

56. *Proceso de Fe de Fray Esteban Sobrino*, bloque 2, hoja 67–68.

57. Ibid., bloque 1, hoja 4.

58. Ibid., bloque 1, hoja 3.

59. Ibid., bloque 4, hoja 5.

60. Elizabeth G. Dickenson and James M. Boyden, "Ambivalence towards Suicide in Golden Age Spain," in Watt (ed.), *From Sin to Insanity*, 102–3.

61. Seaver, "Suicide and the Vicar General," 26–27, 31, 36, 47.

62. Tortorici, "Reading the (Dead) Body," 67; and Watt, "Introduction: Toward a History of Suicide in Early Modern Europe," in Watt (ed.), *From Sin to Insanity*, 2–3. See also Seaver, "Suicide and the Vicar General," 37–38.

63. *Proceso de Fe de Fray Esteban Sobrino*, bloque 1, hoja 1.

64. Puff, "Nature on Trial," 243.

65. Tortorici, "Reading the (Dead) Body," 57.

66. Tortorici critiques the notion that suicide by disenfranchised peoples under colonial rule necessarily equates to an expression of individual agency; see ibid., 72–77.

67. Koslofsky, "Controlling the Body," 53.

2

Sacred Defiance and Sexual Desecration

María Getrudis Arévalo and the Holy
Office in Eighteenth-Century Mexico

Nora E. Jaffary

In the spring of 1797, New Spain's Holy Office initiated an investigation of María Getrudis Arévalo, a poor woman of Spanish descent, for the crime of *heregía mixta*, the heresy, as a contemporary theological guide explains, of "disbelieving that Christ is in the consecrated Host."[1] Arévalo had grave doubts about essential tenets of Catholic dogma, and in a repeated cycle of spiritual desecrations that strike the modern reader as powerfully transgressive, she conducted a series of "proofs" to test for God's existence. Seeking to provoke his wrath—if he was real— she invited God to intervene and prevent her from the repeated defilements to which she subjected the Eucharist and various holy engravings. She began in her adolescence to throw these sacred objects to the ground or tear them up, and then graduated in adulthood to smuggling them out of church in order to hide them in her bedclothes before engaging in sexual acts on top of them, pushing them inside her own vagina, or smearing them with her menstrual blood.

The Eucharist was the most significant sacrament of Catholic ritual in Spanish America, and the celebration of the *Santísimo Sacramento* during Corpus Christi the most important public festival in the viceregal capital. The Church subjected all aspects of the production and consumption of the holy wafer that lay at the center of the rite to a complex series of regulations. Francisco Echarri's authoritative eighteenth-century theological guide detailed the various conditions that might desecrate the Eucharist or render it invalid. For example, the host could be prepared only with toasted or baked wheat flour and water and never with barley flour or milk. Consecrating the host with either vinegar or grape juice instead of wine was "a grave sin." Further, if the priest could not physically perceive the wine and holy water at the moment of consecration, the rite by which the Eucharist was transformed into Christ's body was invalid.[2]

Given the theological centrality of the Eucharist, the understanding that Christ himself was present in the form, and the strict regulations governing its production and consumption, we might anticipate that the Inquisition would not view lightly any act that trifled with the divine host. And María Getrudis Arévalo went far beyond trifling. She subjugated the most sacred object of Catholic ritual practice in the enactment of her own intimate biological and sexual experiences. Although scholars have examined the extent to which lay people and church authorities alike might apprehend various elements of Catholic religiosity in eroticized terms, engaging in orthodox devotion was clearly not Arévalo's objective.[3] Zeb Tortorici explains in his introduction to this volume that contemporaries understood as acts of "natural" sexuality those that took procreation as their objective. Arévalo thus engaged in sexual acts "against nature" in the sense that their purpose was desecration rather than procreation.

Contemporary scholars have characterized such actions as those Arévalo engaged in as subversive because of the symbolic inversion they implied. Nevertheless, the officers of the Mexican Inquisition, the most powerful contemporary promulgator of social control, do not appear to have been particularly concerned by Arévalo or her sacramental desecrations. Instead, they repeatedly absolved her of her crimes, sentenced her comparatively lightly, and, in an unusual act of mercy, even created a charitable fund for her maintenance. In asking why Arévalo did not threaten the tribunal of the Holy Office more than we might have expected, this chapter questions how both the late colonial Inquisition and the subjects whose behavior it policed conceived of natural and unnatural female sexuality, transgression, and religious orthodoxy; it also suggests that in embracing our own era's predilection for viewing such acts as those Arévalo engaged in as subverting normalcy and nature, we anachronistically misapprehend the past.

María Getrudis Arévalo, as she initially told one of her confessors, was born "one year after the expatriation of the fathers of the Company [of Jesus]," or in 1768.[4] She described herself as Spanish, although her ability to pass for a *mulata* when it suited her suggests that her ethnic composition may have been more complex.[5] At about eight years of age, after her father's death, she declared she had fled from her mother's beatings and moved into Mexico City's Poor House, because "she had heard it spoken well of." A few years later, she began working as a servant, but shortly thereafter, as she told the court, she left the house she was working in "to go about in liberty with friends and be with men, starting from then on to prostitute herself."[6] Later in her life, she would return to reside at the Poor House.

Arévalo first brought herself to the attention of the Holy Office in 1797 when, at close to the age of thirty, she denounced herself to her confessor, Manuel Antonio Vidal, while convalescing in the capital city's Hospital General de San Andrés. Vidal wrote Inquisitor Juan Manuel Antonio de Mier y Villar explaining that Arévalo had confessed to him that "from the age of 11 to 25 or 30 . . . she had surrendered herself to lechery with such licentiousness that she had taken communion several times in a spirit of vengeance and irritation against God and in perfect desperation." In this first communication, Arévalo stated that she had long doubted the mysteries of the Virgin Birth and the Holy Trinity and did not believe Christ could be truly present in the Eucharist.[7]

These blasphemies, however, represented only a fraction of Arévalo's sins against God and the church. In subsequent interviews Arévalo declared to Vidal, among other things, that "on five occasions, in vengeance, she had sworn against the Holy Trinity, my lord Jesus Christ, and against the tonsures *[coronas]* of priests because she was angry with God because he did not give her money, and for this reason she had entirely persuaded herself that there was no God."[8] In defiance of this potentially absent divine being, Arévalo began "testing" for his existence by engaging in increasingly outrageous acts. She revealed to Vidal that she had "taken communion on three occasions immediately after having been with a man." She stated that she had taken communion "to take revenge on Jesus Christ and his Holy mother, threatening them that I would be taking communion in mortal sin if they did not perform a miracle upon me."[9] She confessed to having desired to make a pact with the devil and had said she would give her soul to him if he could provide her with money, claiming that "God did not perform miracles because the saints that existed had been saintly since they were children, and the rest were saints because of money, and what poor saint had ever lived?"[10]

The court pardoned Arévalo after this initial confession, instructing Vidal to address her errors by supervising her spiritual penance. Over the course of the next twelve years, however, Arévalo repeated this cycle of private threats to God, defiant actions, and autodenunciation five more times. In subsequent confessions, she also admitted to doubting the existence of heaven and hell ("for who," she asked, "had ever gone there to see them?").[11] She also attested to her practice of daring God or the Virgin Mary to prevent her, if they had the power to do so, from committing the sacrilegious deeds she proceeded to enact. In her anger at God, she had thrown engravings of the saints and of the holy cross and the rosary on the floor, destroying them. On other occasions, she had "placed dogs on [holy] images."[12] When this failed to elicit a divine reaction, she had smuggled them out of church and either hidden them in her bed "when she lay down there with a man" or inserted them into her "unclean vessel" *(vaso inmundo).*[13] In her 1805 autodenunciation, she elaborated on the latter act declaring that "on some occasions, although not always, she had trampled on and destroyed images of the saints and many times the holy cross and the rosary, applying them as well to the most indecent parts of her body, and this she had done to herself with the accomplices of her sordid acts . . . although they had been unaware of it."[14] Ultimately, incensed by the Holy Office's 1805 decision to sentence her with six years' confinement in the Recogimiento María Magdalena, she had taken engravings of the Virgin of Guadalupe and San Luis Gonzaga along with a book of the acts of faith imprinted with the Holy Trinity, cursed them, torn them up, and "used them to clean her 'hidden parts' during a time when she was menstruating" (usó de ellas para limpiarse partes ocultas, estando en la actualidad menstruando).[15] She had then entrusted the stained engravings, contained in a cigar case, to the chief bailiff to send to the priests at the recogimiento, telling him "it was a warning to the priests."[16]

Arévalo's actions intrigue modern-day readers. We are immediately interested in the sexual nature of Arévalo's practices. Whether our consideration is analytic or voyeuristic (or both), in the twenty-first century we are a society (as this volume and others like it attest) fascinated by sex. And for us, ideas of the scandalous, the transgressive, and the outrageous often begin with subjects of a sexual nature. In our current climate, as Ariel Levy has recently examined, women's widespread public performances of sex are widely perceived—and marketed—as transgressive.[17] Similarly, although for different reasons, scholars of Latin American history in the past two decades have generated a predominant interpretation of ritualized bodily acts, such as those Arévalo committed, in terms of symbolic inversion—as challenges to the institutional power of the patriarchal Catholic Church. Jean Franco, for instance, has advanced such an analysis in her discussion of one of Arévalo's contemporaries, Ana de Aramburu, a woman the Inquisition accused of false mysticism in 1801. In her trial, various witnesses described how Aramburu had vomited blood, simulated lactation, and experienced rapture. Several witnesses claimed she had used her own menstrual blood to fake the appearance of stigmata. Franco concluded that if Aramburu had used menstruation in this way, she had threatened the Inquisition by using "the very proof of women's inferiority to enhance her own status," converting "her own body into values that transformed that status of women, that turned the 'low' into the 'high.'"[18]

In this chapter I suggest an alternative approach to apprehending such experiences.[19] Although our temptation and initial interest in Arévalo's case may be, first and foremost with the meaning of the sexual activities it describes, the interpretation I advance here considers whether matters of a sexual nature were foremost on the minds of those most immediately involved in her case—Arévalo herself, her confessors, and her inquisitors. If we are obsessed with sex—if, as a former colleague of mine once commented, it is for our age what death was for the Victorian age—then what was "sex" for people in the eighteenth century? My answer—both obvious and yet curiously underapprehended in contemporary academic readings of figures like Arévalo—is religion, and for people living in New Spain, perhaps in particular the formalized, ritualistic aspects of religion.

Despite what may strike us as their transgressive nature, Arévalo's sexual activities do not seem to have particularly disturbed her inquisitors. One of the striking aspects of Arévalo's trial is its cyclical structure. Arévalo denounced herself a total of five times to the Holy Office, in part because on the first four occasions the Inquisition pardoned her contraventions. Indeed, rather than appearing outraged by her activities, the court repeatedly reacted by treating Arévalo with the greatest leniency possible. After her first denunciation, her confessor, Vidal, informed the court that he had imposed fairly strict spiritual disciplines on Arévalo: every day for one year she was to wear two penitential ropes *(mecates)* around her waist for eight hours, pray the holy rosary on her knees, do one-half hour of meditation on the *novísimos* of the soul, and regularly confess and take communion.[20] Characterizing these disciplines as "very strange and ridiculous" *(mui extraña y ridícula)*, the court responded that Vidal should exercise greater charity. Inquisitor Bergora y Prado instructed Vidal that he should moderate "the penances of his *penitentes* such that they might fulfill them," specifically reducing those of Arévalo to monthly confession for one year, a brief period of daily acts of faith, hope, and charity, and the requirement that she recite the Rosary and the Hail Mary "in whatever way it is possible for her to do so."[21]

The court did not impose harsher punishment than closer spiritual regulation on Arévalo after her two subsequent confessions. Indeed, in December 1799, just a month after receiving the tribunal's absolution for her third autodenunciation, Arévalo again requested an audience with the court. She did this first via her then-confessor, Friar Mariano José Gama, a cleric at the Mexico City Poor House, and a fortnight later, when the court had done nothing to respond to this appeal, by appearing personally at the gates of the inquisitorial palace, adjacent to the Plaza de Santo Domingo in the center of Mexico City. A brief entry in her file dated January 17, 1800, notes that one María Getrudis Arévalo had presented herself at the entryway of the tribunal to denounce herself at the time of Christmas vespers. A notary recorded the court's disinterested response: "she was told that she would be called once the holidays had ended" *(dichosele que se llamaría pasadas las vacaciones)*.[22] Arévalo waited in vain for over five years for the court to call her. Finally, in July 1805, she took action again. At this time, another cleric wrote to the court that Arévalo had yet again denounced herself to him, detailing how she had repeatedly smuggled consecrated hosts out of church to either destroy them or place them in her bed, "and with horrible disobedience had forced them into her filthy vessel [her vagina], cursing them with abominable horror" *(las había entregado en la cama, y con horrible desacato, las había arrojado en el vaso inmundo, maldiciéndolas con horror execrable)*.[23]

Only after this fourth autodenunciation did her inquisitors at last condemn Arévalo's actions, sentencing her with *abjuración de levi* (a public swearing of an oath testifying to her crimes), six years' reclusion in a Mexico City recogimiento, and the regular performance of spiritual exercises, including confession, partaking of the Eucharist, and, for the first year of her seclusion, the weekly recitation of the passion of Christ on Fridays on her knees, as well as a part of the Rosary to Holy Mary.[24] Possibly Arévalo's new admission that she had desecrated the Eucharist itself rather than merely sacred engravings and copies of prayers turned the court against her, for in this action she created an association between herself and a medieval sacrilege the Catholic Church associated with Jews.[25] Nevertheless, in terms of its long-delayed condemnation of her crimes, the court was much more lenient with Arévalo than it was with many of her contemporaries tried for other manifestations of heresy—or for pacts with the devil—in the closing century, and even in the last decades of the court's activities.[26] This may have been because of Arévalo's autodenunciations or because she acted largely in isolation and thus had not accumulated a threatening cadre of followers, but it was also clear that the particular nature of her activities—scandalous as they may appear to us—did not particularly threaten the Holy Office.

The court also demonstrated its leniency toward Arévalo through its unusual determination to create a charitable fund for her maintenance. In her penultimate reversion to her Christian faith, Arévalo testified to the Inquisition in 1805 that after having been sentenced to reclusion in the Recogimiento María Magdelana, she had continued to threaten images of Our Lady of Sorrows with further grievous sins. Then she had learned that the Holy Office and the recogimiento's chaplain had named her a new confessor who would provide her with eight pesos every month to help pay for her living expenses. The act inspired a temporary restoration of Arévalo's faith in Christianity. She declared that she had learned then that "Holy Mary was the powerful mother of God, and she believed that her son was in the holy sacrament."[27] Seven years later, the bailiff of the Presidio Provincial de Santiago wrote to the Inquisition to verify its continued support of Arévalo. The royal criminal court had sentenced Arévalo to six months' confinement in the jail beginning in January 1812 for a separate crime. The bailiff described her as both mentally ill *(loca)* and suffering from physical ailments *(achaques)*, and pleaded that the tribunal should maintain its financial support, which this "wretch of a woman" required in order to feed herself.[28] The Holy Office, however, apparently terminated the fund at this point. The closing document in Arévalo's file is a letter she sent to the court later that year requesting release from the Casa de Recogimiento de Santa María Magdalena, where she had apparently been sent upon leaving the presidio. She described herself as "destitute of all clothing and without food appropriate to my station *[calidad]*," since the tribunal had withdrawn its financial assistance.[29]

As well as the leniency the Inquisition repeatedly extended to Arévalo in its sentencing of her and in the financial support it provided her over several years, the tribunal's lack of concern with the specifically sexual components of Arévalo's activities is also conveyed in the language of her inquisitors' judgments of her crimes. In July 1805, the court's prosecutor *(fiscal)*, Dr. Flores, recommended that the court condemn Arévalo's heretical blasphemies. He began his assessment by stating that the case was "of the greatest gravity, because of the personality of the prisoner, the enormity of her crimes, and because of the four relapses she committed."[30] In his subsequent discussion, Flores focused on Arévalo's condemnable defiance of the Church's power rather than on the specifically sexual and carnal nature of the abuses she committed. Although his summary of her religious crimes included Arévalo's practice of fornicating on top of communion hosts and of placing them in her "vaso inmundo," neither action received his special attention but rather appeared as one item on a long list of errors, as condemnable as throwing communion hosts on the floor or declaring that she did not believe in Jesus Christ or Mary.[31]

In their judgment of August 12, 1805, inquisitors Bernardo de Prado and Isidro Sainz de Alfaro condemned Arévalo for heresy, but once again, any discussion of her sexual behavior in their sentence is notable only by its absence. Only in passing did they refer to Arévalo's sexual activities, writing that "she had extracted in her mouth various consecrated forms for the most execrable and unspeakable uses."[32] Their concern appears to have been more the mere fact that she had abused communion hosts rather than the particular means she had used to abuse them. Arévalo's use of her body's sexual powers to defy the power of the church may captivate modern-day readers of her case, but it does not seem to have been particularly disturbing to her contemporary investigators. The court's final conviction of Arévalo was prompted not by her revelations, in the earliest stages of her case, about her bodily defilement of the Eucharist, but by her audacity in repeatedly mocking God's power and that of his earthly representatives in her cycle of repeated false confessions.

One reason the Inquisition may not have focused on the sexual elements of Arévalo's crimes is that sexual acts were not activities of chief interest to the Holy Tribunal. Solange Alberro, an authority on the history of the Mexican Inquisition, classified 20–24 percent of the total number of crimes the inquisition investigated between 1571 and 1700 as involving acts of "sexual transgression."[33] Seymour Liebman's breakdown of the *Abecedario,* a roughly alphabetical index of subjects the Mexican court investigated between 1528 and the early eighteenth century, classified even fewer cases as involving sexual practices. In his analysis, out of a total of 1755 cases, 98 involved solicitation (priests soliciting sex from confessants), 50 involved "simple fornication" (defined as copulation not directed toward procreation), and 117 involved "scandalous or evil words or deeds."[34] The Inquisition's pursuit of "simple fornicators" was comparatively aggressive in the viceroyalty of Peru during an earlier era, with over one-third of the trials pursued in Lima between 1560 and 1600 dealing with this crime.[35] However, even there, the Church had curtailed its vigorous prosecution of the crime in the seventeenth century.

The court's lack of interest in the particularly sexual nature of Arévalo's offenses may have also been due to its inability to see them as sexual. They were not the kinds of activities that women were normally understood to engage in. Arévalo herself described how she placed religious icons and communion hosts in her vagina. It does not seem to be too much of an interpretive leap to suggest that she was masturbating with these items, especially if we consider the exact language she used in her description ("las había arrojado en el vaso inmundo").[36] But her inquisitors either did not perceive her actions in these terms or were not particularly disturbed by them if they did. A similarly perceived absence of the possibility of women's initiative also marked the Church's perception of what Dyan Elliott describes as the trope of "sex in holy places," a genre of didactic literature in the high and later Middle Ages in which a man and a woman have intercourse in a holy precinct (and are later discovered stuck together in that position). As Elliott writes, in all versions of the episode, throughout the period she examined, "the narrative is gendered male."[37]

In the context of New Spain, as Asunción Lavrin's research on conceptions of sexuality demonstrates, the Church did not understand masturbation to be an activity that women practiced. In the extensive body of confessionals and works on moral theology that she consulted, masturbation, an occurrence that "deeply concerned the church," was "always described as an exclusively masculine problem."[38] Zeb Tortorici, however, discusses female masturbation as an issue that confession manuals, including Bartolomé de Alva's 1634 Confessionario Mayor, explicitly addressed.[39] Yet he, like Lavrin, concludes that although confessionals may have warned of the practice, neither criminal courts nor the Holy Office of the Inquisition "worried much about regulating the manifestations of female sexuality," including masturbation.[40] This is a point that Lee Penyak's doctoral research further substantiates. In his survey of criminal sexuality in Mexico between 1750 and 1850, he examined 369 "sex crime" cases, originating in both criminal and inquisitorial courts. Of this total, "illicit female acts" (those involving masturbation, same-sex relations, cross dressing, and child molestation) formed a tiny proportion: six cases.[41] So in New Spain, most forms of sexual deviancy, and certainly those that most disturbed both the Holy Office and criminal courts, were gendered male; this was especially true for men charged with engaging in sodomy, two dozen of whom were executed for the act between 1530 and 1691.[42]

The one instance in which the court of the Holy Office was prepared to prosecute women for their sexual practices occurred when these involved invocations to the devil. The associations the Catholic Church constructed between female sexuality and diabolism were already ancient by Arévalo's time, dating back at least to the fifteenth-century German text the Malleus Maleficarum. From the sixteenth to the eighteenth century, the Church commonly understood submission to the devil's sexual overtures as an indication of demonic possession.[43] Arévalo declared several times during her trial that she had invoked the devil, explaining that "I wanted to make a pact with the devil, although God had not given me license to, and I called him, ripping off my rosary . . . and putting it into my suspicious part [*parte sospechosa*, vagina] . . . saying that I would give him my soul."[44] Perhaps because by the late eighteenth century the Inquisition was more inclined to view demonic pacts in terms of simple superstition, however, Arévalo's investigators did not focus on this aspect of her behavior.

So, although modern readers may be tempted to fixate on the sexual aspect of Arévalo's actions, perhaps because we have learned to understand such phenomena as both titillating and potentially subversive, when her eighteenth-century investigators examined her case, sexuality was not chiefly in their minds. But what of Arévalo herself? What does evidence from her trial tell us about how she perceived her body, her sexuality, and the relationship of either to the institution of the Catholic Church or the Christian faith? The material from her trial reveals three things about how Arévalo viewed her body and her sexuality. First, unlike her investigators, she clearly understood her body as powerful and practical in the sense that it was the site she selected on which to test the truth of Catholic dogma. Her Inquisition trial suggests that Arévalo's central concern, throughout her life, was in testing the power of the Catholic Church. Although she had clearly developed grave doubts about the dogma and practice of Christianity, as someone raised in the profoundly spiritual climate of baroque Mexico she was unable to completely abandon her faith; instead she was driven to repeatedly design and enact tests of God's existence. Significantly, the method she used for engaging in this testing, perhaps because it was the only medium available for her use, was to pit the force and certainty of her body and those acts she knew it capable of—destroying symbols of Catholic ritual, engulfing communion hosts, engaging in intercourse, menstruating, and masturbating—against the potential power of a God whose existence she sought to determine.

Sonya Lipsett-Rivera has recently documented eighteenth- and nineteenth-century Mexicans' extensive practice of interpreting bodies for information about morality and social status. Clothing, gestures, carriage, and adornment, she shows, all served as indicators that allowed Mexicans to convey respect and disrespect and to enforce subservience or exact deference: "the body served as a metaphor for social order and honor. Because the body was the vehicle for people to mentally map and organize their world, it was a symbol upon which it was worth acting."[45] Lipsett-Rivera's findings support the idea that non-elite Mexicans largely adapted the conventional ordering of the body as outlined in contemporary etiquette guides and sermons, privileging the head (associated with masculinity, the state, and God), which naturally ruled over subservient female "limbs."[46] María Getrudis Arévalo's revelations about her own body's perceived force shows it was possible for colonial Mexican women to imagine alternative associations of their bodies. Whereas she may have been taught her body was weak, she saw it as strong.

Second, the documentation of her case also implies that Arévalo, while she may have questioned central elements of Christianity, had simultaneously absorbed the

Church's contradictory teachings about the meanings of female bodies. She lived in an era in which, as Anne Cruz and Mary Elizabeth Perry write, the Church "reinscribed misogyny by focusing on women's powers to lead men's souls to hell."[47] In this period, the Church struggled to reconcile the possibility of the redemptive role with which spiritual women might use their bodies as the primary vehicle for imitation of Christ's example, on the one hand, with the equally powerful notion that women's weaker flesh subjected them to greater diabolic temptations, on the other.[48] In her assumption that the worst possible defilement she could perform on sacred objects was to bring them into contact with her body—particularly while in the performance of sexual acts—Arévalo displayed an attitude that echoed contemporary orthodoxy about the implications of women's bodies that she likely encountered in the sources of religious knowledge—sermons, art, catechism—with which she would have been the most familiar. Her admission of having rubbed her menstrual blood on sacred engravings represents an enactment of the Catholic Church's long-standing preoccupation with the potentially "polluting" aspects of female corporality, an anxiety represented in the prohibition, adopted at each of the four colonial meetings of the Mexican Provincial Council, on women's admission to the choir of any church during the ceremony of the Eucharist.[49] Arévalo's acceptance of the predominant understanding of the female body, and particularly its genitals, as polluting and shameful are indicated in the language that she—like most of her contemporaries—used to describe it, referring to her vagina with the intentionally imprecise term *partes ocultas* (hidden parts) or the contemptible *vaso inmundo* (filthy vessel) or *parte sospechosa* (suspicious part).[50]

Finally, Arévalo's testimony and actions also reveal that neither her own awareness of her body's powers—sexual or otherwise—nor her acceptance of its associations of depravity were of primary importance to her. Arévalo's chief concerns involved neither her corporality nor her sexuality. In fact, the questions driving her motivation for all the actions in which she engaged were theological. As she declared in her first confession, her own poverty—and the existence she witnessed of misery around her—"entirely persuaded me that there could be no God."[51] As she pondered in the same declaration, "I did not want to believe in the passion because [it was clear that] his majesty had not suffered except for the rich people; for the poor, he did not suffer, but rather left them, desiring that they be left with work and with poverty."[52]

Arévalo was compelled to question fundamental tenets of Christianity, but she did so with constant reference to Catholicism. She was drawn to repeatedly incorporate elements of the sacrament of the Eucharist into her manner of questioning Christianity's legitimacy, and in this action revealed herself to be a representative member of her society, one permeated with Catholic ritual practice. Public rituals and celebrations that symbolically enacted the central mysteries of the Catholic faith—including the worship of saints, holy pilgrimages, confraternal devotions, and the popular festivals of Corpus Christi that celebrated Christ's miraculous embodiment in the communion host—were central elements of popular religious practice in New Spain.[53]

Brian Larkin's research on the religious directives in eighteenth-century Mexican wills emphasizes the degree to which devout "lay Spaniards participated in a largely performative religious culture highly influenced by Catholic liturgy." As he observes, "the basic language of devotion" that the Church established in colonial Mexico "informed many of those rites and rituals performed outside the confines of liturgical celebrations."[54] Larkin uncovered how, in their private religious practices and well into the nineteenth century, a broad sector of New Spain's lay population embraced the Counter-Reformation Church's call for liturgical piety, that is, a religious practice involving the symbolic enactment of the life and death of Christ or the saints, thus forging mystical unions with them. Even during the period of the Enlightened religious reforms of the eighteenth century that sought to rationalize religious devotion, Larkin continued to find strong evidence of ritualized, liturgical devotion in the ongoing centrality of confraternal participation in Mexicans' wills, "reveal[ing] the highly liturgical nature of colonial Catholicism."[55]

In his research, Larkin focuses on the religious practices of ordinary colonial Mexicans. Arévalo's Inquisition trial reveals, however, that similar preoccupations—the fascination with liturgical religion—also informed the religious sensibilities of those extraordinary colonial subjects whom the colonial church convicted of heresy. Arévalo articulated about as radical a set of questions about both the tenets of Christianity and the legitimacy of its worldly officers as one could expect to find in eighteenth-century society. Nevertheless, she remained a subject immersed in the orthodoxy of Counter-Reformation religious practice, as is demonstrated in the orthodoxy of the very heterodox acts she performed. Her practice of taking communion in a self-consciously sinful state, placing the host in her "parte sospechosa," and having intercourse on top of hidden communion wafers all involve reenactments of the liturgy, albeit distorted ones. Indeed, the very cycles of desecration followed by guilt, repentance, and confession were themselves highly ritualized. Just days after having issued her abjuración, for example, Arévalo was transferred to the recogimiento to begin her six-year sentence. An official from the institution, the marqués del Valle de la Colina, wrote her inquisitors to inform them that "on the threshold of the Casa de Recogidas, she called me aside and with great shame told me that I should inform the tribunal that she had reneged once again, and in proof of this, she submitted this engraving that she had destroyed."[56] Arévalo further demonstrated her more quotidian absorption of a mentality that was organized around significant events in the Church's history and calendar: the starting point she uses in remembering the year of her birth is that it was the year following the Jesuits' exile from the viceroyalty.

We live in a period in which people's sexual attributes and activities carry enormous import and one in which we often associate acts of transgression and taboo with deviant or unnatural sexuality. In a time when historians broadly accept the necessity to understand the social construction of all facets of reality, realms of thought and action we hold to be both "natural" and "unnatural" and the distinctions between the two continue to evade our analysis. Arévalo's trial, however, confounds the very category of "nature" and the notion of that which is branded as "unnatural," confirming recent scholarship that demonstrates that colonial Mexicans did not subscribe to immovable categorizations of orthodox and deviant sexuality or morality, even when religious instruction strongly encouraged them to do so. In colonial Mexico, lay people and inquisitors alike inconsistently pursued allegations of such "unnatural acts" as sodomy and bestiality rather than denouncing them to judicial authorities.[57]

Arévalo's investigation reveals that those elements of her case that may most attract contemporary readers because of their seeming outlandishness, their apparent subversion of normalcy and of the natural, were of far less significance in her own day. For us, nothing is worth celebrating as much as a rebel. But those acts we see as rebellious because they appear as challenges to the natural order were not of chief interest to her contemporaries. Where we may fixate on the fact that Arévalo may have *masturbated* with a communion host, the Holy Office was more concerned that her transgression involved the desecration of a *host* than in the particular manner of its desecration. My examination of María Getrudis Arévalo's late-eighteenth-century Inquisition trial suggests that sexual transgression—at least the kind she detailed in her court appearances—was not an issue of primary importance either to the court of the Holy Office or even to Arévalo herself. Although the acts in which she engaged to test the power of God and the Inquisition involved her body and her sexuality, as might be expected for a person who lived in a society permeated with Catholic ritual, doctrine, and morality, her most central concerns were theological and ethical in nature. So too, from the point of view of her judges, was spiritual contravention the chief element of her transgression.

NOTES

1. Francisco Echarri, *Directorio moral que comprehende, en breve, y claro estilo todas las materias de la theologia moral* (Gerona: Por Pedro Morera, 1755), 271. I wish to thank Edward Osowski, Cynthia Milton, and Shannon McSheffrey for their aid in helping me think about how to approach Arévalo's story, and Zeb Tortorici for his helpful input in how to improve this chapter. All translations from Spanish are my own.

2. Ibid., 202–3.

3. For a discussion of eroticized religiosity in the colonial era, see Zeb Tortorici, "Masturbation and Desire: Connecting Sexuality and Religiosity in Colonial Mexico," *Journal of the History of Sexuality* 16, no. 3 (September 2007): 355–372.

4. Archivo General de la Nación, Mexico [hereafter AGNM], Inquisición, vol. 1361, exp. 2, fol. 188. Elsewhere, Arévalo supplied contradictory information about her year of birth. In one court appear-

ance in 1799, she claimed to be only twenty-four years old (birth year: 1775). Then in 1805 she declared that she believed she was thirty years old, though she said that she had been born the year after the death of Viceroy Bucareli (1779), meaning she would have been twenty-six. AGNM, Inquisición, vol. 1361, exp. 2, fols. 198, 212v.

5. Ibid., fol. 212v.

6. Ibid., fols. 212v–213.

7. Ibid., fol. 186–186v.

8. Ibid., fol. 188.

9. Ibid., fol. 188v.

10. Ibid.

11. Ibid., fol. 198.

12. Ibid., fol. 199.

13. Ibid., fol. 208v.

14. "Algunas ocasiones, aunque no siempre, ha pisado y destrozado las estampas de los santos y muchas veces la Santa Cruz, y el rosario: aplicándoselas también a las partes más indecentes de su cuerpo y esto ha hecho asimismo, con los cómplices de su torpeza . . . aunque sin saberlo ellos." Ibid., fol. 214.

15. Ibid., fol. 232. *Recogimientos* were reform houses for wayward women in Spain and Spanish America that sought to restore women to virtue through both spiritual penance and physical service. Nancy E. van Deusen has produced the most comprehensive study of these institutions: *Between the Sacred and the Worldly: The Cultural and Institutional Practice of Recogimiento among Women in Colonial Lima* (Stanford: Stanford University Press, 2001).

16. AGNM, Inquisición, vol. 1361, exp. 2, fol. 232.

17. Ariel Levy, *Female Chauvinist Pigs: Women and the Rise of Raunch Culture* (New York: Free Press, 2005).

18. Jean Franco, "The Power of the Spider Woman: The Deluded Woman and the Inquisition," in *Plotting Women: Gender and Representation in Mexico* (New York: Columbia University Press, 1989), 57, 75. Similar readings of the transgressive power of symbolic inversion are advanced by Ruth Behar, "Sexual Witchcraft, Colonialism, and Women's Powers: Views from the Mexican Inquisition," in *Sexuality and Marriage in Colonial Latin America*, ed. Asunción Lavrin (Lincoln: University of Nebraska Press, 1989), 178–206; Martha Few, *Women Who Live Evil Lives: Gender, Religion, and the Politics of Power in Colonial Guatemala* (Austin: University of Texas Press, 2002); and Steve Stern, *The Secret History of Gender: Women, Men, and Power in Late Colonial Mexico* (Chapel Hill: University of North Carolina Press, 1995). For further discussion of Aramburu's case, see Nora E. Jaffary, *False Mystics: Deviant Orthodoxy in Colonial Mexico* (Lincoln: University of Nebraska Press, 2004.)

19. I was inspired in this attempt to think about Arévalo's actions in a different way by Nancy F. Partner's essay "Did Mystics Have Sex?" in *Desire and Discipline: Sex and Sexuality in the Premodern World*, ed. Jacqueline Murray and Konrad Eisenbichler (Toronto: University of Toronto Press, 1996), 296–311.

20. AGNM, Inquisición, vol. 1361, exp. 2, fol. 191.

21. Ibid., fol. 193.

22. Ibid., fol. 204v.

23. Ibid., fol. 206.

24. Ibid., fol. 225v. The Inquisition imposed the declaration of the *abjuración de levi* as a punishment for those accused of minor heresies and the *abjuración de vehementi* for cases of major heresy.

25. Robert C. Stacey, "From Ritual Crucifixion to Host Desecration: Jews and the Body of Christ," *Jewish History* 12, no. 1 (Spring 1998): 11–28.

26. Along with reclusion and abjuración de levi, for example, the Inquisition sentenced Marta de la Encarnación in 1717 to two hundred lashes and ten years of exile from Mexico City for being an *ilusa* and *embustera* (false mystic): AGNM, Inquisición, vols. 788, exp. 24, and 799, exp. 8. William B. Taylor describes one 1777 trial of a creole from Guanajuato tried for demonic pact and sentenced to public humiliation, two hundred lashes, ten years' exile, eight years' hospital service, and spiritual penances; see William B. Taylor, *Magistrates of the Sacred: Priests and Parishioners in Eighteenth-Century Mexico* (Stanford: Stanford University Press, 1996), 336.

27. AGNM, Inquisición., vol. 1361, exp. 2, fols., 236v–237.

28. Ibid., fol. 279v.

29. Ibid., fol. 282.

30. Ibid., fol. 207.

31. Ibid., fol. 208.

32. "Haverse extrahido de la boca varias formas consagradas para usos los mas execrables y nefandos." Ibid., fol. 225.

33. Solange Alberro, *Inquisición y sociedad en México, 1571–1700* (Mexico City: Fondo de Cultura Económica, 1988), 207. Her numbers were compiled from both the *Abecedario de los relaxados, reconciliados y penitenciados* housed in the Huntington Library and the Index of Cases listed in AGNM, Riva Palacio, vol. 49.

34. Seymour B. Liebman, "The Abecedario and a Check-List of Mexican Inquisition Documents and the Henry E. Huntington Library," *Hispanic American Historical Review* 44, no. 4 (November 1964): 558.

35. See Stuart B. Schwartz, "Pecar en las colonias: Mentalidades populares, Inquisición y actitudes hacía la fornicación simple en España, Portugal y las colonias americanas," *Cuadernos de historia moderna* 18 (1997): 51–67.

36. AGNM, Inquisición, vol. 1361, exp. 2, fol. 206.

37. Dyan Elliott, "Sex in Holy Places: An Exploration of a Medieval Anxiety," *Journal of Women's History* 6, no. 3 (Fall 1994): 8.

38. Asunción Lavrin, "Sexuality in Colonial Mexico: A Church Dilemma," in Lavrin (ed.), *Sexuality and Marriage in Colonial Latin America*, 51.

39. Zeb Joseph Tortorici, "*Contra Natura:* Sin, Crime, and 'Unnatural' Sexuality in Colonial Mexico, 1530–1821," PhD. diss., University of California, Los Angeles, 2010, 294–95.

40. Ibid., 295.

41. Lee Michael Penyak, "Criminal Sexuality in Central Mexico, 1750–1850," PhD. diss., University of Connecticut, 1993, 10.

42. Tortorici, "*Contra Natura,*" 32.

43. See Lisa Sousa, "The Devil and Deviance in Native Criminal Narratives from Early Mexico," *The Americas* 59, no. 2 (2002): 161–79; and Ruth Behar, "Sex and Sin: Witchcraft and the Devil in Late-Colonial Mexico," *American Ethnologist* 14, no. 1 (February 1987): 34–54.

44. AGNM, Inquisición, vol. 1361, exp. 2, fol. 189. She also describes invoking the devil on fols. 107v, 222, 223v.

45. Sonya Lipsett-Rivera, *Gender and the Negotiation of Daily Life in Mexico, 1750–1856* (Lincoln: University of Nebraska Press, 2012), 138.

46. Ibid., 145.

47. Anne J. Cruz and Mary Elizabeth Perry, *Culture and Control in Counter Reformation Spain* (Minneapolis: University of Minnesota Press, 1992), xviii.

48. See Mary E. Giles, "Introduction," in *Women in the Inquisition: Spain and the New World,* ed. Mary E. Giles (Baltimore: John's Hopkins University Press, 1999), 1–15.

49. *Concilio provincial mexicano IV celebrado en la ciudad de México el año de 1771* (Querétaro: Imprenta de la Escuela de Artes, 1898), lib. 3, tit. 18, cap. 3, p. 156. On the history of anxieties involving female pollution, see Elliott, "Sex in Holy Places," 12; Behar, "Sexual Witchcraft," 181.

50. Sonya Lipsett Rivera discusses how common such references were in *Gender and the Negotiation of Daily Life in Mexico*, 162.

51. AGNM, Inquisición, vol. 1361, exp. 2, fol. 188v.

52. Ibid., fol. 189.

53. See discussions of such practices in Linda Curcio-Nagy, *The Great Festivals of Colonial Mexico City: Performing Power and Identity* (Albuquerque: University of New Mexico Press, 2004); and Martin Nesvig, ed., *Local Religion in Colonial Mexico* (Albuquerque: University of New Mexico Press, 2006).

54. Brian R. Larkin, "Liturgy, Devotion, and Religious Reform in Eighteenth-Century Mexico City," *The Americas* 50, no. 4 (April 2004): 494.

55. Brian R. Larkin, "Confraternities and Community: The Decline of the Communal Quest for Salvation in Eighteenth-Century Mexico City," in Nesvig (ed.), *Local Religion in Colonial Mexico*, 208.

56. AGNM, Inquisición, vol. 1361, exp. 2, fol. 234. No engraving remains affixed directly to Valle's submission. However, twenty folios earlier in the file, a torn engraving of Saint Aloysius Gonzaga (San Luis Gonzaga) is included in her file—presumably one that Arévalo herself submitted earlier in her trial.

57. Tortorici, "Contra Natura," 432.

3

The Devil or Nature Itself?

Desire, Doubt, and Diabolical Sex
among Colonial Mexican Women

Jacqueline S. Holler

In 1687, seventeen-year-old Gregoria Rosa de Ubeda found herself a demon lover, or at least so she claimed ten years later when she denounced herself to the Holy Office of the Inquisition of New Spain. Speaking to the Inquisition's commissary in Puebla, the priest don Gerónimo Pérez de Posada, Ubeda described how poverty had driven her to invoke the assistance of the Devil. Obligingly, he immediately appeared in the form of a monkey (a perversion of nature that occurred with relative frequency in demonic visitations). Ubeda told her visitor that she no longer desired to be a Christian or to follow the law of God. The Devil asked her to remove her rosary. Thus began a relationship that lasted about eight months and was marked by ever-increasing physical and affective intimacies. At the outset, there were formalities: Ubeda was asked to kiss the Devil's "indecent parts" and to record in writing (and thereby archive) that her soul was his. He then inscribed their pact on her shoulder, where she felt a great burning *(ardor)*. Like many a mortal lover, he sealed these rites with a proclamation of possession, saying, "now you are mine" *(ya eres mia)*.[1]

Perhaps it is no surprise that sexual contact followed. Interestingly, however, coitus was initiated not by the Tempter, but by the young woman who had summoned him in the first place. In the months that followed her initial invocation, Ubeda said, *she* solicited the Devil for sex *(solicito al dicho demonio para tener actos carnales con el)*. He complied, appearing in her room in the form of a single man to whom she was attracted, whereupon the two had sexual intercourse. The Devil assumed this form over the course of some ten or twelve sexual encounters, much to Ubeda's delight. She reported, "On these occasions she felt such passions in her heart that she thought she would die." Later, the Devil "brought her" other

58

single men, and even one married man, for her delectation; she had only to think about it, and one of these men would appear in her bed. Ubeda was quite certain that whatever form her lover took, he was the Devil, since each lover crept into the room through a small gap in the roof beams, which opened before and closed after him. In each case, Ubeda "had with the said men carnal acts, chats, and kisses."[2]

Ubeda's testimony, as archived, presents itself to the modern reader as a curious mix of the fantastic and the mundane. And for a reader steeped in early modern European demonological lore, this mixture may seem more than a little surprising. The Devil appears as a monkey, but quickly takes on the form of a man—happily, and *naturally,* a man to whom Ubeda is already attracted. The Devil creeps in through a tiny hole in the roof but then lies in bed pleasuring her in entirely banal ways; not only with the simply described "carnal acts" but with the "chat and kisses" of everyday romance. He demands the usual demonic promises, but the crowning moment of the pact is not a wild Sabbath but the Devil's words, as simple and commonplace as those of a lover: "you're mine." Even his assumed identities have an aura of the conventional; while he appeared to Ubeda as a monkey, his sexual activities with her were all conducted in the form of a "natural" male body. In fact, on all but one occasion he had sex with Ubeda in the form of a *single* man, thus eschewing apparent adultery in favor of less problematic fornication. This is not the Devil of the European witch hunts, the triumphant prince of perversions, but a much more personal and anthropomorphized demon lover—a decidedly more "natural" incarnation in that he temporarily took on the form of a human.

This chapter is based on eighteen Mexican Inquisition dossiers involving Spanish and mixed-race women accused of demonic pacts, along with other dossiers in which demonic sex was not the accusation but emerged from testimony. This essay is not a general exploration of Mexican demonism or inquisitorial (in)credulity; the goal of this project, rather, is to explore the ways in which inquisitors, women, and interested others framed sexual contact between women and the Devil, and did so in ways that simultaneously perverted and reified the natural/unnatural divide. Studying demonic sex can show us how learned and plebeian Mexicans, men and women, grappled with notions of the supernatural. On the one hand, standard early modern demonology presumed that sex with the Devil was illicit, unnatural, and abominable. (As we shall see, demonology in Mexico largely accepted this view while eschewing the more dramatic markers of unnaturalness associated with the European witch hunts.) On the other hand, the Devil of demonologists was not necessarily that of plebeians or even of learned inquisitors. When we turn to inquisitorial trials, we discover quite a different Devil. First, he was both unnatural (in his occasional animalism and abilities) and natural (in his sexual embodiment and proclivities). Moreover, "unnatural" demonic sex often ended up naturalizing gender and sexual mores rather than subverting them. And finally, inquisitors "naturalized" the Devil when they turned (as they did with increasing frequency) to medico-emotional explanations for women's encounters with him: explanations that female confessants tended to resist rather than embrace. This chapter thus presents demonic copulation as topsy-turvy: early modern demonology flows not from the pens of inquisitors, who medicalize demonic sex, but from a few rapt and relatively peripheral men; women naturalize the Devil's lovemaking while insisting on the supernatural (rather than medical) character of their troubles. Thus, though there is evidence that European demonological lore was known to both learned and popular Mexicans, there is also strong evidence that many of them denied its model of demonic copulation and, thus, its particular reification of the boundary between the natural and the unnatural. Studying women's encounters with the Devil illuminates the ways in which learned and popular Mexicans grappled with this boundary and, perhaps, the degree to which this boundary remained fluid and contested between and within various groups in colonial society.

TRANSATLANTIC DEMONOLOGY AND DEMONIC SEX

But let us return to Gregoria de Ubeda, alone under the roof beams with her demon lover. However new and thrilling Ubeda's dalliance seemed to her, there was nothing new about women's sexual congress with the Devil. Nor, despite the "demonic" character of the New World itself, was demonic sex an American novelty. Physical contact between demons and human beings has a much earlier genealogy; the challenge of demonic corporeality that such contact presented had already been tackled by Peter Lombard in the twelfth century and by Thomas Aquinas in the thirteenth, the latter concluding that both angels and demons could assume virtual bodies capable of the most intimate acts, extending even to a kind of reproduction by proxy. Demons were thus, in the formulation of Aquinas, *unnatural* bodies capable of *natural* sex.[3]

Still, despite the importance of such discussion of the corporeality of angels and demons, sex itself was not yet the sine qua non of either demonolatry or witchcraft. Indeed, according to Walter Stephens, before 1400 the invocation of demons was largely the privilege of learned men. During the fifteenth century, however, sexual intercourse proved a way to overcome skepticism about the ability of powerless women to invoke demons. After the fifteenth-century publication of Heinrich Krämer's *Malleus Malificarum*—an important medieval treatise on the prosecution of witches[4]—the association between women, sex, and demonic temptation grew stronger. The *Malleus* insisted that women were particularly given to demonic witchcraft, that witches were inspired to malefice by the Devil, and that sexual congress was at the heart of demonic pact. By the sixteenth century, sex between women and demons had taken on the significance it would bear throughout the early modern period.

Although European demonologists came to embroider and alter the *nature* of the sex as the boundaries between the natural and unnatural widened, in the early phases of demonology's ascendancy it was otherwise. If sexual congress between women and incorporeal beings such as Satan and his minions might seem inherently unnatural, for Krämer the Devil was a conventional lover, interested in vaginal intercourse and disgusted by sodomy. Man was indeed the measure of all things, and while the Devil and lesser demons might give a *better* performance than men, their sexual practices were the standard ones. In some senses, then, fifteenth- and early-sixteenth-century conceptions of demonic sexuality emphasized their similarity to "normal" male-female relations and "natural" sexual practices. Demons were more "real" the more pleasure they gave: "More pleasure, more reality"—for surely if demons were all in the imaginations of credulous women, they would not be capable of exciting such sexual delight.

Krämer's views on the ubiquity of sexual contact between women and the Devil were largely accepted among European demonologists by 1570, but his relatively "natural" versions of this unnatural sex were being replaced. The better-known Devil of the late sixteenth century presided over Sabbaths in the form of a goat, penetrating women *and* men with a massive barbed or double-headed member that caused not pleasure but excruciating pain, and taking particular delight in deliberate inversions of "natural" sexuality such as sodomy and bestiality.[5] By the time of the establishment of the American tribunals of the Holy Office, then, perceptions of the "unnatural" potential of demonic copulation were in ascendancy.

By the same time, however, New Spain had its own nascent demonological tradition, the product of hybridization between European demonology and the colonial imposition of Christianity on indigenous peoples. As is well known (but beyond the scope of this essay), many learned Franciscans became convinced of the radical demonism of indigenous religions through the course of the missionary effort. Some had come to the New World with a predisposition to root out demonism. One such missionary was Fray Andrés de Olmos, writer of the Nahuatl treatise *Tratado de hechicerías y sortilegios* (1535). Olmos had been involved in witchcraft proceedings in the Basque country in the 1520s before coming to Mexico, and carried with him a Spanish witchcraft treatise created for the Basque extirpations. He carried with him too the perception that women were particularly susceptible to demonic temptation and that some women—aging spinsters in particular—would "even" engage in sex with the Devil.[6] Thus demonic copulation crossed the Atlantic.

But Olmos's demonology was not merely a transposition of European forms. Listing the forms that the Devil took in his apparition to indigenous people, he described first and foremost how the Devil appeared as an "ancient [Precolumbian] lord."[7] Olmos was obsessed with the idea that indigenous idolatry was at its heart Satanism, an elaborate and mocking subversion of Christianity (complete with a female priestly class).[8] Still, Olmos did not give the Devil too much credit, refusing to believe in his ability to transform human beings into animals (or, for that matter, members of the opposite sex).[9]

While Olmos might have been attuned to demonism from the start, his tendency to conflate indigenous religion with diabolism was not unique. Other missionaries conflated the Devil with indigenous gods, as in Bernardino Sahagún's portrayal of Tlaloc and Huitzilopochtli, while others represented the Devil with bat wings, horns, and a tail. A confusing missionary portrayal of the Devil ensued, not least because this apparently immaterial and supernatural figure was represented in embodied form in Nahuatl missionary theater.[10] Regardless of this confusion, it is safe to say that New Spain's own version of demonology, particularly as articulated by Franciscans, indigenized the Devil (and diabolized the indigenous, as Laura Lewis has argued).[11] The effects, historian Francisco Cervantes claims, were significant: first, indigenous cultural achievements were naturalized while indigenous religion became seen as supernatural. Furthermore, the parsing of the natural/unnatural divide in indigenous society may have had the effect of strengthening the power of the demonic.[12] The influence of this demonology on colonial women and their inquisitorial interlocutors, however, appears to have been limited.

THE NATURAL-BORN TEMPTER: THE COLONIAL WOMAN'S DEVIL

If the notion of demonic copulation crossed the Atlantic, New Spain's devils seem to have been much less given to monstrous forms and perverse sexual behavior than was the Counter-Reformation norm. The women who admitted to demonic pacts[13] had likely never read the *Malleus Malificarum*, which was published only in Latin before the nineteenth century, nor had they delved into Olmos's Nahuatl text. Their demonic relations were therefore an idiosyncratic mixture of folk beliefs and popular demonology, with a generous dose of gendered colonial norms. Women's demonic relations were also, crucially, an expression of desire in all of its complexity. As Zeb Tortorici has written, colonial desire was a complex amalgam of lofty spirituality and quotidian craving—for salvation, for food, for sex, for knowledge of the divine.[14] In fact, it might be argued that eroticism and the desire for pleasure were the quicksilver in this alloy.

Reading Inquisition dossiers this way does not require one to believe in belief: that is, one need not credit the truthfulness of confessants in order to attribute meaning to their testimony. Many of the cases studied here were autodenunciations, suggesting at least some measure of sincerity in women's testimony. But authenticity is not the most interesting question their stories raise. Whether women truly believed they had encountered the Devil or not, their descriptions corre-

devil could be unnatural (goat) or natural (human form)

sponded to some personal notion of desirability. The forms he *did* take were therefore often highly "natural" and would hardly surprise a canny inquisitor. As Armando Maggi has emphasized, it was well known to demonologists that demons assumed the form that was desired by the tempted: "Their physical presence mirrors our deepest yearnings." Thus early modern demonology is in harmony with modern understandings of human psychology. Indeed, a modern reader can hardly fail to see basic human longing and psychic need in women's demonic desires. This was clear to Ruth Behar more than twenty years ago, when she described the Devil as in some colonial Mexican Inquisition cases "a kinder, more loyal, and more interested companion than [women's] true-life husbands."[16] This example of wistful longing is certainly echoed in the cases studied here. The Devil came to women when they were longing for many things. Power, marriage, freedom, and money are prominent but do not exhaust the list of desires that catalyzed initial demonic encounters.

The form the Devil took could be, however, troublingly *un*natural. This was particularly clear when demons appeared in animal form. The assumption of animal forms was standard diabolical practice in European demonology, of course, where the animal of choice was the goat. In the cases studied here, however, other animals were more often described, again suggesting the relative weakness of classic European demonology in New Spain. Given the relationship between demonism and indigenous religion and the importance of shapeshifting to the latter, it is not surprising to find a relatively broad set of animals represented: monkeys, cats, dogs, and bulls. The animals were not necessarily grotesque, but they blurred human-animal boundaries (by speaking, as Ubeda's monkey-Devil did) and natural-unnatural ones (as in the sixteenth-century case of María de Ocampo of Guatemala, whose demon lover terrified her by appearing in the form of a black cat carrying a letter in its mouth—a most unfeline act).

Demonic animalism was also unnatural in that it often trangressed the "proper" hierarchical relationship between animal and human. Behar mentions cases in which the Devil appeared as a friendly little dog-companion; but in Gregoria Rosa de Ubeda's story, where she saw the Devil first as a monkey, the animal-Devil ordered her to kiss his hindquarters and directed her to remove the cross she wore and to offer it indignities.[17] In such a case, the subversion of nature was manifest.

Such a subversion, extended to the sexual realm, would imply bestiality, something understood as clearly unnatural. The goat-copulation of European witch trials is an obvious example, and as Moshe Sluhovsky has noted, in Europe the Devil also took the form of a dog who leapt onto women's beds or crawled under their skirts to commit "crimes against nature."[18] But while the animalism of the Devil was a relatively constant theme in the dossiers, it is noteworthy that in none of the women's confessions examined here did bestial copulation with the Devil occur. When sexual acts occurred, the Devil tended to be "renaturalized" as a man, and an if devil = desires of ♀ (handsome), does that make handsome ♂ unnatural?

64   JACQUELINE S. HOLLER

attractive one to boot. Clearly, then, it seems that we can find in the Devil's forms the quotidian, if generally unexpressed, desires of women. Gregoria Rosa de Ubeda's case is perhaps the most straightforward in this regard, since she expressly stated that the Devil had taken the forms of real-life men to whom she was attracted. But other women also hinted at the Devil's beauty or desirability: the runaway slave Antonia de Sotto saw the Tempter as a handsome young white man dressed in black with a white ruff (a charming costume, if rather out of date in the late seventeenth century). Similarly, in 1668 María Bonifaz gave her lover a picture of the Devil as a long-haired and horned young man dressed as a king (though she apparently also possessed a statue of the Tempter as a monkey).[19] Thus the Devil was often, but not always, an attractive man.

Still, one of his hallmarks was the fluidity of his self-representations, and he could be terrifying in addition to beautiful. Clara Josepha de Jesús Solis denounced herself for a twelve-year diabolical relationship including no fewer than three explicit pacts; for her, the Devil first appeared "in the frightening figure of a black [man]," proclaiming himself the "Prince of obscenity" *(Principe de la torpeza).*[20] Nor was this fluidity confined to the Devil's Mexican exploits; in Cartagena, Paula de Eguiluz experienced her demon lover sometimes as a handsome white man, sometimes as a monstrous creature.[21]

The foregoing suggests the relatively fluid ethnic presentation of the Devil in these dossiers. While a sustained comment on the meaning of race within demonic sex is beyond the scope of this chapter, suggestive themes emerge. First, while Laura Lewis has argued that the Devil was overwhelmingly represented as indigenous or introduced through indigenous intermediaries, there is much more variation in the (admittedly small) sample studied here. Blackness, however, is definitely overrepresented among the Satanic incarnations. This undoubtedly relates to prevailing caste-based notions of blackness, but it is noteworthy that the small sample studied presents cases involving women of varied ethnicities conjuring devils of similar variation. One must be at the very least cautious about assuming simplistic equation of blackness and demonism, or whiteness and desirability. Doña María de Ocampo described her demon lover's appearance as both classed and ethnically determined—a white "gentleman" and "a Black man, dressed as a Black"—but never qualified either form with approval or horror, or suggested differing sexual practices or enjoyment on this basis.

The changeability of the Devil in women's testimony is no surprise, given their need to respond to what they perceived as inquisitors' questions, and also given the profound degree of guilt that many women expressed (and, perhaps, experienced) as a result of these encounters. Yet despite these variations, the Devil of the women of New Spain was most notable for his resemblance in form to a regular man. His behavior was also human and even "normal," corresponding to what was common rather than to the wild perversities confessed in so many witch hunts. As

Sonya Lipsett-Rivera and Lee Penyak have shown, late-colonial Mexican men (and some women) also used the Devil's goading to excuse "unnatural" sexual acts; Zeb Tortorici has documented the use of the Devil to excuse acts such as masturbation and erotic acts involving Jesus and the saints—both categories determined to be "unnatural."[22] But in the cases studied here, Satan's sexual conduct was remarkably restrained; where sexual acts are described by women, they are described minimally and as if they were acts between a man and a woman.[23] Doña María de Ocampo listed many times when the Devil "had access" with her, even when she was sleeping between her parents, but the act itself seems to have been simple coitus. In her case, and in most others, inquisitors did not probe for detail. Perhaps as a result, the fantastical genitalia and imagery of the European Sabbat are virtually absent from the dossiers of New Spain. When doña María described the Devil's penis, it was in terms of the human. The member with which he had access to her, she said, was of the length of a *jeme* (the distance between thumb and forefinger) and slender, "like a finger"—a description that would have disappointed a demonologist accustomed to more spectacular and bestial members and practices.

Thus women confessants provided a mixture of unnaturalness and naturalness in their tales of diabolical sexual activity. On the one hand, their demon lovers were transgressive of the boundaries set by nature, most notably in their assumption of animal forms at initial contact and, often, the concomitant inversion of the human-animal hierarchy. On the other hand, the actual sex between woman and demon tended to replicate the tropes and forms of colonial male-female relations and "natural" sexuality.

NATURALIZING (AND MEDICALIZING) DEMONIC PERSECUTION: THE INQUISITORIAL VIEW

As discussed above, by the time of the Holy Office's official constitution in New Spain, European demonological lore had established the veracity of demonic sex, its inherent unnaturalness and grotesquery, and its importance. As is well known, however, New Spain's inquisitors were less convinced. Even in the sixteenth century, they were far from credulous; and by the late seventeenth century, few were willing to grant much credence to the kinds of fantasies that fueled witch hunts elsewhere. But inquisitorial incredulity is not the focus of this essay. More noteworthy for present purposes is that even in the sixteenth century, inquisitors evinced a highly gendered view of the etiology of demonic pact that emphasized melancholic pathology as an explanation for women's diabolic encounters—and thus naturalized the Devil.

There seems to have been relatively little inquisitorial concern about demonic pact among the colony's women. Gregoria de Ubeda was one of very few women tried by or denounced to the Holy Office of New Spain for this crime. Indeed, such

pacts were overwhelmingly associated with men, particularly men of the multiethnic plebeian world.[24] Of the 112 cases of demonic pact I have identified in Mexico's
Archivo General de la Nación, eighteen involve women, one involves a couple,
three implicate multiple parties of unspecified gender, and ninety involve individual men. Why this emphasis on men? According to Jorge Cañizares-Esguerra, the
ability of the Devil to trick men as easily as women was a New World novelty; one
may also see it as a continuation of an older European tradition that did *not* associate demonic temptation with feminine weakness.[25] The greater mobility of plebeian
men may also have raised fears of the spread of popular demonism. Whatever the
cause, women were a clear minority among those accused of demonic pact.

Women were, however, much more likely to engage in sex with the Devil.
Demons might occasionally help a man commit the "nefarious sin" *(pecado
nefando)* of sodomy, but they were much more likely to help men seduce women
through spells, powders, verses, magic words, or even paintings.[26] Women's under-
representation in this corpus of cases dealing with demonic pacts may be partially
explained by their overrepresentation in cases of witchcraft, where the Devil also
turns up; however, in most such cases the Devil is only a visitor rather than the
inspiring force of the European witch panics. So it seems that while New Spain's
Devil was interested in assisting—and having sex with—women, he was not particularly interested in making long-term pacts. Thus, the Devil's temptations were
gendered: largely confining his own sexual attentions to women, he nonetheless
tended to engage in relatively short-term liaisons. This is, perhaps, further proof
that the Devil's informal engagements with women mirrored the typical forms (for
example, *amancebamiento,* or concubinage) taken by plebeian sexual relationships
rather than the dramatic and orgiastic forms of European demonology. In this the
Devil conformed to norms of masculinity figured as "natural" sexual aggressive-
ness and promiscuity.

The relatively meager attention given to demonic pacts involving women does
not mean that New Spain's inquisitors dismissed either the power of the Devil or
the possibility of his copulating with women. Indeed, the dramatic early colonial
case of doña María de Ocampo included explorations of sexual acts between this
young woman and the Devil.[27] Inquisitors were also clearly versed in demonological norms, as was evidenced in 1598 when Marina de San Miguel was asked to
which legion her demon lover belonged. Conventional demonology had established a script whereby women were contacted by lesser demons, then finally
introduced to the Devil himself. Marina, a learned woman herself, reported that
she had been pursued by Barrabas and Beelzebub, but that her long-term sexual
relationship was with Satan.[28]

But even in the late sixteenth century, New Spain's inquisitors exhibited a
marked lack of fascination with demonic copulation or, indeed, women's relationships with the Devil. In the case of Marina de San Miguel, the inquisitors showed

little interest in the specific *nature* of the sexual acts she had purportedly conducted with the Devil, nor did they press her for details on the corporeality of the body he had used when he copulated with her in the form of an "Angel of Light."

Similarly, in the same year, when the nun María de la Natividad described her constant temptation by the Devil, including his incitement to participate in sexual intercourse with him in the shape of a man, inquisitors seemed wholly uninterested, exhorting her to consider demonic persecution a hopeful sign. The inquisitors made no inquiries about the form the Devil had taken or about his corporeality; instead, they made discreet inquiries about Sor María's mental state.[29] One cannot therefore trace a clear trajectory from inquisitors' avid acceptance of demonological norms in the early colonial period to disillusionment later on. Nonetheless, the Holy Office's already tepid approach to demonic pact among women does seem to have cooled even further over time, as Fernando Cervantes ably documents.[30] What we have here is evidence of inquisitors' devotion to the gendered norms of their society: that is, they viewed women as particularly given to sexual weakness but tended to minimize the extent and importance of demonic hold over women.

Stereotypes of women's weakness also predisposed inquisitors to distrust their testimonies. Therefore, even in relatively dramatic cases, inquisitors exhibited lack of credulity. In 1691, for example, the *mulata* slave Antonia de Sotto of Durango appeared before the local commissary with a picaresque tale of her servitude to the Devil. With the mediation of an indigenous man,[31] Antonia claimed, Satan helped her escape from slavery, after which she apparently lived for six years disguised as a man, gambling, fighting bulls, and committing various crimes including murder. Surely such an inversion of natural gender and ethnic roles should have piqued the inquisitors' interest and, perhaps, convinced them of diabolical involvement. Noting the inconsistencies in her story, however, the *fiscal* (prosecutor) asked that she be examined with particular attention to the many doubts her story raised and considering the possibility that the story might have been dreamed up in order for her to get away from a harsh master.[32]

In contrast to the European witch hunters who viewed sexual contact between women and the Devil as the ultimate proof for accusations of demonism, New Spain's inquisitors seem to have accepted the possibility—and indeed the ubiquity—of demonic copulation without making it their central concern. In the case of young doña María de Ocampo, the inquisitors were much more interested in learning whether María had renounced God than in discussing the details of the Devil's penis or the sexual acts to which María confessed. María was, however, asked whether she had been impregnated by the Devil: a question that smacks of quasi-scientific demonological interest in the boundaries between natural and unnatural sex. But this question was advanced only once and seemingly dropped, even though María's answer (she did not know, but her period was late) was suggestive. Inquisitorial interest in the Devil's "unnaturalism," even in the middle of the sixteenth century, seems to have been quite thin.

Similarly, in a relatively dramatic 1748 case from Coahuila, all of the women implicated admitted to "obscene cohabitation" with the Devil, but testimony was relatively inattentive to sex.[33] Instead, as seen in María's case, the inquisitors' central focus was ascertaining whether the women had renounced God, not whether they had had "natural" or "unnatural" sexual encounters with demons. Thus there is little in the approach of the Holy Office that smacks of the obsessive attention to sexual "evidence" that dominated European demonology between 1500 and 1700.[34] Over time, if the Devil remained responsive to women, the Inquisition became less and less credulous regarding women's congress with the Devil and more inclined to regard their stories as pathological or attention seeking.[35] Indeed, by the late seventeenth century the famous case of the demoniacs of Querétaro revealed a Holy Office that had lost interest in and patience with stories of diabolical possession of women. In that case, women who alleged such became the centerpiece of a fervent Franciscan revivalism—until one of the "possessed" maidens gave birth, confirming inquisitorial suspicions that the demoniacs were shameless frauds. (There was, evidently, little interest in the theory that the pregnancies among the demoniacs might be unnatural: that is, the result of the activity of incubi, who were theoretically capable of impregnation.)

Women's sexual temptation was increasingly seen by inquisitors as a worldly rather than a diabolical issue. Indeed, by the eighteenth century the Mexican tribunal had ceased serious investigation of diabolism.[36] Thus, neither women nor inquisitors pursued an obsession with perverse sex between women and demons, even though, as we have seen, New Spain's demonology accepted demonic copulation, as did, apparently, some colonial women. The few truly "unnatural" Mexican cases of demonic sex—orgiastic copulation in the grand European demonological vein—flowed not from the pens of learned inquisitors but from the allure of demonic explanations among the lower strata of colonial society.

Outside the formal structure of the Holy Office were those men who were more credulous, and for whom classic demonological imagery and particularly unnatural sexuality were important and exciting evidence of the war between good and evil. The first of these cases, a 1598 denunciation, involved a Spanish woman who made friends with a shape-changing indigenous woman and who claimed that for a whole year the two women had gone to parties where goatlike creatures mingled with human beings. At one of these gatherings, the Spanish woman knelt before a demon with long claws and "a penis as big as a club" who importuned her to promise him her loyalty and obedience. Crucially, the case was presented to the Holy Office not by the woman herself, but by a friar to whom she told her story.[37]

A priest's credulity is also the cornerstone of a case from 1752, in which an eighteen-year-old girl apparently described to the parish priest of Zinguilucan her many struggles with the Devil, which included masturbation with holy images and with the consecrated Host as well as sexual congress with animals, which she attempted to incite to copulate with the holy images she herself used so lasciviously. The rapt priest wrote to Mexico City inquisitors, "God knows what I have gone through, and I offer to His greater glory that this woman should confess her sins . . . now, may God be glorified, she is out of the grips of the Enemy." For the priest, languishing far from Mexico City in a minor post, the unnatural torments of this teenaged girl were proof of his own continued importance to the struggle against evil.[38] For the religious men in both of these cases, the raw interaction between women and the Devil served the same function as did holy women's unmediated experience of God. That is, unnatural demonic lust provided essential proof of the workings of the sacred and the demonic in everyday life and served as a means to overcome the weakness of faith that religious men perceived all around them. This same dynamic would operate in the 1691 case of the demoniacs of Querétaro.[39]

One final case of classically unnatural demonic copulation was also mediated by a man, in this case not a clergyman but a Spanish traveler who lodged in Vera Cruz with the *mulata* Francisca Zerdan. He claimed an illicit relationship with her and accused her of having made him impotent with other women. Most damningly, he said that he had perceived her having sexual intercourse with an incubus, breathing heavily and making movements as though she were having sex with a man even though no man could be seen and the door was locked. Afterward, he said, the bed was soaked with semen, as though she had had intercourse with many men, and the odor was so foul it made him want to vomit.[40] This damning evidence, despite its verisimilitude in terms of demonological lore,[41] was not enough to convict Francisca, who was ultimately exonerated on the basis of her more convincing tale of anger and gendered/caste violence and her refusal to admit to any of her accuser's outlandish claims. The case does show, however, that the European demonologists' conceptions of unnatural sex between women and demons were known not only to churchmen but to laymen too. These ideas were not, however, triumphant, either in the daily lives of women or in the Inquisition's dock.

In the end, the demon lover of colonial New Spain was not a replica of the demanding and perversely sexual Devil of the European witch hunts. Rather, in his sexual relations with women the Devil of New Spain was remarkably "natural." For confessing women, the Devil's sexual activities were pursued in the form of a man, and apparently followed the norms of conventional sexuality. For inquisitors, demonic sex not only took relatively pedestrian and uninteresting forms, but also confirmed womanly weakness and the gender order. Indeed, to some degree the Devil was a stand-in for illicit, but "natural," desire; from the earliest days of the colony, learned inquisitors worked with a "natural" and gendered definition of demonic sex that, while it never denied the Devil's existence, tended to emphasize the spiritual and quasi-medical weaknesses of women that predisposed them to temptation. Only a few voices raised the alarm of perversely, grandly unnatural sex between woman and demon.

MELANCHOLY AND ITS MEANING FOR DEMONIC
SEX: NATURAL OR UNNATURAL?

Melancholy played an important role both in demonic sex and in its liminal status between nature and the supernatural. Melancholy crystallized the natural/unnatural divide and its relationship to sexuality; the disorder was also a point of contention between women confessants and (male) inquisitors. While the two groups may seem to have "agreed" on some of the characteristics of demonic sex, the extent to which inquisitors embraced natural or medical explanations of diabolic copulation was a point of rupture between women and the Holy Office. In fact, even sixteenth-century demonologists recognized the slippery borders between the natural and supernatural in demonic temptation, particularly as those borders were straddled by melancholy. As Angus Gowland has noted, the malaise was important to discussions of demonology because of the close causal connection between the two and the resulting implications for the natural/supernatural divide.[42] In European demonology, melancholy's connection with Satanic temptation was extensively parsed, both by those who saw melancholy as the devil's entrée (preserving the power of the supernatural) and by those fewer writers who viewed witchcraft as a melancholic delusion (and thus a wholly natural and medical problem).[43] As a result, by the late sixteenth century melancholy was no longer simply the purview of physicians, but was the domain of churchmen and demonologists.[44]

An individual's physiology, nonetheless, played a strong role in demonic temptation because of the role of individual humors. Each individual was believed to comprise a distinct balance between the four humors, with certain humors associated with age, gender, and ethnic groups. Certain humors predisposed one to particular maladies, which themselves could blur the natural/supernatural divide. Associated with a preponderance of black bile, melancholy was in some ways analogous to demonism and presented symptoms sometimes impossible to tell apart from those of demonic possession.[45] Indeed, until the late seventeenth century black bile played an important role in establishing a causal or sympathetic link between the melancholic and the Devil.[46] Finally, melancholy might be one more affliction with which the Demon attacked the will of the believer.[47] Melancholy thus was recognized to have both natural (primarily humoral) and supernatural causes, and was both a natural and a moral condition, the precise degree of natural and unnatural content a contested matter.

Both humoral and moral factors made women either more vulnerable to melancholy or less able to resist its effects. Women, who were known to be "colder" than men, were physiologically liable to a surfeit of black bile. For demonologists

Graun / Hippocrates
Uncooked ♀

like Krämer, this tendency, combined with women's carnal nature, made women particularly though not uniquely susceptible to demonic sexual influence. Thus sexuality—particularly women's sexuality—and religiosity were linked explicitly with melancholy in demonological discourse. The melancholic woman became the ideal portal for supernatural penetration of the natural world. At a less rarefied or more quotidian level, melancholy was seen by most churchmen and physicians as leading not only to demonic temptation but to a kind of morbid eroticism. Sex, melancholy, and doubt were thus all linked to demonic temptation and to one another in ways that expand our understanding of sexuality and religion and their links to notions of the natural.

Mexico's inquisitors were clearly steeped in contemporary medical and theological understandings of melancholy, as is revealed by their actions in particular cases. Despite doctrinal beliefs regarding its rootedness in original sin, melancholy seems to have been used by the Mexican Holy Office as a lens through which to view—and minimize the importance of—unorthodox or mad behavior. For example, when the nun María de la Natividad denounced herself in 1598 for heresy and blasphemy, her inquisitors launched an investigation that focused on "whether she is *naturally* melancholic," making inquiries regarding possible complexionate factors resulting from humoral imbalance.[48] Throughout the colonial period, others who denounced themselves received similar inquisitorial compassion.[49] Women were particularly likely to be exonerated on the basis of melancholy, both because of their greater moral weakness and because of the bodily infirmities—for example, retention of the menstruum—that might predispose them to the malady.[50]

The confluence of melancholic despair, demonism, and sexuality is seen in many of the cases examined here. Doña María de Ocampo reported that she had called upon the Devil in "anger and sorrow"; while the Devil may have provided some modicum of relief, he also offered the young woman a knife and rope and told her to kill herself. Gregoria de Ubeda, as described at the beginning of this chapter, conjured the Devil in despair at her poverty. A similar trajectory is visible in the case of Sor María de la Natividad. When she denounced herself in 1598, her primary symptom was despair, which, she said, had tempted her to mutilate herself and even to commit suicide. She had also been enticed to believe that God was not in the consecrated Host, which drove her to desecrate the Host. Given the role of Eucharistic desecration in the assertion of the divine presence, one is tempted to read María's desecration as a desperate attempt to provoke a response that might restore her belief. Transubstantiation was not her only stumbling block; she had also been tempted to believe that the Virgin was not pure.

While inquisitors tended to interpret such a confluence of despair, demonism, and sexuality as evidence of medical disturbance, women themselves tended to cling to supernatural causation. Asked by inquisitors whether she felt some sorrow or distress that may have caused her symptoms, María de la Natividad rejected the

biological determinism

tacit diagnosis, firmly identifying the Devil as the cause of her torments. Though she had never seen him except in dreams, she was certain that he had produced her temptations. The inquisitors' apparently compassionate attempts to locate María's disorder in emotional pathology did nothing to cure her symptoms, which drove her to contact the Holy Office repeatedly over a period of years, apparently without cure for her difficulties.[51]

When Mexican women did acknowledge their melancholy, they tended to deny the natural character of that ailment. Marina de San Miguel attributed *all* of her illicit sexual activities, including frequent masturbation, copulation with the Devil, and improper touching (including some acts of mutual masturbation) with both male and female partners, to her melancholy rather than to any desire for pleasure.[52] But she did not understand that melancholy condition as purely natural. Ultimately, Marina, like so many of her contemporaries, took refuge in the supernatural, attributing her doubt and her masturbation to diabolical influence.

Thus, despite inquisitorial indifference, for both the lay population and many clerics the supernatural remained a potent tool for the management of sexual tensions and crises in belief throughout the colonial period. This can clearly be seen in the case of Ana María de Leyba, the teenager who claimed to have masturbated with holy images and with the consecrated Host, consorted sexually with animals, and even attempted to incite animals to sexual contact with the holy images.[53] Though her testimony was recorded by a parish priest and reveals *his* credulity, it is difficult not also to see in Ana's claims an attempt either to conduct or at least to catalogue virtually every possible infamous sexual desecration and unnatural act she could think of. Her motivations remain unclear, because the Holy Office was apparently wholly uninterested in her. However, one is tempted to conjecture. She was apparently without family in the village where she lived, and though she claimed to have family in Mexico City, attempts to contact them showed that they did not exist. Ana was thus revealed as a teenager either willfully or accidentally alone in the world; overcome with despair, at an age when a young woman alone would be inevitably tempted or threatened sexually, she might well have reached for the strange comfort of supernatural persecution. If the acts she described were shocking, disgusting, and unnatural, they nonetheless proved that she existed, that she was worthy of the Devil's attention. The Devil's sexual depravities offered both priest and confessant a bulwark against doubt.

That doubt in addition to melancholy was implicated in women's experience of demonic sexual contact is made clear by some of the final words spoken by Marina de San Miguel to her interlocutors in the Holy Office. Finally, she came to doubt that it had been the Devil who tempted her, wondering instead "whether it was he, or nature itself." Most colonial Mexican women who experienced some admixture of melancholy, religious doubt, and sexual temptation could not contemplate a statement as robustly questioning as this; instead, they and the confessors who contemplated their pain framed their bodily and spiritual suffering in terms that both denied women's responsibility and positioned their bodies not as weak vessels but as battlegrounds for supernatural struggles. Meanwhile, the inquisitors who were bound to hear their testimony moved ever closer toward a medicalized understanding of demonic possession. We can only wonder what inquisitors themselves believed about the Devil, whom plebeians presented to them in a thousand different guises: black, white, indigenous, male or (rarely) female, animal. Inquisitors' own possible doubts appear only between the lines of the thousands of pages given over to the activities of New Spain's Devil.

Learned understandings of the Devil in Mexico were distinct from those of plebeians. But both groups seem to have shared a view of demonic sex that was remarkably "natural" compared to contemporary European versions. With rare exceptions, the Devil of New Spain eschewed the bestial excesses and intentional perversions of European demonology in favor of forms and practices that were much more "natural" and that reveal much about everyday beliefs and desires among New Spain's women. In their relative incredulity as regards the more extreme versions of demonic sex, New Spain's inquisitors moved toward a view of demonic sex as a quotidian symptom of "female trouble" rather than as the crowning proof of dangerous diabolism. In doing so, they revealed the contested nature of the boundaries between natural and unnatural in the varied communities of colonial New Spain.

NOTES

1. Archivo General de la Nación, Mexico [hereafter cited as AGN], Inquisición 449, exp. 10 (1697), fol. 80.

2. Ibid., fols. 78–87. "El mismo demonio le traia diferentes hombres solteros i uno casado i se los entraba por un aguxero que bia este declarante en las bigas i luego se entraba hasta que querian ir y tenia con dichos hombres actos carnales platicas i besos y quando estaba pensando en hello se los traia y ponia delante y en la cama al dichos hombres y que discurre quel dicho demonio tomaba la figura de dichos hombres por ber los entrar por dicho abugero i por las bigas" (fol. 81v).

3. A demon was capable of assuming the form of a woman to receive male semen; thereafter, assuming the form of a man, the demon could transfer the semen to a woman and thereby appear to "father" a child. See Walter Stephens, *Demon Lovers: Witchcraft, Sex, and the Crisis of Belief* (Chicago: University of Chicago Press, 2002), 63–66.

4. Heinrich Krämer and James Sprenger, *Malleus Mallificarum*, trans. Montague Summers (New York: Cosimo Classics, 2007).

5. The *Strix*, however, had already departed to some extent from Krämer's sodomy-abhorring Devil; see Tamar Herzig, "The Demons' Reaction to Sodomy: Witchcraft and Homosexuality in Gianfrancesco Pico della Mirandola's *Strix*," *Sixteenth-Century Journal* 34, no. 1 (2003): 53–72. For discussion of the post-1570 emphasis on the unnaturalness of demonic copulation and the pain caused thereby, see Stephens, *Demon Lovers*, 14–19.

6. Jorge Cañizares-Esguerra, *Puritan Conquistadores: Iberianizing the Atlantic, 1550–1700* (Stanford: Stanford University Press, 2006), 96–97.

7. José Rabasa, *Inventing America: Spanish Historiography and the Formation of Eurocentrism* (Norman: University of Oklahoma Press, 1994), 161.

8. Francisco Cervantes, *The Devil in the New World: The Impact of Diabolism in New Spain* (New Haven, Conn.: Yale University Press, 1994), 5.

9. See Patricia Lopes Don, *Bonfires of Culture: Franciscans, Indigenous Leaders, and the Inquisition in Early Mexico, 1524–1540* (Norman: University of Oklahoma Press, 2012), 184.

10. See the plays in *Death and Life in Colonial Nahua Mexico*, ed. Barry D. Sell and Louise M. Burkhart, with the assistance of Gregory Spira (Norman: University of Oklahoma Press, 2004). The Devil and associated demons frequently appear in characteristically medieval mode, obediently punishing sinners in accordance with the will of God.

11. Laura Lewis, *Hall of Mirrors: Power, Witchcraft, and Caste in Colonial Mexico* (Durham, N.C.: Duke University Press, 2003).

12. Cervantes, *Devil in the New World*, 37–39.

13. Not all of the women who were accused of pacts admitted to them. Indeed, in several cases the Holy Office found absolutely no evidence of such pacts. One such case is discussed below.

14. Zeb Tortorici, "Masturbation, Salvation, and Desire: Connecting Sexuality and Religiosity in Colonial Mexico," *Journal of the History of Sexuality* 16, no. 3 (2008): 359.

15. Armando Maggi, *In the Company of Demons: Unnatural Beings, Love, and Identity in the Italian Renaissance* (Chicago: University of Chicago Press, 2006), 5.

16. Ruth Behar, "Sexual Witchcraft, Colonialism, and Women's Powers: Views from the Mexican Inquisition," in *Sexuality and Marriage in Colonial Latin America*, ed. Asunción Lavrin (Lincoln: University of Nebraska Press, 1989), 191.

17. He often made his initial appearance as an animal, and he demanded written contracts. Gregoria de Ubeda even knew about the kiss to the Devil's hindquarters, a standard of the European Witches' Sabbath.

18. Moshe Sluhovsky, "The Devil in the Convent," *American Historical Review* 107, no. 5 (2002): 1379–1411.

19. AGN, Inquisición 578 (2a parte), exp. 5, fols. 311–35 (Guatemala, 1668).

20. AGN, Inquisición 1137, exp. 33, fols. 368–95 (Denuncia expontanea que de si hizo Clara Josepha de Jesus Solis por herege, 1770).

21. Sara Guengerich, "Paula de Eguiluz: The Witchcraft Trials of a Black Woman in Colonial Cartagena de Indias," in *Afro-Latino Voices: Documentary Narratives from the Early Modern Iberian World*, ed. Kathryn McKnight and Leo Garofalo (Cambridge, Mass.: Hackett, 2009), 175–93.

22. Sonya Lipsett-Rivera, "*Mira lo que hace el Diablo:* The Devil in Mexican Popular Culture, 1750–1856," *The Americas* 59, no. 2 (2002): 201–19: Lee Penyak, "Criminal Sexuality in Central Mexico, 1750–1850," Ph.D. diss., University of Connecticut, 1993; Zeb Tortorici, "Masturbation, Salvation, and Desire: Connecting Sexuality and Religiosity in Colonial Mexico," *Journal of the History of Sexuality* 16, no. 3 (2008): 365.

23. For a case that more closely resembles the European Witches' Sabbath, see Lewis, *Hall of Mirrors*, 128. Described by Lewis as "one of the few reports of a classic Sabbat that I have found," this case is discussed further below. Such lurid details are also found in some of the Cartagena witchcraft proceedings of 1620, which involved African suspects subjected to torture. See Heather Rachelle White, "Between the Devil and the Inquisition: African Slaves and the Witchcraft Trials in Cartagena de Indias," *North Star: A Journal of African-American Religious History* 8, no. 2 (Spring 2005): 1–15.

24. For discussion of this point, see Cervantes, *Devil in the New World*, 88–91.

25. Jorge Cañizares-Esguerra, *Puritan Conquistadors: Iberianizing the Atlantic, 1550–1700* (Stanford: Stanford University Press, 2006), 96–97.

26. For spells, powders, herbs, and incantations designed to help men succeed with women, see Cervantes, *Devil in the New World*, 87–88. For a friar accused of painting "obscene images," see AGN,

Inquisición 1104, exp. 18, fols. 247–62. For a case involving another priest and "verses," see AGN, Inquisición 1019, exp. 9, fols. 213–14.

27. AGN, Inquisición 35, exp. 1, fols. 1–385 (Contra doña María de Ocampo, hija de Francisco Chavez y contra Francisco del valle Marroquin, Santiago de Guatemala, 1557). The case is mentioned in Cervantes, *Devil in the New World*, 125, though it is cited there as vol. 31. I discuss this case further below and in a manuscript currently in preparation.

28. Jacqueline Holler, "The Spiritual and Physical Ecstasies of a Sixteenth-Century *Beata*," in *Colonial Lives: Documents on Latin American History, 1550–1850*, ed. R. Boyer and G. Spurling (New York: Oxford University Press, 2000), 89.

29. AGN, Inquisición 166, exp. 5 (Relación de María de la Natividad, monja profesa en el convento de Regina Celi, contra si misma por aver dicho y hecho cosas contra la fe, Mexico, 1598).

30. Cervantes, *Devil in the New World*, 126. Cervantes sees the decline in inquisitorial credulity as precipitous, taking place within a generation; the evidence presented here suggests that the situation may be more complex

31. For the role of indigenous people in demonism, see ibid., 64–69, 91; also Lewis, *Hall of Mirrors*, 103–31.

32. AGN, Inquisición 525, exp. 48, fols. 500–520 (Denunciacion que contra si hizo Antonia de Sotto mulata esclava de Francisco de Noriega vezino de la ciudad de Durango de diferentes echos, con pacto con el demonio, 1691). Cervantes (*Devil in the New World*, 89) discusses this case, seeing it as evidence of "the devil's reputation as a dispenser of markedly masculine skills." The degree of gender inversion in the case is certainly noteworthy.

33. AGN, Inquisición 886, exp. 9, fols. 46–113 (Relación de la causa de Rosa Flores, Villa de Santiago de Monclova, Coahuila, 1748).

34. I am thus expressing partial disagreement with Ruth Behar's claim that "if the confessions touched on sex, all the better, since the lusts of the body, both in thought and in deed, were particularly singled out for close inspection and castigation" (Behar, "Sexual Witchcraft," 184). In the cases addressed here, worship and belief, rather than sex, were of primary importance.

35. By the eighteenth century, the medical category of "melancholic hysteria" was deployed to explain the behavior and beliefs of such women, and stringent tests were applied to cases of purported possession. See Nora Jaffary, *False Mystics: Deviant Orthodoxy in Colonial Mexico* (Lincoln: University of Nebraska Press, 2004), 137–64; and Alejandra Araya Espinoza, "De espirituales a histéricas: Las Beatas del siglo XVIII en la Nueva España," *Historia* [Chile] 37, no. 1 (2004): 5–32.

36. Cervantes, *Devil in the New World*, 113–27.

37. Lewis, *Hall of Mirrors*, 128.

38. AGN, Inquisición 981, exp. 22, fols. 327–46 (Contra Ana María de Leyba por el delicto de pacto con el Demonio y otros errores, Zinguilucan, 1752).

39. For the role of the demoniacs in furthering Franciscan religious revival within Querétaro, and particularly for friars' credulity, see Cervantes, *Devil in the New World*, 113–24.

40. AGN, Inquisición 619, exp. 1, fols. 1–67 (Testifacion remitida por el commissario . . . Francisca Zerdan mulata vezina de la ciudad de Nueva Veracruz, 1672).

41. As mentioned above, incubi were presumed to deliver the semen that succubi removed from sleeping men, and therefore were thought at least theoretically capable of insemination. In the famous Querétaro case, this claim was tested and found wanting when Juana de los Reyes, the girl at the center of the possession, became pregnant. See Cervantes, *Devil in the New World*, 122.

42. Angus Gowland, "The Problem of Early Modern Melancholy," *Past and Present* 191 (May 2006): 83–84.

43. Ibid., 92–93.

44. See Krämer and Sprenger, *Malleus Mallificarum*, 32; also Jennifer Radden, *The Nature of Melancholy: From Aristotle to Kristeva* (New York: Oxford University Press, 2002), 96.

45. Dolores Bienko de Peralta, "Un camino de abrojos y espinas: Mística, demonios, y melancolía," in *Transgresión y melancolía en el México colonial*, ed. Roger Bartra (Mexico City: Centro de investigaciones interdisciplinarias en ciencias y humanidades [UNAM], 2004), 100–101.

46. See, inter alia, Antonio Contreras Mas, "*Libro de la Melancolía* by Andrés Velázquez (1585). Part 2. Its Context and Importance," *History of Psychiatry* 14 (June 2003): 189.

47. As in Jean Gerson's insistence that melancholy was produced when the Devil sabotaged mystical meditation. See Noel Brann, "Alchemy and Melancholy in Medieval and Renaissance Thought: A Query into the Mystical Basis of Their Relationship," *Ambix* 32, pt. 3 (November 1985): 127–48.

48. Witnesses were specifically asked to comment not only on her temperament and relationships within the convent, but also on her complexion and build, both of which might indicate a humoral or complexionate predisposition to the disorder. Thus inquisitors combined moral and medical approaches. See AGN, Inquisición 166, exp. 5 (Relación de María de la Natividad, monja profesa en el convento de Regina Coeli, contra si mismo por aver dicho y hecho cosas contra la fe, Mexico City, 1598).

49. Maria Cristina Sacristán, "Melancolía religiosa y culpabilidad en el México colonial," in Bartra (ed.), *Transgresión y melancolía*, 43–62.

50. On the exoneration of *ilusas* and heretics, see Jaffary, *False Mystics*, 146. The retention of menstrual flow appeared as the cause of mental disturbances in Farfán's 1592 *Tratado breve de medicina y de todas las enfermedades*.

51. María was undoubtedly a sufferer from scrupulosity, a condition that was often related to acedia or religious melancholy. Scrupulosity is beyond the scope of this essay, but I regard it (at least in the early modern context) as a subset of melancholy. Today, scrupulosity is regarded as a form of OCD. See two recent books on scrupulosity among contemporary Catholics: Joseph Ciarrochi's *Doubting Disease: Help for Scrupulosity and Religious Compulsions* (Mahwah, N.J.: Paulist Press, 1995) and William Van Ornum's *A Thousand Frightening Fantasies* (New York: Crossroads Press, 1997).

52. In her seventh confession, Marina claimed that she didn't believe that she had sinned mortally with her male partners because she had been pure of intention and melancholy. Unfortunately, inquisitors were quite uninterested in her melancholia and did not pursue further questions on its manifestations.

53. AGN, Inquisición 981, exp. 22, fols. 327–46 (Contra Ana Maria de Leyba por el delicto de pacto con en Demonio y otros errors, Zinguilucan, 1752).

4

Female Homoeroticism, Heresy, and the Holy Office in Colonial Brazil

Ronaldo Vainfas and Zeb Tortorici

Translated by Luiza Vainfas and Zeb Tortorici

For the purposes of elucidating the social contours of the sins against nature in the early modern Lusophone world, it is necessary to analyze the links between sodomy and heresy in colonial Brazil, especially in relation to gender. This chapter therefore has two primary goals: (1) to outline the ways in which sodomy was often treated *as if it were* heresy in Portugal and its colonies; and (2) to discuss the comparative archival absence of female sodomy cases in the colonial Brazilian historical record—a fact that is linked to the very definition of "sodomy" in the Lusophone context.[1] Regarding the first of these goals, it is not so important to determine whether or not the Portuguese Inquisition technically considered sodomy itself a heresy. Rather, our emphasis should be on the conceptual aspects involved in this debate. The proposed question—of whether or not "sodomites" were heretical—should be analyzed not only through a theological perspective but also through a historical approach. This polemic leads us to the meanings and changes that the concept of heresy has acquired over time and that are, in fact, the preoccupation of the historian. It also allows us to understand why some Inquisitions chased the so-called sodomites throughout the early modern era, though they did so far more frequently with men than with women.

We agree with scholars such as Luiz Mott, who affirm that within a theological perspective the concept of heresy—as a deviation of faith, which implied the spread of beliefs and ideas that countered the dogma and tenets of the Catholic Church—was always intimately related to religion.[2] It is worth noting that, at least within the field of theology, the concept of heresy has always had its own subdivisions and subclasses. Take, for instance, the contrast between formal heresy and material heresy: formal heresy was ultimately related to the notion of free will and the presence of erroneous beliefs on the part of an individual, whereas material heresy referred specifically to a mistake made largely out of ignorance rather than from a conscious disagreement with official dogma. Another example lies in the difference between heresy and apostasy. According to Saint Thomas Aquinas, apostasy refers to the abandonment of Christianity in order to embrace another religion. In contrast, heresy implies the abandonment of an article of faith but without renouncing Christianity. In this case, in spite of his or her erroneous choices and belief, the suspected heretic essentially remained a Catholic.

Medieval and early modern scholars and theologians who wrote about the topic of heresy had tended to agree that, in general, only a baptized Christian could be accused of either apostasy or heresy, in that only a member of the Christian community could abandon the faith or reject its laws and beliefs. Yet even this seemingly basic rule has not always been observed by theologians throughout history. For example, the Dominican Francisco Larraga, who published an important theological manual in 1706, the *Promptuário de Theologia Moral* (Treaty of Moral Theology), wrote: "The sins against faith are heresy, apostasy, infidelity, and Judaism." This statement, according to its author, amounts to law within Catholic theology, though it can equally be considered nonsensical and contradictory from a historical and theological perspective. In fact, a historical approach allows us to better comprehend the meanings of those terms than a strictly theological approach. For instance, here it is worth thinking through the strong distinctions between infidelity and Judaism, since, as we know, according to the Catholic Church, the law followed by the Jews belonged to another religious tradition, that of "the Law of Moses," and likewise the Muslims, who followed "the Law of Muhammad." But Larraga was not naive; perhaps he preferred to stress Judaism in order to denounce the so-called crypto-Judaism practiced by the New Christians (those who had converted to Christianity from Judaism or Islam) in the Iberian Peninsula and *not* actual Judaism as practiced by the self-defined Jews. Therefore, the best way to understand the conceptual definitions proposed above by the Dominican Larraga is through the historical context of the Iberian world in the sixteenth and seventeenth centuries, whereby "heresy" took on specific meanings that were localized in ways not evident if we limit our analysis to medieval scholasticism.

By making such assertions, we intend to stress two important principles in the debate regarding the potentially heretical nature of sodomy. First, the definitions of heresy provided by scholars and theologians only make sense when considered alongside historical perspectives and local considerations of both place and time. Therefore, that which could be considered heresy by Thomas Aquinas in his thirteenth-century *Summa Theologica* would not necessarily include those heresies laid down by the Iberian tribunals of the Inquisition from the sixteenth century on. Historical specificity makes all the difference, and such an approach considers the local social changes that theology sometimes ignores. Second, even in the field of theological writing, it is possible to perceive some important subtleties, classifications, and subspecies of "heresy" among both famous and lesser-known theologians. It is not by chance that, within the history of medieval and early modern inquisitions, it becomes possible to prioritize one particular crime over another, thereby considering it to be more or less heretical than its counterparts. Theological thought was expansive enough to include or exclude various sins from the list of possible errors of faith. The expression *pecados contra a fé* (sins against the faith), as used by the Dominican Larraga, is a good example of these oscillations and inaccuracies, because "heresy" and "sin" are very different concepts. Moreover, what was considered a simple sin or even a serious sin in the fourteenth century might be considered heretical two centuries later. In the Middle Ages, what was seen as a religion of infidels—Muslims during the Crusades, for example—became a heresy in Portugal or Spain, since that religion began to be practiced by *moriscos* (Muslims who were baptized as Christians) during the sixteenth century. Once again, history makes the difference.

If our analysis is correct, the discussion of whether sodomy was considered heresy by the Inquisition, under a strictly theological approach, is almost nonsensical. The answer depends entirely on the time period, on the author, on the circumstance, and on history and historical context. Luiz Mott has rightly argued that sodomy became a crime for the Inquisition only in the sixteenth century— around 1509 in Spain, and in the middle of the same century in Portugal. Nevertheless, it is worth adding that it did not happen uniformly in all Iberian Inquisitions. In the Spanish Inquisition, for instance, despite its centralized power in Madrid, the Church's jurisdiction over sodomy was not uniform. While the courts of Barcelona, Saragossa, and Valencia received papal briefs authorizing them to prosecute the "nefarious sin," in the kingdom of Aragon sodomy remained a *mixti fori* crime that could be prosecuted by either a royal or an ecclesiastical court, depending on which initiated the process. Already for the Inquisition of Castile, as well the inquisitorial courts in Spanish America, sodomy (so long as it did not involve a priest or the crime of solicitation in the confessional) did not fall under the jurisdiction of the Inquisition, leaving this crime to royal justice instead.[3]

Nonetheless, sodomites could not freely express their erotic choices in the Castilian domains. Serge Gruzinski, in his work on sodomy in early colonial Mexico, gives us the valuable information that in 1658 fourteen sodomites were condemned to the stake by the royal justice system in Mexico City, and Zeb Tortorici has shown, via archival records and secular court proceedings from New Spain, that at least three dozen men were executed for sodomy between 1530 and 1786. In comparison, around thirty sodomites were executed throughout the entire history of the Portuguese Inquisition, over the course of nearly three centuries. The criminal cases from New Spain and the Inquisition cases from the Lusophone world paint a picture of largely sporadic and irregular outbursts of repression—for moral and social reasons—directed toward sodomites in the early modern period. The Inquisition certainly would prosecute sodomites, but mainly because of religious reasons (such as same-sex solicitation in the confessional, which desecrated the sacrament). In essence, we must acknowledge these oscillations of theological knowledge over time and in historical perspective. I (Vainfas) have therefore argued that sodomy in Portugal and colonial Brazil, like other crimes against Catholic morals, fell under the Holy Office's jurisdiction precisely because it came to be associated with suspicions of heresy. With great caution, I suggest that sodomy was assimilated with heresy, but sodomy itself was never formally declared a heresy. Assimilation, as we know, is not the same phenomenon as identification. To assimilate assumes the existence of differences between objects, suggesting comparable resemblances rather than absolute identities.

When the General Inquisitor of Portugal, Cardinal Henrinque, instructed the Holy Office's ministers to prosecute sodomites in 1555—calling them *filhos da dissidência* or "sons of dissidence"—in the same way inquisitors used to prosecute heresies, he nonetheless clearly distinguished both crimes. It seems clear that when he recommended similar procedures for different offences, he assimilated the act of sodomy to an error of faith. After all, what kind of "dissidence" could be considered erroneous enough to be judged as heresy by the Holy Office? The answer is simple: deviations of faith, even if only presumed, because the Inquisition was a court that specialized in prosecuting enemies of the faith. In my book *Trópico dos pecados,* I tried to demonstrate for colonial Brazil the somewhat arbitrary expansion of the concept of heresy at the level of inquisitorial Portuguese judiciary practice (following the examples of some Spanish tribunals). Through this conceptual amplification, many behaviors that definitely did not imply deviations of faith were metamorphosed into heresy, as if practitioners of sodomy held some convictions against the official Catholic faith.

Therefore, several deviations from the Catholic faith were transmuted as such, even if the suspects had no intention of questioning the faith. That was the case of the men who, talking about their sexual relations with single women, used to say—typically using colloquial words and vulgar terms—that simple fornication was not a sin. Inquisitors, seeming genuinely concerned about the possible heresies present in these "proclamations," would always ask if those men had learned such things from Lutherans or from Lutheran books. Inquisitors did not care so much about the acts of illicit sex committed by such defenders of simple fornication, but rather focused on the errors of faith contained in such propositions. But we must ask: did not the act of simple fornication insinuate an act against family, the institution of marriage, and Christian values, just like the sin of sodomy? Of course it did; but it was not because of the sexual relationships per se, but rather the presumption of a doctrinaire mistake that led the Holy Office to prosecute these verbal defenders of fornication during the sixteenth century. As a tribunal of faith, inquisitors assumed jurisdiction over this matter because they suspected these men subscribed to heretical beliefs.

The same argument pertained to bigamy, the crime most frequently prosecuted by the Portuguese Inquisition after crypto-Judaism. It is obvious that men or women who had married two or more times, even though the first spouse was still alive, did so not with heretical intentions but for personal reasons. In this framework, bigamy was facilitated by individual mobility throughout the Portuguese colonial empire. Yet Portugal's Holy Office prosecuted bigamists, from the sixteenth century on, as if they were heretics.

A third example can be seen in cases of *solicitação ad turpia*—the solicitation of sexual favors in the confessional—a crime prosecuted by the Holy Office in the sixteenth, seventeenth, and eighteenth centuries.[4] In this case, we might ask why the Inquisition would prosecute those priests who had tried to seduce women (or men) in the confessional—an offensive behavior that went against the family and Church morals—while they meted out little or no punishment to priests who had reneged on their vows of celibacy or who engaged in concubinage. The answer is the same: as a tribunal of faith, the Inquisition suspected that this crime contained not only a sexual component but also an error of faith and a desecration of the sacrament. Particularly for the Inquisition, this behavior could suggest contempt in relation to the sacrament of penance. Just like the boastful fornicators who were suspected of defying the sixth commandment, the scandalous sodomites suspected of challenging the nature of sex, or the bigamists suspected of denying the sacrament of matrimony, the priests who had tried to seduce women in the confessional *were treated as if they were heretics*, unlike the so-called crypto-Jews who clearly fell under the formal category of heresy. Their actions were compared to and assimilated to heresies. Through these examples we see that the broadening of the concept of heresy in inquisitorial practices was somewhat arbitrary.

When we shift our analysis along the axis of gender, we see that the decision of the Holy Office on whether to prosecute female sodomites was also highly arbitrary in Spain, Portugal, and their overseas colonies. The doubts and dilemmas of inquisitors in their judgments of the crime of sodomy were, above all, of a conceptual order. To uncover and interrogate those accused of sodomy signified, on the one hand, proceeding against individuals suspected of practicing a specific sexual act: anal penetration with ejaculation, which between men was known as "perfect sodomy." However, the sexual act performed between two women was typically defined as "imperfect sodomy," whether or not "ejaculation" had taken place. On the other hand, it implied a whole variety of sins between individuals of the same sex. The Portuguese *Regimento* of 1640, which dealt exclusively with the issue, clearly suggests that the Holy Office direct its attention toward men who practiced sodomy. The Inquisition could, however, also prosecute instances of *molície*—a vast and imprecise theological category that could refer to individual or mutual masturbation, fellatio, or cunnilingus—to see if they might be indicative of sodomy. *Molície* was, in essence, any act that provoked ejaculations outside of the anus or the vagina (as "vessels" or receptacles), whether enacted between men and women or between members of the same sex. Yet, as we shall see below, the overall uncertainty of inquisitors in this domain would prevail.

Inquisitors throughout the Lusophone world were largely baffled by the very notion of *sodomia foeminarum*, or sodomy between women, as were secular authorities throughout colonial Spanish America, as the essay by Chad Black in this volume demonstrates. Until the second half of the seventeenth century, the Portuguese Inquisition, which had jurisdiction over all of colonial Brazil (given that no independent tribunal of the Inquisition was ever established there), had still not prosecuted many cases of this type. The rare exceptions are the inquisitorial processes initiated by Heitor Furtado de Mendonça, who was sent by Lisbon's Holy Office to Brazil in an infamous visitation toward the end of the sixteenth century. Further demonstrating the uncertainty of inquisitors regarding the topic of female sodomy, in the seventeenth century the tribunal of Goa found it necessary to formally ask the General Council of the Holy Office in Lisbon if and how it should proceed against women who engaged in copulation, sodomitical acts, or who had used instruments in their "natural" or "posterior" vessels (i.e., vagina or anus).[5]

Archival evidence shows that inquisitors throughout the early modern Lusophone world navigated a sea of uncertainty when it came to sodomy and the female body. Such hesitation is evidenced by a 1646 debate, held by the inquisitors in Évora, Portugal, on how to proceed in cases of *sodomia foeminarum*. The majority who debated the topic in Évora were of the opinion that the Inquisition could only prosecute those cases in which one woman introduced "semen" into the "posterior vessel" of another, indicating that the vagina was insufficient for the effectuation of the "said crime."[6] In other words, most inquisitors insisted that anal coitus was the *authentic* sodomitical act. In this peculiar debate, some claimed that the Holy Office only would be able to judge such cases if one of the women had used an "instrument" to penetrate another woman, as an artificial phallus or a dildo; others stated that perfect sodomy among women could occur only if the penetration with a fake penis was in the *vas preposterum* (the "posterior vessel"), as opposed to the vagina; and one inquisitor even claimed that an act of sodomy existed only if intercourse had been consummated with a natural penis, never with an artificial phallus, and therefore women were deemed unable to practice perfect sodomy. Against this last opinion, one sole inquisitor, Veríssimo de Lencastre, said that all intercourse among women, with or without instruments, into the anus or into the vagina, was nefarious and "against nature" and, for this reason, could be classified as sodomy.[7] In part because of this debate, from the middle of the seventeenth century on, Portuguese inquisitors followed a course of prosecuting only sodomy between men and, much more rarely, between women and men.

However, before the General Council of the Inquisition would acknowledge the inability of the Holy Office to prosecute cases of female sodomy, a number of cases fell into the hands of inquisitors, especially in colonial Brazil. During the visitation of the Holy Office in northeastern Brazil between 1591 and 1595, the inquisitorial visitor, Heitor Furtado de Mendonça, listed a total of twenty-nine female suspects through denunciations and self-denunciations. Only seven of these women responded to the charges. While there are no spectacular cases of transvestism or instances of love within the confines of the convent, as have been found in early modern Europe, the twenty-nine women who were charged with sodomy do allow us to reconstruct through documentary evidence certain important aspects of the everyday lives of women during Portuguese colonialism in Brazil.

The majority of relationships that were confessed to Mendonça involved girls of nine or ten years of age and *donzelas,* or young maidens, between the ages of eighteen and twenty. A number of other women who were either married or widowed confessed to relationships and caresses with childhood friends. Such was the case with Madalena Pimentel, a woman of forty-six, widow of a plantation owner, who admitted to having had, as a young girl, "foolish friendship *[amizade tola]* out of ignorance with other girls of her same age," some of which involved "carnal contacts."[8] We see something similar with Guiomar Pisçara, the thirty-eight-year-old wife of a farm laborer who, when she was around thirteen years old, took carnal delight with a girl named Méscia, a "black *ladina* from Guinea," who was the domestic slave of the family.[9]

From what the documentation suggests, some women on the path to marriage spontaneously expressed other aspects of their sexuality in homoerotic relationships enacted with younger girls. Such was the experience of Catarina Baroa in her youth before marrying the tailor Diogo Rodrigues: at around fifteen years of age she used to "play" *(brincar)* with girls who were ten years old or younger, juvenile frolics that one of her "ex-partners" thought necessary to denounce to the inquisitorial visitation. Something similar occurred with Catarina Quaresma, daughter of a rich *fazenda* owner in Bahia who was married to a wealthy sugar mill owner. She confessed that when she was still single and only nineteen years old, she maintained frequent relations with girls the same age or younger.[10]

Archives also hold the singular yet illustrative case of a *mameluca* or mixed-race woman, Maria de Lucena, who at age twenty-five was living in the house of a female relative who was married to a plantation owner from Pernambuco. Although she was still single at that time, she had already known men sexually and, according to one of her denouncers, had given birth before she got married. It appears, however, that love of other women excited her desires most, especially with the indigenous slaves Margaryda and Vitória whom she courted and pestered. The unique singularity of this case resides in the fact that Maria de Lucena was caught in the act, something that was exceedingly rare in archival documentation. Maria had

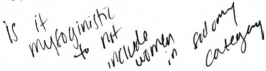

acquired the infamy of "sleeping carnally with the *negras* [indigenous women] of the house," and more than once she was caught in flagrante delicto with her female partners. On one occasion another indigenous slave, Mônica, surprised Maria and Margaryda in the act. Mônica, upon seeing them, spat at them and screamed that they "not do that for lack of men."[11]

Another notable case is that of Paula de Siqueira, age thirty-eight, wife of the accountant of the Fazenda del Rei in Bahia. Paula was uncommon in that she was literate, a rare trait among women and men of that time. Her favorite book was *Diana*, a pastoral romance written in Spanish by Jorge de Montemayor in 1559, which quickly made its way into the Inquisition's list of prohibited literature due to its depictions of love and romance between shepherds and shepherdesses. Considered a "dishonest book" by the censors of the Holy Office, *Diana* narrated, among other things, the candid and intense love story between two young girls. In fact, Paula had spoken so frequently and openly to her friends about her penchant for *Diana* that she was eventually tried for having the book in her possession. Courageous as she was, Paula openly defied the inquisitor, saying that she did not see any reason why the Holy Office had prohibited the book, that she enjoyed reading it very much, and that for her part she would continue to read it always.

Passionate and intrepid, Paula de Siqueira would not hesitate to verify in practice some of the passions that her favorite book had described. She was supposedly seduced by a certain Felipa de Souza, a woman who, knowing how to write, sent her several "letters of flattery and love" *(cartas de requebros e amores)* and also repeatedly gave her kisses and hugs with lascivious intentions. Over the course of two years, in 1588 and 1589, Paula and Felipa limited themselves to one another's caresses, kisses, and letters, until one "holy day" *(Dia de Deus)* Paula, who was alone, received a visit from her friend. Recognizing the desires that Felipa had already expressed in writing, Paula invited her into her bedroom, where they engaged in numerous sexual acts throughout the day. According to Mendonça, the inquisitorial visitor sent by the Holy Office to the northeast of Brazil, Paula was never with Felipa nor with any other woman again.[12]

And yet the case of Paula and Felipa is not the most scandalous that we have notice of from the files of the Inquisition, especially in comparison to that of Francisca Luiz and Isabel Antônia. Isabel, who was unmarried, arrived in Bahia, Brazil, by means of banishment in 1579 for having sinned with other women. Defamed and dishonored in Porto, Portugal, where she was born, she quickly gained a similar reputation in Bahia de Todos os Santos, where she came to be known by the nickname Isabel "a do veludo," or "of the velvet." Isabel did not garner such a nickname because she wore velvet or because she had sold cloth made of velvet, but rather because it was publicly known that she tended to use a velvet-covered "instrument" in her sexual relations with others. Isabel's case proves that debates among inquisitors and theologians about the potentially sacrilegious nature of such "instruments" were not merely theoretical exercises (or forms of wishful thinking).

Isabel's partner, Francisca Luiz, a freed black woman *(negra forra)* also from Porto whose husband had abandoned her, came to offer Isabel a place to live for a short period. They were friends and occasionally lovers in Porto, and they continued being so in Bahia. Their romance appears to have been difficult, especially after a public scandal that took place when Isabel "of the velvet" resolved to go out with a man. When she returned home from one of her meetings with this man, Francisca Luiz confronted Isabel at the front door of their house and began to scream: "*Velhaca!* How many kisses do you give to your *coxo* [lame man], and hugs you give me none?! Don't you know that I want a *cono* [vagina] more than all the *caralhos* [penises] that there are?!" Francisca lost control and began to use physical violence, grabbing Isabel by the hair and pulling her inside the door with violent blows and slaps, all within sight of her neighbors.

The fight between the two made its way to the ecclesiastical judge, who, given such strong "nefarious" evidence, exiled the two women in 1580. The sentence, however, was never carried out. It did not take long for Francisca to send a conciliatory message to Isabel, saying that she would do anything to have her back, irrespective of earthly or divine punishments. But the love between the two women did not continue, and Isabel died before the arrival of the Holy Office's visitation in 1591.[13]

Perhaps the most flagrant female sodomite in Bahia was Felipa de Souza, the same who had sent "letters of flattery and love" to the wife of the royal accountant. Born in Tavira, Portugal, in the Algarve, she was around thirty-five years old at the time of the visitation of the Holy Office in Brazil. Felipa, a humble woman who "made her living with the needle," had been widowed by her first husband and lived with her second husband, a modest day laborer. In spite of having been married two times, she liked women, and had the nerve to admit this to Mendonça, saying that she sought out women "for the great love and carnal affection that she felt" *(pelo grande amor e afeição carnal que sentia)* upon seeing them.

And to that end, she did not lose any opportunity to flirt with, seduce, and seize certain women who crossed her path, using her varied luck to provoke the partners she coveted and to be unfaithful to her husband and to theirs as well. Such was the case with Maria Peralta, an eighteen-year-old *donzela,* or maiden, with whom she took shelter on one occasion in the house of a certain Gaspar da Vila. It was the same with Paula de Siqueira, whom she courted over a period of two years with love letters prior to sleeping with her one hot Sunday in Salvador. And something similar happened with Ana Fernandes, who was married to a blacksmith and whom Felipa grabbed and kissed within the walls of the monastery of São Bento, all the while insisting that the two sleep together.

One particularly interesting encounter took place with Maria Lourenço, who was married to a coppersmith and who took shelter with Felipa for several days when the

English sacked the city of Salvador. According to the testimony of Maria, who denounced her lover to the Inquisition, right away on the first night when the women were alone together Felipa got close to her and began to speak "love and lascivious words" *(amores e palavras lascivas),* words that the visitor of the Holy Office unfortunately did not record in the case proceedings. Felipa whispered to her, "It is better than were I a pimp to your lover" *(melhor do que se fosse um rufião à sua barregã),* and then showered her with "kisses and hugs." She then led Maria to the bed, an act to which she consented. The following night their amorous encounter became more complicated: Felipa's husband was home, a fact that made some deception necessary. Lying with her husband, Felipa feigned *doente da madre*—menstrual cramps—and with this she succeeded in getting Maria to lie with her elsewhere in order to "cure her." According to Maria's testimony, the two then engaged in a series of discreet sexual acts.

Acting in this way, Felipa de Souza confessed to having had six female partners over the eight years prior to the inquisitorial visitation in northeastern Brazil. Some of these women denounced Felipa to Mendonça. According to what they confessed—something that Felipa herself never denied—she regularly "boasted about" *(se gabava)* being with women, declaring that "she went out with and had [several] ladies" *(namorava e tinha damas).* The visitor Mendonça had no hesitation in classifying her as a woman who was "accustomed to committing [the nefarious sin] and courting woman" *(useira em cometer e namorar mulheres),* and for this he sentenced her to be publicly whipped in the city streets and banished her in perpetuity from the *capitania* of Bahia.[14]

Up until this point, upon narrating the amorous encounters and profiles of women accused of practicing the "nefarious sin," we have necessarily avoided going into much detail about the specific sexual acts that the archival documents speak to. It would be extremely interesting, for example, to see how these women dealt with, understood, viewed, and experienced the female body and feminine corporeality. In general, the corpus of inquisitorial documents is rich with such information and lends itself well to anthropological readings of this kind. Nevertheless, the same cannot be said for those documents of the Holy Office that deal with *sodomia foeminarum.* As Chad Black's essay in this volume also demonstrates, this absence of detail signals a methodological problem in terms of researching female sodomy in colonial Latin America: the sources themselves point more to official attitudes toward women, their bodies, and their desires than they do toward explicit representations of female sexuality. This is perhaps yet another instantiation of the misogyny of inquisitors in the Lusophone world.

Of those extremely rare cases of female sodomy that the Portuguese Inquisition tried, the majority originated with the efforts of Mendonça, the inquisitorial visitor to Brazil, in the late sixteenth century. In the decades that immediately followed, no woman was tried for sodomy either in the kingdom of Portugal or in its colonies. By the middle of the seventeenth century, the Portuguese Inquisition by and large relinquished its jurisdiction over the crime of female sodomy, considering women incapable of engaging in sodomy with members of the same sex due to their anatomy. Yet even in the late-sixteenth-century cases that were brought to light by Mendonça, we can perceive a relative disdain toward female sexuality that, paradoxically, worked to the advantage of those women who were inclined toward "nefarious acts" *(atos nefandos)* by practically decriminalizing female homoerotic relations, at least in the domain of the Holy Office of the Inquisition.

This inquisitorial disinterest toward female sodomy is only partly evidenced by the gap between the number of women implicated (29) and the number who were actually tried (7), as this disjuncture is also seen with the denunciations and proceedings in relation to other forms of deviancy dealt with by the Holy Office. And of the seven women whom Mendonça formally tried, only three were punished for the crime of sodomy. The remaining four women were punished for other errors of faith, including Lutheranism, reading prohibited books, certain irreverent acts, and, among other things, eating meat on days prohibited by the Church. Lastly, of the three women who were punished for the crime of female sodomy, only one of them, Felipa de Souza as we saw above, suffered harsh punishments.

Mendonça's contempt for the *crime nefando,* the "nefarious crime," of these women—an attitude that in itself shows a certain impudence toward female sexuality—can be gleaned less from the numbers of cases that were tried and more from the theories that guided those inquisitorial proceedings. In contrast to the large number of male sodomy cases tried by the Inquisition, the cases of sodomy among women present some subtle but important differences. A superficial comparison of the two series of archival documents appears to indicate that among men interactions were largely sexual, with a high frequency of sexual partners and seemingly brief encounters, and relatively few instances of affection between men. In the case of women, on the other hand, at least in those cases that involved adult women, we find clear evidence of lovers' entanglements, explicit passions, love letters, and a comparative silence surrounding the details of the sexual acts.

While the denunciations, testimonies, and confessions of men accused of sodomy tended to be graphic in nature, the opposite is true in the case of women accused of sodomy. This perhaps points to a certain level of discretion among women, especially regarding the nature and experience of sexual acts, and also to differences in terms of legibility and visibility between male-male and female-female sodomy. While many of the men accused of sodomy were witnessed in flagrante delicto committing the "nefarious act," or else they had given off certain signals of their predilections by their attitudes, their "scandalous" gestures, and their gendered performances (which occasionally included transvestism), the same cannot be said for women, who were rarely caught in the act and who often maintained romantic relationships in secrecy. This disjuncture points to the different ways that male and female sexuality in colonial Brazil came to be witnessed, transcribed, documented, and archived, especially within the context of sodomy and homoeroticism.

Furthermore, the archival documents indicate that the ways women related to one another sexually was remarkably similar. Lying in bed or at times on the floor or in a hammock, the women were described as being one on top of the other, with their "underwear pulled down" *(fraldas arriadas)* and their "shirts lifted" *(camisas levantadas);* they then "joined their front vessels [vaginas]" *(uniam seus vasos dianteros),* moving themselves against one another until they achieved "pleasure" *(deleite)*—something that many of the women admitted to upon interrogation. In all, this is the rough profile that the documentation of the Inquisition's sixteenth-century visit to colonial Brazil offers us. There are almost no allusions to "instruments" and no explicit references to sexual caresses, mutual masturbation, the erotic use of hands, or cunnilingus (which fell under the category of *molície,* according to theologians). The documentation primarily and perhaps euphemistically describes the "kisses and hugs" *(beijos e abraços)* between some of the women and, less commonly, the "words of love" *(palavras de amores)* that passed between some women, without registering exactly what those words were.

The confessions of the women were shaped more by the circumstances of seductions and amorous encounters than by the narratives of sexual acts, which is very much in contrast to the highly sexualized narratives that made their way into the transcripts of male sodomy cases. In this sense, female sexuality as registered in the archival documentation of the Inquisition is barely perceptible, even opaque. The descriptions of sexual acts in this corpus of cases show clear signs of inquisitorial jargon and formulaic language, such as "kisses and hugs" or "one woman was on top of the other, as if they were man on woman" *(ficava uma sobre a outra, como se fosse macho sobre fêmea)*—a clear projection of the model of male-female copulation that was judged to be "natural" by theologians.

Here we wish to briefly return to the center of the controversy of whether or not sodomy was assimilated to heresy by the Portuguese Inquisition. Was the case of sodomy an exception in the traditions and procedures of the tribunals of faith? There is no doubt that the confusion between heresy and sodomy had already begun, in a subtle manner, in the late Middle Ages, and that oftentimes sodomy was seen as evidence (or an aggravating factor) of heresy. This can be seen in John Boswell's book *Christianity, Social Tolerance, and Homosexuality,* which remains one of the most erudite and well-documented studies on the subject.[15] Agreeing with Boswell, Luiz Mott affirms that "from the twelfth to the thirteenth centuries. . . Christianity developed a real and aggressive horror of sodomites, as well as of Jews and other heretics, making them into scapegoats for the main evils and calamities afflicting Europe at that time."[16] Around this same time, Pope Innocent

III (1198–1216), who fought the Cathars in France and convoked the Fourth Lateran Council in 1215, considered heresy to be a poison and a social infection, thus adopting the lexicon of contagion and the stigmas associated with sodomites in general during this period.[17] In his 1198 edict *Urgentis et senium,* he classified heresy as a crime that was no less serious than the crime of lèse-majesté.[18]

Here we might also remember the articles of the Ordenações Filipinas, book 5, chapter 13: "Every person, whatever his quality, that commits the sin of sodomy, for whatever reason, shall be burned and made by fire into dust, so that from his body and grave never shall arise any memory . . . just like those who commit the crime of Lèse-majesté."[19] The association is very clear. In the bull of Innocent III, as we saw, the heresy came to be associated with lèse-majesté. In the Ordenações Filipinas sodomy was also associated with the same felony of lèse-majesté. Heretics could be condemned to the stake and also have their properties confiscated, and this *same punishment* was applied to sodomites, showing that since the late Middle Ages sodomy and heresy have been associated with one another in complicated and ambiguous ways. According to the Church, both "sodomites" who had given in to an unnatural sexual desire and those "New Christians" who had maintained their Jewish beliefs because of their impure ancestry were considered *suspects* of heresy.

The Inquisition's problem in the face of sodomy can be summarized by the following question: How abominable did the practice of sodomy have to be considered to signify an opposition to the Catholic faith? There were many doubts and few certainties, even in the crucial details concerning what technically counted as sodomy. The inquisitors, for example, wanted to know if certain individuals had been forced to commit an act of sodomy or if they had forced others to do so. The ages of the culprits and other factors such as the presence of alcohol surrounding the details of same-sex erotic activities could either mitigate or aggravate the severity of the charge. Another great concern of the inquisitors was whether the defendant had repented such "abominable acts," whether he had accused his partners, whether or not he had enjoyed these acts of intercourse, and so on. The Holy Office literally thrived on seeing the defendant submissive, contrite, and humiliated in the face of the tribunal's authority.

As Mott has correctly argued, sodomites, when punished by the Inquisition, did not abjure their errors except in the event that they were also punished for errors of consciousness, belief, or thought beyond the crime of sodomy. While Mott uses this evidence to sustain the theory that sodomy categorically was not a heresy, we see this as proof that the Inquisition, as a tribunal of *faith,* could not ascertain exactly where the sodomite's error of faith resided. Most of the time, those punished for the crime of sodomy had previously provoked gossip in a community, usually among their neighbors, being seen as those who challenged the family, marriage values, and ecclesiastical authority. But this was the inquisitors'

only certitude. On several other issues they remained in doubt as to how to proceed. The case of the Inquisition's treatment of female sodomites throughout the
Lusophone world is a poignant case in point: through the theological and juridical
negation of their own sodomitical potential, Portuguese inquisitors rendered these
girls and young women marginal to the discussion of sodomy and the heresies
with which it was associated.

The overall disinterest of the Portuguese Inquisition in the question of female
sodomy is in itself an important cultural phenomenon, a trace of the triumph of
misogynistic knowledge that was constructed around female bodies and desires.
This, of course, echoes much of the scholarship on female same-sex eroticism in
colonial Spanish America as well. Scholars including Lee Penyak, Jacqueline Holler, Nora Jaffary, Zeb Tortorici, and Ursula Camba Ludlow, for example, have independently researched the topics of female sodomy, masturbation, and autoerotic
religious visions in colonial Mexico, but all have run up against the same methodological issues tied to the relative dearth of archival documentation on these
topics.[20] In 1993, Lee Penyak observed that in comparison to the relative scarcity of
cases of female sodomy for early modern Europe, "Data for deviant female activities are equally difficult to locate in Mexico."[21] Almost twenty-five years later, it
seems that not much has changed in terms of the extant archival documentation
on these topics.

In my own research on some 325 criminal and Inquisition cases dealing with the
"sins against nature" in colonial New Spain from 1530 to 1821, I (Tortorici) have been
able to locate only *one* unambiguous archival reference to a criminal case of female
sodomy: the judicial summary of a 1732 case against a woman named Josepha de
Garfias for "the crime of sodomy she perpetrated with other women" *(por el crimen
de sodomia que perpetró con otras mugeres).* Although the original case file is lost,
the summary shows that the court pronounced the "definitive sentence" that Garfias serve the sick for a period of two years in the Hospital of San Juan de Dios in
Mexico City, that she fulfill a series of spiritual "medicinal penances," and that
"among other things certain instruments which she used for her sordid crime be
burned" *(mandó entre otras cosas se quemasen siertos instrumentos de que usaba
para su torpe delicto).*[22] Fascinating as this succinct eighteenth-century Mexican
judicial summary is, the intimate details of this case of female sodomy ultimately
elude us (in ways that are not unlike the colonial Brazilian documentation). Female
sodomy in colonial Latin America continues to be characterized by archival
absences—absences to which a small number of archival presences point.[23]

The Portuguese Inquisition in essence negated the possibility of female sodomy, relegating these acts to the category of mere *molície.* The women, sinning
among themselves without men and without phalluses, could not commit the
crime of perfect sodomy, a sin that was treated as if it were a heretical error of
conscience that only men could commit. Whatever the case may be, the Holy

Office of the Inquisition in Portugal broadened the concept of heresy in its judicial practice, and perhaps this elasticity is why the institution lasted for so many centuries. Without heresies—real or not—and especially without heretics, the Holy Office would have lost its sole reason to exist. What is clear, however, is that for the majority of Portuguese jurists and ecclesiastics, the desires and sexual acts of women when directed toward other women did not fall under this category. The same might be said, by and large, for the rest of colonial Latin America.

[handwritten annotation: Constructions of sex & truth about sex established the Holy Office]

NOTES

1. The first part of this essay is largely a synthesis and revision of the scholarship previously published in Ronaldo Vainfas, "Homoerotismo feminino e o Santo Ofício," in *História das mulheres no Brasil*, ed. Mary del Priore (São Paulo: Editora Contexto, 2004), 115–40; and Vainfas, "Inquisição como fábrica de hereges: Os sodomitas foram exceção?" in *A Inquisição em xeque. Temas, controvérsias, estudos de caso*, ed. Ronaldo Vainfas, Bruno Feitler, and Lana Lage da Gama Lima (Rio de Janeiro: Universidade do Estado do Rio de Janeiro, 2006). We wish to thank Lee Penyak for his suggestions and comments on this essay.

2. Luiz Mott, "Sodomia não é heresia: Dissidência moral e contracultura," in Vainfas, Feitler, and Lima (eds.), *A Inquisição em xeque.*

3. Rafael Carrasco, *Inquisición y represión sexual en Valencia. Historia de los sodomitas (1565–1785)* (Barcelona: Laertes Ediciones, 1986). For more in clerical sodomy in colonial Brazil, see Veronica de Jesus Gomes, *Atos nefandos: Eclesiásticos homossexuais na teia da Inquisição* (Curitiba: Editora Prismas, 2015).

4. The most complete work on the history of solicitation and the Portuguese Inquisition in colonial Brazil is the doctoral thesis of Lana Lage da Gama Lima, "A confissão pelo avesso: O crime de solicitação no Brasil colonial," University of São Paulo, 1990.

5. Biblioteca Nacional de Lisboa, Secção de Reservados, códice 869, fols. 361–64.

6. For more on the notion of female semen and its role in the conceptualization of female sodomy, see Fernanda Molina, "*Femina cum femina:* Controversias teológicas, jurídicas y médicas en torno a la sodomía femenina en el mundo hispano (Siglos XVI–XVII)," *ARENAL* 21, no. 1 (2014): 153–76.

7. Biblioteca Nacional, Secção de Reservados, códice 869, fols. 361–64. "Consulta: pode a Inquisição proceder contra mulheres que umas com as outras tiverem cópula e atos sodomíticos sendo íncubas ou súcubas agentes ut viri com instrumento ou sem ele por vias anteriores ou posteriores?" (1646).

8. *Primeira visitação do Santo Ofício às partes do Brasil. Confissões da Bahia, 1591–1593* (São Paulo: Ed. F. Briguiet, 1935), 206–9.

9. Ibid.

10. Arquivo Nacional Torre do Tombo/IL, processo 1289.

11. *Primeira visitação do Santo Ofício às partes do Brasil*, 47–50.

12. Arquivo Nacional Torre do Tombo/IL [hereafter cited as ANTT/IL], processo 3077.

13. ANTT/IL, processo 13787.

14. ANTT/IL, processo 1267.

15. John Boswell, *Christianity, Social Tolerance, and Homosexuality: Gay People in Western Europe from the Beginning of the Christian Era to the Fourteenth Century* (Chicago: University of Chicago Press, 1981).

166. Mott, "Sodomia não é heresia," 274.

17. Javier Paredes, ed., *Diccionario de los papas y concilios* (Barcelona: Ariel, 1998), 210.

18. A *lesa majestade* crime could be defined as any crime against the king or even a simple attempt to cause him any harm.

19. Silvia Hunold Lara, ed., *Ordenações Filipinas—Livro V* (São Paulo: Companhia das Letras, 1999), 91.

20. Lee Penyak, "Criminal Sexuality in Central Mexico, 1750–1850," Ph.D. diss., University of Connecticut, 1993; Jacqueline Holler, "'More Sins than the Queen of England': Marina de San Miguel before the Mexican Inquisition," in *Women in the Inquisition: Spain and the New World*, ed. Mary E. Giles (Baltimore: John Hopkins University Press, 1999); Nora E. Jaffary, *False Mystics: Deviant Orthodoxy in Colonial Mexico* (Lincoln: University of Nebraska Press, 2004); Zeb Tortorici, "Masturbation, Salvation, and Desire: Connecting Sexuality and Religiosity in Colonial Mexico," *Journal of the History of Sexuality* 16, no. 3 (2007): 355–72; and Ursula Camba Ludlow, "Gregoria la Macho y su 'inclinación a las mujeres': Reflexiones en torno a la sexualidad marginal en Nueva España, 1796–1806," *Colonial Latin American Historical Review* 12, no. 4 (2003): 479–97.

21. Penyak, " Criminal Sexuality in Central Mexico," 189.

22. Archivo General de la Nación, México, Indiferente Virreinal, caja 1482, exp. 7, fol. 9v.

23. For more on colonial sexuality, female sodomy, and archival absence, see Zeb Tortorici, "Archival Seduction: Indexical Absences and Historiographical Ghosts," *Archive Journal* 5 (Fall 2015).

PART II

Unnatural Crimes

5

Experimenting with Nature

José Ignacio Eyzaguirre's General Confession
and the Knowledge of the Body (1799–1804)

Martín Bowen Silva

"I wanted to put it in my mouth . . . like dogs do." This line, written in June 1802, is in a small notebook kept in Chile's National Archive.[1] What José Ignacio Eyza-guirre, the author of these notes, wanted to put in his mouth was his own penis, and he not only fantasized about it but he "tried to" one or two times. The manu-script, a collection of sins produced by a young member of the Chilean elite, contains other examples of unorthodox eroticism, including when he searched for pleasure by putting a cigar on his member, or when he thought of crafting a little bag to masturbate on. These thoughts and actions probed the natural limits of bodily pleasure—by forcing it to adopt an animal-like posture or by pro-viding it an artificially induced sexual satisfaction. And as such, they were classi-fied as "sins." In this chapter, I argue that these forms of eroticism offer interesting examples of how the conceptual tool of the "unnatural," and the broad range of transgressions that term encompasses, can give us a better understanding of the history of sexuality in colonial Spanish America. Indeed, Eyzaguirre's notes, to quote from Zeb Tortorici's recent discussion of "visceral archives," contain "acts and desires that tend to be queerer, less legible, and more historiographically mar-ginalized . . . than other types of criminalized sexuality in the past" (for example sodomy, adultery, or incest).[2] The unnatural can help us to queer the colonial archive, as long as we use the term *queer* to identify, as Tortorici puts it elsewhere, "processes through which historians seek to de-privilege and de-center heteronor-mative ways of reading and writing history."[3] Thus, a close reading of Eyzaguirre's manuscript may help us in the ongoing process of reshaping the categories and classifications we use to understand the history not only of sexuality, but also of desire.

In this essay I will show how Eyzaguirre's own archive of his unnatural deeds came to be constituted. I will then analyze some of his sins in order to understand how Eyzaguirre experimented with and tried to know more about the body, particularly the nature of sex and the human genitalia. I suggest that Eyzaguirre's attempts to know more about the "low"—the body—reveal the intimate link between the natural and the unnatural. During this discussion we will see the very different sins that could be considered among Eyzaguirre's unnatural acts. I will then show how these unnatural acts and desires were part of a more general list of sins, which responded both to the theological injunction to confess all sins and to Eyzaguirre's personal use of writing as a mnemonic technique. I conclude with a discussion of the unnatural as a fruitful concept for rethinking how we conceive the history of sexuality.

Let us begin by uncovering who the author of this notebook was, and why he decided to assiduously document his sins within it. José Ignacio Eyzaguirre was born in 1779 in Santiago de Chile, one of nine children of a merchant, Domingo Eyzaguirre, and Rosa de Arechavala, a rich aristocrat. In patriarchal late-colonial society, the personal trajectories of José Ignacio's four brothers enlighten us as to what was expected of a male member of the Chilean elite.[4] Miguel, the eldest, was president of the Real Universidad de San Felipe, Santiago de Chile's university, and *fiscal* (representative of royal interests) of Lima's Real Audiencia, and therefore a man of much political importance for the Spanish empire.[5] Once the revolutionary process had begun in Chile in 1810, the second brother, Agustín, acted as head of the government on three different occasions. Domingo, the third brother, was renowned for his philanthropic work and is considered to be the founder of the village of San Bernardo, south of Santiago. José Alejo, José Ignacio's only younger brother, was an important priest who came to be Santiago de Chile's bishop for a short period of time. From the 1820s onward, all the brothers (with the exception of Miguel, who died in 1821) were members of the national congresses of the recently declared independent state of Chile.[6] Like his brothers, José Ignacio was a prominent member of the local elite. His son, José Ignacio Víctor Eyzaguirre, described him as "one of the founding fathers" of the Chilean nation, listing his services as deputy, senator, "member of the State Council," "secretary of the Finance and War Departments," and "director of Chile's mint," among other administrative and honorific distinctions. He died in June 1848.[7]

José Ignacio's notebook is preserved in Chile's national archive, the Archivo Nacional Histórico de Chile, in the collection left by the historian Jaime Eyzaguirre after his death and donated in 1970 to the institution by Jaime's widow.[8] The document is exceptional in several ways, not the least of which is how it highlights the ways in which one particular individual enumerated and enunciated his experiments with his own body. Produced outside the institutions in which scholars usually find evidence of marginalized forms of sexuality, this manuscript provides

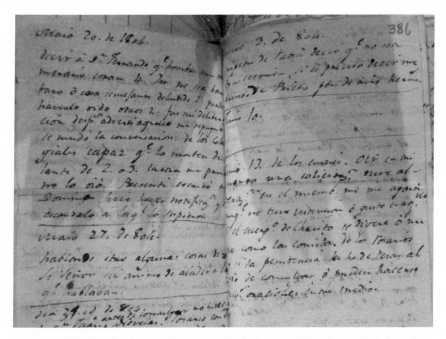

FIGURE 2. Folio from José Ignacio Eyzaguirre's *Confesión Generalísima* (1799–1804), from the Archivo Nacional Histórico de Chile. Photo by Martín Bowen Silva.

us with an unexpected window into the presence of the unnatural in colonial archives. On the one hand, it is a rare example of a confession written down without any literary intentions; on the other, it is an eloquent and original demonstration of how a Catholic man organized, catalogued, and analyzed his own corporeal practices. Among these, those related to what we call sexuality were especially important, and help us explore the liminal space between "natural" and "unnatural" acts and desires. Through them we can study how a young boy in a Catholic context built his own knowledge of the low by experimenting with his own body and with the bodies of others.

JOSÉ IGNACIO EYZAGUIRRE'S *GENERAL CONFESSION*

José Ignacio Eyzaguirre's manuscript is not a homogeneous corpus of writing. Rather, it can be divided into at least three parts. The first is a small notebook with generally short, dated annotations (fig. 2). The first date to appear in this part of the document is August 26, 1799, and the last is July 22, 1804. This would mean that José Ignacio, age twenty when he began, kept this notebook for about five years, cataloguing his past sins in it. The dates, rather than representing the day on which a specific sin was committed, indicate the day the comment was written. For example, on February 6, 1803, he wrote: "Angry with father, I called him a bloody old man [viejo de mierda], I disobeyed his call to pray the Rosary." This could be considered an entry in a diary if it weren't for the fact that José Ignacio's father had died in 1800.[9] Another fragment, which deals with a political conflict, is dated 1804, though we know from José Ignacio's letters that the conflict occurred in 1803.[10] In other words, these fragments are in fact memories, written down to establish an account of past events that he felt needed to be confessed.

The second part of the manuscript (as it is found now in the archives) is written in a larger format than the previous section and has a title: "Confesión Generalísima" (General Confession; fig. 3). In contrast with the first part, in which the sins are written down confusingly and without any order, in this second section they are organized and classified according to eight kinds of sin. This classification seems to be taken from one of the many authors who published books to guide and instruct both confessors and penitents during the early modern era.[11] Paolo Segneri, an influential Italian Jesuit, for example, reordered the ten precepts of the Church into eight items to be confessed by merging the sixth and ninth and the seventh and tenth precepts.[12] This part of the document is better organized and easier to understand than the first, though it still cannot be considered a coherent document. It also has dates, but they cover only June and July 1804. This document is followed by a short fragment of writing titled "Confession from Passion Sunday to Holy Saturday" (fig. 4). After this, another "Confesión generalísima" begins (fig. 5), in which Eyzaguirre states the same sins already confessed in the small notebook. Two pages consisting of sins written in Latin interrupt this fragment. Finally, the document as it is conserved today ends with a couple of pages filled with fragmentary and seemingly haphazard writings on Eyzaguirre's sins.

The apparent disorder of the document is one of its most interesting features, distinguishing it from the standard confessional discourse of early modern Spanish America. The manuscript is not an autobiographical piece of writing with literary intentions, nor is it an intimate account of a rich internal life.[13] Thus, it differs from what Alain Corbin defined as the "autobiographical narration" of general confessions, an account that was supposed to be, following the obsessions of the period, a "sexual autobiography" of the sinner.[14] On the contrary, it is an example of the use of writing as a cognitive tool to comply with the precept that all sins be confessed. Its confusing nature is the result of the difficulties that this obligation posed to Catholics. For this reason, it should be considered a nonmediated testimony on the problems of memory and confession in the modern period.

Following the imposition of annual confession, it was mandatory (in theory) for every Catholic to remember and confess all his or her sins.[15] Paolo Segneri stated that a confession had to satisfy certain conditions to be considered "successful." Among those conditions, one of the most important was "to be complete."

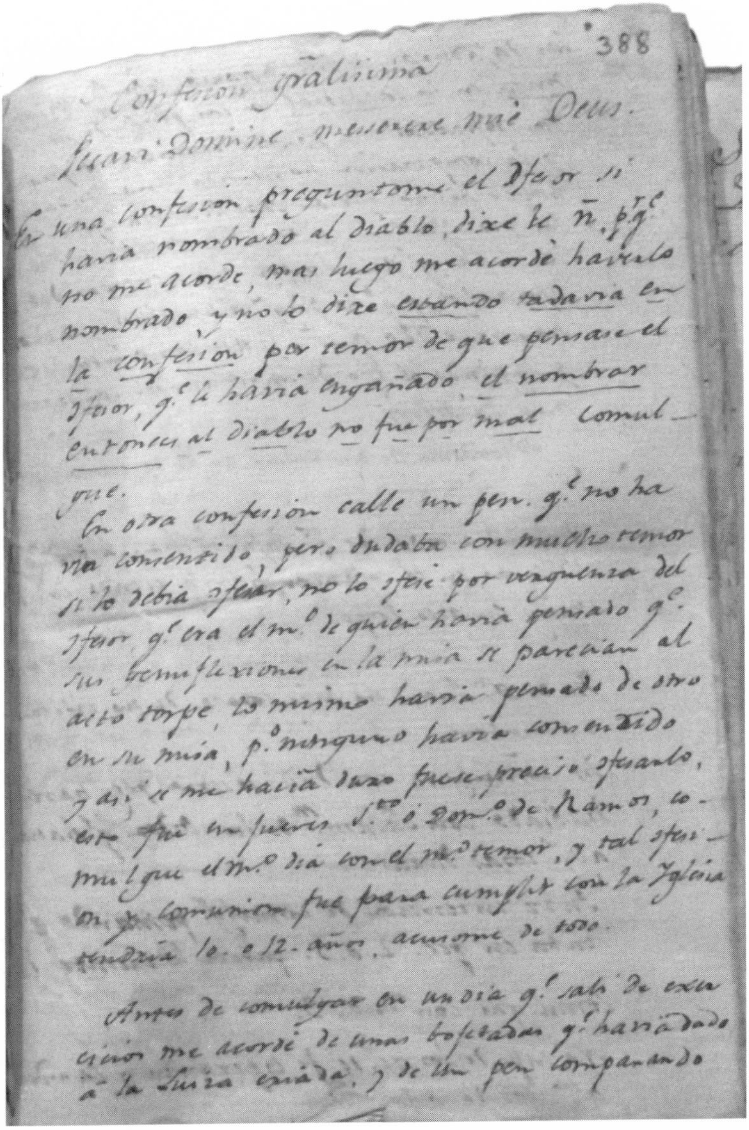

FIGURE 3. Folio from José Ignacio Eyzaguirre's *Confesión Generalísima* (1799–1804), from the Archivo Nacional Histórico de Chile. Photo by Martín Bowen Silva.

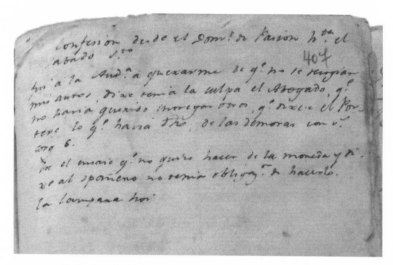

FIGURE 4. Folio from José Ignacio Eyzaguirre's *Confesión Generalísima* (1799–1804), from the Archivo Nacional Histórico de Chile. Photo by Martín Bowen Silva.

This meant that both the penitent—by examining his bad deeds—and the confessor—by posing the right questions—had to achieve the fullest possible account of the penitent's bad actions and thoughts.[16] It was sacrilege, one of the worst sins for Catholics, not to confess all of one's faults. According to Jean Delumeau, the efforts of early modern Catholic thought to build a complete knowledge of all possible sins and to establish a list of their corresponding punishments or penances was a result of the fear of being condemned because of some unnoticed sacrilege.[17] It was necessary to know all the weaknesses of human nature and all the tricks of the Devil so as to save oneself from hell. Paolo Segneri highlighted this fact for his readers when writing that "Saint Teresa used to say that because of sacrilegious confessions, Hell was constantly fed; and, writing to a Preacher, she warned: Father, preach many times against wrong Confessions, because the Devil has no other snare as effective as this to hunt souls."[18]

Two things were at stake in the problem of sacrilegious confessions: first, the cognitive process that would help the penitent and the confessor to properly identify and classify any bad action or deed; and, second, the penitent's memory, as he or she was called to remember all of his or her sins. This was even more important in the case of general confessions. A general confession according to the *Diccionario de autoridades*, published in 1729, was "that of the whole past life, from the age when the penitent was able to sin and to receive the Sacrament of Penance, to the day of the confession; or that where particular confessions of a certain time are repeated, out of necessity or devotion."[19] Thus a general confession was the practice of remem-

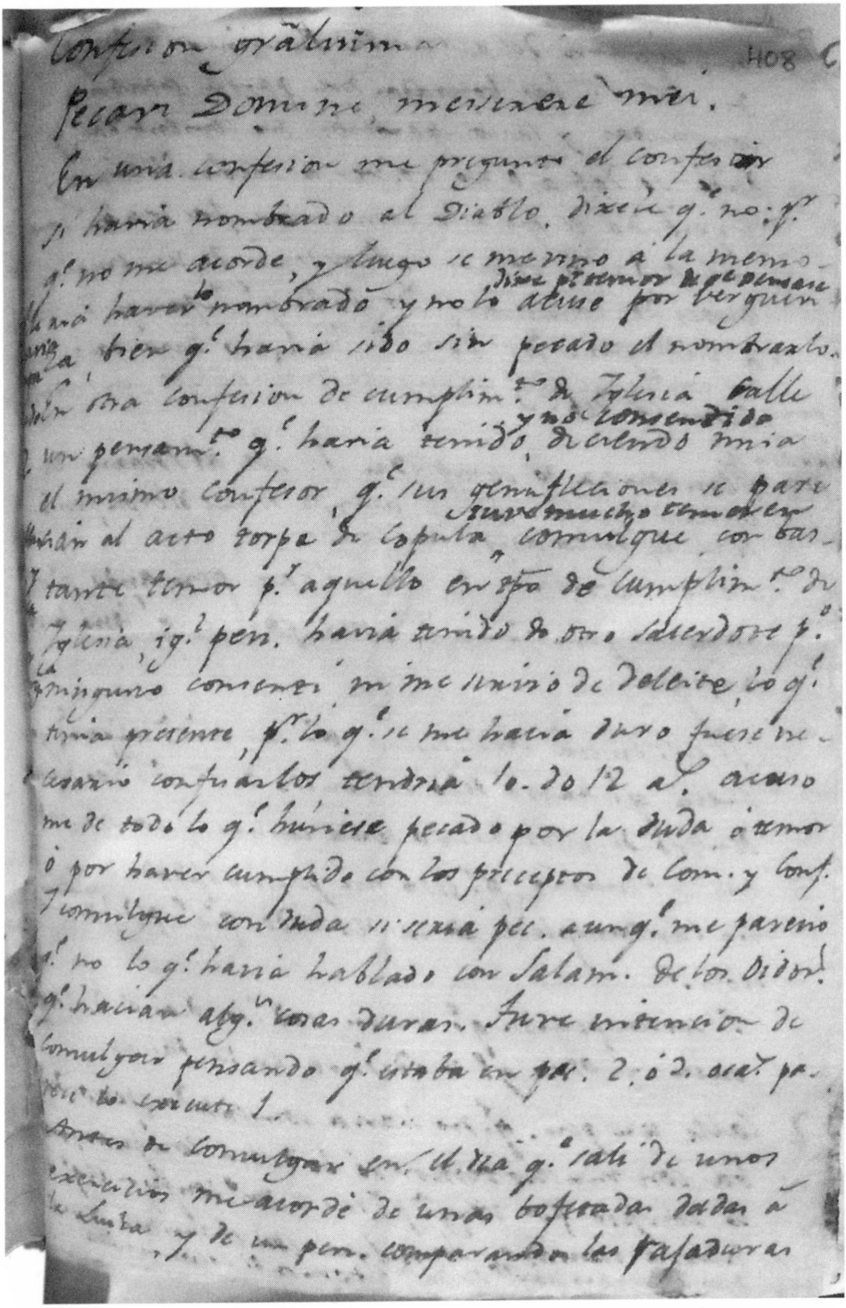

FIGURE 5. Folio from José Ignacio Eyzaguirre's *Confesión Generalísima* (1799–1804), from the Archivo Nacional Histórico de Chile. Photo by Martín Bowen Silva.

bering all past sins, or sins from other specific confessions. For the *Diccionario de la lengua castellana* of 1780, it was only about confessing "sins of all past life, or those of an important part of it."[20] Sometimes, a general confession was considered an obligation, as when a penitent had not confessed all his sins in previous confessions.[21] But it was also recommended when the penitent felt that his ordinary confessions were insufficient, or as part of the celebration of particular religious festivities or events.[22]

Eyzaguirre followed these precepts. At the beginning of the first fragment entitled "General Confession," the most coherent piece of writing in the manuscript, he stated some of his potentially unnatural transgressions of the first commandment that had not been properly confessed:

> In a confession, the confessor asked me if I had invoked the Devil. I said no, because I didn't remember; but later I remembered having invoked him, and I had not told him while still in the confession, because I feared the confessor might think that I had lied to him. . . . In another confession, I did not confess a thought . . ., but I doubted greatly whether I should confess it; I did not do it because I was ashamed, [because it was about] the confessor, whose genuflections at Mass I had thought looked like a lewd act. . . . I was 10 or 12 years old, I accuse myself of all this.[23]

Later, he mentions other general confessions, made perhaps as a result of some devotional practices: on one occasion he wrote that he wondered whether "in making a general confession I should have confessed all sins already confessed," while on another occasion he briefly mentioned some sins "from the last general confession."

As we can see, Eyzaguirre wrote down those actions and thoughts he had failed to confess previously. He is remembering old sins, some of them committed when he was a boy. At the same time, he was trying to correct old confessions that he deemed to be incomplete. It is important to point this out, as it reveals Eyzaguirre's doubts regarding whether his potentially unnatural acts and thoughts were in fact sins. To confess his sins, José Ignacio had to identify them as such in the first place: he was therefore forced to confront his own deviations from the norm and to determine whether they should be classified as unnatural. This confirms that Eyzaguirre's writings obey the terms of a general confession and that what guides his writing is the obligation to remember all his unconfessed or wrongly confessed bad thoughts and actions.

BUILDING A KNOWLEDGE OF THE "LOW"

Most of the sins confessed by Eyzaguirre were related to what we today call sexuality. This may be the result of the obsession with lust—as a sin—that was developed by Catholic theologians of the eighteenth and nineteenth centuries.[24] Eyzaguirre followed very closely the instructions and precepts of the ecclesiastical discourse on confession, which may have influenced his approach to the subject. But his focus on sexuality may also be the result of his age, given that he was a young man confessing the sins of his childhood. We have to bear in mind here that he was between twenty and twenty-five when he wrote this document. According to Segneri, one reason for making a general confession was to confess the sins of childhood, as some penitents "do not confess some faults committed by them when they were little boys; even if they remember them, because until then they were ashamed of them."[25] Be that as it may, the preeminence of sexuality in Eyzaguirre's manuscript allows us to analyze the sometimes contradictory relationship between knowledge of the body and the unnatural.

Many bodily experiences confessed by Eyzaguirre were experimental in nature, and can therefore be framed as natural explorations of the body, both male and female. At least in the way Eyzaguirre writes of them, these actions seemed to have been dictated by his will to explore and understand his own autoerotic body and its attending pleasures. He wrote, "I put a cigar on my member once or twice"; and "Pollution [ejaculation], I was awake, I left my excited member against my thigh, in order to see if it peeled itself [si se mondaba]," perhaps referring to the pulling back of the foreskin. The vocabulary Eyzaguirre uses to confess his sins in this fragment is worth noting. What I have translated as "peel" is the verb mondar, which Eyzaguirre always used when referring to his penis. Mondar was a verb that signified "to clean or to purify something, removing from it what is superfluous or strange to it."[26] As we shall see, José Ignacio's vocabulary reflects on his efforts to understand the human body without transgressing the boundaries of the official discourse.

At this point, Eyzaguirre's account takes on several layers of meaning, as it not only reproduces the ecclesiastical discourse on the body that prompted it in the first place, but also offers an alternative archive, formed by a series of practices and discourses that the penitent experienced as sin but that constructed his own knowledge of the body. In the fragments cited above, Eyzaguirre was not just accusing himself of having sexual desires for other humans; he was also attesting to practices of exploration guided by curiosity that technically fell within the theological category of "sins against nature." Indeed, as historiography has shown, the formulation of "sins against nature" was a very complex category that encompassed not only sodomy and bestiality but also unorthodox sexual positions and masturbation. These were considered to be among the most offensive sins because they transgressed God's intention for nature.[27] Eyzaguirre's sins—like masturbating and ejaculating or, as he recalls elsewhere in the manuscript, touching another man's penis and ejaculating him—were very serious crimes from a theological point of view. But they were also the result of the very restrictions that Catholicism imposed on the knowledge of the body.

Indeed, Eyzaguirre's research on his own body seems to have been guided in part by ignorance. Whether this is because he was raised in a very Catholic and pious family or because it was normal for the time, the fact is that many of Eyzaguirre's confessions are the result of his will to understand not only his body but also the mysteries of sex.[28] On April 9, 1800, for example, he wrote the following sentence: "I wished to know the way to sin with a woman one or three [times]. I tried it out from behind with my finger *[por atrás con el dedo]*." This means that he did not know exactly how to have sex, and that he tried to find out by experimenting with himself, introducing his finger into his anus—a potentially pleasurable "unnatural" act of autopenetration that had the ultimately "natural" aim of better understanding how to sin with a woman. He seemed to be accusing himself of the same sin when he wrote, "I used my finger [to find out] if it could be done in the ass *[culo]* two or four [times], with excitement." The fact that he did not know exactly how things worked when having sex is confirmed when he writes that, at the age of thirteen or fourteen, he was afraid "of getting stuck in the act, and not being absolved afterward."

Eyzaguirre's will to understand his body and the mysteries of sex and to experience its pleasures are revealed not only in confessions regarding experiments with himself, but also in his interactions with other people. We know that when he was a small boy he tried to obtain information about this sin in his own household. In these confessions, we see the different children who shared the domestic space in a classic Hispanic-American patrician household: his own sisters and brothers, the slave-born children, and the children of the free servants.[29] The interesting nature of their interactions is reflected in Eyzaguirre's notes. He wrote, for example:

> Having heard from Dolores, a slave, that Antonia had told of what women did with men, I asked her what she had said, [and] a sister of mine, who had heard it, rejected it, saying to her that she should not tell it, that it was wrong, and I urged the slave to tell me, and even though I think she did not tell me when my sister was there, she did so later. I do not know if I insisted again. I heard attentively, I do not know whether with pleasure, that women fondle the man's member. . . . I was 9 or 10 years old, and the one who told it was 8 [years old].

This part of Eyzaguirre's confession shows his strong desire to know. Being a nine- or ten-year-old boy, he pushed an eight-year-old slave to tell him what women and men do, even after facing the resistance of one of his sisters. The manuscript shows us how the first learning about sexuality happened within the domestic unit (at least in this confession). It also shows us how this knowledge was built not only by means of the spoken word. José Ignacio, one of his brothers (Alejo), three slaves (a boy and two girls, one of them the aforementioned Dolores), and other servants also practiced a sort of polymorphous sexuality:

> I touched a four- or five-year-old brother, like he who gelds a bull, I saw his member . . . and I touched him [later]. I invited four girls to do the same, one four or five years

old, a sister of hers, six- or seven-year-old daughters *[sic]*, the slave Dolores five or seven years old, and another slave aged eight or ten. The first two were daughters of a free servant. I saw and touched their members, all of them, eight or twelve times . . . ; I also once saw and touched the member of Xavier, an eight- or nine-year-old slave. . . . It seems to me that Xavier once said this could be a sin, and I denied it once or twice. We hid. Xavier, the slave, once asked why he didn't do the same thing to me, I agreed, I lay down for him to touch me.

We can see here how different individuals from the household—all of lower status than José Ignacio, as he touched his younger brother, slaves, and servants—practiced some form of early sexuality. It should not surprise us that Eyzaguirre accused himself of these childhood practices. For early modern Catholicism, childhood was not exactly an innocent age, free of sins.[30] Moreover, Eyzaguirre was aware of having shown signs of doing wrong, by hiding with the other children, a manifestation of personal guilt according to Paolo Segneri.[31]

It was within the all-male institution of the Santiago de Chile Seminary that José Ignacio would take his bodily experimentations to the next stage. The seminary was one of Chile's most prestigious educational institutions, reserved for the instruction of the children of the local elite.[32] Most of Eyzaguirre's sexual transgressions are linked with other students from the seminary.[33] This is not necessarily surprising: according to Alessandro Stella, the directors of these institutions did not pay too much attention to students' sexual adventures, which they judged normal for their ages.[34] As we shall explore later, one of Catholicism's most important contradictions during the early modern period was that, under certain circumstances, unnatural sins could be socially considered as natural.

In the manuscript, it becomes clear that José Ignacio Eyzaguirre was still constructing his own knowledge of the body and sexuality while studying in the seminary, even though that knowledge was considered a sin. Some examples are quite clear: for instance, he asked one particular student, Manuel José Fraga, "what is that sort of crown of the member?" *(qué significa aquella como corona del miembro?)* and also "what's that sort of *grano* [spot, pimple] that he had on his member, and whether everyone had it" (both sentences may be asking the same question, expressed differently in each case). Eyzaguirre also accused himself of wanting "to see Vilvado's member. . . . Having heard from him that a women had asked him to fornicate, I wished to know if he had fornicated with her, and I tried to undo his trousers with my hand."[35] Once again, here, the natural and the unnatural coalesce through the corporeal experiments of Eyzaguirre and his schoolmates.

In fact, the students in the seminary told each other their sexual (mis)adventures. According to Eyzaguirre, one of them once recounted "that on having women, he found himself incapable [of having sex], and that he was angry at his member." Eyzaguirre also accused himself of having heard, from the same student, "two obscene tales of fornications." Another student told him that, wanting to have sex with a reluctant peasant woman, he lifted her skirt up "and fornicated [with] her," that is, he raped her.[36] As in the rape case mentioned above, power relations were also important in Eyzaguirre's sexual explorations with his schoolmates. As current historiography on sodomy has shown, during this period sexual intercourse was very much informed by hierarchy and social status.[37] Consequently, Zeb Tortorici has found that "many of the spaces in which sodomy became a possibility were defined by asymmetrical power relationships: the school, the ship, the prison, the hacienda, the slave's quarters, and the confessional."[38] Santiago's seminary was one such place as well.

One of the main figures in Eyzaguirre's confession is the aforementioned Manuel José Fraga. He was some five years older than José Ignacio, as he had entered the seminary in 1790, aged sixteen.[39] As we have seen, Fraga appears to be informing and teaching Eyzaguirre about the male body and sexuality. Eyzaguirre wrote, "I heard from him that he woke up to search for a woman. I heard from him of fornications, etc." José Ignacio not only heard his stories, but also asked Fraga questions, as in the following fragment: "I asked him how it was, and I heard from him, attentively and with pleasure, that when he was a young boy, a woman made him fornicate, and of the pleasure he had; I don't know if I wished to do the same." The "pedagogical" role fulfilled by this older student is more clearly revealed in other fragments of José Ignacio's confession, such as: "I wanted to know how one fornicates with women twice or four [times]. I asked Fraga once; I heard his explanation once or twice." Fraga not only told Eyzaguirre how to have sex, he also proposed practical experiences, as when Eyzaguirre noted: "he offered to take me to his women to fornicate."

But the relationship with Fraga went a little further, showing us how eroticism and exploration of the body were closely related and how acts that theologically fell under the category of the unnatural could perhaps be seen by many as normal adolescent experimentation. Eyzaguirre writes, "I saw Fraga's member four or six [times], I touched it three or six, I measured it two or three." Another fragment of the manuscript is more explicit: "Fraga asked me if I wanted him to pollute [ejaculate]. I said do as you wish. I was alone in my bedroom, I was twelve or thirteen years old. Fraga did it. I watched how he did it two or three [times] and its spilling once. I consented to the same thing in my room two or three [times]. I was probably excited. I listened to what he was saying." Eyzaguirre also writes, about Fraga: "I let him rub my member; it wasn't my initiative, but I laughed and I didn't do anything to avoid him or to escape."

We must bear in mind here that Fraga was five years older than José Ignacio. As the last two fragments show, their relationship was not equal. In this case, the power imbalance inside the educational institution was not between students and teachers,[40] but between older and younger students. And as in other contexts, power imbalances can redefine the crimes committed. It has long been debated whether authorities in Spain and Spanish America considered "passive" and "active" sodomy to be equally grave sins. But what seems clear is that male individuals who practiced sodomy saw the active (penetrative) role as more compatible with their masculine identity than the passive one.[41] Similarly, Anne-Marie Sohn has found that in nineteenth-century French *lycées*, male students viewed "initiating" younger schoolmates as a way to affirm their virility.[42]

Eyzaguirre's sins were perhaps usual among students in this kind of school. Alessandro Stella has suggested that same-sex educational institutions lay the foundations for homoerotic behavior among priests and nuns.[43] Even if Stella's analysis is debatable,[44] certainly these institutions were places where unorthodox forms of desire *could* take place.[45] In fact, studies of early modern and modern Europe's educational institutions have shown that the kind of relationship established between Eyzaguirre and Fraga, like the experiences he had with other schoolmates, were usual among male students.[46]

Even the characteristics of José Ignacio's sexual experiences were not necessarily rare. Most were focused on the penis. In his notes, we see him watching, touching, measuring, and examining his and others' penises. Female genitalia are almost absent from his manuscript.[47] This "focalization" on the male member can also be found in testimonies of men accused of sodomy in early modern Spain,[48] and in the sexual practices of young students in France.[49] Moreover, theologians seemed to have been confronted with such sins repeatedly enough that they incorporated them into their confession manuals, as a way to guide the priest in his questioning of the penitent. Thus, Eyzaguirre's sins with other boys at the Santiago de Chile Seminary were the same ones that Leonardo da Porto Maurizio, a Franciscan friar, mentioned in a sort of standard confession he wrote to guide penitents. Only "perfect sodomy" (sodomy with another man) is absent from Eyzaguirre's manuscript, but a panoply of other "unnatural" acts and desires found their way into the text.[50]

Eyzaguirre's manuscript, as argued here, does not only reveal these practices; it also shows how a Catholic built up knowledge of his body and of his sins. Although it has been claimed that, due to a lack of privacy, sex was no secret for children during the early modern period,[51] Eyzaguirre's notes reflect a different, more nuanced reality. He asked about sex and human anatomy, sometimes revealing great anxiety about it, as when he questioned one of his house slaves for more information on what men and women do together. He also tried to know the limits of his body and others' bodies by touching and exploring them. But even actions that we would consider "natural," like seeing his own genitals, he incorporated into his catalogue of sins, as in the following fragment: "I saw my member during the night once in the room; in Don Juan's room once; in the stable once; in the corner where the stocks were once. I also saw it four times when I peeled it [*quando lo mondé*] at school, four or five [times], and twice I saw it when I peeled it [*quando lo mondé*] in the Dormitory. . . . Seen ten or twelve times [*son vistas diez o doce*]."

For someone like Eyzaguirre, a member of Spanish America's Catholic elite, to know more about the human body entailed important risks. And, as we shall see in the next section, it also led to serious paradoxes.

THE HIGH, THE LOW, AND THE BODY

Eyzaguirre's admissions enable us to understand how an individual of the late eighteenth and early nineteenth centuries approached forbidden knowledge of the body, merging the quest for experience with natural and unnatural desires for women and men. As we saw in the previous section, this will to know about the human body led Eyzaguirre to natural and unnatural sins and desires. Experimental practices, explorations of his own and others' bodies, questions addressed to those more experienced than him, and stories heard from others: all these situations reflect how an individual constructed his own knowledge of the body.

However, Eyzaguirre learned of the body not only from interpersonal relationships: "I read González Téllez on how to determine a woman's virginity. I got excited several times. I was studying the subject. I read with fear." Here Eyzaguirre seems to be writing about Manuel González Téllez's *Commentaria perpetua in singulos textus quinque librorum Decretalium Gregorii IX*, a book of canon law first published in the seventeenth century.[52] The fact that approved literature like this one could be put to unsanctioned ends is not necessarily surprising. Members of Chile's elite denounced the moral dangers of reading casuistry literature, mainly because it described different kinds of sins, especially those regarding lust, in great detail.[53] This immoral use of casuistry literature reveals one of the contradictions of early modern Catholicism's knowledge of sins: in order to fight sins, it was necessary to identify and understand them.[54] For example, the treaty on marriage by the Jesuit Tomás Sánchez, *Disputationes de sancto matrimonii sacramento*, published between 1602 and 1605, was considered, according to Fernanda Alfieri, "to be something to be both praised (for the profundity of the issues addressed) and reproached (for the detail with which the 'unspeakable' sphere of sexuality [was] dealt)."[55] Eyzaguirre's notes reflect this paradox, as he identifies as sins the very actions by which he tried to understand the secrets of sex and sexuality. He had to mobilize a form of knowledge about the body (in this case, a theological one) in order to accuse his own efforts to know more about it.

As Carlo Ginzburg has demonstrated, in the economy of knowledge of the early modern era the "high" matters—the divine truths, the high political issues—were not open to everyone's curiosity. They could even be conceived as forbidden knowledge. For example, José Ignacio's brother Miguel, when finishing his studies in theology at the Real Universidad de San Felipe in Santiago, was reminded "not to abuse the license obtained to interpret the Sacred Scriptures because of the danger and harm that may ensue."[56] It was against this prohibition that the motto

Sapere aude!—"Dare to know," later considered as the Enlightenment's leitmotiv—was used from the seventeenth century onward.[57] But what is often disregarded—or seen as a self-evident attribute of early modern societies—is that, in some cases, it was also forbidden to investigate or to learn about the "low," the corporeal, the sinful parts of existence, and that this social prohibition affected the relationship between individuals and their bodies.

Sapere aude! is a motto that could also qualify Eyzaguirre's explorations of his body in all of its "natural" and "unnatural" manifestations. He dared to know what was supposed to be kept secret from him. He pushed other people to tell him what he did not know. He explored his body. Eyzaguirre's own scrutinizing of his past explorations, as we have seen, is the result of an institutional obligation, but the obligation to talk about sex in the confession is mirrored here by the audacity and experimental practices of a Catholic. Eyzaguirre wrote, for example, that he stared at a donkey and a mule that were copulating out of "curiosity," the keyword for sins related to forbidden knowledge.[58]

This tension between the official and the unofficial knowledge of the body becomes quite clear in Eyzaguirre's vocabulary. In some contexts, words used to describe sex or sexual encounters have proven to be very interesting for understanding historically how individuals and societies have made sense of sexuality.[59] Eyzaguirre's vocabulary is interesting because he usually described his sexual acts using words such as *polución* (pollution, meaning the spilling of semen), *fornicación* (fornication), or *alteración* (alteration, meaning erection), all part of the official discourse on lust.[60] This official vocabulary confirms the fact that José Ignacio, educated in the Santiago de Chile Seminary, was very much aware of the theological discourse on confessions.[61] But at the same time, other words, such as the already mentioned *mondar,* contaminate his account, coming as they do from outside the official discourse. We do not know if other contemporaries used that verb in this same context, but we *do* know that Eyzaguirre accused himself of using unofficial words to describe the human anatomy. Once, for example, he heard someone associating the "women's member" (the vagina) with the term *trucha* (trout), and he did the same thing a couple of times. In Spanish, *trucha* is similar to *chucha,* a vulgar term used in some parts of Spanish America, including Chile, for the vagina.[62] More explicitly, Eyzaguirre also accused himself of having given the name "Don Juan" to the penis, and in another fragment he mentions having given it the name of "Santo." What seems interesting here is that the very act of naming female or male genitalia could be considered a sin, even while the theological discourse provided José Ignacio with a vast array of concepts to define sexual acts.

Eyzaguirre's confession shows that we should not assume that individuals had a clear and immediate knowledge of their bodies. A body, even one's own, could be a difficult enigma to solve. The "low," which is opposed to the "high" in modern theology, could also be an arcane matter, and not necessarily due to prohibition alone.[63] Furthermore, we can see from José Ignacio Eyzaguirre's writings that the relationship between modern individuals and their bodies was far from transparent. As Thomas Laqueur has shown, even in those aspects where the body was expected to provide clear and visible signs, like the sexual division between men and women, those signs could prove difficult to read.[64] In this sense, Eyzaguirre's manuscript confirms that the body was both intimate and strange, that "nature" paradoxically engendered unnatural sins and desires.

The difference between the "high" and the "low" worked as an anthropological construct for modern culture. The fact of being conceived as two poles of human experience paradoxically attracted them to each other and helped to develop a constant dialogue between them. This is made particularly clear in comic practices that mixed the low and the high, producing laughter as a result.[65] This kind of operation was also present in Eyzaguirre's own manuscript when he accused himself of comparing the appearance of a church's sanctuary to the unholy "parts" of our Lord,[66] and of having thought that a priest's "genuflections" in mass resembled a sexual act *(acto torpe)*.[67] Given the structural parallel between the "high" and the "low," it is not surprising that Dolores Peña y Lillo, an eighteenth-century Chilean nun, also made the same comparisons.[68] Historians, too, have seen this parallelism. In an inquisition case from the seventeenth century in which a Mexican woman declared that she had had sexual and mystical relationships with Jesus, the Virgin Mary, and some saints, Zeb Tortorici noted a "simultaneous sacralization and vulgarization" of religious devotion.[69] Nora Jaffary's essay in this volume explores similar themes.

The natural and the unnatural were equally connected. Even if Eyzaguirre did not use these concepts himself to describe his actions and desires, in his manuscript he links sins that fell under the category of the unnatural—like masturbation and pollution—with his will to know more about the body and sexuality. The unnatural lurked beneath the natural body; it was inscribed in every effort to know more about it. When Eyzaguirre tried to perform oral sex on himself "like dogs do," he was trying to know more about his body and testing its limits at the same time. Such explorations on the natural body led to unnatural actions and desires. It is interesting to note that Eyzaguirre kept the scenes and practices he used to explore his body and to learn about sex in his memory for years, a sort of archive of his sins, inscribed (as memory is inscribed) on his body. In other words, all the practices that helped him to understand sex were also understood as sins. In a way, Eyzaguirre's notes confirm the analysis by Michel de Certeau, who thought of the body as a surface where the Law comes to be inscribed and of paper as a substitute for human skin.[70] We can say that Eyzaguirre had his transgressions written in his body, in the form of memory, before he turned them into paper and ink.

WRITING DOWN UNNATURAL SINS

José Ignacio's confession is not a document about sexuality, but rather a list of sins. The transgressions of the "sexual" norms—in fact, of the sixth commandment (lust)—I have been describing here were part of a larger set of deviances from the norm, which included such sins as contesting paternal authority, having sacrilegious thoughts, and being dishonest. It is important, then, to analyze why Eyzaguirre wrote down all of these sins, in order to fully grasp what meaning they had for him. In this process, the concept of the unnatural can give us a better understanding of Eyzaguirre's confession than the more traditional concepts in the history of sexuality (including perhaps the very concept of "sexuality" that I have been using thus far).

Writing was not an art for Eyzaguirre. Rather, it is what made it possible for him to give an account of his sins. Writing a confession down was not such an unusual practice. By the end of the eighteenth century, in Valdivia (a city south of Santiago), the merchant José Lopetegui Villar "made a general confession each month, and took pleasure in writing these down, carefully keeping the manuscripts" for himself.[71] At the end of the nineteenth century ordinary people also wrote down their confessions, like the criminal Jean Bladier, whose papers the historian Philippe Artières studied.[72] Moreover, individuals—including José Alejo Eyzaguirre, one of José Ignacio's brothers—often wrote down everyday actions to keep account of their way of life.[73] All of these texts served what Spanish historian Antonio Castillo-Gómez has described as one of the main purposes of modern "ordinary writings": to help the individual memory.[74]

However, the difference between Eyzaguirre's manuscript and a finished personal confession is that in this case we have only a fragment of the process of introspection, of remembering sinful acts and desires. This becomes clear in Eyzaguirre's will to recount the exact number of faults he committed. In the modern period, a general confession was not only an account of bad actions and deeds; the penitent had also to state the exact number of times he committed each sin in order to give a measurable dimension to his faults and, consequently, to gain the possibility of redemption by an equivalent penance.[75] As Segneri put it, the "completeness" of a general confession consisted "not only in a manifestation of all mortal sins remembered after a diligent examination of oneself, but also of their number." He added that if the penitent could not remember the exact number of times he had committed each fault, he should state "the most probable number that comes to memory."[76] This imposed on sinners the obligation to remember all of their sins with specificity. Alain Corbin, in his study of confessors' manuals, called this relationship between confession and numbers "the arithmetic of faults": God had an account of the sins of each human being, and this account was numerically exact.[77] It is not surprising, then, that in her analysis of Spanish American confession manuals Martine Azoulai discovered a true "obsession for counting" sins related to the sixth commandment.[78] Yet we must bear in mind that numbers were not important only for Catholics. In fact, they were widely present in the modern period's interpretations of Christian salvation, as we can conclude from Lucia Dacome's study on the arithmetic of salvation in eighteenth-century England.[79]

There is no doubt that Eyzaguirre was trying to establish a definitive (or at least probable) number of his sins before confessing. This was the case in the fragment cited above where José Ignacio specified the number of times he had seen his own penis, adding them to get to a final count of "ten or twelve views." Sometimes Eyzaguirre seemed unable to remember the exact number of times he committed a sin. When facing this problem, he proved again that he was well aware of the theological exigencies of the practice of confession, for he wrote down the length of time instead of the number of times he committed the sin—as, for example, when he wrote that he had had bad thoughts about a "single" woman "for a month and a half." This was the solution recommended by theologians like Paolo Segneri.[80]

Eyzaguirre was thus constructing a list of his sins, trying to stabilize his memory and to duplicate honestly at least, if not exactly, God's own great archiving of the sins of humanity. Writing was the tool that allowed him to address the arithmetic nature of Catholic confessions, just as khipus—knotted strings used by the Incas to store administrative information—were used by the indigenous peoples of colonial Peru to present faithful accounts of their sins to the priests.[81] Like colonial khipus, which were seen by Spanish authorities as having a dangerous capacity because of the social dynamics that surrounded them in Andean communities, writing could be useful and at the same time potentially dangerous; indeed, writing was regarded by some early modern authors as a tool for penitents willing to make general confessions, as long as they kept their narrations concise in style.[82] Otherwise, writing down the sins in explicit detail might put the penitent at risk of reigniting old desires and provoking new sins. This had important consequences for the way José Ignacio dealt with his potentially unnatural sins. Like colonial khipus, Eyzaguirre's writing was aimed at recounting his sins rather than at exploring their nature. Indeed, José Ignacio seems to have been enumerating his faults, such as when he wrote about his sexual interactions with male partners during his childhood and adolescence: "I saw Fraga's member four or six [times], Xavier's once or twice, Alexo's once or twice, Olivo's once. . . . I grabbed Fraga's [member] three or six [times], Benites's once, Xavier's once or twice, Alexo's once or twice, Fantóbal's once. How long did it last? Mine was grabbed by Fraga two or three [times], by Xavier I don't know [how many times], by Benites once." In this fragment, as in almost the whole document, Eyzaguirre is remembering his bad actions, not taking any time to analyze his feelings or experiences. The unnatural desires for the same sex that may have accompanied these actions were not necessarily analyzed as such; instead, they were integrated into a list of bad actions in which the number of faults seem to be more important than their nature. In this sense, the author is creating a catalogue of his actions—one that enumerates same-sex desires without necessarily naming them through the official language of theological discourse.

Eyzaguirre's manuscript is thus the result of a cognitive process that consisted of remembering, counting, and cataloguing each sin according to the exigencies of ecclesiastical discourse. This included, as I mentioned above, a wide range of actions and desires, not only those considered "sexual" in nature. Even if most of the sins asserted by Eyzaguirre were by far transgressions of the sixth commandment, they do not explain by themselves the existence of his confession. This confirms Nora Jaffary's assertion in this volume that the centrality we, as historians, ascribe to the realm of sexuality may prove to be anachronistic, imposing an inadequate *grille de lecture* on past documents. Moreover, by focusing our attention on what *we* consider as "sexual," we may be ignoring desires and practices that may not be easily catalogued in a history of sexuality. As Eyzaguirre's document is a list built upon a very specific set of assumptions—remembering, counting, and cataloguing—it allows us to see what is usually included in a history of sexuality—sexual intercourse with male or female partners, for example—as well as what could be *left aside* if we were to focus solely on those kinds of acts. Indeed, his confession includes practices and desires that the traditional history of sexuality might have trouble incorporating into its narrative. For example, Eyzaguirre accuses himself of having touched and looked at two different women's feet, a kind of sin that, for us, hardly seems to fit the more general history of sexuality. The same could be said about his will to perform oral sex on himself, or about his desire to have a "beautiful member." José Ignacio's heterogeneous set of actions and desires thus reinforces the need to rethink the way we study sexuality, in order to recognize the historicity of desire and the different historical modes of experiencing the body.[83]

The unnatural can prove to be a useful analytical tool in this task, as it incorporates a larger set of practices and desires into the historian's scope of analysis. It encompasses many of the unexpected, visceral, and sexual practices of the individuals of the early modern era, as well as their minor transgressions and their strange and polymorphic desires.[84] Being a "negative" category—defined more by what it is transgressed than by anything else—it also highlights the intimate links within the transgression and the discourses and institutions that defined what was normal and what was not. As we have seen in Eyzaguirre's manuscript, the relationship between the norm and the transgression, the high and the low, the natural and the unnatural, is fundamental to understanding not only the meaning of historical sexual desires and practices, but also the reasons behind the very existence of the documents and archives we are using to analyze them. As I have demonstrated here, even if the unnatural does not cover all of José Ignacio's sexual sins (many of them, like looking at a woman's feet, do not fulfill the requirements as such), and even if the term "against nature" *(contra natura)* does not appear in his text, the unnatural is nevertheless a useful concept to interrogate not only the content of this particular document, but also its structure and the general meanings behind Eyzaguirre's experiments with the nature of the body.

My purpose here has been to show how the sex-related sins of Eyzaguirre's manuscript are intimately bound to confession-writing practices, to ecclesiastical discourse, and to acts and desires that the Church would have called natural or unnatural, without such a distinction having been made by the subject himself. The high and the low, the natural and the unnatural, are dimensions that must be studied together in any reading of the manuscript. Eyzaguirre wrote this archive of his bodily sins because he wanted to save his soul, and for this reason he was forced to remember the practices and occasions that allowed him to learn and to build his own knowledge of the body and its desires. Eyzaguirre's manuscript, between these two intertwined sets of knowledge of the body, shows us, albeit in a fragmentary way, how bodily experiences could be inscribed in a modern Catholic individual's subjectivity, and perhaps how the natural and the unnatural were never quite as far apart from one another as we might think.

NOTES

A first version of this text was presented at the international workshop "Archives of the Body: From Medieval to Early Modern," held at Cambridge University on September 8–9, 2011. An earlier draft of this paper was published under the title "An Archive of Sins: Experimenting with the Body and Building a Knowledge of the 'Low' in José Ignacio Eyzaguirre's *General Confession* (1799–1804)," in *Epistemocritique* (2013).

1. The document can be found in the Archivo Nacional Histórico (Chile), Fondo Jaime Eyzaguirre [hereafter cited as ANJE], vol. 4, fols. 360–413v. All quotes from this manuscript have been taken from the modernized version I published in Spanish: Martín Bowen Silva, *Experimentar el cuerpo y escribir los pecados: La confesión general de José Ignacio Eyzaguirre (1799–1804)* (Lima: IFEA/IEP, 2014).

2. Zeb Tortorici, "Visceral Archives of the Body: Consuming the Dead, Digesting the Divine," *GLQ* 20, no. 4 (2014): 432.

3. Zeb Tortorici, "Against Nature: Sodomy and Homosexuality in Colonial Latin America," *History Compass* 10, no. 2 (2012): 169.

4. That colonial Spanish America was a patriarchal society has been stated many times. An interesting account of the power relations between genders can be found in Steve Stern, *The Secret History of Gender: Women, Men, and Power in Late Colonial Mexico* (Chapel Hill: University of North Carolina Press, 1995). For the Chilean case, see Tomás Cornejo, *Manuela Orellana, la criminal. Género, cultura y sociedad en el Chile del siglo XVIII* (Santiago: Tajamar Editores/Dibam, 2006); Sarah C. Chambers, "Los derechos y los deberes paternales: Pleitos por alimentos y custodia de niños en Santiago (1788–1855)," in *Justicia, poder y sociedad en Chile. Recorridos históricos,* ed. Tomás Cornejo and Carolina González

(Santiago: Ediciones Universidad Diego Portales, 2007); and Sol Serrano, Macarena Ponce de León, and Francisca Rengifo, *Historia de la educación en Chile (1810–2010)*, vol. 1 (Santiago: Taurus, 2012), esp. 193.

5. The Audiencias were the highest courts in the Spanish Americas.

6. Francisco Taforó, "Don José Alejo Eyzaguirre," in *Galería Nacional, o colección de biografías y retratos de hombres célebres de Chile*, ed. Nicolás Desmadryl, vol. 2 (Santiago: Imprenta Chilena, 1854); Vicente Chaparro, "Elojio fúnebre del señor Dr. Don José Alejo Eizaguirre," in P. G. de la Fuente, *Oratoria sagrada, o colección escogida de sermones de oradores sagrados americanos*, vol. 1 (Santiago: Imprenta del Independiente, 1866); Anonymous, *Homenaje a la memoria de don Domingo Eyzaguirre (9 de febrero de 1884)* (Santiago: Imprenta Nacional, [1884?]); Jaime Eyzaguirre, "El maestre de campo don Domingo de Eyzaguirre," *Revista chilena de historia y geografía* 69 (1930); Jaime Eyzaguirre, "El doctor don Miguel de Eyzaguirre, universitario y magistrado, 1770–1821," part 1, *Boletín de la Academia chilena de la historia* 52 (1955); Jaime Eyzaguirre (ed.), *Archivo epistolar de la familia Eyzaguirre, 1747–1854* (Buenos Aires: n.p., 1960); Jaime Eyzaguirre, *El alcalde del año diez* (Santiago: Editorial Andrés Bello, 1968).

7. José Ignacio Víctor Eyzaguirre, *Historia eclesiástica, política y literaria de Chile*, vol. 2 (Valparaíso: Imprenta Europea, 1850), 249–50.

8. The document has a modern title in the institutional catalogue, "Diario íntimo de Miguel de Eyzaguirre." After a few years of researching this document, I have come to discover that its real author was José Ignacio Eyzaguirre and not Miguel. Also, it was not a journal or personal diary, but a general confession. These claims are more fully developed in Bowen Silva, *Experimentar el cuerpo y escribir los pecados*. On the donation of Jaime Eyzaguirre's personal archive, see *Guía de fondos del Archivo nacional histórico. Instituciones coloniales y republicanas* (Santiago: Archivo Nacional de Chile/Centro de Investigaciones Diego Barros Arana/DIBAM, 2010), 80.

9. See Anonymous, *Relación de los méritos y servicios de don Josef Ignacio de Eyzaguirre, abogado de la Real Audiencia de Santiago, y ensayador de la Real Casa de Moneda de este reyno* ([Madrid?]: n.p., [1804?]). This relación was certainly published in Madrid by the efforts of José Ignacio's older brother, Miguel, who was at the time visiting the court. It was made in order to obtain a job for him in Santiago de Chile's mint. It closely follows the instructions given by Miguel to another brother, Agustín, in a letter from June 8, 1803, reproduced in Eyzaguirre, *Archivo epistolar*, 54.

10. For the letter, see Eyzaguirre, *Archivo epistolar*, 55.

11. On the origins of this literature, see Jean Delumeau, *Le péché et la peur. La culpabilisation en Occident (XIIIe–XVIIIe siècles)* (Paris: Fayard, 1983), 222–29. For eighteenth-century Spanish confession manuals, see Antonio Morgado, "Los manuales de confesores en la España del siglo XVIII," *Cuadernos dieciochistas* 5 (2004). A general catalogue of the Spanish confession manuals can be found in Antonio González Polvillo, *Análisis y repertorio de los tratados y manuales para la confesión en el mundo hispánico (ss. XVI–XVIII)* (Huelva, Spain: Universidad de Huelva, 2010).

12. Pablo Señeri, *El confessor instruido. Y el penitente instruido* (Madrid: Gabriel Ramírez, 1743), 229–37. According to Alejandra Araya, Paolo Segneri's works were very popular in Chile and Spanish America; see Alejandra Araya, "El discurso sofocado: El epistolario confesional de una monja del siglo XVIII," *Mapocho* 53 (2003): 169. We know that Miguel Eyzaguirre, José Ignacio's older brother, had a copy of this book; see "Nota de dos caxones de Libros," n.d., ANJE, vol. 4, fol. 416. In this article, I will be using Segneri's work as a key to understanding Eyzaguirre's manuscript, as I have found important coincidences between the theologian's advice and Eyzaguirre's confession. Anyway, we must consider that, judged by the number of reprints and different translations, Segneri's manual was far less popular than other works such as Martín de Azpilcueta's *Manual de Confessores*. For a comparative table, see González Polvillo, *Análisis y repertorio*.

13. I am referring here to works like those of Sor Juana Inés de la Cruz (1651–95) or Sor Úrsula Suárez (1666–1749).

14. Alain Corbin, *L'harmonie des plaisirs. Les manières de jouir du siècle des Lumières à l'avènement de la sexologie* (Paris: Flammarion, 2010), 364, 385, and 411.

15. The obligation for Catholics to confess their sins annually was first established by the Fourth Lateran Council in 1215, and by the seventeenth century it was a firmly established institution in the Catholic Church. For the importance of confession in early modern Spain, see Patrick J. O'Banion, *The Sacrament of Penance and Religious Life in Golden Age Spain* (University Park, Pa.: Penn State University Press, 2012).

16. Señeri, *El confessor instruido*, 192.

17. Delumeau, *Le péché et la peur*, 220–21.

18. Señeri, *El confessor instruido*, 136.

19. *Diccionario de la lengua castellana, en que se explica el verdadero sentido de las voces, su naturaleza y calidad . . .*, vol. 2 (Madrid: Imprenta de Francisco del Hierro, 1729), 497.

20. Real Academia de la Lengua Española, *Diccionario de la lengua castellana compuesto por la Real academia española* (Madrid: Joaquín Ibarra, 1780), 256.

21. Señeri, *El confessor instruido*, 226. On general confessions, see 226–41.

22. Alain Corbin, "Le secret de l'individu," in *Histoire de la vie privée*, ed. Philippe Ariès and Georges Duby, vol. 4 (Paris: Le Seuil, 1999), 421; Corbin, *L'harmonie des plaisirs*, 406–16.

23. "En una confesión preguntome el confesor si havia nombrado al diablo, dixele no, porque no me acordé, mas luego me acordé haverlo nombrado, y no lo dixe estando todavia en la confesión por temor de que pensase el confesor que le havia engañado. . . . En otra confesión callé un pensamiento que no havia consentido . . ., pero dudaba con mucho temor si lo debía confesar, no lo confesé por vergüenza del confesor, que era el mismo de quien havia pensado que sus genuflexiones en la misa se parecían al acto torpe. . . . Tendría 10 o 12 años, acúsome de todo." Here and throughout, the punctuation in the English translation has been emended for clarity.

24. Corbin, *L'harmonie des plaisirs*. According to Jean Delumeau (*Le péché et la peur*, 238–46), during the early modern period lust, while not the most important sin, was already subject to theologians' warnings.

25. Señeri, *El confessor instruido*, 26.

26. Real Academia de la Lengua Española, *Diccionario de la lengua castellana*, 631.

27. Francisco Tomás y Valiente, "El crimen y pecado contra natura," in Francisco Tomás y Valiente et al., *Sexo barroco y otras transgresiones premodernas* (Madrid: Alianza, 1990); Thomas W. Laqueur, *Solitary Sex: A Cultural History of Masturbation* (New York: Zone Books, 2003); Fernanda Molina, "Los sodomitas virreinales: Entre sujetos jurídicos y especie," *Anuario de estudios americanos* 67, no. 1 (2010): 25; Tortorici, "Against Nature"; María Ruiz Ortiz, "Pecados femeninos y vida privada: Discursos sobre la conciencia y la vida cotidiana en la España moderna (ss. XVI–XVIII)," *Cuadernos de historia moderna* 39 (2014): 62.

28. On the conservative nature of the Eyzaguirre family, see Eyzaguirre, "El doctor don Miguel de Eyzaguirre," 79.

29. On these different members of the Spanish American elite households and their conflicts, see Alejandra Araya, "Sirvientes contra amos: Las heridas en lo íntimo propio," in *Historia de la vida privada en Chile*, ed. Rafael Sagredo and Cristián Gazmuri, vol. 1 (Santiago: Taurus, 2005).

30. Delumeau, *Le péché et la peur*, 296–303; Francisco Vásquez and Andrés Moreno, *Sexo y razón. Una genealogía de la moral sexual en España (siglos XVI–XX)* (Madrid: Akal, 1997), 91–94.

31. Señeri, *El confessor instruido*, 226.

32. Alejandro Fuenzalida, *Historia del desarrollo intellectual en Chile (1541–1810)* (Santiago: Imprenta Universitaria, 1903), 208; Eyzaguirre, "El doctor don Miguel de Eyzaguirre"; Luis Lira Montt, *Los colegios reales de Santiago de Chile: Reseña histórica e índice de colegiales* (Santiago: n.p., 1977), 18–21. For a more general overview on Chile's colonial education, see José Toribio Medina, *La instruc-*

ción pública en Chile desde sus orígenes hasta la fundación de la Universidad de San Felipe (Santiago: Imprenta Elzeviriana, 1905); and Serrano et al., *Historia de la educación en Chile*, 1:25–60.

33. For a list of this seminary's students, which includes José Ignacio Eyzaguirre, see Lira Montt, *Los colegios reales de Santiago*, 41–56. For the other students that seem to be mentioned in Eyzaguirre's confessions, see Bowen Silva, *Experimentar el cuerpo y escribir los pecados.*

34. Alessandro Stella, *Le prêtre et le sexe. Les révélations des procès de l'Inquisition* (Brussels: André Versaille, 2009), 109–20.

35. The "Vilvado" Eyzaguirre mentions here could be either Bernardino Bilbao or Rafael Bilbao, both students at the seminary during that time. See *Libro de Constitución y entrada de colegiales de este seminario de la Iglesia Catedral de Santiago de Chile bajo la advocación del Santo Ángel de la Guarda,* Archivo Nacional Histórico (Chile), Fondo Varios, vol. 235, fols. 42 and 71v.

36. The work of Georges Vigarello (e.g., *Histoire du viol, XVIe–XXe siècle* [Paris: Le Seuil, 1998]) shows that violent stories of this kind, told in an all-male context, were not uncommon, nor were they necessarily criticized.

37. See, for example, Rafael Carrasco, *Inquisición y represión sexual en Valencia. Historia de los sodomitas (1565–1785)* (Valencia: Laertes, 1985). Although much more controversial, see also Cristian Berco, *Sexual Hierarchies, Public Status: Men, Sodomy, and Society in Spain's Golden Age* (Toronto: University of Toronto Press, 2007).

38. Tortorici, "Against Nature," 166.

39. *Libro de Constitución*, fol. 41v.

40. See the examples given by Stella, *Le prêtre et le sexe*, 109–20.

41. See Carrasco, *Inquisición y represión sexual en Valencia.*

42. Anne-Marie Sohn, *Sois un homme! La construction de la masculinité au XIXᵉ siècle* (Paris: Le Seuil, 2009), 159.

43. Stella, *Le prêtre et le sexe*, 113.

44. For example, is it the same-sex nature of these institutions or the power relations that they enabled that engendered those forms of sexuality? More important, were these practices seen as "homoerotic," and therefore linked with same-sex institutions, or were they part of a different understanding of sexuality?

45. See, for example, Sarah Newman, "'The Freshman Malady': Rethinking the Ontology of the 'Crush,'" *Rethinking History* 16, no. 2 (2012): 279–301.

46. Sara F. Matthews-Grieco, "Corps et sexualité dans l'Europe d'Ancien Régime," in *Histoire du Corps*, ed. Alain Corbin, Jean-Jacques Courtine, and Georges Vigarello, vol. 1 (Paris: Editions du Seuil, 2005), 167–234; Jean-Claude Caron, "Young People in School: Middle and High School Students in France and Europe," in *A History of Young People*, ed. Giovanni Levi and Jean-Claude Schmitt, vol. 2, trans. Carol Volk (Cambridge, Mass.: Belknap Press of Harvard University Press, 1997), 159–63; Sohn, *Sois un homme!*

47. See Bowen Silva, *Experimentar el cuerpo*, 71.

48. See Carrasco, *Inquisición y represión sexual en Valencia.*

49. Sohn, *Sois un homme!*, 147–52.

50. For Porto Maurizio's standard confession, see Corbin, *L'harmonie des plaisirs*, 410–11. A similar confession can be found in Señeri, *El confessor instruido*, 229–41.

51. See, for example, Laura Gowing, "Knowledge and Experience, c. 1500–1750," in *Routledge History of Sex and the Body, 1500 to the Present*, ed. Sarah Toulalan and Kate Fisher (Florence, Ky.: Routledge, 2013), 241.

52. The book ran through several editions. See Manuel González Téllez, *Commentaria perpetua in singulos textus quinque librorum Decretalium Gregorii IX* (Lyon: Annison & Posuel, 1715).

53. See Francisco Antonio Pinto, "Apuntes autobiográficos del general don Francisco Antonio Pinto," *Boletín de la Academia Chilena de la Historia* 8, no. 17 (1941); and José Miguel Varas, *Lecciones elementales de moral* (Santiago: Imprenta de la Independencia, 1828).

54. And to talk about them. See Michel Foucault, *Histoire de la sexualité*, vol. 1 (Paris: Gallimard, 1976).

55. Fernanda Alfieri, "Urge without Desire? Confession Manuals, Moral Casuistry, and the Features of *Concupiscentia* between the Fifteenth and Eighteenth Centuries," in *Genders and Sexualities in History: Bodies, Sex, and Desire from the Renaissance to the Present*, ed. Kate Fisher and Sarah Toulalan (London: Palgrave Macmillan, 2011), 153.

56. Cited in Eyzaguirre, "El doctor don Miguel de Eyzaguirre," 85.

57. See Carlo Ginzburg, "High and Low: The Theme of Forbidden Knowledge in the Sixteenth and Seventeenth Centuries," *Past & Present* 73 (1976): 28–41.

58. On curiosity and religion in the Iberian Atlantic World, see Stuart Schwartz, *All Can Be Saved: Religious Tolerance and Salvation in the Iberian Atlantic World* (New Haven, Conn.: Yale University Press, 2008), 82–84. On the dangers of curiosity in early-nineteenth-century Chile, see Martín Bowen Silva, "Pouvoir, communication et système politique: L'espace public au Chili pendant l'âge des révolutions," Ph.D. diss., Ecole des Hautes Etudes en Sciences Sociales, Paris, 2014, 581.

59. See, for example, Carrasco, *Inquisición y represión sexual en Valencia*; and, for a different context, Lisa Z. Sigel, "Name Your Pleasure: The Transformation of Sexual Language in Nineteenth-Century British Pornography," *Journal of the History of Sexuality* 9, no. 4 (2000): 395–419.

60. Laqueur, *Solitary Sex*.

61. For example, in his documents Eyzaguirre proves to have been aware of the theological meaning of concepts such as scandal and contrition. See Bowen Silva, *Experimentar el cuerpo*, 52–64.

62. According to the Real Academia de la Lengua Española's 22nd edition of the Spanish dictionary, available online at www.rae.es, *chucha* means vagina in Peru and Colombia. I have seen it used in Chile with the same meaning.

63. See, for example, the case of the abbot of Nuestra Señora de la Asunción Monastery in New Spain, Diego Núñez, who in 1737 was deeply intrigued by his feces. This case is described in Ruth Behar's thought-provoking article "Sexual Witchcraft, Colonialism, and Women's Powers: Views from the Mexican Inquisition," in *Sexuality and Marriage in Colonial Latin America*, ed. Asunción Lavrin (Lincoln: University of Nebraska Press, 1989), 178–206.

64. Thomas W. Laqueur, *Making Sex: Body and Gender from the Greeks to Freud* (Cambridge, Mass.: Harvard University Press, 1992).

65. M. M. Bakhtin, *Rabelais and His World*, trans. Hélène Iswolsky (Cambridge: MIT Press, 1968). The images of defecating people inside medieval churches seem to be one of these junctions of the high and the low. See Welleda Muller, "The Iconography of Gothic Choir Stalls: An Enhancement of the Body in All Its States in a Sacred Space," presentation at the conference "Archives of the Body: From Medieval to Early Modern," Cambridge University, September 7–9, 2011.

66. "Pensamiento comparando las rajaduras de un Sagrario *estando oiendo misa en la Cathedral* a las partes de N.S." N.S. may be an abbreviation for "Nuestra Señora" (Our Lady) or "Nuestro Señor" (Our Lord).

67. "Genuflexiones en la misa . . . se parecían al acto torpe."

68. Cf. Dolores Peña y Lillo, *Epistolario de Sor Dolores Peña y Lillo (Chile, 1763–1769)*, ed. Raissa Kordic (Madrid: Universidad de Navarra/Iberoamericana, 2008).

69. Zeb Tortorici, "Masturbation, Salvation, and Desire: Connecting Sexuality and Religiosity in Colonial Mexico," *Journal of the History of Sexuality* 16, no. 3 (2007): 367.

70. Michel de Certeau, *L'invention du quotidien*, vol. 1, new ed. (Paris: Gallimard, 1990), 205–9.

71. Memoirs of Lopetegui's grandson, Antonio Barrena Lopetegui, reproduced in Jorge Molina, *Vida de un soldado. Desde la toma de Valdivia (1820) a la victoria de Yungay (1839)* (Santiago: RIL, 2009), 16.

72. Philippe Artières, *La vie écrite. Thérèse de Lisieux* (Paris: Les Belles Lettres, 2011), 44.

73. Chaparro, "Elojio fúnebre del señor Dr. Don José Alejo Eizaguirre," 454; "Diario autografo de don Mariano Egaña," National Library of Chile, Sala Medina, ms. BA 50, vol. 115, fols. 21–68. Manuel Peña Díaz has seen in this kind of written pieces—also present in early modern Spain—an "interioriza-tion" of guilt directly linked with the Catholic confession. See Manuel Peña Díaz, "Normas y transgre-siones: La cultura escrita en el Siglo de Oro," in *Grafías del imaginario. Representaciones culturales en España y América (siglos XVI–XVIII)*, ed. Carlos Alberto González Sánchez and Enriqueta Vila Vilar (Mexico City: Fondo de Cultura Económica, 2003), 129.

74. Antonio Castillo-Gómez, "Entre public et privé: Stratégies de l'écrit dans l'Espagne du Siècle d'Or," *Annales. Histoire, sciences sociales* 56, nos. 4–5 (2001): 803–29. The relationship between writing and memory was of fundamental importance during the modern era. On the tension between written memory and its erasure during this period, see Roger Chartier, *Inscription and Erasure: Literature and Written Culture from the Eleventh to the Eighteenth Century*, trans. Arthur Goldhammer (Philadelphia: University of Pennsylvania Press, 2007).

75. On penitential regimes and the equivalences between sins and penances (often numerical), see Delumeau, *Le péché et la peur*, 218–21.

76. Señeri, *El confessor instruido*, 192.

77. Corbin, *L'harmonie des plaisirs*, 412–13.

78. Martine Azoulai, "Manuales de confesión americanos: Prácticas y costumbres amorosas de los indígenas, siglos XVII y XVIII," *Cuadernos para la historia de la evangelización en América Latina* 2 (1987): 14–15.

79. Lucia Dacome, "Resurrecting by Numbers in Eighteenth-Century England," *Past & Present* 193 (2006): 73–110.

80. Señeri, *El confessor instruido*, 12.

81. *Khipus* were knotted strings used by the Incas to store administrative information. For their use as means of confession, see John Charles, "Unreliable Confessions: *Khipus* in the Colonial Parish," *The Americas* 64, no. 1 (2007): 11–33; Regina Harrison, "Pérez Bocanegra's *Ritual formulario*: *Khipu* Knots and Confession," in *Narrative Threads: Accounting and Recounting in Andean Khipu*, ed. Jeffrey Quilter and Gary Urton (Austin: University of Texas Press, 2002); Juan Carlos Estenssoro, *Del paganismo a la santidad. La incorporación de los indios del Perú al catolicismo, 1532–1750*, trans. Gabriela Ramos (Lima: IFEA/Pontificia Universidad Católica del Perú, 2003).

82. Corbin, *L'harmonie des plaisirs*, 411–12. The relationship between written culture and both the imposition and transgression of social norms is studied in Peña Díaz, "Normas y transgresiones." On the dangers that, according to some priests, the use of *khipus* represented for confession, see Charles, "Unreliable Confessions." For the general critiques on *khipu* reliability during colonial times, see John Charles, "Tying the Truth in Knots: Truthworthiness and Accountability in the Inka Khipu," in *Decep-tion: From Ancient Empires to Internet Dating*, ed. Brooke Harrington (Stanford: Stanford University Press, 2009).

83. For similar calls to the "historicization" of desire, see Newman, "'The Freshman Malady'"; and Tortorici, "Masturbation, Salvation, and Desire." On the philosophy behind the way Eyzaguirre under-stood his desires and the need to confess them, see Alfieri, "Urge without Desire?"

84. Tortorici, "Visceral Archives of the Body."

6

Prosecuting Female-Female Sex in Bourbon Quito

Chad Thomas Black

In the closing decades of the eighteenth century, royal authorities in the Audiencia of Quito dramatically increased their interest in the sex lives of their subjects.[1] In addition to numerous trials for prostitution, adultery, cohabitation, and incest, the Audiencia's prosecutions also included a number of so-called sodomitical relationships.[2] This chapter focuses on two of those cases, involving two couples of young women—highlighting how the "unnatural" act of female sodomy, though underreported and frequently dismissed by colonial authorities, was not entirely ignored by colonial society. Furthermore, as we shall see, the very notion of female sodomy pushed the boundaries of the legibility of so-called "natural" and "unnatural" acts, especially as they were grafted onto the bodies and behaviors of women.

One Saturday night in December 1782, the *alcalde de barrio*, or neighborhood magistrate, of the parish of San Roque surprised Andrea Ayala and Rosa Hidalgo, invading the home of Juan de Salazar on a tip and finding the women sleeping together in the same bed.[3] Ayala and Hidalgo had allegedly maintained a sexual relationship for more than five years, prompting Hidalgo to abandon her husband and married life. Five years later, in late July 1787, the neighborhood magistrate of the parish of San Marcos arrested another pair of young women, Manuela Palis and Josefa Lara, when he found them sharing a bed.[4] The alcalde reported the next day to don Fernando Quadrado, an *oidor* or judge of the Audiencia, that he discovered the two asleep together after entering their room in response to neighborhood objections to their continued relationship and the presumed abominable crime of sodomy.

Prosecutions of female sodomy are exceedingly rare in the colonial Spanish American historical record.[5] Male sodomy is much less rare. Deviant female sexu-

120

ality was frequently an object of judicial scrutiny by both ecclesiastical and civil authorities. Women were routinely prosecuted in Quito during the Bourbon period for adultery and illicit cohabitation, along with their male lovers. Acts that were perceived by authorities as unnatural, such as masturbation *(polución)*, cross-dressing, female-female sex, sex with demons, anal sex with a male partner, and the like, are much harder to locate in the archives. Prosecutions of female-female sex are not only comparatively rare, but they also challenge the prevailing norms of criminal sodomy during the colonial period and their modern interpretations by historians. Thus, the fortuitous concurrence of two female sodomy cases in Quito in the 1780s offers an interesting point of comparison regarding how judicial authorities and plebeians perceived sodomy during the Bourbon period, as well as the normative expectations for courtship, economic citizenship, and sociality among the young.

The defendants in the two cases were denounced, investigated, and tried on the weight of neighborhood and familial suspicions and gossip. Evidence for the allegations was completely circumstantial and broke into two categories: unnatural gender inversions and general moral turpitude. Technically, prosecutions of sodomy in the early modern Spanish empire required in-the-act proof of penetration. Cases such as those under consideration here presented late colonial authorities with "penetrational ambiguity."[6] In response, magistrates looked to prove unnatural acts by documenting the inversion of gendered behaviors and evidence of the general moral depravity of defendants as confirmation of sexual activities. Sodomy, like the attendant sins of masturbation and bestiality, was a crime and sin "against nature" *(contra natura)*. As such, prosecutions of female sodomy serve to validate what were perceived as "natural" forms of sex and courtship. However, these prosecutions also testify to underlying toleration of aberrant female sexuality and sociality.[7]

CONTEXTUAL MATTERS

The cases of Andrea Ayala and Rosa Hidalgo and of Manuela Palis and Josefa Lara offer important additions to the growing scholarship on sodomy and sexualities in colonial Latin America. As Zeb Tortorici has noted, the question of penetration and active/passive roles in sodomitical relationships has formed an anchor for key debates in the historical literature on Spain and its empire.[8] In part, this has been because the literature overwhelmingly centers on male-male sodomy, a reality driven by availability of archival sources that also reinforces the invisibility of female homoeroticism in colonial Latin American society.[9] Additionally, much of the extant literature operates under a gendered model of dominance/passivity that connects penetrative "tops" and penetrated "bottoms" not only to masculinity and femininity respectively, but also to larger models of honor and shame born out of anthropological explorations of modern Mediterranean honor codes. As the pieces in this collection demonstrate, natural/unnatural may be a more appropriate analytical binary.[10]

Tortorici has critiqued the binary identification of actives and passives by noting "penetrational ambiguity" within a group of prosecuted indigenous men in New Spain, individuals who switched roles with various partners, thereby dissembling fixed positions as masculine tops and feminized bottoms.[11] Furthermore, the association of the active/passive model to an ideologically defined patriarchal binary of honor/shame presents its own problems. In 2001, Nesvig expressed concern over the uncritical acceptance and applicability to same-sex desire of the patriarchal assumptions inherent in the Mediterranean honor code model, which gives preeminence to penetration, or guarding others (women) from penetration, as the gendering prerogative of masculinity.[12] (This skepticism is certainly not accepted by all. Berco, for one, has argued forcefully in the case of early modern Valencia that patriarchalism and sodomy are inextricably intertwined.)[13]

The honor code regime is further challenged in recent contributions to early modern Spanish historiography that do not deal with sodomy.[14] Poska has argued that the application of the Mediterranean honor code by early modern Spanish historians, with its emphasis on female fertility as the collective basis of both male and female honor, was overly influenced by their acceptance of normative elite and Catholic Reformation discourses, which she claims "had little resonance among the majority of the Spanish population."[15] Taylor has argued that, contrary to the honor model, credit worthiness and fair pricing were essential elements of women's honor in seventeenth-century Castile, as evidenced by criminal records of verbal and physical assaults.[16] Modern anthropologists began to jettison the construct two decades ago, critiquing it as a product of Anglo-American imputations of the deviance of southern Europeans, built upon the ethnographers' own ethnocentrism and sexism.[17] Indeed, Cole has noted that the concepts of honor and shame portrayed as the markers of Mediterranean identity bear a striking resemblance to the ideologies propagated by the Catholic Church and the fascist states of Iberia during the period in which the foundational anthropological texts were produced.[18] Finally, adherence to a dominant/passive cum honorable/shameful model of patriarchal enforcement, generalized as a cultural structure of Spanish empire, has led to some of the more tedious characterizations of sodomy as a crime inherently violent, hierarchical, and endemic to Mediterranean societies, committed as a form of conquest and for the maintenance of age-graded patriarchal authority.[19]

The cumulative impact of the critiques of the dominant honor/shame rubric of masculinity and femininity makes problematic the use of prescriptive normative discourses in assessing lived gender and sexual desire. Prescriptive norms must be contextualized in their institutional roots and interrogated by the tensions presented by the very behaviors they sought to control. In the case of the sodomy prosecutions in late-eighteenth-century Quito, the institutional context of our evidence is that of an aggressive judiciary interested in projecting royal authority by controlling and ordering the sex lives of the city's barrios.[20] This judiciary presumed guilt and proceeded in its prosecutions accordingly. But beneath the boilerplate language and judicial activism of magistrate investigations, competing popular norms of a spectrum of tolerated sexual behaviors loom in the ancillary details and defendant confessions of the cases. The disjuncture between judicial expectations and popular toleration becomes starkly evident in their procedural flow. During the initial investigation *(sumaria)*, magistrates' presumption of guilt controlled the portrayal and condemnation of the alleged relationships. During the confession, and with witnesses provided by the accused, that control was cracked, with alternative narratives of sociability and sexuality emerging. Finally, postconviction appeals brought about reconciliation with judicial and religious norms. Cases of female or male sodomy and bestiality, grouped together as "crimes against nature," followed the same formulaic procedures as any other contemporary sex-based or non-sex-based prosecutions. As the Ayala/Hidalgo and Palis/Lara cases moved through the process of denunciation, arrest, investigation, confession, sentencing, and appeal, they conformed to regular judicial procedural standards.[21]

CASE I: MANUELA PALIS, JOSEFA LARA

As with many of the sexual prosecutions in late colonial Quito, the case against Manuela Palis and Josefa Lara began with a targeted complaint to the local neighborhood magistrate.[22] On July 29, 1787, the barrio alcalde of San Marcos, Antonio Freyre de Andrade, reported to Audiencia judge don Fernando Quadrado that the night before, in response to "repeated complaints" about Manuela and Josefa's illicit cohabitation *(concubinato)* and implication in the "abominable offense of sodomy," he had apprehended the two young women sleeping together in one bed, although his report does not claim they were caught *in flagrante delicto.*[23] It is likely Freyre surprised the women during the course of his nightly rounds, a responsibility shared by the city's various magistrates.[24] Despite the confidence with which Freyre pronounced the charges, the opening of the case evidences a certain discomfort with (and confusion about) characterizing the relationship between Manuela and Josefa. On the original cover page, the relationship and charges against the women are described as "incestuous cohabitation" *(incestuoso concubinato)*, while within the folios their relationship is usually referred to by the less confrontational phrase "illicit friendship" *(amistad ilícita).* The term *sodomy* was avoided by Freyre after its initial use.

In the sixteenth century, Archbishop of Mexico City Juan de Zumárraga condemned three types of sins against nature, involving male-male, and female-female, and male-female nonprocreative sex. He defined the sin against nature (*pecado contra natura*) as "a very abominable placing of the virile member in the dirtiest and ugliest part of the body of the person who receives the man; that part is delegated for the expulsion of feces."[26] This definition, while not discounting the participation of a woman as receiver in the act, would seem to exclude sex acts between women, as female sodomy represented the ultimate condition of penetrational ambiguity. That female-female sex was included under the broader definition of sins against nature, but not within the specific definition of the sodomitical act, demonstrates both that unnatural sex acts constituted a spectrum of behavior and that there was uncertainty in comprehending and classifying illicit sex between women. Unsurprisingly, this uncertainty carried into the eighteenth century.

Some eighteenth-century criminal prosecution manuals dispense with female-female inclusion altogether. The 1764 manual *Libro de los principales rudimentos* from Mexico City, for example, explicitly avoids the term "sodomy," opting simply for the term "nefarious" *(nefando)*. The anonymous author defined offenders by stating that "they are *putos*, meaning that there is one [on top] who acts as the man, and [on bottom] who acts as the woman."[27] The manual continues with instructions for investigation and prosecution of the offense, which the author determined must be started by accusation by the individual or individuals who caught the defendants in the act. Based on the statements of the accuser and witnesses, the defendants were then questioned separately. If one or both denied their involvement, they were to be questioned face to face or in front of the accuser and witnesses, and could also be physically examined to establish the fact of penetration. The physical examination called for the insertion of a certain surgeon's instrument or a large chicken's egg into the anus, euphemistically called the "rear eye" *(ojo de atrás)* in the presence of the judge and the notary.[28] Again, these instructions, including the physical examination, determined criminal culpability through penetration in a form unlikely to implicate female-female sex.

In bestiality cases, the *Libro* also looked to a combination of eyewitness testimony and physical evidence in order to determine culpability. Bestiality appears in the *Libro*, and in the actual litigation in Bourbon Quito as well, as a crime requiring penetration of the animal by a man. Magistrates were counseled to examine the defendant as quickly as possible for evidence that the animal was penetrated, but also to apprehend and hold responsible both the individual and the animal. The human involved was to be questioned to determine if he understood the nature of the allegations. Witnesses were to be questioned in a manner to determine the specific possibility of penetration: Were the defendant's pants off? Was his "member" moist? There was an overwhelming interest in establishing through physical and verbal evidence the veracity of penetration.[29]

The investigation of Palis and Lara reinforced the ambiguity of female-female sex acts, and the difficulty of establishing culpability without direct evidence or admission of penetration. On August 1, 1787, oidor Quadrado ordered the barrio

TABLE 1 Initial Witnesses and Their Relationship to the Accused

Name	Age	Relationship
Ysabel Robles	50	Manuela Palis's landlord
doña Rosa Robles	70+	Ysabel Robles's mother, and a resident in her house
Flora Lara	30	Josefa Lara's sister
Juana Palis	40	Manuela Palis's sister
Ygnacia Cordero	50	Josefa Lara's aunt
Martina Campoverde	25	Josefa Lara's cousin

SOURCE: ANE SC 129.6, 29-vii-1787

alcalde to gather information in the company of Audiencia lawyer Doctor don Manuel Josef de Borja and notary Ramón de Maya. The investigation began in earnest three days later as Freyre and Borja took the statement of the first of six women. Each of the witnesses against Manuela and Josefa were intimates of the accused (table 1). Over two days of testimony, Freyre and Borja assembled a dossier of allegations against the two women.

Given the tightly knit group of initial witnesses, it comes as no surprise that the nature and content of the allegations repeated during the testimony were fairly uniform. This is a function of a number of elements in the investigatory phase of a case. The investigation may have been initiated by judicial authorities (de oficio), as was commonplace in sexual criminal complaints, but it was predicated on a denunciation. In this case (as well as the one that follows), the barrio alcalde never identified the denouncer, though contextual clues suggest it was one of the opening witnesses. It is not always the case that the identity of the denouncer remains opaque. For example, a 1788 male-male sodomy case against one Custodio Legendres begins with a formal petition of complaint by Mariano Espinosa submitted to the president of the Audiencia indicting the accused for "degenerating the nature of man with infamy for Religion" by "maintaining nefarious cohabitation [concubinato nefando] with one Justo Santana, with notorious scandal."[30] In the absence of a formal petition of complaint, the barrio alcalde would merely reference neighborhood objections. Regardless, the accusations logged by verbal or written complaint formed the basis for the interrogatories used by magistrates, who parroted said allegations. Additionally, magistrates gathered recommended and relevant witnesses via the complaint and thence further via the testimony of the witnesses that the complaint recommended. Functionally, this stacked the deck against the accused, compounding the systemic presumption of guilt with hostile questions and hostile witnesses who very likely knew one another ahead of time.

The intimates arrayed against Palis and Lara included blood relatives, Palis's landlord, and the landlord's mother. All were women, ranging from twenty-five to over seventy years old, from whom barrio alcalde Freyre learned of the circumstantial evidence indicating a sexual relationship between Palis and Lara. The testimony amounted to a series of behavioral allegations: (1) they were physically and verbally abusive with each other; (2) they on occasion slept together in the same bed; (3) they went for strolls and drank *aguardiente* to the point of intoxication; (4) they financed each other the way a man would his mistress; (5) their relationship was well known in the neighborhood, as was Palis's preference for women and previous relationships; (6) Palis had solicited Lara; (7) they frequently spouted verbal obscenities; (8) they had abandoned work and the payment of ecclesiastical taxes; and (9) their passion for one another had driven them to penury.

According to the testimony, Palis and Lara had maintained their illicit relationship for more than a year. Four of the witnesses testified to the severity of their physical confrontations, often accompanied by drunkenness *(ambas ebrias)*; they were frequently heard fighting with obscene, raised voices, wracked with jealousy to the point of beating each other up.[31] Just as on the night of their arrest, several of the witnesses noted the two women frequently slept together. The fighting, drinking, and sleeping together combined with public strolling and spending money on each other, "taking care of the expenses as men do for their concubines and lovers," as evidence of courtship. This accusation was also a key element of evidence against Custodio Legendres in his sodomy case. Almost all of the eight witnesses against Legendres, witnesses who were also accused as his lovers, admitted that Legendres provided them with clothing, fine shoes, a place to stay, a bed to share, and money for food and incidentals.[32] These were inversions of the normative gendered roles of courtship and romantic love, and particularly of the form men customarily engaged in with their own illicit affairs. And as inversions, they were unnatural.

The allegations that indicated inverted gender relations were combined with those that implied a general depravity and inability to control passions and live productively. Physical and verbal abuse, out-of-control drinking, abandonment of work, and an inability to pay ecclesiastical or civil taxes were evidence of the depravity of *zelos* (jealousy), or passions run amuck. Such passions threatened the capacity of royal officials to maintain a tenuous colonial order in the wake of Quito's Rebellion of the Barrios. Parading and courtship behaviors, which could include abuse, joined together with sleeping in the same bed as evidence of gender inversion, though it is completely unclear which partner was playing the supposedly masculine, dominant role in the relationship. In fact, the lack of clear roles calls into question modern scholars' reliance on a binary that demands adherence to masculine or feminine roles in same-sex relationships. Palis, the younger of the two women, solicited the relationship with Lara in the wake of losing another lover. The testimony also suggested that Palis would take Lara out on strolls through the streets, an act associated with public courtship, and it was implied that the two always slept together in Palis's bed. The supporting evidence of an illicit relationship was not determinative from the perspective of masculinizing and feminizing roles. They were both masculinized by hitting and verbally abusing each other, going out drinking, and paying for each other's excesses. Their wanton spending combined with abandonment of their trades to bring the couple to the point of destitution. Witnesses against Palis and Lara cited their lack of economic productivity as evidence of the ruinous turpitude stemming from their sexual deviance.

Finally, the testimony indicates that several of the witnesses had attempted to intervene in the relationship previously, both face-to-face and by appealing to ecclesiastical authorities. Flora Lara claimed that on numerous occasions she had implored her sister to abandon Manuela Palis, "because of the gravity of the sin in which she found herself, as well as for the corporal ruin it was causing her." In desperation, Flora Lara asked her confessor for advice on how to deal with the situation. In response, the parish priest advised Flora that he had excommunicated Manuela Palis for failing to meet her annual ecclesiastical tax obligation, a humiliation that Lara would soon face too if she failed to confess her sins. Likely, this threat motivated the appeal to judicial intervention. The parish priest's willingness to conflate Palis's evasion of ecclesiastical duties with the threat to Lara's soul caused by her alleged sexual impurity makes economic idleness a corollary to immorality, and evidence of general moral turpitude.

The weight of this evidence was enough for the magistrate to take the women's confessions, despite its circumstantiality. Stage two of the prosecution broke the discursive control of the denunciation as the accused provided compelling explanations for their questionable behaviors. Josefa Lara's confession was taken first, on August 6 at the women's jail at the Recogimiento of Santa Marta.[33] Freyre asked a series of thirteen questions, forcing Lara to defend the allegations against her. Following criminal procedure, the confession began with a standard identity question eliciting the defendant's name, residence, marital status, occupation, age, and if the confessant was aware of the reason for their arrest. Lara was a twenty-five-year-old widowed seamstress from Quito, and was cognizant that she was being held for having an illicit relationship (comercio ilícito) with Manuela Palis. As the questioning continued, Lara repeatedly denied this relationship was in any way sexually illicit. She claimed that her friendship with Manuela Palis was based on their mutual interest in alcohol, which by extension explained the rest of their suspicious behaviors. Lara claimed the two women frequented a bar owned and run by a woman named Brigida Alban, where they would drink to the point of drunkenness in the company of many others, mostly other women. Aside from this, they never went on courtship strolls (paseos).

Freyre asserted their relationship had begun when the two women met at a shop on the Portal in the center of Quito, when Palis solicited Lara by buying and offering her some escabeche. This too Lara denied, though she admitted that after

they became friends the two would go to Alban's bar and pitch in together, each ½ *real*, to share escabeche. It is very likely that both Palis and Lara were telling the truth. Their actions, though, left them vulnerable to neighborhood and magistrate interpretations with far greater implications than the capriciousness of youth. Importantly, in Quito in the 1780s, mundane behaviors came to define secret unnatural acts. The magistrate alleged that Lara had gone broke, pawning property to make money to keep Palis. Again, Lara repudiated the assertion, claiming that she was broke because of her attachment to liquor, not Palis. Lara further brushed off the allegations of public fighting, contending that the two of them were never involved in jealous fits, but that she had been hurt on one occasion by Manuel Alban, a suitor who hit her in the face, leaving a mark. As to the assertions that her sister Flora Lara had implored the couple to separate, Lara again claimed the issue at hand was alcohol and drunkenness, not illicit sex, and that Flora blamed Manuela Palis for her sister's drinking.

Josefa Lara did admit that she had slept together with Manuela Palis on various occasions, but only as good friends *(camaradas)* and only because neither of them had more than one bed in their respective houses.[34] Furthermore, she claimed the practice of girlfriends sleeping together was customary and innocent. Lara stated that on the night they were caught in bed, she had stayed because she was in the neighborhood checking out a rowdy party *(fandango)*. She admitted that both she and Palis were avid partygoers and regulars at the city's fandangos, but in this case she did not know the hosts and decided not to attend, retreating to Palis's room instead. Because of the late hour, she decided to stay. It was that innocent.

Manuela Palis's confession later that same day supported Lara's contentions. Palis, a nineteen-year-old single seamstress, was appointed a guardian ad litem by the court in accordance with judicial procedures for all minors. In the presence of her guardian, Palis acknowledged she was being held for suspicion of sodomy or "nefarious intercourse" *(comercio nefando)*, but like Lara, she repudiated the charges arrayed against her. Palis admitted a fondness for alcohol and for drinking at Brigida Alban's in the company of other men and women. She denied gifting Lara escabeche as a means of soliciting a relationship. She claimed she ate escabeche in the Portal only with Flora Lara and another young woman, Francisca Alban, though on some occasions Josefa Lara joined them, each pitching in for the expense. When confronted with the financial allegations, including that she had abandoned her profession for an idle life, Palis responded that she had actually abandoned her parents' house because of an abusive sister and that she found herself without enough money to pay for her room and board. As a consequence, she admitted to pawning a few things to raise cash, and had even redeemed and repawned the goods on a number of occasions. Further, Palis claimed, "this is nothing strange, because poor women often manage their affairs in this way." Their behavior was thus explained by customary norms of the popular classes. Finally,

Palis recounted the same story as Lara concerning their fights, sleeping together, the neighborhood party, and the circumstances surrounding their discovery by the magistrate.

Five days later, on August 11, the oidores sentenced Josefa Lara to two years' service in the Royal Tobacco Factory of Quito and Manuela Palis to two years' reclusion in the city's Poor House, "for the correction of [their] excesses." Thus, the magistrate reinscribed a sodomy allegation into a condemnation of all of their inappropriate behaviors. Sexual impropriety was subsumed into a larger set of unnatural acts and attitudes, including fighting, drinking, cavorting, and dereliction of economic responsibilities. In the execution of the order, the venues of incarceration somehow changed, as Palis ended up in the Tobacco Factory and Lara in the Casa de Misericordia. Six months into her sentence, Palis wrote from the factory to President Villalengua to appeal for mercy and commutation. Her tenor had completely changed from raucous defiant to humble supplicant. Palis explained that she had suffered during her confinement and that in her poverty and suffering she looked to Villalengua's "Divine Magesty" and "Angelic and charitable heart" *(pecho Angelical, y caritativo)* for the mercy of release to care for her one surviving family member, an ailing father "of advanced age, who finds himself alone with no one to care for him, and at risk for his life" due to his failing health. Furthermore, she claimed to have corrected her ways and completely abandoned her improper relationship *(mala amistad)* with Josefa in order "to live as God has commanded, without a bad reputation." Finally, she appealed to the president to treat her with the same charity and mercy that is usually reserved for the Passion of Jesus, the sufferings of Mary, the devotion of Joseph, the Virgin of Quinche, and the like. Villalengua received the petition on March 15 and shelved it.

Five months later, the president received two petitions from Josefa Lara over the course of a few days. Writing from the Casa de Misercordia, Lara complained that the effects of one year of confinement had seriously jeopardized her health. Facing a second year, she appealed to the president, "crying out to the Angelic piety of my lordship, that by Our Lady of Mercy and the Soul of Father Fray Francisco de Thomas y Bolañoz . . . to pardon me of the rest [of my sentence] and grant me release." Lara wanted nothing more, she claimed, than "to live with some peace and quiet." Apparently fearful that this first petition was not reverent enough, or that the court would simply order her moved to another venue to finish her sentence, Lara wrote again to Villalengua. This time she added significant rhetorical flourishes demonstrating her piety and humility right from the start, opening with "Josefa Lara, a widowed citizen of this City, with the most reverent and humble submission by means of this sad petition," appealing to Mary, her Queen and Lady of El Quinche, the blood of Christ's circumcision, and the suffering of his Holy Mother as her intercessors. She then, with great pomp and circumstance, reenumerated the afflictions and torments caused by her year imprisonment, her great devotion and piety, and her "promise to make complete amends and live as God has commanded, as I must give account to my God."

On August 18, 1788, one year after their imprisonment, the ministers of the Audiencia granted clemency to both Josefa Lara and Manuela Palis on the condition that they live ordered lives, and under threat that if they returned to their former ways they would be punished without mercy. The reengendered public appeals of Lara and Palis encoded them as properly devout women dedicated to honorable living. When the appeals are read in the context of the Audiencia's offensive against sexual deviance and in dialogue with the witness testimony that placed the women in jail, it becomes evident that the language of both accusation and appeal interpolated institutional values not necessarily representative of popular norms. The confessions of Lara and Palis testified to a popular life in Quito that included girls drinking, dancing, and spending nights out on the town. The two women were not alone in their cavorting, but indeed part of a group of revelers that often met at Brigida Alban's bar and attended parties. Such behavior was not in and of itself enough to bring the women under judicial scrutiny, as it was only under suspicion of their relationship crossing into illicitness that judicial authorities took note. Finally, just as the appeals for leniency seem crafted to charm the Audiencia, the gendered character of the women's suspect behaviors must also be considered in this light. It may well be that the witnesses, whether responding to the facts they were presented by the inquiry or by crafting their characterization in terms they expected to appeal to the authorities, presented a gendered indictment of Lara and Palis responsive to institutional values interpolated from magistrates, notaries, or the witnesses' mutual confessor.

CASE II: ROSA HIDALGO, ANDREA AYALA

Some five years earlier, on the night of Saturday, November 30, 1782, the barrio alcalde of San Roque, don Francisco Vicente de Salazar, made a surprise visit to the house of Juan de Salazar, intent on finding Rosa Hidalgo and Andrea Ayala in bed together.[35] Salazar took with him don Eduardo de Aguilar, an assistant warden of the Audiencia's court jail *(teniente alguacil mayor de corte)*, and Josef Hidalgo, the husband of Rosa Hidalgo's sister, Josefa Benalcazer. The three men were responding to a verbal denunciation made against Rosa Hidalgo for being involved in an "illicit, sodomitical relationship *[ylicito comercio sodomitico]* with Andrea [Ayala] for the space of six years, in complete abandonment of her husband, causing notable scandal to the public."[36] The women were apprehended and taken to the Recogimiento de Santa Marta. As in the case of Palis and Lara, the women were arrested after their alleged relationship had been going on for quite a while, and at the prompting of a denunciation to a barrio alcalde. And as in the case five years later, the constitution of the witnesses and allegations deployed against the defendants were cast by this denunciation.

TABLE 2 Initial Witnesses and Their Relationship to the Accused

Name	Age	Relationship
Leonardo Zapata	24	Rosa Hidalgo's husband. Indian. Quichua-only speaker.
Vicente Barreyro	41	Rosa Hidalgo's godfather (padrino)
Tomas Rivera	30	Eyewitness of the kidnapping. Illiterate.
Don Eduardo de Aguilar	40	Teniente Alguacil Mayor de Corte. At the arrest.
Josef Hidalgo	22	Rosa Hidalgo's brother-in-law
Manuela Parrales	60+	Rosa Hidalgo's adoptive mother

SOURCE: ANE SC 99.3, 2-xii-1782

The verbal complaint against Rosa Hidalgo was sparked by a public incident and lodged by her disaffected husband, Leonardo Zapata, who had felt humiliated by it. Earlier that evening, Ayala had appeared, dressed as a man, at Zapata's home and forcibly taken Rosa Hidalgo. The act was accompanied by violence between the participants and resulted in a legal denunciation by Zapata of Hidalgo and Ayala's alleged illicit relationship. Unlike the later case, the barrio alcalde and subsequent judicial officials were clear on the sodomitical nature of this alleged relationship. But they also were unable to overcome the penetrational ambiguity of the allegations to prove the unnatural act, resorting again to circumstantial behavioral evidence of gender inversion and moral turpitude.

That the denunciation originated with Hidalgo's husband resulted in a very different slate of witnesses, though with no less continuity of testimony (table 2). Of the six witnesses questioned, five were men, and four were eyewitnesses to the event. Although the testimony centered on Ayala's sequestration of Hidalgo, the witnesses confirmed several other behaviors that evidenced an illicit sexual relationship. As in the case of Lara and Palis, these behaviors constituted evidence of gender inversion and moral disorder, together with testimony of earlier face-to-face interventions by the people in Rosa Hidalgo's life. The testimony also centers more on allegations against Andrea Ayala, as the cross-dressing aggressor in the relationship.

All of the witnesses agreed on two points, with a third added to the magistrate's quiver during the confession. First, Hidalgo and Ayala acted as a couple, and Ayala in particular acted as the man. Second, the relationship caused Hidalgo to abandon her husband for more than five years. Given the ages of Rosa Hidalgo (25) and her husband, Leonardo Zapata (24), the alleged relationship must have lasted for much of their marriage. The witnesses testified that there was physical violence motivated by jealousy between the two women, and that they were also publicly affectionate and known to "carouse together" (alegrandose en junta). It emerged during the testimony that on numerous occasions Hidalgo would leave Ayala and return to her husband's house for a few days, temporarily assuaging the indignity of marital abandonment. It is unclear why. Nevertheless, it was one such sojourn under Zapata's roof that prompted judicial action. Andrea Ayala appeared at the house, dressed as a man, intent on taking Hidalgo. What is more, from the street she called for Hidalgo by whistling loudly through her fingers, provoking a confrontation that resulted in Hidalgo leaving with Ayala. The witnesses make much of the combination of cross-dressing, whistling, and taking *(sacar)*. The verb *sacar* shows up in criminal records most frequently to indicate removing something from its proper authority. This could be movable property, such as clothing or money.[37] More often, however, the verb appears as the operative word in crimes that involve removing people from institutions (jail, monastery, convent) or relationships of authority (husband, father, parents, employer).[38] In the latter case, *sacar* is most often used to characterize male actions in illicit relationships.[39]

Thus, Ayala's particular and dramatic forms of gender inversion occurred on the street, at the door of the house of her alleged lover, where she showed up dressed in men's clothing, whistled loudly to beckon her lover, and attempted to sequester her from the authority of her husband. These actions, combined with years of intermittent infidelity, led Rosa Hidalgo to abandon her husband and her marital obligations. Such abandonment typified moral disorder in the Bourbon period and is not tied directly to gender. The obligation to attend to marital life was mutual, and its abandonment was considered key evidence of one's devotion to bad living and mistreatment of one's spouse.[40] Abandonment of marriage indicated an individual had opted for immoral living, and had done so without concern for his or her public image.[41]

Armed with testimony against Ayala and Hidalgo, on December 5, 1782, Audiencia judge Quadrado ordered the barrio alcalde to take the women's confessions. As in the case of Palis and Lara, the women explained their untoward behavior as a combination of drunkenness and customary normalcy. They explained away any violence as either accidental or as the fault of men. And they denied vehemently anything illicit about their friendship. Hidalgo, who it turns out was Indian, as was her husband, admitted to being in bed with Ayala, but only because the two had passed out in drunken stupors from an evening of celebrating Ayala's saint's day. November 30, the night of their arrest, was the fiesta de San Andrés, and thus a pretext for celebration for Andrea Ayala. After a night of drinking aguardiente, Hidalgo slept in Ayala's bed out of convenience—the same argument used by Palis and Lara. In fact, she claimed that anytime they had slept together it was innocent and in plain view of other people in the room, who sometimes were in the bed with them as well. When asked if she had abandoned marital life to pursue an illicit friendship with Ayala, Hidalgo denied the allegation, claiming she "had maintained living marital life with her husband" all along, with occasional stretches of a week up to a month away here or there after arguments with Zapata. When asked about the allegations of jealous fits of rage and fighting between the two women, Hidalgo maintained that she had only ever hit Ayala because Ayala had hit her husband or lied to her. Moreover, Hidalgo maintained that the real source of jealous violence in her friendship with Ayala was a third party with whom the two of them frequently drank at a shop owned by Hidalgo's husband. This mysterious third person was a young woman from Riobamba named Marica *(una Muchachaa Riobambeña nombrada Marica)*. The mention of "Marica" in the context of a friendship with a cross-dressing woman is tantalizing given that the term *marica* could be used pejoratively to designate effeminate sodomites.

During the mid to late eighteenth century, the term *maricón* came into more general usage to describe effeminacy. In November 1791 it even made an appearance in a printed letter to the *Mercurio Peruano,* one of Lima's two original newspapers.[42] The letter writer complained, "They appear in the streets dressed in extravagant outfits. Their hands on their hips, they disguise themselves in a cape. With a definite feminine air they proceed with their head erect and their shoulders swaying from side to side like windmills as they, in time to this movement, make a thousand ridiculous swaggers with their bodies, directing their stares in all directions."[43] The quote is interesting in this context for the association of the term *maricón* with dress and affectation. In the first dictionary of the Real Academia Española (RAE; 1726–39), *maricón* was defined as an "effeminate and cowardly man" and was a synonym for *marica. Marica,* the root for *maricón,* carried a number of performative meanings. It was a synonym for *(h)urraca,* a songbird and a term used to lampoon women's and children's styles of talking. It also meant an effeminate man who lacked the energy or capacity *(de pocos brios)* to subjugate, rule, or subordinate as he should *(que se dexa supeditar y manejar).* There is no explicit indication of sexual behavior in these early definitions, but definitely a gender inversion. The definitions of *marica* and *maricón* held constant until the early years of the nineteenth century, when *marica* changed in the 1803 RAE dictionary to: (1) the same as the name María; (2) a synonym of *urraca;* and (3) an effeminate man lacking energy and strength *(ánimo y esfuerso). Maricón* at this point meant simply an effeminate and cowardly man. It was not until the 1899 edition of the Royal Academy's dictionary that *maricón* was defined as a sodomite *(sodomita)*—the first mention of or association with sexual behavior. In that same edition, *marica* continued to be a synonym of *urraca* and an effeminate man.[44]

Who was this Marica who went out drinking with Ayala and Hidalgo on numerous occasions? In her own meandering confession, Ayala mentions that she was accompanied at times when she went to retrieve Hidalgo by a man named Chepe Cuñado, a name made up of two nicknames, on whom she blamed the whistling. Like Hidalgo, Ayala denied that there was anything inappropriate about the two women's friendship, going so far as to state that it was "plain and simply without illicit intent, with neither inappropriate touching nor kisses." She did admit to caring for Hidalgo, giving her something to eat and a place to stay when in need.[45]

The crown attorney rejected Ayala's initial confession on account of her age. In this confession, Ayala claimed to be twenty-two years old, which made her still a minor. The barrio magistrate at that point should have appointed her a guardian ad litem, which he did for a second confession. On the occasion of her second confession, though, Ayala claimed that, based on her mother's statements, she must be eighteen years old, and further she claimed legal status as a single, unmarried women who worked as a seamstress. She again denied not only the illicitness of her friendship with Hidalgo, but also ever dressing like a man or whistling. She also claimed that any injuries she had sustained were from drunkenly falling into a streetside doorframe at Hidalgo's home and that all other fighting was between Hidalgo and her husband.

After confessions, the case was interrupted by an official recantation by Leonardo Zapata, who had initiated the case with his verbal denunciation to the barrio alcalde but after two months of seeing his wife in jail reneged. He asked for liberty for both Hidalgo and Ayala, but most pointedly for his wife, whose absence had left him with "a lack of support in paying Tribute."[46] In response to the retraction, the crown attorney recommended returning Hidalgo to her husband, in part due to "the nature [of Zapata and Hidalgo as Indians], their naivety and rusticity, [and] that the aforementioned Rosa is the wife of Indian Leonardo Zapata, who, having been the one to lodge a verbal complaint against his wife, today recants." Indigenousness, and especially tributary status, was a mitigating factor, and Hidalgo was given to her husband with a warning advising her of the "enormity of the crime to which she has been accused" and that should such accusations be made again she would face the death penalty. Ayala, for her part, was excused due to "her condition and nature" as a single woman, but given the same warnings as Hidalgo and recommended a year's seclusion in a monastery, where she could "live honestly and in fear of God." The Audiencia concurred with the attorney's recommendations, particularly in light of Leonardo Zapata's need to pay tribute, and ordered accordingly. With that, Andrea Ayala was handed to the custody of the office of the bishop of Quito, who placed her in the Monasterio de la Concepción on February 13, 1783.

CONCLUSIONS

What, then, can be concluded from the details of just two criminal cases against just four women in Quito in the 1780s? If anything, these cases demonstrate the difficulties confronted by judicial authorities seeking to prosecute (and conceptualize) sodomy between women. Though sexual encounters between two individuals of the same sex were considered unnatural, the penetrational ambiguity of two women made the instance of female sodomy extremely difficult to prove juridically. As a result, judicial authorities steered witnesses toward circumstantial evidence of the inversion of gendered behaviors associated with courtship, sarto-rial practice, and illicit love, and evidence of general moral disorder and deprav-ity—all unspecific markers of the "unnatural." This form of prosecution mirrored that of male-male sodomy and also bestiality cases where the defendants were not caught in the act but turned in through some precipitating event. In both of the cases considered here, the relationships were long-lived and only came to judicial scrutiny because of some crisis moment that made the relationship formally pub-lic—bringing it to ecclesiastical attention, in the first instance, or creating a big scene at nine o'clock on a Saturday night, in the second.

Likewise, the procedural form and flow of criminal prosecution laid bare a cen-tral tension at the heart of neighborhood perception and toleration of potentially illicit sexual activities. The presumption of guilt and overdetermined nature of wit-nesses during the opening investigatory phase of a trial set discursive terms of a debate predicated on judicial and ecclesiastical norms built on a notion of natural-ness. But during the confession phase, when defendants had the option of explain-ing their actions and providing counterwitnesses, that institutional discursive con-trol was challenged by an appeal to custom and popular norms, where plebeian women drank together with friends, slept in one bed where only one bed was available, and watched out for one another against threatening men. The heart of these two female-female sex cases is this tension between interpretations of sets of behavior as either "unnatural" or "customary."

In both of these cases, authorities were unable to prove penetrative sex had occurred, and none of the defendants were found guilty of sodomy. They were, however, still punished for their "excesses"—excesses that in a court of law were understood within a framework of female same-sex intimacy as inherently "unnat-ural," like male-male sodomy though less legible. Those punishments were miti-gated in their severity once judicial authorities believed that all the social actors involved had been or were capable of being "rehabilitated" (at least in theory) and incorporated back into prescriptively "normal" society. The women reassumed their proper place in the colonial order by both abandoning gender-inverting behaviors and morally reforming through economically productive work and reli-gious instruction.

Ultimately, they were not punished for sexual dalliance, but for the excesses of their public behaviors of drinking, partying, economic unproductivity, and inabil-ity to meet social and marital obligations. Finally, the ancillary evidence of the cases suggests that the sustainability of "unnatural" sexual relationships depended on factors that existed outside of the legal or moral acceptability of those relation-ships. In both cases, reputation for sexual preference was secondary to other exter-nal factors in the denunciations that brought the defendants under scrutiny. Regardless of acceptance, these particular "unnatural" relationships existed in public consciousness just as illicit cohabitations did, but they did not become notorious until threats from a parish priest or a row over some other dispute arose. The prosecution of same-sex relationships within this context engendered the accumulated evidence against the condemned parties in terms defined by normative institutional discourse of naturalness, but revealed countervailing popular customary norms where young women drank, worked, and paid tithes while they cared for their friends as comrades and more.

NOTES

1. Chad Thomas Black, *The Limits of Gender Domination: Women, the Law, and Political Crisis in Quito, 1765–1830* (Albuquerque: University of New Mexico Press, 2010), 83–93. Similar scrutiny has been found in other parts of the empire. For Venezuela, see Kathy Waldron, "'The Sinners and the Bishop in Colonial Venezuela: The Visita of Bishop Mariano Martí, 1771–1784," in *Sexuality and Marriage in Colonial Latin America*, ed. Asunción Lavrin (Lincoln: University of Nebraska Press, 1989), 156–77; and Arlene J. Diaz, *Female Citizens, Patriachs, and the Law in Venezuela, 1786–1904* (Lincoln: University of Nebraska Press, 2004), 40–41. For Mexico, see Michael Scardaville, "'(Habsburg) Law and (Bourbon) Order: State Authority, Popular Unrest, and the Criminal Justice System in Bourbon Mexico City," *The Americas* 50, no. 4 (April 1994): 501–25; and Lee Michael Penyak, "Criminal Sexuality in Central Mexico, 1750–1850," Ph.D. diss., University of Connecticut, 1993.

2. In early modern Spain, sodomy as a broad category of sexual offense theoretically included a whole range of "unnatural" offenses, including bestiality, same-sex relationships, and male-female anal sex. For examples from this period, see Archivo Nacional de Ecuador [hereafter cited as ANE], Serie Criminales [SC], Caja 129, Expediente 6 (129.6), 29-vii-1787, "Autos criminales seguidos pro el Alcalde de San Marcos contra Josefa Lara y Maneula Palis por el delito de concubinato yncestuoso"; ANE SC 99.3, 2-xii-1782, "Causa criminal seguido de oficio contra Andrea Ayala, y Rosa Hidalgo (o Benalcázar), sindicado del pecado nefando"; ANE SC 131.12, 7-ii-1788, "Autos criminales seguidos por el Gov.r de Guayaquil contra Joseph Sisneros por el delito del Nefando"; ANE SC 132.13, 20-v-1788, "Autos seguidos sobre el feo, y abominable Delito de el crimen nefando de Sodomia contra natura, que se le atribuye haver cometido á Custodio Legendres, con varios Muchachos"; ANE SC 84.4, 25-viii-1779, "Exp. en donde se lleva la información reservada, solicitada por el Fiscal de la Audiencia, sobre las actividades del governador de Guayaquil"; ANE SC 84.12, 11-viii-1779, "Autos seguidos en Guayaquil por el Sr. Fiscal de esta Audiencia contra la Persona y malos procedimientos de Pasqual Cardenas, conocido por el Cusqueño"; ANE SC 179.9, 6-x-1800, "Autos criminales seguidos p.r el Gov.r de Guayq.l contra Pedro Mexia p.r el delito de bestialidad"; ANE SC 206.8, 22-viii-1806, "Causa criminal seguido por el Gob.r de Cuenca contra Geronimo Berverian por el delito de Bestialidad"; and ANE Prisiones [PR] 8, 9-i-1806, "Exp. de D.n Ygnacio Martinez de Barbete y Boya apelando los autos del Alcalde de 1.o Voto."

3. ANE SC 99.3, 2-xii-1782, "Causa criminal seguido de oficio contra Andrea Ayala, y Rosa Hidalgo (o Benalcázar), sindicado del pecado nefando." Colonial Quito was divided into seven parishes: El Sagrario, San Roque, San Sebastian, San Marcos, San Blas, Santa Barbara, and Santa Prisca. For descriptions of the barrios in the eighteenth century, see Martin Minchom *The People of Quito, 1690–1810: Change and Unrest in the Underclass* (Boulder, Colo.: Westview Press 1994), 22–27. I have chosen to leave the Spanish text in its original orthography. All translations from Spanish are my own.

4. ANE SC 129.6, 29-vii-1787. The case was mislabeled on its original front page as incestuous cohabitation, the implications of which are discussed below.

5. Penyak, "Criminal Sexuality," 291–97, documents a small number of cases from Inquisition and criminal records of late-eighteenth-century Mexico City. For Spain proper, see Sherry Velasco, *Lesbians*

in Early Modern Spain (Nashville: Vanderbilt University Press, 2011). See also the chapter in this volume by Ronaldo Vainfas and Zeb Tortorici.

6. I've borrowed the phrase "penetrational ambiguity" from Zeb Tortorici, "'Heran Todos Putos': Sodomitical Subcultures and Disordered Desire in Early Colonial Mexico," *Ethnohistory* 54, no. 1 (2007): 36–67.

7. I use the term *toleration* as Martha Hodes defines it, as "a measure of forbearance for that which is not approved." Martha Hodes, *White Women, Black Men: Illicit Sex in the Nineteenth-Century South* (New Haven, Conn.: Yale University Press, 1997), 3.

8. Zeb Tortorici, "Against Nature: Sodomy and Homosexuality in Colonial Latin America," *History Compass* 10, no. 2 (2012): 165.

9. Much of the work done on female homoeroticism in the early modern Spanish empire has come from literary studies. See, for example, the collected essays in María José Delgado and Alain Saint-Saëns, eds., *Lesbianism and Homosexuality in Early Modern Spain* (New Orleans: University Press of the South, 2000); Josiah Blackmore and Gregory S. Hutcheson, eds., *Queer Iberia: Sexualities, Cultures, and Crossings from the Middle Ages to the Renaissance* (Durham, N.C.: Duke University Press, 1999); Velasco, *Lesbians in Early Modern Spain*; Lisa Vollendorf, "The Value of Female Friendship in Seventeenth-Century Spain," *Texas Studies in Literature and Language* 47, no. 4 (2005): 425–45; and Sylvia Molloy and Robert McKee Irwin, eds., *Hispanisms and Homosexualities* (Durham, N.C.: Duke University Press, 1998). Work by historians includes Ronaldo Vainfas, "Homoerotismo feminino e o Santo Oficio," in *Historia das mulheres no Brasil*, ed. Mary del Priore (São Paulo: Editora Contexto, 2004); Penyak, "Criminal Sexuality," 245–310; and Stephanie Kirk, *Convent Life in Colonial Mexico: A Tale of Two Communities* (Gainesville: University Press of Florida, 2007), chap. 3.

10. Martin Nesvig, "The Complicated Terrain of Latin American Homosexuality," *Hispanic American Historical Review* 81, nos. 3–4 (2001): 691. For an example of the active/passive model in full force, see Laura A. Lewis, "From Sodomy to Superstition: The Active Pathic and Bodily Transgressions in New Spain," *Ethnohistory* 54, no. 1 (2007): 129–57. Cristian Berco argues that sodomitical relationships in early modern Valencia reveal the extent to which "patriarchal culture and sodomy were inextricably linked, producing each other in a system of individual and collective reinforcement." See Berco, "Producing Patriarchy: Male Sodomy and Gender in Early Modern Spain," *Journal of the History of Sexuality* 17, no. 3 (2008): 352. For foundational anthropological work on the Mediterranean honor code, see John K. Campbell, *Honour, Family, and Patronage: A Study of Institutions and Moral Values in a Greek Mountain Community* (Oxford: Clarendon Press, 1964); John G. Peristiany, ed., *Honour and Shame: The Values of Mediterranean Society* (Chicago: University of Chicago Press, 1966); and, most notably, Julian Pitt-Rivers, *The Fate of Shechem, or the Politics of Sex: Essays in the Anthropology of the Mediterranean* (Cambridge: Cambridge University Press, 1977).

11. Tortorici, "'Heran Todos Putos,'" 44–48. See also Kimberly Gauderman, "It Happened on the Way to the *Temescal* and Other Stories: Desiring the Illicit in Colonial Spanish America," *Ethnohistory* 54, no. 1 (Winter 2007): 177–86.

12. Nesvig, "Complicated Terrain," 691.

13. Berco, "Producing Patriarchy," 352. Berco does note that his argument applies only to male-male relationships. He excludes female-only relationships because of their rarity in the documentary record and because of the complexity of interpreting and theorizing their position in the gender regime

14. For critiques of the application of Pitt-Rivers's honor/shame model to early modern Spain, see most recently Scott K. Taylor, *Honor and Violence in Golden Age Spain* (New Haven, Conn.: Yale University Press, 2008), esp. chap. 1; see also Allyson Poska, *Women and Authority in Early Modern Spain: The Peasants of Galicia* (Oxford: Oxford University Press, 2005), 5–13; Allyson Poska, "Elusive Virtue: Rethinking the Role of Female Chastity in Early Modern Spain," *Journal of Early Modern History* 8, nos. 1–2 (January 2004): 135–46; Scott Taylor, "Credit, Debt, and Honor in Castile, 1600–1650," *Journal of*

Early Modern History 7, no. 1–2 (January 2003): 8–27; and Abigail Dyer, "Seduction by Promise of Marriage: Law, Sex, and Culture in Seventeenth-Century Spain," *Sixteenth-Century Journal* 34, no. 2 (Summer 2003): 439–55. For works on Italy equally skeptical of the honor model, see Elizabeth S. Cohen, "Honor and Gender in the Streets of Early Modern Rome," *Journal of Interdisciplinary History* 22, no. 4 (Spring 1992): 597–625; and Thomas V. Cohen, "Three Forms of Jeopardy: Honor, Pain, and Truth-Telling in a Sixteenth-Century Italian Courtroom," *Sixteenth-Century Journal* 29, no. 4 (Winter 1998): 975–98.

15. Poska, "Elusive Virtue," 136.

16. Taylor, "Credit, Debt, and Honor," 10–11.

17. Sally Cole, *Women of the Praia: Work and Lives in a Portuguese Coastal Community* (Princeton: Princeton University Press, 1991), 78–79. See also Michael Herzfeld, "The Horns of the Mediterraneanist Delima," *American Ethnologist* 11, no. 3 (August 1984): 439–54; and the collected essays in David Gilmore, ed., *Honor and Shame and the Unity of the Mediterranean*, Special Publication No. 22 (Washington, D.C.: American Anthropologist Association, 1987).

18. Cole, *Women of the Praia*, 79.

19. This line of interpretation is exemplified by Richard C. Trexler, *Sex and Conquest: Gendered Violence, Political Order, and the European Conquest of the Americas* (Ithaca, N.Y.: Cornell University Press, 1995); and Cristian Berco, *Sexual Hierarchies, Public Status: Men, Sodomy, and Society in Spain's Golden Age* (Toronto: University of Toronto Press, 2007).

20. Black, *Limits of Gender Domination*, 72–120.

21. For procedural overviews of prototypical criminal litigation and templates in the primary legal literature, see Alonso Villadiego, *Instrucción política y práctica judicial, conforme al estilo de los consejos, audiencias y tribunals de corte y otros ordinaries del reyno* (Madrid, 1747), 58–93, 477–85; Joseph Juan y Colom, *Instrucción juridical de escribanos, abogados y juices ordinaries de juzgados inferiores* (Madrid, 1795), 200–203; Charles R. Cutter, ed., *Libro de los principales rudimentos tocante a todos juicios, civil, criminal y executivo: Año de 1764* (Mexico City: UNAM, 1994), 29–70. For secondary literature examinations, see Black, *Limits of Gender Domination*; Charles R. Cutter, *The Legal Culture of Northern New Spain, 1700–1810* (Albuquerque: University of New Mexico Press, 1995), 109–38; Colin M. MacLachlan, *Criminal Justice in Eighteenth-Century Mexico: A Study of the Tribunal of the Acordada* (Berkeley: University of California Press, 1974), 21–25; Asunción Lavrin, "Sexuality in Colonial Mexico: A Church Dilemma," in Lavrin (ed.), *Sexuality and Marriage in Colonial Latin America*, 69–73.

22. It is the case that all of the nefarious crime prosecutions began with a third-party denunciation (see the list of cases above in note 2). Motivation for the denunciations varies from personal embarrassment to calculated acts of retribution radiating from other disputes.

23. All details from the case in this section are from ANE SC 129.6, 29-vii-1787.

24. For other examples of sexual prosecutions radiating from neighborhood patrols, see ANE SC 109, 22-ii-1785, "Expediente formado por Maria Josefa Suares, contra Manuel Manrique su marido y Maria Yturrabalde, sobre concubinato en que se han mantenido estos"; ANE SC 115, 6-ii-1786, "Autos criminales contra Miguel y Fernando Lagos, y Petrona Ayala sobre adulterio"; ANE SC 117, 26-viii-1786, "Autos seguidos por el Alcalde ordinario contra D.n Fran.co Xavier Acusabi y D.a Thomasa Domingues sobre concubinato"; ANE SC 135, 16-vi-790, "Doña Mariana Flore dela Bandera or falsa ynforme de Juaquina Enrriquez sobre adulterio con José Chagaray." Sometimes the invasive presence of the ronda provoked violent response from residents, to the point that participants were beaten or even assaulted with weapons. See, e.g., ANE SC 122, 9-vii-1787, "Autos criminales contra Visente, Felipe, y Lorenzo Basques Alban y Palis por haver insultado al Alcalde de San Sebastian y Ministros de Justicia."

25. Nesvig, "Complicated Terrain," 694.

26. Juan de Zumárraga (1543), quoted ibid.

27. Cutter, *Libro*, 38.

28. Ibid.

29. Ibid., 38–39.

30. ANE SC 126, 10-v-1788.

31. ANE SC 123, 29-vii-1787, "Con crecido desahoy, y vozes las mas impuras se tomaron zelos mutuamente, preciendo muchos golpes entre las dos."

32. ANE SC 126, 10-v-1788.

33. For more on Santa Marta, see María Isabel Viforcos Marinas, "Los recogimientos, de centros de integración social a cárceles privadas: Santa Marta de Quito," *Anuario de estudios Americanos* 50, no. 2 (1993): 59–92.

34. The excuse of only having one bed was used in other cases to justify questionable sleeping arrangements. See, e.g., ANE SC 115, 6-ii-1786, "Autos criminales seguidos contra Miguel y Fernando Lagos, y Petrona Ayala sobre adulterio," in which an alcalde found Fernando Lagos in bed with his sister-in-law, Petrona Ayala, her husband passed out drunk on the floor. The trio argued that nothing untoward was occurring, but rather that they were poor and only had one bed for everyone to sleep in.

35. This section is based on ANE SC 99.3, 2-xii-1782, unless otherwise noted.

36. Various surnames were used for both women during the case. Andrea Ayala was alternately named Montenegro or Ayala, and Rosa was variously Hidalgo or Benalcazar. For continuity's sake, I have used the last name settled on by the middle of the case.

37. Diego Aras, for example, was arrested in July 1770 for having "removed all the clothes by trickery" from the possession of his victim. ANE, Juicios de Primer Notaría [1NJ], 45, 1767. For an example involving money, ANE SC 56.8, 11-xii-1765, "Sumaria inciada por el alcalde ordinario de Quito por la pérdida de dinero usual y corriente sacada de una escribanía y perteneciente a las Cajas Reales." Or there is the arrest of Fernando Manos Albas in 1769 for having falsely taken 190 pesos in league with a slave. See ANE 1NJ 45, 1767. See also ANE 1NJ 235, 15-xi-1806, "Criminales seguids pr Dn Manuel Molineros, contra Cristoval Ruiz pr haverle sacado ciento nov.ta ps con cartas falsas de Da Man.a Benites X.a."; and ANE SC 122.7, 21-vi-1786, "Expediente relativo sobre que Fray Antonio Zambrana Religioso de Sn Agn quebrantó la Carzel atropellam.to dela jurisdiccion real de sacarse un Yndio preso deudor de tributos."

38. For example, Quito's arrest rolls for 1768 include Pedro Flores, who "took a married women from the authority of her husband." The year 1769 includes Joseph Gualli, Manuel Peña, and Manuel Theran for having "taken a married woman." In February 1770, Ramon Montenegro was arrested for having "taken a women from a monastery." One month earlier it was Pedro Mariano who had "taken a young women *[doncella]* from the authority of her parents." ANE 1NJ 45, 1767. In Cuenca in 1725, charges were brought against Alejo Renjifo Pezantes and his sons for refusing to return a young woman they had taken from the home of the woman who raised her. The young woman, Melchora Arias, was engaged to marry another man. See ANE SC 22.8, 18-vii-1725. See also ANE 1NJ 277, 3-viii-1814, "Autos criminales seguidos por Antonio Guacollame, yndio natural del pueblo de Cotocollao, contra D.n Fran.co Carcelen por la saca de una hija."

39. See, e.g., ANE 1NJ 97, 31-xi-1787, "Autos criminales seguidos por parte del Cap.n de Granaderos d.n Carlos Presenti, . . . contra Manuel Cruz por concubinato reinsidido con Jensa Ramos"; ANE SC 129.19, 13-ix-1797, "Autos criminales de oficio . . . contra Maria Yepes alias la Chunchulli por Alcagueta y Amansabamiento"; ANE SC 120.6, 28-i-1786, "Expediente seguido por Maria Jimenez contra Josef de Leon por estupro de su hija menor de edad"; ANE SC 120.9, 6-ii-1786, "Autos criminales seguidos contra Miguel y Fernanado Lagos, y Petrona Ayala sobre adulterio."

40. See, e.g., ANE SC 117.13, 4-vii-1785, "Recurso de Josef Joaq.n de Alarcon con Micayla Valles su muger, sobre su mal vivir." *Mala vida* has traditionally been interpreted as the "abuse of power by a spouse," usually indicating a husband ducking his responsibilities to provide material sustenance or engaging in inordinate physical abuse or sexual dalliance. See Asunción Lavrin, "Introduction," in Lavrin (ed.), *Sexuality and Marriage in Colonial Latin America,* 20–21. See also Richard Boyer, *Lives of*

the Bigamists: Marriage, Family, and Community in Colonial Mexico (Albuquerque: University of New Mexico Press, 1995), 128–32, 158–60. I would suggest that *mala vida/mal vivir* were not terms tied to the abuse of power as much as they were a linguistic trope of debased moral charachter. When women in Quito wished to indict their husbands' abuse of power, they used the phrase *mal tratos* or *maltratamientos* (mistreatments), rather than *mala vida*.

41. Black, *Limits of Gender Domination*, 105.

42. "Carta sobre maricones," *Mercurio peruano* 94 (November 27, 1791), 230–32; in Jacinto Calero y Moreira, *Mercurio peruano: De historia, literatura, y noticias publicas que da á luz la sociedad academica de Amantes de Lima*, vol. 3 (Lima: Imprenta Real de los Niños Huérfanos, 1791).

43. Quoted in Johanna S.R. Mendolson, "The Feminine Press: The View of Women in the Colonial Journals of Spanish America, 1790–1810," in *Latin American Women: Historical Perspectives*, ed. Asunción Lavrin (Westport, Conn.: Greenwood Press, 1978), 198–218. The *Mercurio Peruano* circulated in Quito in the 1790s, though that is of little consequence here.

44. Definitions were tracked using the Real Academia de Español online historical dictionaries at http://buscon.rae.es/ntlle/SrvltGUILoginNtlle (accessed February 3, 2009).

45. The same claims were made by Custodio Legendres in his sodomy trial.

46. ANE SC 99.4, 2-xii-1782, "Y aserme falta para Soportar la paga de Tributos."

7

Sodomy, Gender, and Identity in the Viceroyalty of Peru

Fernanda Molina

Translated by Lucía Cordone

The aim of this chapter is to explore the sexual practices of sixteenth- and seventeenth-century sodomites in the viceroyalty of Peru in order to evaluate in what way the definition of sodomy, which was seen as an inherently *unnatural act* by theologians and jurists of the time, evinces the myriad experiences undergone by individuals accused of the "sin against nature."

Authors such as Michel Foucault have suggested that sixteenth- and seventeenth-century sodomites were driven primarily by lust, that it was their incapacity to subdue to the flesh that made them commit lascivious and disordered acts. Unlike nineteenth-century homosexuals—whose "perversity" was thought to originate deep in the (medicalized and pathologized) essence of their being—the "modern sodomite" of the sixteenth and seventeenth centuries was simply a juridical subject whose condition was determined by the execution of a series of acts that, to a degree, could even be considered external to the sodomite.[1] Even though such a statement does place sexual practices between individuals of the same sex in historical perspective—thus counteracting essentialist and ahistorical perspectives that tend to project contemporary experiences on the past—it also contributed to the crystallization of a narrow image of the "sodomite."

This chapter suggests that sodomitical practices, being both personal and intimate experiences, not only constituted diverse phenomena—impossible to reduce to one single meaning tied to "nature" and the "unnatural"—but also influenced gender identities and, in the passion of sexual encounters, strengthened erotic and affective bonds in the long term. These lived realities of sodomy in colonial Peru go beyond and challenge the notion of sodomy as simply an act "against nature." Even if there are theoretical and methodological limits to studying the intimate

141

everyday experiences of subjects in the past, it is undeniable that research of this kind contributes to further reconsideration of the canonized visions of the history of (homo)sexuality.

THE ACT

During the period I focus on here, sodomy constituted one of the "lustful sins" as defined by to Saint Thomas Aquinas, who believed that lust was the use of venereal pleasure against reason. Its origin lay, on the one hand, in the denial of its use for its natural aim, that is to say, the production of offspring, and, on the other, in the wrong choice of the recipient vessel of the venereal act.[2] Nevertheless, sodomy, along with bestiality and *molicies* (onanism), constituted the most abominable forms of lustful sins, for they implied the obstruction of divine purposes associated with creation. Such an interpretation rests on the fact that even though God had created all existence in complete perfection, such creation was yet unfinished. In this sense, males, created in God's own image and likeness, and carriers of the seeds of procreation, capable of accomplishing the mandate "be fruitful and multiply," became direct collaborators with creation.[3] Hence, any deviation from the task given by God was understood as an alteration of both the natural order created by God and the social order.

This last consequence made sodomy not only a sin, but also a crime. After all, social order was but an extension of divine order, and the alteration of one necessarily affected the other. This duality with regard to sodomy stemmed from the juridical culture of the time, which, fed by both canonic and Roman law, rendered the boundaries between the notions of sin and crime unclear.[4] From the juridical perspective, even though sodomy consisted of coitus through the "unnatural vessel," either between persons of the same sex or between men and women, there was a distinction between "perfect" and "imperfect" sodomy.[5] The majority of doctors considered, as did Aquinas, that this crime in its perfection consisted of coitus between two persons of the same sex, while imperfect sodomy referred to coitus between men and women either through the unnatural vessel (the anus) or outside it.[6] In either case, it involved the spillage of seed, hence the seriousness and materiality of the crime. Nevertheless, controversy frequently arose over how to define the act—or rather, how to determine in which contexts sodomy was and was not consummated. For some it had to do with the emission—or lack thereof—of semen inside or outside the unnatural vessel, while for others the simple act of touching sufficed. Some jurists and theologians, for example, still designated certain instances of *tocamientos impúdicos*—impure acts of touching—with the term *pecado nefando* ("nefarious sin").[7] Yet some doctors believed that anal coitus between men and women could not be considered pure sodomy but merely "sodomitical acts."[8] In this sense, for many theologians this phenomenon was not restricted to a simple act based on penetration and the emission of semen.

This tendency is reflected in the evolution of secular laws in relation to accusatory proofs. The *Pragmática* issued by Ferdinand and Isabella in 1497 established that "should no proof be found of such crime, but proof of acts very close to it, the criminal will be judged and sentenced."[9] The Philippine *Pragmática* of 1598 was more radical in this aspect, given the difficulty of proving a crime of this nature: the accused should be "punished accordingly even if the crime was not proved with witnesses but rather through other forms established and proven by law which show proof to impose the customary sentence."[10] This pragmatic sanction thus recognized circumstantial evidence and suppositions declared by witnesses, overestimating their plausibility over concrete proof. This implies that any other acts approximating sodomy would almost certainly lead to a sentence. Just as in the theological debates over sodomy, this legislation has a tendency to underestimate the existence of the "juridical act" and overestimate the intentionality or the volition of the acting subject.

Both theological controversies as well as the tendency to underestimate the material proof of sodomy suggest the need to look beyond erudite or formal definitions of sodomy. Even though some theological and juridical formulations were hegemonic during the period I analyze, they were not monolithic; indeed, various interpretations competed with the dominant views of the time. Even if there had been a singular mode of defining the phenomenon of sodomy, surely the practices and experiences of men accused of the crime were more diverse and complex.

THE VICEROYALTY OF SODOMITES: BEYOND THE JURIDICAL SUBJECT

To a certain extent the interpretation of the "juridical subject" proposed by Foucault seems to fit with the concept that gender systems have the capacity of superimposing sexual experiences. Even though it is true that channeling sexual desire through persons of the same sex does not necessarily imply an alteration of gender behavior—as would feminization—it is no less certain that sexuality has an active role in conforming gender identities. As Eve Kosofsky Sedgwick puts it, "Sexuality extends along so many dimensions that aren't well described in terms of the gender of object-choice at all."[11]

Following these premises, the aim of this section is to analyze the contexts in which both systems maintain their relative autonomy, and in which the sodomitical sexual experience could affect both gender identities and the subjectivities of sodomites in the viceroyalty of Peru. I analyze below the various judicial processes dealing with sodomy in the viceroyalty of Peru during the sixteenth and seventeenth centuries, alongside reports and other documents produced by the administration of justice, in order to bring to light a series of characteristics that show, on the one hand, the narrow dominant theological and juridical definitions of sodomy at the time, and on the other, the complexity that characterized the phenomenon in daily practice.[12]

Hugs, Kisses, and "Words of Love"

One of the recurrent aspects evident in the corpus of trials I analyze is the presence of affection between those accused of sodomy. This is a revealing element, since it is largely absent from many studies on this subject for early modern Spain. In his research on sodomites in Valencia, for example, Rafael Carrasco observes that one of the characteristics of the nefarious practice is the radical separation between affection and sex, for, according to Carrasco, such practices constituted a means of satisfaction rather than one of affection.[13] Even though there is plenty of evidence revealing economic and material dependence—especially between younger and older men, but also between persons of different socioeconomic status—the number of cases in which there were unambiguous affective ties between the accused is significant, and invites a reconsideration of sodomy in the early modern period as being simply sexual in nature.

Notwithstanding, these emotional ties could only be observed through exterior signs of affection, of which we hear from some witnesses. Among such signs, hugs and kisses are the most common, either given by the accused or solicited by an unrequited lover. An example of the first comes to us in a 1608 case, in which Doctor Gaspar González de Sosa, clergyman of La Plata, and Diego Mejía (also referred to as Mexia in the records), his closest confidant, were implicated in charges of sodomy.[14] Their relationship had become so public that some witnesses expressed outrage because, among other things, "they are not ashamed of holding hands under the table."[15] Neither were they ashamed of kissing and hugging each other in public, for which they became infamous in the region through a popular *copla* that told the story of a *negro* called Cajamarca (referred to as Caxamalca in the records) who was accused of having committed the nefarious sin in Cuzco. Every night when the doctor and Diego Mejía retired to their chamber, their servants, neighbors, and relatives would mockingly chant, "give him your tongue, Caxamalca" (*dale lengua Caxamalca*), suggesting that the two were kissing.[16]

In 1590, also in La Plata, some witnesses mentioned having seen the *oidor* or judge of the Real Audiencia, Doctor Manuel Barros de San Millán, in a similar relationship with his slave, Andrés Cupín, "who was so much loved by Doctor Barros, that Doctor Barros was once seen in the horse shed, one arm behind the black man's neck and the other holding his hand."[17] These were cases of requited love, but soldier Pedro González, in spite of repeated attempts to achieve sexual contact—whether asking for a kiss or caressing the hair of his loved ones or organizing actual "romantic dates"—was not as lucky.[18] Equally unlucky was the provincial of the Dominican convent Nuestra Señora del Rosario in Ciudad de los Reyes in

1596. According to witnesses, "the provincial, fray Domingo de Valderrama, was seen many times lying on the bed holding the hands and face of Juan de Silva, flattering him *[regalándose con él]*."[19] According to Juan, a young novice, those acts were against his will: "Fray Domingo approached him by force to kiss him, pushing him against a table, and he said he feared he would come and kiss him by force because he was sick and very young."[20]

These hugs, kisses, and caresses indicate that rather than being merely a subject of lust, on certain occasions the sodomite could be an individual wanting a relationship beyond the sexual encounter. In some cases of unrequited love, however, it appears that kissing and hugging functioned as a tactic to engage in more sexual acts. Even in cases when authority was used to force intimate encounters, many so-called sodomites showed special affection for their chosen partners, as the cases above demonstrate. This was clearly understood by the judges and attorneys concerned with establishing the existence—or lack—of affection between the men and boys accused of sodomy.

Apart from exterior signs of affection, those accused of sodomy also expressed their feelings toward their sexual partners verbally. Such feelings operated on several often contradictory levels, including unconditional love, yearning for the loss of a loved one, and anger or jealousy for real or suspected cheating. For example, nostalgia for a loved one could become especially intense as a result of actions secular justices took to prevent future sodomitical acts between two people. One of the methods used to immediately "remedy" the situation was banishment of one or both of the accused from the land where the scandal had taken place. This is what happened with Luis de Herrera, who, in 1603, was banished from Provincia de Chayanta to la Villa de Potosí when his illicit relationship with don Diego Díaz de Talavera, his master, was discovered.[21] Even though friends and relatives had suggested to don Diego that he dismiss his servant, he refused, stating that wherever Luis de Herrera went, "he would go with him" *(avia de yr con el)*.[22] He thus fell into deep melancholia, which further increased his feelings for his servant, to whom he wrote love letters over the course of some ten months, pleading him to return. A witness recalls how, on wishing for his servant's return, don Diego "had not wanted to have lunch" *(no avia querido almorçar)*, for he was very sad at the table.[23]

Such relationships were so intimate, it seems, that any type of physical separation could become unbearable for one or both of the men involved. Melancholia was not, however, the only response. Doctor Gaspar de Sosa, for example, did not hide his anger when a guest sat at the very spot where Diego Mejía, his lover, used to sit. According to witnesses, when asked about his lack of appetite he replied: "I cannot eat, for he who feeds me has sat somewhere else."[24] Such a response did not surprise the people present, who on more than one occasion had observed the "communion" between the two: "eating together from the same plate and drinking from one single cup, first the doctor and then, giving it to don Diego, telling him, drink this, Diego, *por amor de mi por vida mia* [for love of me, for my life], and the same he would do with food, the doctor bit first and don Diego followed suit."[25]

Yet the relationship between the accused was not always one of yearning or passion, either. Jealousy, its affective counterpart, constituted a means through which some men expressed their deepest feelings, especially when the affection given was not reciprocated as hoped for. One night, after attending a comedy, Diego Mejía returned home very late, having accompanied a lady to her dwelling place. This situation provoked rage in the doctor, who, not caring about any repercussions his actions might have, reprimanded Mejía: "I share my hacienda with you and I have bought you a regiment to take rest with you *[holgarme con bos]*, and you go out with women and return at midnight."[26] He then forbade Mejía to enter the house, as if he were a betrayed wife. After this incident they remained distant for two days, during which Mejía kept his head low, not daring to look the doctor in the eye. Nevertheless, "they eventually talked and were happy together again,"[27] for according to witnesses, they could not live without each other. Doctor Barros suffered a similar downfall when his slave, Andrés Cupín, married a *mulata* called Pascuala, putting an end to the happy days in which they "were at leisure with" *(holgaban)* one other. As punishment—and as a way of channeling his disillusion—Doctor Barros ordered his slave to be whipped, then replaced his position as pageboy with another *negro* named Pedro.[28]

While in some cases, as the ones mentioned above, the partner in question was conceived of as an unfaithful lover and was therefore punished with indifference, jealousy, or violence, in others the other partner was seen as a war trophy in a contest between two impassioned men. In 1596, for example, Juan González, a druggist in Potosí who was part of a clandestine network of sodomites that circulated between Villa Imperial and La Plata, was fought over by nurses Domingo Hernández Bautista and Alonso López del Valle. According to the testimony of González, "jealousy between the said Baptista and the said Alonso Lopez del Calle over this witness caused them to fight."[29]

Curiously enough, it can be observed that the relationship between many sodomites was a central aspect in their constitution as subjects—in terms of feelings and affective ties especially, which ranged from unconditional love to jealousy. Whatever the nature of such feelings, it indicated the existence of a bond that transcended mere sexuality. It is highly likely that the types of affection described in the hearings and found in many of the court cases documenting sodomitical relationships was part of a wider process of change, in the perception both of love and of sexual relations.[30]

Dangerous Cohabitation

Just as the bonds between these men went beyond sexual relations, such bonds extended over time (in some senses imitating the rituals of heterosexual courtship). In this sense, they transcended the isolated act that defined sodomy in "juridical terms," thereby complicating theological and juridical conceptions of sodomy as "unnatural." This was true not only of individuals maintaining a recurrent same-sex behavior (as a sexual preference) but also of individuals maintaining long-lasting sexual and affective relationships with one cohabitating partner.

Some of the protagonists that I analyze here, including Díaz de Talavera, Doctor Barros de San Millán, and Doctor González de Sosa, shared not only the same chamber in which they slept with another man, but also the same bed, which, in the eyes of witnesses, served as a kind of spousal bed. It is highly likely that the amorous words and acts previously described were even more audacious in private, as was the case with Cristóbal de Zamorano and his servant. According to witnesses, "they have committed dishonest and filthy acts of *tocamentos* [touching] in their private parts, they have kissed, laid on the same bed, and told each other dishonest words."[31]

Even though in some cases they kept up appearances, fictionalizing with "separate beds," close and indiscreet witnesses could give accounts of what was going on inside the chambers. In the case of Diego Díaz de Talavera and his servant Luis de Herrera, a witness revealed that during the time the servant was dwelling in the house of Talavera, one of the beds was never slept in: "Luis de Herrera did not sleep in it, but he slept with Diego Díaz, in the same bed."[32] They maintained the same behavior when, for various business matters, they had to leave the house and travel. Everybody knew that "when they traveled there was only one bed for them."[33] Doctor Gaspar González de Sosa and Diego Mejía were also caught by an eyewitness who saw, through the chamber window, how they both lay naked on the same bed, under the sheets and blankets. The scene of "two men in that form, as if they were man and woman . . . embracing and kissing one another, and talking" caused the witness great distress.[34]

The scandalized discomfort that witnesses experienced through such manifestations of intimacy also responded to changes that started to take place in the sixteenth century. Until then, the bedroom was part of people's everyday life: it was not uncommon to receive visitors in the room containing the beds and even have a guest sleep in the same chamber where the hosts—both men and women—slept.[35] Nonetheless, during the early modern period the bedchamber became one of the most private and intimate spaces, where spouses carried out their "spousal duties." In this context, sharing the bedroom could entail an attack on one's decorum and on individual intimacy. The experiences of men and women in the viceroyalty of Peru oscillated between medieval conceptions of the body and of bedroom intimacy, on one side, and the new tendencies that began to emerge during the first half of the sixteenth century, on the other. Even if sharing the same bedroom or the same bed was considered part of everyday routine, some witnesses distrusted the fact that the accused escaped from everybody's sight to shut themselves within the intimacy and secret of their chamber. For what kind of acts could take place behind closed doors? Juan de Salas, witness in the case against Díaz de Talavera and his servant, explained that "as a lawyer he can say he has seen and he knows there is enough proof to go against the accused and proceed with much rigor," referring to the fact that both of the accused men regularly slept together in the same bed.[36]

In general, colonial sodomitical relationships tended to develop between persons of unequal social status and ethnic background. Therefore, the relationships of power and submission between, for example, masters and slaves, lords and servants, priests and parishioners, masters and apprentices, Spaniards and Indians, manifested themselves in sexual relationships.[37] Notwithstanding, in some of the criminal and Inquisition cases studied—such as those of Doctor González de Sosa and Diego Díaz de Talavera—even if they did involve persons of unequal social strata linked by power relationships, did not necessarily constitute coercive relationships. To the contrary, in these and other examples in which sexual violence is not key, not only was the sodomitical relationship far from being a form of abuse for the "dependent," but it also constituted a way of balancing existing social differences. In connection to this, one of the witnesses in the case against Díaz de Talavera and his servant offered the magistrate a peculiar vision: "This witness knows that Diego Dias and Luis de Herrera are not master and servant but equals; they are never far from one another, and nothing that Luis de Herrera does not want to do is ever done."[38]

What this statement shows is both that hierarchies could be altered and that social dependencies constituting master and servant relationships could be contradicted, or at least destabilized. Another attempt to balance social differences was the one developed by Doctor González de Sosa regarding Diego Mejía. According to many witnesses, before meeting the doctor his "assistant" was a miserable and shabby-looking subject whose surname was "Pobrete" and not "Mejía," as he would later be baptized. But after their encounter in the Villa imperial jail, where Diego Mejía was imprisoned, Doctor González de Sosa placed him under his protection and showered him with wealth, banquets, clothing, and numerous other gifts. Most surprising about this case is that the doctor decided to change the identity of the ex-convict. One witness remembered how "the doctor' had ordered 'Diego Pobrete' be addressed as 'don Diego Mexia,' and he found it very funny for having seen him wearing the garments he wore in jail."[39] The purpose of this form of address, "don," was to elevate the status of Diego Mejía, thus moderating the social differences among the two of them. This did not mean, however, that the rules of social relationship between the persons involved disappeared. In both cases, affective and sexual relationships lay within more encompassing social relationships, thus generating continuous tensions and contradictions.

Passivity and "Enemies" of Women

A third characteristic element found in this corpus of trials was the lack of interest in establishing sexual ties and roles considered by many to be "masculine." Given that this tendency became, in some cases, a recurrent behavior, it contradicts the idea of the sodomite as a subject driven by lust who, in order to satisfy his uncontrollable sexual desire, was capable of committing the *pecado nefando* within what would be called a "heterosexual" structure. On the contrary, the sample of cases presented here by the defendants reveals a clear lack of interest in such structures, as shown in two distinct types of behavior: on the one hand, they occasionally expressed disgust for having had sexual relations with women (who were clearly not objects of desire), and on the other, a preference for being the "passive" partner in the sodomitical relationship.

Out of the 123 individuals involved in sodomy cases found in the viceroyalty of Peru's registers from the sixteenth and seventeenth centuries, 54 percent were categorized in the documentation as passive or *paciente*, almost 35 percent were identified as active or "agents," and a mere 5 percent were recognized as having assumed both roles.[40] This proportion must not lead us to the conclusion that most sodomites preferred passive to active roles, since, in many cases, more than one person was solicited by the so-called agents, especially when an unequal power relationship applied, as between a priest and the members of his parish. In this sense, the decision to assume passive roles should be analyzed in qualitative rather than quantitative terms—which is by no means less significant. For example, in 1595, in Potosí, Alonso López del Valle confessed to having committed the *pecado nefando* with the above-mentioned Juan González and declared "that Juan González always played the role of woman *[serbia de muger]* and that fray Luis had another strange condition, that he did not want to ride *[no queria cabalgar]* the said Juan González, but rather wanted to be ridden by the said Juan González."[41] This shows the clear preference on the part of some sodomites for being penetrated, a role that many considered to be that of the female. In the case of Juan González, he also confessed how, coming from Spain on the high seas, he had committed the nefarious sin with a friar named Juan de Valenzuela, "being this confessant passive *[paciente]* and the friar the agent *[agente]*."[42]

This preference was also manifest on more than one occasion by Juan Ponce de León, from Huamanga, who in 1620 was taken to the secular courts under the charge of sodomy. According to one witness, Ponce de León had no problem asking one of his accomplices to do it to him *por el culo*, "in the ass."[43] According to the declaration his own master made to the magistrates of his city, Ponce de León had used similar words in his interactions with an unidentified black slave.[44] Another slave named Francisco narrated yet another peculiar proposal made by Ponce de León: "Do you want to go to the horse shed and ride me in the ass *[cabalgarme por el culo]* and so that I will buy you from your master and make you free?"[45] Similar sexual conduct can be seen in the declarations of fray Pedro Coronado, who was imprisoned in the Inquisition jails in Lima. Coronado confessed to having committed the crime of sodomy in various occasions with his "sons of confession," with whom he "had not been passive because they did not want to, even though he had asked and begged for it."[46] Both behaviors establish a clear distinction with the traditional image of the active sodomite.

With respect to affective and sexual relationships with women, some individuals were absolutely reluctant to have such ties. This tendency can be seen through a quantitative approach, which shows a great disproportion between married and unmarried men. Out of the 123 registered sodomites, only 10 individuals declared that they were married, 106 were unmarried, and there is no data for 7 of them. The high number of single men (86%) can be explained in part by the number of underage males involved—though the vast majority of them were old enough to be married, that is, they were over fourteen years old. Among the adult sodomitical males, moreover, we need to distinguish ecclesiastic population: out of the 83 single adults, 16 were ecclesiastics, representing 19 percent of single adult males and 13 percent of the total register.

In sum, the 67 single sodomites eligible for marriage (i.e., the secular population over fourteen years of age) amount to 54 percent of those detailed in the register—a number that seems to confirm a lack of regard for formal relationships with women. Nevertheless, even when sodomites did marry, an aversion to sexual contact with women can sometimes be observed. This is expressed, for example, by an indigenous man who had been courted by a *vecino* (citizen) of Huamanga, one Juan de La Plata; this man certified "that it was a long custom of Juan de La Plata to seek the company of male Indians *[indios]* from the Guanta valley and that he disregarded his wife because he kept requesting the *indios*."[47] Though such individuals were married men, the preference for having sexual contact with other males leads us to think about matrimony as a social mandate imposed by a society bound by gender restrictions rather than as a "natural" condition of the sodomitical experience.

Doctor Gaspar González de Sosa experienced a similar situation, even when the ecclesiastical dress he wore forbade, in theory, formal or informal ties with women. Given his preference for having sexual contact with other men, when he had carnal access with a woman, he tried to enact sodomitical relations. According to the statement of a *mulata:* "The said doctor fumbled to grab her ass *[culo]* to penetrate it with his *carajo,* then she tried to turn around, facing down, and said she didn't want it that way but the usual way, through the *coño,* and the doctor said he only wanted it in the ass *[por el culo]*."[48]

Such forms of behavior seem to indicate a resistance to choosing the socially expected object of desire, which is confirmed by the statements of many sodomites. The apothecary from Potosí, Juan González, told how on his way to Villa Imperial, a few years before being tried as an accomplice of Doctor Gaspar González de Sosa, he had committed the nefarious sin with a man named Escobar from Ciudad de Panamá. In order to give further details to his interrogating judges, he described his sexual partner as a man of "no more than thirty years of age more or less with a broad back and black beard and a very big moustache."[49] He also described another subject with whom he had committed the same crime, someone whose name he could not recall but who was a "tall and slim boy [mozo] with a black beard." The description González gave went beyond juridical requirements; the attention he paid to physical details—"broad back," "tall and slim"— perhaps showed his attraction to the male body and looks (or he may have merely been responding to the tribunal's request for explicit detail).

A similar case was that of Alonso de Rentería, a Franciscan friar who, in 1597 at thirty-one years of age, confessed to the Inquisition judges of having practiced sodomy for a long time. According to his own declaration, "I sought out the biggest mozo and took him with me for him to give me protection, and at night I asked him to sleep by my bed and when the lights were out I called him."[50] If in this case the erotic was materialized through discourse, in other cases it was materialized anatomically. Such was the case with Damián de Morales, protector de naturales from the city of La Plata, and Antón de Tierra del Congo, who declared how Morales "fumbled through the pocket and said, 'You are fat Antón,' and fumbled and grabbed his buttocks and he went to the front to grab his parts."[51]

The rejection of women was not limited only to the personal experience of sodomites in terms of an object of desire. A social perception, too, connected any rejection of females with just the hint of nefarious sexual desire. For example, the inhabitants of the cities of Panamá and Santo Domingo accused Doctor Barros de San Millán—future judge of La Plata—of committing the crime of sodomy, "saying that he chased women but he was, in fact, their enemy" for, as an Audiencia official, having dealt with a series of scandalous amancebamientos, or cases of concubinage.[52] If, however, being the "enemy" of women could define the condition of sodomy, a "friendship" with them could dissipate any doubt in that regard. In this manner, the head of the case presented for the defense of one Antonio de Fuentes, accused of committing the nefarious sin, interrogated the persons testifying in the following terms: "Item. If [the witnesses] know the cause of what was expressed in the questions prior to this, and Antonio de Fuentes being also a Christian and such a person as it was said, and given that he is married and has a wife, and if he is a friend of women [amigo de mugeres] and can live with them; the witnesses believe and know for fact that Antonio de Fuentes did not commit and did not want to commit the crime against nature [i.e., sodomy]."[53]

The defense lawyer of Andrés Cupín, a slave of Doctor Barros, responded in a similar manner: "He [Cupín] could not possibly have committed such a crime, for he is a good Christian and he is fearful . . . and he has always been involved with women and he is married to a free *mulata* and he has always loved women, which he still does, and he is always with them."[54] In addition, Juan Ponce de León's mother stressed the futility of the process, given that her son was married to Catalina Marroquín, his legitimate wife.[55] The arguments of the defense show how the fact of being "married" or of being a "friend of women" could constitute a legal argument to favor those accused of sodomy.

Nevertheless, if the social discourse of the sixteenth and seventeenth centuries recognized the existence of individuals prone to a feminine (or feminized) sexuality, it is because there were also other types of men for whom women did not constitute a pole of sexual attraction. In this sense, these sodomites seem to be more than sexually disordered: they are individuals who chose to live a nefarious sexuality, but in a largely exclusive manner.

Pelilargos, Afeminados, *and Transvestites*

A fourth element to take into consideration is the effeminate tendency of some so-called sodomites. According to David Halperin, the "effeminate" was a man who, apart from having a sexual preference for persons of the same sex, deviated from the norms of the surrounding European-elite-based militarist culture by preferring love to war; they were considered "soft men."[56] Here, however, the concept of effeminacy will be analyzed in connection to sodomitical practices, defining men who alter their roles, identities, or personal style in favor of the opposite sex, thus constituting a definition that is closer to the notion of "sexual inversion" proposed by Halperin.[57] In the end, the concepts of "effeminate" and "inverted" are tools of analysis that may require reformulation and redefinition, as some cases analyzed in this work show.

One of the main concerns of civil and ecclesiastic authorities was the uninhibited manner in which men approached their physical appearance. In 1648, the archbishop of Ciudad de Los Reyes prepared a document in which he informed the king of the state of his church members: "When I was reestablished in this Holy Church, by order of His Majesty, one of the first things I observed that needed to be remedied was the scandalous excess of hair and locks and other horrendous inventions with which many, and especially the young, profaned the holy dress, which is why in the general document for public sins I have added a clause forbidding such dress to the clergymen, due to the indignity of its state."[58]

This disposition generated a series of criminal cases in the ecclesiastical courts in which clergymen were reprimanded for how they wore their hair and dress. To illustrate this, I turn to a series of cases from the Archivo Arzobispal de Lima in which men were charged with the following: "wearing long hair, tied at the back, and locks," "wearing long hair in *guedejas y tufos* [long hair and locks]," "wearing the hair down to their shoulders," "wearing the hair long at the back," "wearing satin garments," etc.[59] An endless number of quotes is possible, since ecclesiastical processes for this cause were initiated in 1646 and reached extraordinary proportions after 1664. Between 1664 and 1666 alone, for example, of the 82 criminal cases registered in the ecclesiastical courts in Los Reyes, fully 27 dealt with clergymen's hair and dress (32.9 percent of the cases in those two years).

Even though this regulation could have been the result of a conservative attempt to resist new fashion trends and the needs imposed by the moral reformation of the clergy, the motivations were clear: "do not feminize yourselves by wearing long hair, and locks and other abuses of the hair" or by "provoking scandal with this superfluous and effeminate aspect."[60] What can be inferred from these quotes is that the concern involved an alteration not only in masculine aesthetics but also possibly in gendered roles and behavior.

Similarly, sixteenth- and seventeenth-century society also established a clear association between an effeminate appearance—as expressed through dress—and sodomitical sexuality. This was made clear by Alonso Fernández de Córdoba during the trial against the *protector de naturales* Damián de Morales. According to Fernández de Córdoba, the *corregidor* from the province of Carabaya "must have been a *puto* [one who was accustomed to committing sodomy], since he had given a local official *[alguacil]* named Hernando necklaces and blouses with lace that he had had made for himself."[61] The cellmates of Doctor Barro's slave Andrés Cupín, who had been systematically solicited by him, expressed similar sentiments. Since Cupín acted at night, his cellmates claimed to have recognized him by a beaded necklace that he wore over his doublet, which tinkled when he moved.[62] In this manner, effeminate dress not only allowed for a certain recognition of the individual who wore it, but also led witnesses to anticipate acts of sodomy.

The connection between "feminine dress" *(hábito mujeril)* and sodomy is clearly seen in the cases of Ponce de León and Damián de Morales, who tried to obtain sexual favors wearing women's clothing. According to Antón de Tierra del Congo's statement, one night Damián de Morales told him to go to a back room where an *india*—a female indigenous housemaid—was waiting to offer him sexual pleasure. Antón was greatly surprised when he discovered that the *india* was no other than Damián de Morales himself, who had "painted his hands and face black and wore an Indian woman's dress and *azo [acsu] y lliquilla [lliqlla]* and lay in her bed and called Antón saying, 'Come here, I love you very much, Antón.'"[63] Also obscured by the darkness of night, Ponce de León stopped an *indio* called Yanque in an alley and said to him, "'Come, I will give you a *patacón*,' even though the witness did not see the money, 'I am a woman dressed in men's clothes, let us do it, do it to me,' and the witness was scared away."[64] In both cases, the men requesting sex had adopted feminine attire and behaviors, although it is not clear whether this was a way of living for them or merely a strategy of seduction to obtain desired results, or both.

The famous trials initiated in Mexico City on September 27, 1657, also cast some light on the ways in which women's dress may have indicated sodomitical desires.[65] According to the statements registered, Juan de la Vega was "an effeminate *mulato* popularly known as 'Cotita,' which is the same as 'Mariquita,'" who would dress as an Indian or *mestiza* woman in the city, wearing a piece of cloth called a *melindre* on the head and a white doublet with color laces hanging from the sleeves.[66] Interestingly, the *melindre*, used to tie the hair back, was defined in a 1611 dictionary also as "delicate food, often used as a sweet. From it derives the affected manner in which women talk, which is the reason why they are called *melindrozas.*"[67] Cotita's feminine airs could be observed in the *melindre* or head covering he donned, in the way he moved his hips *(quebraba la cintura)* when he walked, and in the position he assumed when he sat to make tortillas.[68] Similarly, there was Juan de Correa, a septuagenarian *mestizo* who hung around the city dressed as a woman and, together with other sodomites, "visited each other as if they were women and called themselves *niñas* [girls] and adopted the names of the pretty women in this town."[69]

Even when effeminate behavior did not constitute a necessary element for the definition of sodomy in this period, the adoption of feminine behavior or the use of womanly dress appeared as possible indications of nefarious desires. Even if such characterization preceded the stereotypes of gender and the definitions of the "feminine" and the "masculine," it is also true that the sodomitical practice and the desire of some men to become sexually involved with other men not only may have jeopardized (or reinterpreted) their masculinity but also may have favored a redefinition of their gender identities.

Putos, Bujarrones, *and* Enredados

One of the last elements I want to examine here is how sodomites identified and self-identified. As mentioned above, particular power relationships and colonial courts identified sodomites as subjects of lust: criminals or sinners circumscribed by a particular act, that act alluded to in euphemistic terms—"nefarious sin," "act against nature," "very atrocious act." They usually referred to sodomites with the terms *bujarrón* and, more frequently, *puto*. Bujarrón is not included in the Palencia (1490) and Nebrija (1495) dictionaries, while the Covarrubias dictionary (1611) defines it as "perforated"; thus it was used in colloquial language to identify persons who had been sexually penetrated. The term *puto*, however, is found in all three dictionaries. Whereas in the Palencia dictionary it is related to the idea of being rotten, in the Nebrija it is more accurately defined as one who suffers *catamitus*—a term used in Antiquity to refer to the sexually inverted.[70] The Covarrubias dictionary, in contrast, associates the term *puto* with the "nefarious," a more subtle term used in cultivated language and official discourse. Even when *puto* was included in the dictionaries of the time, its usage was restricted to colloquial contexts and to some erudite expressions.

Throughout the trials, the term in question is found to refer to the accused as a specific type of person who, even though belonging to a small group, was considered dangerous. Most of the deponents were clear in this regard and, when referring to those accused of sodomy, had no problems identifying them as such—speaking, for example, of "other persons whose names he does not remember, but treated as and called *putos*."[71] The reason they termed them *putos* was to identify a group of men different from their gender peers, individuals whom they saw as embodying an identity opposite to theirs. During the trial against Damián de Morales, a witness said that he had heard a certain *negro* (an individual of African descent) from the mines of Aporoma proclaim that "in that province there are *putos*."[72] A similar reaction was attributed to a slave who was in jail with Cupín when he woke his fellow inmates saying, "there are *putos* here" *(aquí ay putos).*[73] This distinction was used to separate men who disgraced their gender, turning them into a special kind of male who had to be punished by justice. The leaders of the trials paid attention to these accusations and, leaving aside the euphemisms of the day, asked the accused if "they had been involved in this trade of the *puto* for a long time."[74]

The scope of this term was not limited to external identification; it was also used for self-identification. This was manifested by Luis de Herrera, Diego Díaz de Talavera's servant, who on several occasions declared publicly "that he was a puto" *(que era puto).*[75] Probably their adoption of the term facilitated recognition among those who practiced sodomitical sexuality and encouraged them to identify as a group and even give assistance to one another. However, to speak of sodomitical identification in terms of an individual versus a collective perspective constitutes a problem that is methodologically hard to resolve. On the one hand, we can only have access to the vision that sodomites had of themselves through external signs—behaviors and acts—that were mediated through the words of others (including judges, attorneys, witnesses, notaries, etc.), which imposes significant limitations. On the other hand, there is the risk of extrapolating the current concept of "gay" identity to individuals in the past and through a kind of universal and transhistorical essence of homosexuality. But even if in an Old Regime society an identity of this kind could not emerge, this does not necessarily preclude other ("pre-modern"?) modes of recognition and subjectivity that sodomites of the period might have indeed developed and employed.

Some indications of this, albeit indirectly, can be traced in the case studies. One of the characteristics observed among sodomites in viceregal Peru is the tendency to group themselves socially and culturally around questions of sexual practice and preference. This can be seen in masculine spaces such as jails, ships, and monasteries, where sodomites attempted to come closer to one another and establish ties among themselves.[76] Even if this inclination can be interpreted as an efficient strategy to satisfy their sexual needs without suffering denunciations, it would be erroneous to reduce it so simply. The tendency to group can also suggest a process of self-recognition and the predisposition to generate ties of solidarity. In this sense, it is worth mentioning the accusations against Doctor Barros de San Millán in the trial against the slave Andrés Cupín, accused of sodomy in 1590. Based on a few statements, Doctor Barros was accused of having favored some sodomites while he was acting as *oidor* at the Audiencia de La Plata. First, he was accused of having negligently postponed the judicial process of a man named García Sánchez, from Panamá, who was granted freedom in spite of having been found guilty of the nefarious sin and was even granted a commission to take account of the inventories of deceased persons' estates.[77] Second, in the sodomy case against the slave of Licenciado Maldonado de Torres, not only was San Millán accused of having postponed the judicial process—which eventually led to the slave escaping prison—but he was also accused of being particularly worried about the slave and of having sent him food while he was in jail.[78]

In addition, there is some evidence of sodomitical social networks in the archival record, such as in the earliest trials against Doctor Gaspar González de Sosa for the nefarious sin of sodomy.[79] These trials took place in 1595, in Potosí, where the doctor was found guilty of committing such a crime with Juan González, apothecary of Villa Imperial. One of the most significant aspects of this case is the number of sodomites involved—about ten individuals, more than double the number generally implicated in sodomy cases. Another aspect to bear in mind is the rotation of sexual partners, which favored the fact that in one way or another, *putos* got to know each other socially. Finally, there is a significant correlation in terms of the professional activities of accused sodomites: an apothecary, two male nurses, two students, two priests, etc. These elements found in the first criminal trial of Doctor Gaspar González de Sosa suggest the existence of a network that was known and navigated by sodomites in Potosí—and which had echoes as well in the neighboring city of La Plata.[80]

BETWEEN JURIDICAL SUBJECTS AND SPECIES

In the criminal cases I have analyzed here, we observe that the everyday reality of "sodomites" exceeded the limits imposed by the theological and juridical discourses of power. In this sense, sodomites could assume different forms and identities, even when there existed hegemonic notions of sodomites as immoral subjects who were incapable of controlling their sexual instincts, but who, nevertheless, retained typically masculine appearances, behaviors, and attitudes.

As previously mentioned, Michel Foucault was an advocate of these types of interpretations and his work was a turning point in the distinction between the phenomenon of sodomy and the construction of homosexuality. Although his work constituted a logical proposal in reinterpreting the experience of sexual relations between men in modern Europe, many researchers have taken his model as an invitation to embark on their own historical reconstruction and analysis of the periodizations that have marked the difference between the experience of "sodomy" and that of "homosexuality."[81]

However, several factors—the manifestations of affect and eroticism among the sodomites studied here, the extension over time of their affective and sexual relations, the cases of feminization and of sexual preference for other men of "passive" roles, and the recognition and self-recognition as a special group of individuals—go beyond the concept of the unnatural "juridical subject" and show that, in some cases, sodomites maintained a *modus vivendi* that turned them into certain kinds of subjects. This delimitation also included the common population, which, as several witnesses observed, recognized the existence of peculiar men who were different from the norm. Even lawyers recognized this way of living when they stated that "the circumstances of sin are incredible and so old that many had lived like this for forty years, others thirty, or ten, twelve or eight."[82]

As Halperin has put it, the criticism of the radical distinction between sodomites and homosexuals does not imply an inversion of terms, that is to say, a rejection of any type of historical specificity or extrapolation of contemporary concepts to the past.[83] These individuals clearly did not constitute a "species," as nineteenth-century sexology saw homosexuals, nor were they a group with a political or collective identity, as the gay movement in the second half of the twentieth century would have it. However, they were not merely juridical subjects: some sodomites within the viceroyalty moved between both definitions.

The problem with the radical distinction between the sodomite and the homosexual lies within the notion of an apparently uniform sexuality—whether "heterosexual" or "deviant," "natural" or "unnatural"—whose fiction could only be sustained thanks to the systematic attempts to regulate and set norms for sexuality, whether through sixteenth-century juridical terms or nineteenth-century medical concepts. But what is evident from the analysis of documentation is the complexity of social phenomena and, particularly, the plurality of the ways of embodying the "sodomite" in the sixteenth and seventeenth centuries in the viceroyalty of Peru. Given that sodomy was intimately connected to the phenomenon of sexuality, perhaps it could not be any other way. Since sodomy was not merely restricted to the sexual act, but it also affected the physical, emotional, and psychological sensitivity of sodomites, the erotics and the pleasures sought through the act were as varied as the subjects themselves. Despite the discourse of jurists and theologians of the time, the criminal and Inquisition cases analyzed here reveal that through their experiences, some colonial Peruvian sodomites contradicted the dominant discourse regarding the "unnatural" nature of sodomy as well as gender and identity performances.

NOTES

1. Michel Foucault, *The History of Sexuality*, vol. 1 (New York: Penguin Books, 1978), 43.

2. Saint Thomas defined sin as every voluntary action opposing divine and human reason, preventing the natural course of things as established by nature. Saint Thomas Aquinas, *The Summa Theologica*, vol. 2 (London: Burns Oates & Washbourne Ltd., 1921), 122.

3. Francisco Tomás y Valiente, "El crimen contra natura," in *Sexo barroco y otras transgresiones premodernas*, ed. Francisco Tomás y Valiente (Madrid: Alianza Universidad, 1990), 35.

4. Bartolomé Clavero, "Delito y pecado: Noción y escala de trasgresiones," in Tomás y Valiente (ed.), *Sexo barroco*, 59.

5. Juan Pedro Gury, *Compendium theologiae moralis* (Barcelona: Apud Jacobum Subirana, 1864), 182.

6. Juan Donoso, *Diccionario teolójico, canónico, jurídico, litúrjico, bíblico, etc.* (Valparaíso: Imprenta y Librería del Mercurio de Santos Tornero y Ca., 1859), 532; Pedro de Calatayud, *Doctrinas prácticas que solía explicar en sus misiones el V.P. Pedro de Calatayud* (Madrid: Imprenta de Don Gerónimo de Ortega, 1798), 198.

7. Calatayud, *Doctrinas prácticas*, 198–99.

8. Miguel Ángel Chamocho Cantudo, "El delito de sodomía femenina en la obra del padre franciscano Sinistrati D'Ameno 'De Sodomía Tractatus'," *Revista de estudios histórico-jurídicos*, no. 30 (2008): 387–424.

9. *Novísima recopilación de leyes de España* (Madrid, en la Imprenta de Sancha, 1805), 428.

10. Ibid., 429.

11. Eve Kosofsky Sedgwick, *Epistemology of the Closet* (Berkeley: University of California Press, 1990; updated ed. 2008), 35.

12. The documentation analyzed for this paper was obtained from various repositories. On the one hand, I have analyzed the criminal processes remitted to the Royal and Supreme Council of the Indies for resolution, as well as cause of faith relations that Peruvian inquisitors brought to the Supreme and General Inquisition Council—currently kept at the Archivo General de Indias (AGI) and Archivo Histórico Nacional de Madrid (AHN), respectively. On the other hand, I have studied criminal processes initiated and dictated locally, which are kept mainly at Archivo y Biblioteca Nacionales de Bolivia (ABNB) and Archivo Arzobispal de Lima (AAL). Although for the qualitative analysis of this paper only twenty proceedings from AGI, three from AHN, two from ABNB, and five from AAL are quoted, the quantitative projections were based on the analysis of thirty-seven criminal proceedings initiated between 1550 and 1690 by civil, inquisitorial, and ecclesiastical justice within the jurisdiction of the viceroyalty of Peru. Such material allows us to study further the lives of 123 sodomites. I would also like to mention the thirty criminal proceedings conducted by Archiepiscopal Justice in Lima between 1646 and 1669 against ecclesiastics for wearing "womanly" garments.

13. Rafael Carrasco, *Inquisición y represión sexual en Valencia. Historia de los sodomitas (1565–1785)* (Barcelona: Laertes, 1986), 114.

14. Geoffrey Spurling has also analyzed the case of Dr. Gaspar González de Sosa, although he does so under the honor/dishonor paradigm, which was defined in terms of gender. Even though such an honor system originated from and was founded on relationships we would now call heterosexual, it was also used as a rubric to interpret the sodomitical relationships within which some men considered themselves more masculine than others. Geoffrey Spurling, "Honor, Sexuality, and the Colonial Church," in *The Faces of Honor: Sex, Shame, and Violence in Colonial Latin America*, ed. Lyman L. Johnson and Sonya Lipsett-Rivera (Albuquerque: University of New Mexico Press, 1998), 45–67.

15. AGI, Charcas 140, fol. 5v (personal foliation).

16. Ibid., fol. 2v.

17. AGI, Escribanía, 917B, fol. 357.

18. AGI, Escribanía, 119C, fols. 4, 37v.

19. AHN, Colección-Diversos, 45, N. 2, fol. 2.

20. Ibid., fol. 9v.

21. ABNB, EC.1603.14.

22. Ibid., fol. 33v.

23. Ibid., fol. 17v.

24. AGI, Charcas 140, fol. 2v.

25. Ibid.

26. Ibid., fol. 5.

27. Ibid.

28. AGI, Escribanía 917B, fol. 226v.

29. AGI, Charcas 140, fol. 1v.

30. Philippe Ariès, "Love in Married Life," in *Western Sexuality: Practice and Precept in Past and Present Times,* ed. Philippe Ariès and André Béjin, trans. Anthony Foster (Oxford: Blackwell, 1985), 138.

31. AGI, Escribanía 451A, fol. 4.

32. ABNB, EC.1603.14, fol. 33.

33. Ibid., fol. 16.

34. AGI, Charcas 140, fol. 1v. During the period studied, the expression "as if they were man and woman" was commonly used to describe male sodomitical relationships. After all, sodomy was not considered a peculiar way in which to live sexuality; it was considered an abhorrent and degenerate parody of relations enacted by members of the opposite sex. See Fernanda Molina, "Más allá de la sodomía: Notas para el estudio de las (homo)sexualidades (pre)modernas en América Latina," *Revista Sudamérica,* no. 1 (2012): 199–219; and Zeb Tortorici, "'Heran Todos Putos': Sodomitical Subcultures and Disordered Desire in Early Colonial Mexico," *Ethnohistory* 54, no. 1 (2007): 46.

35. Norbert Elias, *The Civilizing Process* (Oxford: Blackwell, 1994; rev. ed. 2000), 138.

36. ABNB, EC.1603.14, fol. 33.

37. Status, work, and age dependence also led to sexual submission and subordination. In these cases the relationships of power were turned into nonconsensual sexual ties in which the socially more powerful individual sodomized the less powerful one. Even though this was a common paradigm in sodomitical relationships during colonial times, there is evidence of cases in which the socially dominant individual disregarded his role of "agent" and not only inverted the passive/active paradigm in sexuality but also altered the consolidated social positions.

38. ABNB, EC.1603.14, fol. 16.

39. AGI, Charcas 140, fol. 5v: "el dicho doctor avia mandado que el dicho Diego Pobrete le llamasen don Diego Mexia de que se rio mucho este testigo por lo aver visto en el avito que le vio en la carzel."

40. Given the fragmentary state of the sources—either because they have been lost, deteriorated, or destroyed—the quantitative data is partial and approximate.

41. AGI, Charcas 140, fol. 1v. "Fray Luis" is unidentified.

42. "Siendo este confesante paciente y el dicho fraile agente": AGI, Charcas 140, fol. 2.

43. AGI, Escribanía 504C, fol. 23.

44. Ibid.

45. Ibid., fol. 21.

46. AHN, Libro 1028, fol. 202v.

47. AGI, Escribanía 504C, fol. 1v.

48. AGI, Charcas, 140, fol. 2. The terms *carajo* and *coño* in early modern Spanish are colloquial terms used respectively to refer to the penis and the vagina.

49. Ibid., fol. 2v.

50. AHN, Inquisición, Libro 1036, fol. 314.

51. ABNB, EC. 1612.9, fol. 3v.

52. AGI, Escribanía 917B, fol. 356. In many cases the accusation of sodomy—whether real or fictitious—constituted an efficient way of damaging a rival or competitor's reputation, which is why it usually took place in social situations of conflict.

53. AGI, Justicia 855, N11, fol. 66.

54. AGI, Escribanía 917B, fol. 220.

55. AGI, Escribanía, 504C, fol. 89.

56. David Halperin, *How to Do the History of Homosexuality* (Chicago: University of Chicago Press, 2002), 104–37.

57. The premodern terms for the inverted were *catamita* and *pática*, for men, and *tribada* for women. The term *inversion* was coined by sexology in the late nineteenth century. See David Halperin, "Homosexualidad una categoría en crisis," in *Dictionnaire des cultures gays et lesbiennes*, ed. Didier Eribon and Arnaud Lerch (Paris: Larousse, 2003).

58. AGI, Lima, 302, s/f.

59. AAL, Causas Criminales, Legajo XV, expediente 27; Legajo XVI, expediente 21; Legajo XXII, expedientes 2, 14, and 18.

60. AAL, Causas Criminales, Legajo XXII, expedientes 5 and 11.

61. ABNB, EC.1612.9, fol. 9v.

62. AGI, Escribanía 917B, fol. 208.

63. ABNB, EC.1612.9, fol. 7v. The *acsu* (dress) and *lliqlla* (wide woolen shawl) were clothes worn by indigenous women.

64. AGI, Escribanía 504C, fol. 3v.

65. Although the quoted case has been lost, the information on this case was found in a copy of a letter sent by the viceroy of Albuquerque to the king on November 15, 1658; another missive from the *alcalde del crimen*, Juan Manuel de Sotomayor, dated November 19, 1658; and a list of the accused and a summary of the statements currently kept at the Archivo General de Indias in Seville. See Serge Gruzinski, "The Ashes of Desire: Homosexuality in Mid-Seventeenth-Century New Spain," trans. Ignacio López-Calvo, in *Infamous Desire: Male Homosexuality in Colonial Latin America*, ed. Pete Sigal (Chicago: University of Chicago Press, 2003), 197–214; Federico Garza Carvajal, *Butterflies Will Burn: Prosecuting Sodomites in Early Modern Spain and Mexico* (Austin: University of Texas Press, 2003), 171–83.

66. AGI, México 38, N. 57, 3, fol. 1.

67. Sebastián de Covarrubias, *Tesoro de la lengua castellana o española* (Madrid: por Luis Sanchez impresor del Rey, 1611), 545. Other dictionaries define it as: "melindre: delicado, suave, limpio" (delicate, soft, clean)—for example, Baltasar Henríquez, *Thesaurus Utriusque Linguae Hispanae et Latinae, Omniun Correctissimus* (Madrid: in the typography of Juan García Infançón, 1679), 149v. Years later, *melindre* would refer to, among other meanings, "la afectada y demasiada delicadeza en las acciones o el modo" (the affected and exaggerated delicacy in actions or manner): Real Academia Española, *Diccionario de la lengua castellana. Tomo IV* (Madrid: por lo herederos de Francisco de Hierro, 1734), 534.

68. AGI, México 38, N. 57, 3, fols. 1–2.

69. Ibid., fol. 3.

70. In the Palencia dictionary, *catamita* is defined as defined as "the weak among the weak" *(floxo dende los floxos)* and is associated with the mythological hero Ganymede, a young and handsome Trojan prince and Zeus's lover. Alfonso de Palencia, *Universal vocabulario en latín y en romance*, vol. 2 (Sevilla, 1490), fol. ccclxxxxviii. Cf. José Antonio de Nebrija, *Vocabulario español-latino* (1495; Salamanca, 1995), fol. lxxxv.

71. ABNB, EC.1603.14, fol. 6.

72. ABNB, EC.1612.9, fol. 6v.

73. AGI, Escribanía 917B, fol. 205v.

74. AGI, Justicia 1181, N. 2, R. 5, fol. 6v.

75. ABNB, EC.1603.14, fol. 28.

76. Fernanda Molina, "La sodomía a bordo: Sexualidad y poder en la Carrera de Indias (Siglos XVI–XVII)," *Revista de Estudios Marítimos y Sociales* 3, no. 3 (2010): 9–20; and idem, "El convento de Sodoma: Frailes, órdenes religiosas y sexualidad en el Virreinato del Perú (Siglos XVI–XVII)," *HISTOIRE(S) de l'Amérique latine* 9 (2013): 1–17.

77. AGI, Escribanía 917B, fol. 312v.

78. Ibid., fol. 310.

79. AGI, Charcas 140.

80. A sodomitical network is also revealed by Serge Gruzinski in his study of *novohispano* sodomites, "Las cenizas del deseo," 275–77.

81. A brief account of the studies that worked under this paradigm can be found in Helmut Puff, *Sodomy in Reformation Germany and Switzerland, 1400–1600* (Chicago: University Chicago Press, 2003), 3–6. See also Randolph Trumbach, "Gender and the Homosexual Role in Modern Western Culture: The Eighteenth and Nineteenth Centuries Compared," in *Homosexuality, Which Homosexuality?*, ed. Dennis Altman, Carole S. Vance, Martha Vicinus, and Jeffrey Weeks (Amsterdam: Dekker/Schorer, 1989), 151–53.

82. AGI, México 38, N. 57, 1, fol. 1–1v.

83. Halperin, *How to Do the History of Homosexuality*, 28.

8

Incestuous Natures

Consensual and Forced Relations in
Mexico, 1740–1854

Lee M. Penyak

*As a weak and miserable man I had the misfortune to become involved with
my first cousin and . . . after promising to marry her . . . she finds herself
pregnant. I fear her father will kill her or cause a scandal if he finds out. . . .
[I want] to save my soul and remedy this [situation] by marrying her and
restoring her honor.*

JOSÉ RAFAEL DE URIBE, HUICHIAPAN, 1772[1]

*Some factors work in Patricia Nieto's favor [to receive a reduced sentence
after confessing to daughter-father incest and bearing a child], such as her
crude and poor upbringing, total subjugation to her father, and . . . her abandonment by a family that cannot be expected to provide any assistance.*

MAGISTRATE, QUERÉTARO, 1854[2]

The expression "crime against nature" is usually associated with sodomy, the sexual sin in colonial Mexico that included homoerotic activities, bestiality, masturbation, and nonprocreative heterosexual intercourse. The 1817 *Diccionario de la
lengua castellana* makes clear, however, that incest—"a carnal sin committed by
relatives within prohibited degrees"—also received the designation *contra natura*.[3]
Despite placing sodomy and incest in the same category, ecclesiastical and civil
officials roundly condemned the former but maintained a nuanced perspective on
the latter. Generally speaking, they found incest nefarious and unnatural when
committed by close relatives and when violence was involved, but they considered
it understandable and natural when cousins sought to marry their social equals.
Incest cases from late colonial and early modern Mexico reveal how patriarchy
and marriage buttressed order and stability in these periods, how social elites
manipulated the concepts of honor and purity of blood for their own benefit, how

ecclesiastical officials balanced the desires of parents and children in spousal selection, and how males occasionally subjected wives, children, and other vulnerable household members to violence.

Seventy-four criminal and ecclesiastical incest trials from the central region of Mexico are examined in this study, forty-eight prior to Mexico's independence in 1821 and twenty-six from after independence until 1854. The years under investigation correspond to Mexico's "middle period." This era allows scholars to analyze changes and continuities in laws and social attitudes as Mexico moved from colonial to independent status. Thirty-eight cases involve incestuous relationships between in-laws, parents and children or step-children, half-siblings, uncles and nieces, and a grandmother and her stepson. One man engaged in sexual activity with two sisters; another man with a woman and her daughter. Sixteen trials concern females who were raped by male family members. The remaining eighteen cases focus on marriage petitions (dispensations) to enable close relatives to marry. Spaniards, creoles (children of Spaniards born in the New World), and Indians make up the majority of those people examined in this study, representing 40 percent and 37 percent respectively. *Mestizos* (Spanish and Indian ancestry) account for 17 percent, mulattoes (European and African ancestry) 4 percent, and *castizos* (European and mestizo ancestry) 2 percent. Tables 3 and 4 distinguish nonviolent and violent incestuous relationships (excluding dispensation requests) and provide sentences and ancillary information. Incomplete trial records account for discrepancies in the total number of cases and the number of cases in the tables.

Prohibitions against incest generally stem from the desire to forbid the propagation of the species within the same family. The Old Testament threatens with death and curses those who engage in sexual relations with their parents, siblings, grandchildren, and in-laws. The Old and New Testaments state that children should separate from parents and form new families.[4] Doctors of the Catholic Church such as Saint Augustine and Saint Thomas Aquinas viewed incest as the product of innate selfishness and lust. Augustine wrote, "The demands of charity are most perfectly satisfied by men uniting together in the bonds that the various ties of friendship require." Aquinas concurred, and added, "There is essentially something unbecoming and contrary to natural reason in sexual intercourse between persons related by blood [though] there is not the same essential unbecomingness attached to other persons who are related to one another not directly but through their parents."[5] Vicente Ferrer, a Spanish Dominican friar, in his *Suma moral para examen de curas y confesores*, published in Mexico City in 1778, relied on the writings of Aquinas to examine forms of lust, including incest, that led to mortal sin. Ferrer wrote that the abject nature of incest increased according to the degree to which two people were related to one another.[6] Accordingly, ecclesiastical officials in colonial Mexico distinguished between direct and collateral lines, the former running through one's parents' parents and the latter through one's cousins.

TABLE 3 Nonviolent Incest Cases (Excluding Dispensation Requests): Relationships and Sentences*

Sister and Brother
   Woman banished (1809)

Sister-in-Law and Brother-in-Law
   Sentence not provided (1755)
   Both imprisoned and then set free; to cease further contact (1755)
   Sentence not provided (1755)
   To cease further contact; woman banished (1791)
   To cease further contact; both told to pray (1796)
   Both sentenced to 6 months in prison (1832)
   Both imprisoned and then set free; to cease further contact (1837)
   Both imprisoned and then set free; to cease further contact (1842)
   Both imprisoned and then set free; told to confess (1842)
   Woman 1 year of *recogidas;* man 2 years of military service (1843)
   Both sentenced to 4 months in prison; to cease further contact (1848)

Cousins
   Imprisoned, excommunicated; to cease further contact, pay court costs (1740)
   Marriage license denied; man banished (1758)
   Dispensation granted and couple married (1784)
   To cease further contact; both told to pray (1790)
   Both freed after unspecified time in prison (1843)

Father and Daughter
   Man given 50 lashes and sentenced to 4 years in prison (1798)
   Woman sentenced to 8 years of *recogidas* (1839)
   Both sentenced to 1 year in prison (1841)
   Man sentenced to 6 years in prison; woman to 2 years of seclusion (1843)

Father-in-Law and Daughter-in-Law
   Sentence not provided (1756)

Step-Grandmother and Step-Grandson
   Man freed from unspecified prison term; to cease further contact (1832)

Stepfather and Stepdaughter
   Sentence not provided (1756)
   Dispensation denied; further contact prohibited (1790)
   Pardon granted; woman banished (1821)
   Pardon denied; unspecified prison terms for both (1821)

Uncle and Niece
   Dispensation granted (1796)

Unrelated Man Has Sex with Two Sisters
   Man sentenced to 3 years in prison then freed to marry 2nd sister (1838)
   Man sentenced to 2 years on public works projects; 2nd sister sentenced to 1 year in prison (1841)

Unrelated Man Has Sex with Woman and Her Daughter
   Man sentenced to 1 year in prison (1839)

*Relationships not provided in 23 cases

TABLE 4 Violent Incest Cases: Relationships and Sentences*

Brother-in-Law Raped Sister-in-Law
Sentenced to 3 years on public works projects (1806)

Male Cousin Raped Female Cousin
Sentenced to 5 years in prison (1791)

Father Raped Daughter(s)
Sentenced to 10 years in prison (1771)
Sentenced to death for raping two daughters (1790)
Sentenced to 3 years on public works projects (1809)
Man pardoned after unspecified time in prison; woman banished (1820)
Sentence not provided (1820)
Man sentenced to 6 years in prison; woman to 3 years of seclusion (1854)

Half-Brother Raped Half-Sister
Sentenced to 8 years in prison (1789)

Husband of First Cousin Raped Victim
Sentenced to 6 years in prison and 200 lashes (1770)

Stepfather Raped Stepdaughter
Man freed after unspecified prison term; woman forced to leave house (1763)
Sentenced to 4 years in prison (1789)
Mother of girl dropped charges; man freed after unspecified time in prison (1796)
Man to reunite with wife and cease further contact (1805)
Man fled area; unresolved (1810)

Uncle Raped Niece
Man pardoned after unspecified time in prison and fined (1820)

*Sentence is for man unless otherwise specified

Spanish law codes and confessional manuals delineated the types of incestuous relationships condemned by the state and the church. Castile's thirteenth-century law code, the *Siete Partidas,* defined *incestus* as "a sin a man commits when he knowingly lies with one of his female relatives, or with a female relative of his wife, or with any other woman within the fourth degree; or where he lies with his step-mother, or with his mother, daughter, sister-in-law, or daughter-in-law; or where anyone lies with a woman belonging to a religious order; or with his adopted daughter or with his godmother. The same rule applies to women."[7] The 1733 confessional manual by Agustín de Quintana, a Dominican missionary and philologist from Oaxaca, categorized blood relations into four degrees:

First Degree (grandfather, grandmother, father, mother, son, daughter, grandson, granddaughter, older brother, younger brother, older sister, younger sister); Second Degree (uncle, father's brother; uncle, mother's brother; aunt, father's sister; aunt, mother's sister; male first cousin, female first cousin; nephew, son of brother; nephew, son of sister; niece, daughter of brother; niece, daughter of sister); Third and Fourth degrees (indistinct from one another because the same words are used for both) . . . such as uncle, aunt, cousin, nephew, [and] niece.[8]

Quintana also listed relations by marriage or affinity included in the category of incest: "father-in-law, mother-in-law, brother-in-law, sister-in-law, son-in-law, daughter-in-law, step-father, step-mother, step-son, step-daughter, father-in-law of one's son or daughter, mother-in-law of one's son or daughter, spouse of one's own brother-in-law, spouse of one's own sister-in-law, godfather, godmother, god-son, goddaughter."[9]

Priests relied on confessional manuals to administer the sacrament of penance properly, and these primers left little room for confessants to claim ignorance of Church doctrine. A manual published in 1731 by Angel Serra, a Franciscan missionary from Michoacán, for instance, listed questions pertinent to discussions about the sixth commandment, such as, "[have you had intercourse] with your relatives . . . with your in-law by baptism or confirmation . . . daughter-in-law . . . your own father . . . a relative of your husband . . . son-in-law . . . father-in law?"[10]

Spanish monarchs considered marriage the linchpin of all cultural institutions and a vehicle with which to establish responsibilities and rights inherent in paternity and filiation. The *Siete Partidas* detailed why marriage is indispensable for a well-regulated community:

> Wherefore, since God Himself, by Himself, established this regulation of matrimony, it is one of the noblest and most honorable of the seven Sacraments of the Holy Church and for this reason it should be honored and observed, as being the first of them, and because it was made and ordained by God Himself, in Paradise, which is, as it were, His own particular house; and, also, as it is the support of the world, and causes men naturally to live a regular life and one free from sin, and without which the other six Sacraments can neither be maintained nor observed. For this reason we have placed it in the middle of the Seven Partidas of this book, just as the heart is placed in the middle of the body where is situated the spirit of man, from which life proceeds to all his members.[11]

Courts in colonial Mexico promoted and protected the institution of marriage in the belief that moral individuals in stable families buttressed the order and stability of the realm. Ecclesiastical tribunals investigated incidents of unnatural sex and unnatural unions because they violated God's laws and ridiculed the institution of marriage.[12]

Betrothed couples in late colonial Mexico were required to submit a *diligencia matrimonial,* or marital investigation, to their parish priest to prove that no impediments existed.[13] The first step required meeting with the parish priest, who noted their names, ages, origins of birth, racial statuses, current residences, and whether or not they were baptized, legitimate offspring, and had chosen freely to marry one another. The priest then asked if they were related to each other by blood or by spiritual ties. Couples within the fourth degree of consanguinity were required to provide extensive information on their family histories, which officials sometimes fashioned into a chart or diagram. The priest also read the banns from the pulpit on three Sundays or days of holy obligation to inform the community of the impending marriage and give parishioners the opportunity to prevent the celebration of an unnatural union.[14] Couples related to each other within prohibited degrees of kinship required episcopal dispensation to marry.[15] Direct blood descent—a dire impediment—generally excluded couples from marriage. Cousins who sought to marry—a preventive impediment—usually received favorable outcomes. Couples with dire impediments who had initiated sexual relations were arrested and subjected to lengthy trials. Couples with preventive impediments who had initiated sexual relations prior to submitting the *diligencia matrimonial* were sometimes incarcerated for brief periods of time, though more frequently they were forbidden to see each other until their case was resolved and told to confess their sins to a priest.[16]

Privileged Spanish and creole youth were groomed to adopt the values, beliefs, and norms of their parents and peers, and were predisposed to court and marry members of their kinship group.[17] They rationalized discrimination against indigenous, African, and multiethnic peoples on the grounds of race, honor, and legitimacy. Racial purity demanded one's ability to prove "clean blood" *(limpieza de sangre),* that is, the absence of Moorish, Jewish, Indian, and African ancestry. Honor and reputation, according to the *Siete Partidas,* were afforded to "a man who lives justly and according to the law and good customs, and has no defect or blemish in his character."[18] Propriety demanded the observance of Christian sexual standards, including engendering legitimate children. Illegitimate children were disqualified from prestigious and lucrative positions in society, and largely excluded from inheriting their father's wealth.[19]

Spaniards and creoles occasionally complained about the difficulty of finding suitable mates to marry within their kinship group. Marrying one's cousin was much preferable to the unnaturalness of marrying a social "inferior," and some members of the dominant class initiated romantic relationships with cousins prior to seeking dispensations to marry. Churchmen—the vast majority Spaniards and creoles themselves—accepted the racial and social constructs that maintained Spanish hegemony and generally sympathized with the plight of these couples.[20] Nora Jaffary examined more than two hundred routine dispensations in the Archdiocese of Mexico from 1765 to 1776. Most concerned petitioners from the white ruling class, and nearly all received episcopal approval. "The most common argument these applicants used to legitimate their dispensation applications," she noted, "was the canonical justification of *exigüidad del lugar,* or smallness of the place." In a case from Huexutla, for example, petitioners stated that "the *cortedad* (smallness) of such towns makes it difficult for those of *sangre limpia* (clean blood) to marry equally." In another instance, a creole petitioner who sought to marry his cousin stated that he was unable to find nonrelatives to marry, since "we are related to everybody in this region."[21] Cousins continued to seek dispensations to marry well into the nineteenth century because of the supposed lack of suitable partners. In 1842, a judge in Temascalcingo noted that "it would not be easy for [the couple] to find consorts because [their town] is practically composed of relatives."[22] In that same year, a priest from San Pedro Tejupilco asked the archbishop to grant a dispensation given "the smallness of the place . . . almost everyone is related."[23]

A 1772 dispensation case from San Juan del Rio demonstrates that some parents denied their progeny in order to maintain propriety. In that year, don Antonio Carabeo sought a dispensation to marry doña María Manuela de Espínola, who was pregnant with their child. One of the first documents in this dossier, however, is a copy of don Antonio's 1742 baptismal record stating that he had been born to "parents unknown."[24] Why would a man who had been orphaned at birth and who could not trace his ancestry need a dispensation to marry a close relative? As it turned out, don Antonio claimed to have recently learned the identity of his birth father, and that that man and the mother of doña María Manuela were brother and sister. Don Antonio then recounted the events surrounding his upbringing and current predicament. Abandoned at the home of one doña Francisca Méndez, this woman briefly cared for the orphan until he went to live with her daughter and her daughter's new husband, don José Joaquín Carabeo. From that moment forward, this couple raised young Antonio, and he adopted the Carabeo surname. In all likelihood, don Antonio was actually the illegitimate son of don José Joaquín and doña Francisca's (unnamed) daughter, and don Antonio's baptismal record indicated unknown parentage as a means to safeguard the reputations of his parents and their families. Raised in the Carabeo extended family, don Antonio claimed to have unwittingly fallen in love with his first cousin, doña María Manuela, and they now sought a dispensation to marry.

The prosecutor doubted that the couple had only recently learned the truth about don Antonio's birth family. "They had sufficient reason," he said, "at least to have doubts about their immediate kinship." He also wondered if don Antonio "committed incest to facilitate the dispensation." Questioned anew, don Antonio denied previous knowledge of his parentage and that he had commenced sexual relations to achieve a dispensation. He also reminded the court that "discredited and pregnant, it is doubtful [doña María Manuela] can find another man to marry." His comment underscored the limited options for women who had lost their virginity prior to marriage. No one involved in the case inquired into or commented on the identity of don Antonio's birth mother. Since her son did not intend to marry one of her blood relatives, there was no reason to humiliate her or her family. The archbishop granted the dispensation.[25]

FIGURE 6. Genealogy of José Rafael de Uribe and María Gertrudis de Uribe (1774). Mexico Historical Manuscripts, 1649–1886, Rare Book & Manuscript Library, Columbia University in the City of New York, exp. 747.

TABLE 5 English Translation of Genealogy of José Rafael de Uribe and María Gertrudis de Uribe (fig. 6)

Antonio de Uribe, brother of and father of	1st	Tomás de Uribe and father of
María Gertrudis de Uribe	2nd	José de Uribe suitor
Antonio Romero, brother of and father of	1st	Pedro Romero and father of
Polonia Romero mother of	2nd	Luisa Romero mother of
José Rafael de Uribe suitor	3rd	María Gertrudis de Uribe

Some couples assumed, correctly, that the Church usually granted dispensations freely. In a trial from 1774 (quoted in the first epigraph), don José Rafael de Uribe said that fragility led to "the misfortune to become involved with my [paternal] first cousin and [maternal] third cousin named María Gertrudis de Uribe." Officials compiled a chart (fig. 6, translated in table 5) to record this couple's shared genealogy. Don José admitted knowing their degrees of relatedness prior to their relationship, but "did not think it would be so difficult to get it [the dispensation]."[26] He said he had "taken her honor," "the aforementioned [María Gertrudis] finds herself pregnant," and feared that her father would "kill her or cause a scandal" if he found out about their relationship before the couple married.[27] As with the previous trial concerning the orphan don Antonio, the prosecutor inquired if Rafael de Uribe and María Gertrudis de Uribe had commenced sexual relations with the intention of forcing the bishop's hand, an accusation the couple denied. In an unusual move, the prosecutor asked don Rafael if he would be willing to contribute one thousand pesos to doña María Gertrudis's dowry as a precondition to the dispensation.[28] Don Rafael agreed, but said he could only do so if they married, since that amount represented one-fourth of his total wealth. The archbishop ordered spiritual penance for the couple and approved the request.[29]

Officials did not, however, rubber stamp all dispensation requests. Individuals who divulged information about their incestuous relationships but then ended their engagement risked punishment. In 1757, for instance, Agustín de Medina implored the ecclesiastical court to allow him to marry his first cousin, Gertrudis Eustacia de Zúñiga. She was already seven months pregnant, he explained, and he wished to marry her to protect their honor and to prevent any violence directed against him from the woman's parents. "Her parents don't want her to marry me," he stated, "and my uncle . . . and his son have threatened to kill me if I try." The ecclesiastical judge interceded on their behalf and suggested that the small size of their town (Tlachinol) made it difficult to find appropriate spouses, since "there are not more than five families of *gente de razón*" (nonindigenous, "rational" individuals) and "all are related to one another." Agustín's plans were frustrated, however, when Gertrudis Eustacia told court officials that she no longer wished to marry Agustín. He was banished thirty leagues from his home town for a period of six years, forced to give a general confession of his sins, and required to pray a third part of the Rosary every Friday for a year. Gertrudis was permitted to remain at her home, but was also required to confess and pray.[30]

A case from Toluca in 1800 demonstrates that even siblings might seek dispensations to marry, but that they risked dire consequences when admitting to their illicit relationships. José Rafael de Lara, a nineteen-year-old soldier, and his half-sister María Josefa Dolores Lara were arrested for living together and engendering a child. Lara sought permission to marry from a local priest, who threatened him with violence if they dared to continue their relationship. They did not heed his warning and were subsequently jailed and sentenced to two years on public works projects.[31]

Determining whether couples were related, and to what degree, often proved laborious. Magistrates in a 1740 incest case from Xilotepec drew a diagram (fig. 7, translated in fig. 8) to determine the family ties of Toribio de Roxas, a forty-seven-year-old mestizo, and Juana de Ximénez, a thirty-five-year-old castiza widow. Arrested after living in "illicit copulation" for more than a year, Toribio was immediately sent to jail and Juana to a *casa de depósito* (a home that provided supervisory custody).[32] Testimony by neighbors, relatives, and the couple revealed that Juana's first husband was Toribio's uncle; the prosecutor thus determined that they were related to one another by affinity. In their own defense, Toribio and Juana claimed to be ignorant of this blood tie when they began the relationship—an assertion refuted by witnesses and ultimately rejected by the judge. He ordered that a decree of their excommunication be affixed to the door of their parish church "until the aforementioned duly request mercy" and said that their punishment should serve "as an example to others." They were also forbidden to see each other. Unlike other couples who asked permission from the Church to sanctify their unions, this couple had lived together without originally intending to request a dispensation, and they were punished for their insolence.[33]

Many couples claimed to commence sexual relations only after securing a *palabra de casamiento*, or promise to marry, from each partner. The *Siete Partidas* had recognized the legitimacy of oral marriage promises, and the medieval Church considered couples bound together in unconsummated marriage once promises had been exchanged.[34] But the Council of Trent (1545–63) deemed marriages sanctified only when performed by a priest. Women who trusted their lovers to follow through with the promise did not necessarily risk the loss of honor as long as premarital sexual intercourse remained private before the wedding ceremony. If a man reneged on his commitment after the couple had begun sexual relations, however, a woman's reputation was usually tarnished and she faced familial and societal condemnation, especially if she were pregnant. Women who could prove that their partner had broken a promise to marry usually received a sympathetic hearing from officials. Generally speaking, Church and state officials encouraged these couples to marry or to cease further contact with one another.[35]

Though *palabra de casamiento* cases were more common among nonrelatives, a woman abandoned by her cousin might take him to court to make him honor his pledge. Such was the case with Juana Isabel Vega in 1784. A mestiza, she desired to marry her creole cousin, Mariano Vega. She claimed they had begun a sexual relationship after he had given his *palabra*. For his part, Vega admitted to the sexual relationship, but said he had not taken her virginity and had never made a promise to marry. Moreover, since he was a creole and she a mestiza, he told officials he preferred punishment to such an unnatural marriage. Mariano changed his mind after spending a month in jail. The final entry in this trial document notes that he obtained a dispensation to marry Juana Isabel.[36]

Three cases from Mexico City demonstrate the broad definition of incest employed in Mexico during the years of this study. On October 24, 1841, Pantaleón Márquez wrote a letter to magistrates from jail complaining about the injustice of

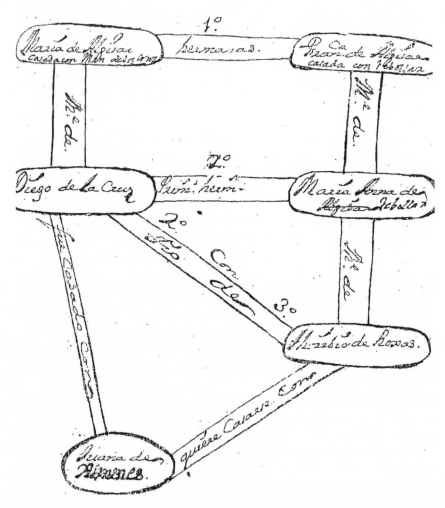

FIGURE 7. Genealogy of Toribio de Roxas and Juana de Ximénez (1740). Archivo General de la Nación, Mexico, Matrimonios, vol. 75, exp. 120.

his three-year sentence for incest. All he had done, he stated, was maintain a (sexual) *amistad* (friendship) with the sister of his former female lover. The public prosecutor replied that Márquez had been charged appropriately, since "the incest in question is by affinity in illicit copulation." Another example of the expansive definition of incest can be seen in the 1838 trial of Bartolo Cabrera, who was sentenced to three years for having had sexual relations with two sisters. In 1839, Ignacio Ortiz was sentenced to one year in prison because of the incestuous relation-

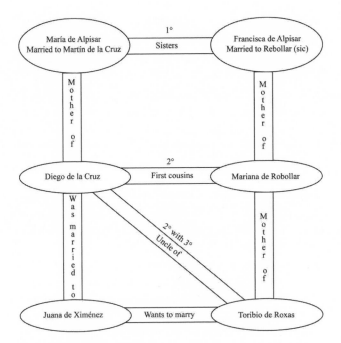

FIGURE 8. English translation of the genealogy of Toribio de Roxas
and Juana de Ximénez (fig. 7).

ship he had maintained first with a woman and later with her daughter.[37] Magistrates
in early national Mexico continued to use the expanded definition of incest developed by medieval jurists.

In cases of incestuous adultery, the guilty person and his or her spouse were
banned from participating in marital relations until the archbishop granted a dispensation entitling them to resume marital privileges. In 1790, for instance, Ignacio Blas Méndez forgave his wife, Marcela Enríquez, for her "incestuous adultery"
with his first cousin. Their punishment and absolution show how the institution of
marriage served to regulate individual behavior and to consolidate the foundation
for social order. Don Juan Cienfuegos, the vicar general of Mexico City, upon confirming that the adulterers had confessed to their offense and that the guilty
woman requested the resumption of her marriage, wrote,

> I hereby condemn her and her accomplice by way of healthy spiritual penance . . .
> [and they are] seriously and effectively warned that the full extent of the law will be
> applied if they repeat the same error, making sure to cease communication in any
> form . . . nor giving the husband reason for a new complaint; in order to proceed
> with the resumption of their marriage, I order that these materials be sent to the
> Chamber Secretary and to the office of the Excellent Lord Archbishop for him to

authorize, if in his superior capacity he deems appropriate, this woman fit for the use of her marriage, in which case she will be returned to her husband with the necessary charge that he treat her with the charity and love which he has promised.[38]

Ecclesiastical officials followed this protocol throughout the middle period. In 1842, José García and his sister-in-law María de Jesús López were apprehended in Temascalcingo for "having known one another carnally." The archbishop granted absolution from the sin of incest and authorized García "to ask and receive the conjugal debt [from his wife] to which he had been deprived."[39]

Magistrates were more concerned with preserving the marriage unions of incestuous adulterers than with punishing wrongdoers with severity. Eleven cases of incest involving sisters- and brothers-in-law reveal judicial leniency. Those found guilty typically spent only a few weeks or months in jail and were told to cease further contact with their accomplices. The 1832 trial involving Luis Islas and his sister-in-law Hilaria Ramírez was typical. The two confessed to having lived together for a period of two weeks "as if husband and wife."[40] The public prosecutor tried to persuade the judge to sentence the man to three years of service on public works projects and the woman to two years in jail. The defender assigned to represent Islas and Ramírez, however, argued that they should not spend more than six months in jail. His reasoning was instructive:

Who would doubt that the marriage of Islas and Gabriela Ramírez [the accused woman's sister and Islas's spouse] would be lost forever if the penalty asked by the minister were applied? No sacrifice is too great in order to conserve the peace of their marriage, and religion reinforces this. Gabriela Ramírez knows nothing about this now, [but] if she sees that her husband has been given the grave [penalty] of three years on public works she will infer that there was adultery . . . [and] two things will result: the first that perhaps she will never reunite with him, and the second that perhaps she will detest her sister Hilaria—things which truthfully should be avoided at all cost.[41]

The judge accepted the argument used by the defense and sentenced the man and his sister-in-law to jail for six months rather than three years. The preservation of marriage was the great panacea to the problem of illicit sexual activity.

Another method used to preserve the marriages of incestuous adulterers was to expedite the proceedings and banish the nonmarried partner from the area. A 1791 case from Xochimilco is representative of this type of resolution. In that year, Alejandro Dionicio and his sister-in-law Pascuala de Espíritu Santo were convicted after having maintained an affair during the previous year. Pascuala was now pregnant. As in the trial above that affected Hilaria Ramírez, the judge withheld information from Dionicio's (unnamed) wife to protect "the honor of the marriage [and the] tranquility and peace of these wretches."[42] He banished the sister-in-law from town and forbade any further contact between the accused. Dionicio was forced to pay the costs of his sister-in-law's relocation, but not the costs of raising their child.

The judge's decision probably meant that this child would never know his father or members of his mother's family, and that the mother and child were destined to struggle against impoverishment. But these were not primary concerns to magistrates. The *Siete Partidas* noted that women bore the moral and economic consequences of raising such children:

> Relatives in the direct descending line of the father are not bound to provide for those who are born [out of wedlock] of other women, as, for instance, in adultery, incest, or other fornications, unless they desire to do so, except where they act through courtesy, being naturally induced to bring them up and show them kindness as they would do to strangers, to keep them from perishing. But the mother, as well as the relatives in the direct ascending line of the latter, are obliged to provide for such children, when they have the means. This is the case because the mother is always sure that a child born of her is her own, and the father is not, so far as children born of this kind of women are concerned.[43]

Alejandro Dionicio's wife must have suspected that her husband and sister had participated in an incestuous relationship: they had been simultaneously imprisoned for three months, and once released, her noticeably pregnant sister suddenly moved away. Most important for our purposes, however, was that magistrates set aside personal convenience and parental responsibilities in the interest of preserving the sanctity of marriage and maintaining the Christian sexual code.[44]

The previous incest cases provide information about the lives of women and men who consciously entered into "unnatural" sexual relationships. Incest-rape trials present a very different scenario: females who without any complicity were forced into particular "unnatural" acts by male relatives. Officials used various words and phrases to describe rape. They usually employed the word *estupro* when a man coerced or tricked a young female virgin into having sexual intercourse, and *violación* when a man sexually assaulted a married woman, widow, or nonvirgin female. But the distinction between the two terms was never straightforward. *Estupro* was occasionally used to describe the sexual act of a female virgin who voluntarily participated in a consensual relationship. Some cases of marriage promise begin with an accusation of *estupro* or *violación*, even though it is clear that the woman was not raped. The term *rapto* was sometimes employed when women were abducted by strangers or willingly eloped with suitors. François Giraud analyzed these terms for his study on sexual violence in colonial Mexico and defined rape as "a sexual relation imposed upon a woman by force, without her consent."[45] This definition was used when selecting the sixteen incest-rape documents for this study. It must be noted, however, that some male relatives in "nonviolent" incest cases probably intimidated females into complying with unsolicited sexual advances.

Eight mothers and one father notified authorities of sexual assaults against their daughters. Three daughters denounced their fathers to magistrates. Priests began investigations in two cases. In one case, male and female family members carried the victim to the police station, and in another case an anonymous person, "jealous to protect God's honor," made a denunciation.[46] Data on race, marital status, age, occupation, and sexual activity are inconsistently noted in the case documents. Of the eleven men accused of rape for whom occupations are listed, four were low-ranking soldiers, four were tailors or weavers, one worked in a ciga-rette factory, one was a shoemaker, and one hauled materials at a mine. Available information on these men's ethnicity reveals that four were of Spanish descent, four were Indians, and one was a castizo. Only one of the sixteen men (a Spaniard) accused of rape could sign his name. The average age of rapists (out of a sample of ten) was 34.8, the youngest 25 and the oldest 46. The average age of victims (of a sample of eleven) was 13.4, the youngest 9 and the oldest 20. By comparison, men and women who entered consensual incestuous relationships were much closer in age: 31 and 27 (out of samples of eleven and eight), respectively.

Incest-rape trials reveal that sexual abuse was just one of many forms of vio-lence that existed in the households of victims. As Asunción Lavrin notes, "What we know today about [sexual behavior] was what became out of control, spilling from private chambers or hideouts to the public arena."[47] Spousal abuse, adulter-ous affairs, and illegitimate children became part of the public record once incest-rape cases were tried. In 1810, for example, María Urbana Pérez exposed the rou-tine domestic violence that occurred in her home prior to her husband's arrest for raping her daughter from a previous marriage. Although he had previously beaten his wife so severely that she suffered a broken arm, and she was also cognizant of his adulterous relationship with a neighbor, María Urbana Pérez finally refused to remain silent about the violence he committed against her thirteen-year old daughter, María Apolinaria García. While the mother was out of the house, Luis Antonio Paredes had entered the girl's bedroom and threatened to kill her if she resisted his sexual advances, and then raped her.[48]

An 1820 incest case shows how family members hid activities including unnatu-ral sex from neighbors and even relatives in order to maintain the illusion of a safe and functional home. In that year, María Ignacia Jaen told her mother: "You already know the bad life and beatings my father has given me." But what the mother did not know, she said, was that "three months ago, when you were not at home, he locked me in a room and threatened to kill me and . . . he satisfied himself for the first time and [then] three other times in other places and with the same threats."[49] As the trial unfolded, another well-kept family secret came to the fore: the victim's maternal aunt, María de la Cruz, who had lived with the family years previously and had died in childbirth, had also been raped by María Ignacia's father, but family members "had hidden [the truth] so as not to jeopardize the marriage."[50]

María Ignacia told her confessor about the rape after the first assault, and he spoke to her father, who "gave his word he would not commit that act again, and he controlled himself for a few days but he then returned with the same desire."[51] When María Ignacia told the priest of continued rapes, he arranged for her to go to a *casa de depósito* and then to a local convent, where she remained for about five months. When the same pattern resumed on her return home, she revealed the secret to her mother, who notified civil authorities. María Ignacia's father was imprisoned but released after only a few months, the recipient of a general pardon extended to most prisoners. As a condition of his pardon, however, he needed to secure his wife's forgiveness. She agreed to his release, as his absence, she stated, had caused "great [economic] need to me and my poor family." María Ignacia was not consulted by the judge prior to her father's release.[52] The priest was not reprimanded for failing to report the unnatural crime of father-daughter incest to authorities.

The failure to consider María Ignacia's physical safety and psychological well-being was characteristic of the subordinate position of children, especially girls, in the household. Civil and ecclesiastical law and confessional manuals recognized husbands and fathers as the ultimate authority in the home. A husband, by virtue of *patria potestas,* noted the *Siete Partidas,* ruled the household and dominated "all those who live underneath him."[53] The Fourth Mexican Provincial Council (1771) further affirmed the divine nature of patria and the "obedience, reverence, and honor owed by children to parents."[54] Fathers were sometimes asked during confession, "Have you spared the rod and failed to scold your children when they erred or when they were bad?[55] Children were asked, "Have you been disrespectful to your father or mother? Have you conducted yourself with anger and arrogance toward [them]?"[56] Obedient daughters were educated to respect and demur to their father's wishes.

Obviously, though, a father's authority did not include the right to engage in unnatural sex with his daughter. He who did so broke the social contract that justified patriarchy, damaged the myth of the home as a safe haven for women, and made a mockery of society's principal institution.[57] A tragic case from San Luis Potosí in 1771 demonstrates how officials intervened to punish this type of perpetrator and to restore order. María Ignacia García reported that José Antonio Manuel de Acosta, a man with whom she had had an illicit relationship ten years previously, had raped their daughter, María Olaya. Apparently, García and Acosta ended their relationship shortly after their daughter's birth, and García married another man. Following her husband's death, however, she and Acosta resumed their former relationship. The mother, returning home one day from an errand, noticed the daughter all bloodied and asked "who had done such damage," and María Olaya replied, "Daddy" *(Tata).*[58] Asked by officials to elaborate, young María testified that her father grabbed her, forced her onto the bed the family shared together, slapped her across the face, placed his hand over her mouth when she screamed, and threatened to kill her if she told anyone. To cover up his act, he washed his own blood-soaked shirt and doused the girl with water to hide the physical evidence of the assault. Her mother arrived while the girl was endeavoring to cleanse herself of the horror.[59]

Acosta responded in the way most men did when accused of rape: he denied everything. He rejected the accusation that he had raped the girl and said he and García had not had sexual relations ten years previously, which made it impossible for him to be María Olaya's father. When presented with the bloodied garments, however, he changed his story: he now confessed to having had sexual relations with María Olaya. Claiming they were consensual, he said she screamed and defended herself but that he could not restrain himself once his "member" *(miembro)* was inside her. He continued to insist that the charge of incest was irrelevant because the girl was not his daughter. María was sent to a *casa de depósito* during the remainder of the trial.

Acosta's court-appointed lawyer now adopted the typical stance of most public defenders: everyone was to blame except his client. The first scapegoat was the victim herself. Defenders scrutinized a woman's sexual reputation because they knew that judges gave lighter sentences to men who raped nonvirgins and sometimes no punishment at all if the women had reputations for promiscuity.[60] María Olaya, accordingly, was said to be curious about sex and the provocateur. He also argued that she would have struggled more if she had been raped. The lawyer referred to Law XII, Title I, Partida IV of the *Siete Partidas*, which, he said incorrectly, stated that girls as young as seven could marry "if *malice* makes up for age." The lawyer used the word *malice* to imply that ten year-old María Olaya was a temptress, ready for sexual intercourse, and of marriageable age under the circumstances.[61]

Acosta would probably have been found innocent if the trial had centered on his word against María Olaya's. A few factors, however, worked to María's advantage. First, the medical examiner determined she was the victim of *estupro*, in this case an indication that the child lost her virginity due to the assault. Second, two witnesses placed Acosta at the scene of the crime. Third, the girl's clothing was used as evidence and, indeed, ultimately forced Acosta to admit to having had sexual relations. And finally, the magistrate had caught Acosta in a lie: he said both that María Olaya was a willing participant and that she put up a struggle. Acosta was sentenced to ten years in prison.[62]

Acosta's lawyer had argued that María was sexually precocious because she shared a bedroom with her mother and other family members. While he used this tactic to mitigate his client's punishment, intimate living spaces did expose women and girls to sexual aggression that most people assumed only occurred outside the home. Females who relied on patriarchs for protection from external dangers frequently faced peril from within. Members of large extended families often lived together. Brothers and sisters sometimes shared the same bed or same sleeping area on the floor. Husbands and wives occasionally slept next to their children and their children's spouses. Aquinas wrote about the potential danger that existed when blood relatives "live in close touch with one another." "If they were not barred from venereal union," he reasoned, "opportunities of venereal intercourse would be very frequent."[63] Bishops and other members of the Church hierarchy at the Fourth Mexican Provincial Council (1771) implored clerics to prevent "the mixing that occurs when members of the two sexes sleep without [sufficient] separation in huts."[64]

Unfortunately, prohibitions against incestuous relations did not deter sexual abuse within the home. Nine-year-old María Candelaria, for example, lived in the same house as her thirty-year-old brother-in-law, Nicolás Varela. On Sunday, August 3, 1806, between three and four in the afternoon, Varela threw María Candelaria onto a bed, covered her mouth, and raped her. The court clerk carefully recorded the events: "having left her injured and bleeding copiously, he immediately made her comb her hair, in which place she left a lake of blood." Midwives who examined María said the rape "damaged the entire interior of her uterus." Varela was sentenced to three years on public works projects.[65]

As the above trials suggest, judges in colonial and early national Mexico relied on testimony from midwives to establish guilt and render judgment in sex crime cases. Midwives ascertained whether the female had recently had intercourse, whether she had been a virgin at the time, and if force had been used.[66] When in 1805 fifteen-year-old María Hilaria de Jesús accused her stepfather of raping her, the midwife determined that she had not been a virgin *(doncella)* at the time because she showed signs of "having had intercourse some time ago"—a statement that helped exonerate her accuser.[67] In another incest case, the lawyer who prosecuted Pantaleón Márquez (accused of having sexual intercourse with two sisters separately in 1841) noted that a midwife had determined that one of the sisters "had lost her virginity" to Márquez, a finding that contributed to Márquez's two-year prison sentence.[68]

Judges employed the *careo* (face-to-face confrontation) when the accuser and the accused provided conflicting testimony. Placed one in front of the other, they were given the opportunity to refute each other's previous statements. The *careo* was not foolproof, as accusers and the accused sometimes insisted on their own version of events. But this method worked in other instances, especially when judges uncovered discrepancies in testimony. Such was the case in an 1820 trial in Chalco. The ecclesiastical judge informed civil authorities that forty-five-year-old Gregorio Antonio Estebañez had "forced and taken the virginity of his eighteen-year-old stepdaughter," Victoriana María. She testified that Estebañez on three separate occasions had threatened to beat her if she did not have sex with him. "Placed in front of her father," Estebañez responded that "it was true that he had been with her but that he had done so out of rage because she had fled to Mexico [City, without his permission] but that he had not taken her virginity." Victoriana María said she had run away from home, but had done so after the first rape. Estebañez spent five months in jail prior to being released under a general pardon. Victoriana María was relocated to another town.[69]

Lawyers and judges sometimes emphasized extenuating circumstances, such as a person's indigenous background, as a means to explain a perpetrator's unnatural sex and lessen punishment. Indians of any age were automatically treated as minors before the law and assigned a *curador* or legal protector to represent them. Spanish kings, viceroys, and judicial officials looked upon Indians as a group worthy of special consideration and treated them as children in court. In 1784, Viceroy Matías de Galván sounded the paternalistic trumpet, declaring that protecting "the miserable Indians" was his primary concern. He also called attention to "their lack of education and the pernicious example of their parents."[70] The lawyer assigned to represent Manuel de Dios, accused of incest with his sister-in-law in 1843, emphasized his client's Indian status to petition for a light sentence. He noted the "immemorial practice of our courts to punish leniently all crimes of *incontinencia* especially with respect to the Indians whom even the Church has viewed with much indulgence on this matter."[71] Manuel de Dios and his sister-in-law, María Francisca Velázquez, were released from jail. Twenty years after independence, therefore, lawyers and magistrates still considered the Indians a group that needed special protection and consideration because of their presumed moral weakness and inability to adhere to Christian sexual ethics.

One's socioeconomic class and lack of education were also used in incest cases to explain behavior, as suggested in an 1841 trial against father and daughter, Crecencia Pacheco and Vicente Vargas. Their lawyer argued, "I have already stated in this case and in others of a similar nature, and I do not tire of repeating, that with this type of crime much consideration should be given to the offenders, especially when they belong to the miserable class and do not receive any education and are ignorant even of the basic rudiments of the Christian religion."[72] In 1848, Ignacio Cuseño y Palacios, the court-appointed spokesman for Vito Gutiérrez, used similar terminology to describe his client's incestuous relationship with his sister-in-law. "Belonging to the low class of people," he stated, "what knowledge could he have of the prohibitions established by law concerning persons who find themselves within a certain degree of relatedness and much less when this is by affinity?"[73] Gutiérrez was let go.

Sex crime suspects sometimes blamed the devil for their actions. Since at least medieval times, Europeans had associated the devil with jealousy, unnatural sex, and violence, and had blamed him for inducing sexual desires. A father who raped his virgin daughter claimed that the devil had "tempted" him. A step-father who committed a similar act said that the devil had "put this bad thought in his head."[74]

Some people may have believed that the devil made them stray from their usual good behavior. Most, however, seem to have stated what they believed officials wanted to hear or used this excuse because they were at a loss to explain their actions by other means. While lawyers and judges were quick to note the ethnic and economic backgrounds of their clients, they never mentioned that the devil could be held responsible for the errors of men and women. As scholar Fernando Cervantes has observed, the devil ceased to play a prominent role in Inquisition trials by the period under consideration here. As early as the 1730s, argues Cervantes, inquisitors viewed the devil and Satanic intervention as "the product of those 'fantasies and hallucinations' that were so characteristic of the rabble." By the second half of the eighteenth century, he continues, "It was not Satanic intervention . . . but human ignorance and weakness that was to blame for religious error . . . men were [now] free and rational agents."[75]

Three- to ten-year prison sentences seem minimal and general pardons unconscionable for rapists. For many of these men, however, a few years in Mexico's wretched prisons could actually be a life sentence. In 1804, Alexander von Humboldt estimated that only eight out of every one hundred persons of Spanish descent and six out of every one hundred Indians lived until the age of fifty.[76] In 1842, only 9 percent of the population overall reached the age of sixty.[77] The average age of men accused of incest-rape, out of a sample of eleven, was 32.2 years. Spain's paternalistic judicial system, moreover, sought to enforce laws while demonstrating benevolence and forgiveness. "Mercy and justice," according to the *Siete Partidas*, were the "two great qualities which every man especially kings and great lords should possess," and "grace . . . moves kings to pity toward those who have need of it." A king might issue a general amnesty to all prisoners to celebrate a royal birth, a military victory, peace accord, or because of his "love of our lord Jesus Christ."[78] The heinous actions of some perpetrators, such as José María Quijas, guilty of raping his two virgin daughters in 1790, were so damaging to society, however, that authorities were unable to show mercy. Quijas, for one, was sentenced to death. The judge said that this punishment would teach "a lesson to the public" and serve as "an example to those who witness it." Viceroy Juan Vicente de Güemes Pacheco de Padilla y Horcasitas sustained the verdict.[79]

Lawyers and judges in late colonial Mexico continued to acknowledge the importance of the *Siete Partidas* when determining culpability and imposing sentences, though nineteenth-century jurists conceded that the harsh punishments included in this ancient law code were seldom enforced. In 1843, in-laws María Francisca Velázquez and Manuel de Dios benefited from the more magnanimous spirit of early-national legal scholars. "Although a law from the third *Partida* imposes the death penalty on those who commit incest," stated the prosecutor, "it is well known that the rigor of this [law] and of similar laws on this matter has been completely diminished by virtue of the gentleness of our subsequent customs." The judge agreed; he referred to the *Partida* when rendering his verdict of guilt but sentenced this incestuous couple to "time served."[80]

Chronologically, the final case of incest in this study (quoted in the second epigraph) concerns the 1854 trial of Francisco Nieto and his daughter Patricia Nieto, whose relationship resulted in the birth of a child. This document demonstrates continuities in family dynamics and legal opinions in such cases until the mid-nineteenth century. Incest, especially in this degree, was depicted in this trial as "profoundly grave," "nefarious," and "so repugnant that it highly offends morality and for that reason public vengeance must be satisfied."[81] The tenor of this document suggests that this crime remained abhorrent, not because of the violation of this woman's body but because of its assault on the moral and social codes of the community.[82] The father's dominant position in the household was complete, as reference to his daughter's "complete subjugation" made clear. Despite her victimization, the judge noted that there was no recourse from harsh reality for unwed mothers like Patricia: she found herself in "an unfortunate situation due to having a baby to feed, suffering all of the subsequent hardships related to child rearing, and abandonment by a family that cannot be expected to provide any assistance." The view prevailed decades after independence that men like Francisco Nieto must reunite with their wives. Nor did the sentence include any provision that the father provide sustenance to his illegitimate offspring. Like magistrates before him, the judge acknowledged the existence of extenuating circumstances such as Patricia's "crude and poor upbringing" in order to mitigate her punishment. Finally, the close, if increasingly strained, working relationship between state and Church continued during the first decades of independent Mexico, as suggested by the motto "God and Liberty" used by the Ministry of Justice and Ecclesiastical Affairs, and found at the end of the document.[83]

Mexican magistrates during the middle period maintained nuanced perspectives about incest out of necessity. Not surprisingly, they made careful distinctions between the incestuous relationships of cousins who wished to marry and those between intimate family members, especially in cases of rape. Officials understood the class, race, and social demands of elites: endogamous relationships were essential to maintain the hierarchical construct of society. As Nora Jaffary notes, churchmen routinely granted dispensations allowing otherwise forbidden relationships, since "it was more important to preserve the sanctity of marriage in the potentially unstable social atmosphere of the colonial setting than to rigidly apply Trent's regulations on acceptable and unacceptable marital unions."[84] Sexual relations between in-laws and parents and children, however, clearly violated religious and cultural taboos. These unnatural relationships could not be tolerated because they threatened to destroy the survival of the institution of marriage, which, as stated in the *Siete Partidas,* served as "the support of the world and causes men naturally to live a regular life."[85]

More difficult to comprehend are the astounding measures taken by officials to preserve marriage unions in the face of horrendous violations of human dignity, such as lying to wives about their husbands' adultery, expecting wives to reunite with batterers and sexual predators, and depriving the victims of incest and their offspring of financial and moral support. Given that husbands and fathers exercised ultimate authority by virtue of *patria potestas*, many wives and daughters were forced to endure household violence or acquiesce to extreme demands. Economic dependence on males prevented women from calling attention to their situation and caused most to accept violent men back into the home. Women must have recognized the difficulty of confronting all-male courts, where officials had a vested interest in protecting patriarchal rights and preserving marriages whatever the cost. As a result, we do not know about those situations where women and children remained silent, received no support from family members who knew of abuse, or lived with family members who ignored or condoned crimes against nature. Even when violent incest cases forced magistrates to intervene in household governance, they never questioned patriarchal structure and the near indissolubility of the marriage bond, thereby bringing incest into conformity with "nature" in the process.

NOTES

The author wishes to thank Zeb Tortorici, Walter J. Petry, and Pamela Chapman for their helpful suggestions; Nora E. Jaffary for sharing select primary documents; and Ernesto Cabrera Villoro for providing research assistance.

1. Columbia University in the City of New York [hereafter CU], Mexico Historical Manuscripts, 1649–1886, Rare Book & Manuscript Library, exp. 747. All translations by author. Spelling of Castilian modernized and standardized for consistency.

2. Archivo General de la Nación, Mexico [hereafter cited as AGNM], Justicia, vol. 416, exp. 76, fols. 276–77.

3. *Diccionario de la lengua castellana compuesta por la Real Academia Española*, 5th ed. (Madrid: Imprenta Real, 1817), 487: "pecado carnal cometido por parientes dentro de los grados prohibidos . . . pecado contra natura o contra naturaleza."

4. Incest prohibitions in the Old Testament are found in Leviticus 18–20 and Deuteronomy 27, and in the New Testament in Matthew 14, Mark 6, 1 Corinthians 5, and Luke 3. On the need to form new families, see Genesis 2:22–24 and Mark 10:7–9.

5. St. Augustine and St. Thomas quoted in St. Thomas Aquinas, *Summa Theologica*, Pt. II-II, Q154, Art. 9, in *St. Thomas Aquinas, Summa Theologica: First Complete American Edition in Three Volumes*, trans. Fathers of the English Dominican Province (New York: Benzinger Brothers, 1947), 2:1823–24.

6. Vicente Ferrer, *Suma moral para examen de curas y confesores que a la luz del sol de las escuelas Santo Tomás dio al público*, parts 1–2 (Mexico City: Imprenta Nueva Madrileña de D. Felipe de Zúñiga y Ontiveros, 1778), 306.

7. *Siete Partidas*, Part IV, Title II, Law XIII, in *Las Siete Partidas*, trans. Samuel Parsons Scott (Chicago: Comparative Law Bureau of the American Bar Association; Commerce Clearing House, 1931), 891.

8. Agustín de Quintana, *Confessonario en lengua mixe, con una construcción de las oraciones de la doctrina christiana, y un compenedio de voces mixes, para enseñarse a prononciar [sic] la dicha lengua* (Puebla: Viuda de Miguel de Ortega, 1733; reprint Alençon: E Renaut-De Broise, 1890), n.p.

9. Ibid.

10. Angel Serra, *Manual de administrar los santos sacramentos a los españoles, y naturales en esta provincia de los gloriosos apóstoles San Pedro, y San Pablo de Michuacán [sic] conforme a la reforma de Paulo V y Urbano VIII* (Mexico City: Joseph Bernardo de Hogal, Ministro e Impressor *[sic]* del Real, Apostólico Tribunal de la Santa Cruzada en Toda Este Reino, 1697, 1731), 116, 120.

11. *Siete Partidas*, Part IV, "Here Begins the Fourth Partida Which Treats of Betrothals and Marriages," in Scott (trans.), *Siete Partidas*, 877.

12. A. Knecht, *Derecho matrimonial Católico*, trans. T. Gómez Piñán (Madrid: Editorial Revista de Derecho Privado, 1932), 1–3; Asunción Lavrin, "Introduction," in *Latin American Women: Historical Perspectives*, ed. Asunción Lavrin (Westport, Conn.: Greenwood Press, 1978), 36–37.

13. Dire impediments to marriage included consanguinity (direct blood descent), affinity (relations through marriage such as step-parents and step-children), previous religious vows (a promise to God of clerical vocation or chastity), different religious affiliation, bigamy, polygamy, male impotence, criminal activity, misrepresentation, and coercion. Marriages could be annulled if impediments were discovered after the fact.

14. Martine Segalen, *Historical Anthropology of the Family* (Cambridge: Cambridge University Press, 1986), 198.

15. Children born prior to the dispensation, however, were not legitimized by the marriage. In these cases, parents had to petition and purchase a separate dispensation to legitimate their children (a process referred to as *gracias al sacar*) in order for these offspring to "inherit equally with their legitimate full-blood siblings." Subsequent marriage legitimized the offspring of incestuous couples after 1803. See Ann Twinam, *Public Lives Private Secrets: Gender, Honor, Sexuality, and Illegitimacy in Colonial Spanish America* (Stanford: Stanford University Press, 1999), 233, 130.

16. Ramón A. Gutiérrez, *When Jesus Came, the Corn Mothers Went Away: Marriage, Sexuality, and Power in New Mexico, 1500–1846* (Stanford: Stanford University Press, 1991), 243–47; Richard Boyer, *Lives of the Bigamists: Marriage, Family, and Community in Colonial Mexico* (Albuquerque: University of New Mexico Press, 2001), 62; Christine Hunefeldt, *Liberalism in the Bedroom: Quarreling Spouses in Nineteenth-Century Lima* (University Park: Pennsylvania State University Press, 2000), 94. The *Siete Partidas* (Part IV, Title VI, Law IV, in Scott [trans.], *Siete Partidas*, 907) notes that cousins "on one side can marry those on the other, beyond the fourth degree."

17. A royal decree on marriage promulgated by King Charles III in 1776 strengthened parental consent for persons under the age of twenty-five who wished to marry. See Susan M. Socolow, "Acceptable Partners: Marriage Choice in Colonial Argentina, 1778–1810," in *Sexuality and Marriage in Colonial Latin America*, ed. Asunción Lavrin (Lincoln: University of Nebraska Press, 1989), 210–12.

18. *Siete Partidas*, Part VII, Title 6, Law I, in Scott (trans.), *Siete Partidas*, 1333.

19. Ann Twinam, "The Negotiation of Honor: Elites, Sexuality, and Illegitimacy in Eighteenth-Century Spanish America," in *The Faces of Honor: Sex, Shame, and Violence in Colonial Latin America*, ed. Lyman L. Johnson and Sonya Lipsett-Rivera (Albuquerque: University of New Mexico Press, 1998), 77.

20. Cousins who wished to marry and churchmen who granted dispensations shared "collective knowledge and accepted patterns of behavior." See Linda A. Curcio-Nagy, "The Language of Desire in Colonial Mexico," in *Emotions and Daily Life in Colonial Mexico*, ed. Javier Villa-Flores and Sonya Lipsett-Rivera (Albuquerque: University of New Mexico Press, 2014), 44.

21. Nora E. Jaffary, "Incest, Sexual Virtue, and Social Mobility in Late Colonial Mexico," in *Gender, Race, and Religion in the Colonization of the Americas*, ed. Nora E. Jaffary (Hampshire, Eng.: Ashgate, 2007), 95, 99–100.

22. AGNM, Bienes Nacionales, vol. 890, exp. 2, fol. s/n (9/7/1842).

23. Ibid. (9/19/1842).

24. CU, Mexico Historical Manuscripts, 1649–1886, exp. 75B.

25. Ibid.

26. Ibid., exp. 747.

27. Ibid.

28. A man found guilty of raping a woman or reneging on a promise to marry after he had taken a woman's virginity was sometimes ordered to contribute money to his victim's dowry. See, for example, the 1790 rape trial of María Gertrudis Calderón, who received 25 pesos (Archivo Judicial del Tribunal Superior de Justicia, Mexico City [hereafter cited as AJTSJ], Penales, leg. 6, exp. 31, fols. 1–6), and the 1797 marriage promise trial of María Francisca Castillo, who likewise received 25 pesos (AJTSJ, Penales, leg. 8, exp. 52, fols. 1, 5–6, 16–17). For additional information on dowries and their relative value in colonial Mexico, see Asunción Lavrin and Edith Couturier, "Dowries and Wills: A View of Women's Socioeconomic Role in Colonial Guadalajara and Puebla," *Hispanic American Historical Review*, 59, no. 2 (1979): 280–304.

29. CU, Mexico Historical Manuscripts, 1649–1886, exp. 747.

30. AGNM, Criminal, vol. 640, exp. 1, fols. 4, 11, 14.

31. AGNM, Criminal, vol. 534, exp. 6, fols. 146, 166. No further information was provided on María Josefa Dolores Lara.

32. For additional information on this protective and punitive institution, see Lee M. Penyak, "Safe Harbors and Compulsory Custody: *Casas de Depósito* in Mexico, 1750–1865," *Hispanic American Historical Review* 79, no. 1 (February 1999): 83–99.

33. AGNM, Matrimonios I, vol. 75, exp. 120, fols. 409–30.

34. *Siete Partidas,* Part IV, Title I, Law I, in Scott (trans.), *Siete Partidas,* 879.

35. Asunción Lavrin, "Sexuality in Colonial Mexico: A Church Dilemma," in Lavrin (ed.), *Sexuality and Marriage in Colonial Latin America,* 47, 58, 61; Elizabeth Anne Kuznesof, "Gender and Ethnic Influences on 'Spanish' Creole Society in Colonial Spanish America," *Colonial Latin American Review* 4, no. 1 (1995): 166.

36. AGNM, Criminal, vol. 641, exp. 2, fols. 13–18.

37. AJTSJ, Penales, leg. 12, exp. 28, fol. 22; AGNM, Justicia, vol. 224, exp. 10; AGNM, Justicia, vol. 225, exp. 9.

38. AGNM, Matrimonios III, box 156 (29), exp. 41, fols. 12–13. Each party agreed to this decision.

39. AGNM, Bienes Nacionales, vol. 890, exp. 2, fol. s/n (9/13/1842).

40. AJTSJ, Penales, leg. 12, exp. 33, fol. 2.

41. Ibid., fol. 4.

42. AJTSJ, Penales, leg. 6, exp. 72, fol. 13. Alejandro Cañeque analyzes the "rhetoric of wretchedness" and the obligation of authorities to civilize and protect the *persona miserable* in *The King's Living Image: The Culture and Polititcs of Viceregal Power in Colonial Mexico* (New York: Routledge, 2004), esp. 185–210.

43. *Siete Partidas,* Part IV, Title XIX, Law V, in Scott (trans.), *Siete Partidas,* 974.

44. AJTSJ, Penales, leg. 6, exp. 72, fol. 13.

45. François Giraud, "La reacción social ante la violación: Del discurso a la práctica," in *El placer de pecar y el afán de normar* (Mexico City: Grupo Editorial Planeta, 1988), 316.

46. AGNM, Criminal, vol. 705, exp. 5, fol. 38.

47. Asunción Lavrin, "Sexuality in Colonial Spanish America," in *The Oxford Handbook of Latin American History,* ed. José C. Moya (Oxford: Oxford University Press, 2011), 138.

48. Paredes was arrested but escaped from jail one month later and eluded authorities. AGNM, Criminal, vol. 41, exp. 5, fols. 322–35.

49. AGNM, Criminal, vol. 530, exp. 2, fol. 24. The father later confessed to having raped his daughter on eighteen occasions.

50. Ibid.

51. Ibid.

52. Ibid.

53. *Siete Partidas*, Part, Title XXXIII, Law VI, in Scott (trans.), *Siete Partidas*, 1473. Patriarchy existed as an ideal and in law, but not necessarily as household practice, since not all families were headed by men. For a further discussion of the impact of patriarchy on people in all social strata, see Elizabeth Dore, "The Holy Family: Imagined Households in Latin American History," in *Gender Politics in Latin America: Debates in Theory and Practice*, ed. Elizabeth Dore (New York: Monthly Review Press, 1997), 102–8.

54. Libro IV, Título 1: "De los esponsales y matrimonios, Parágrafo V," in *El Cardenal Lorenzana y el IV Concilio Provincial Mexicano*, ed. Luisa Zahino Peñafort (Mexico City: Universidad Nacional Autónoma de México, 1999), 254.

55. Quintana, *Confessonario en lengua mixe*, 43–44.

56. Ibid., 41.

57. Lynn Sacco, *Unspeakable: Father-Daughter Incest in American History* (Baltimore: Johns Hopkins University Press, 2009), 29–30, 34; Joanne M. Ferraro, *Nefarious Crimes, Contested Justice: Illicit Sex and Infanticide in the Republic of Venice, 1557–1789* (Baltimore: Johns Hopkins University Press, 2008), 60.

58. AGNM, Criminal, vol. 548, exp. 1, fols. 4, 38. Economic necessities of lower-class life probably left girls more exposed to victimization, especially when they ran errands for their parents or were left unsupervised at home. For an incest-rape trial where a girl was raped while on an errand, see AGNM, Criminal, vol. 305, exp. 8, fol. 168. In another trial, an eleven-year-old servant was referred to as a "woman of disproven proven honesty . . . she is a servant who runs errands"; see AGNM, Criminal, vol. 705, exp. 5, fol. 44.

59. AGNM, Criminal, vol. 548, exp. 1, fols. 4–5, 9, 37.

60. Bianca Premo also found, for late colonial Lima, that virginity and sexual comportment were generally more important determinants in rape cases than the age of the victim. See Bianca Premo, "Minor Offenses: Youth, Crime, and Law in Eighteenth-Century Lima," in *Minor Omissions: Children in Latin American History and Society*, ed. Tobias Hecht (Madison: University of Wisconsin Press, 2002), 124.

61. AGNM, Criminal, vol. 548, exp. 1, fols. 9, 14–16, 25, 29, 34 (emphasis added). In fact, *Siete Partidas*, Law XII, Title I, Partida IV, refers to a girl's *intelligence*, not "malice," as this lawyer stated. The law prohibits "the female relatives of the betrothed woman from marrying the man who is betrothed" and vice versa, and concludes with commentary on the legitimacy of betrothals for youngsters as young as seven if they "have acquired sufficient *intelligence* to be content with the betrothal." Scott (trans.), *Siete Partidas*, 885 (emphasis added).

62. AGNM, Criminal, vol. 548, exp. 1, fols. 5, 37–39. Spousal abuse in colonial Mexico is examined in Lee M. Penyak and Verónica Vallejo, "Expectations of Love in Troubled Mexican Marriages during the Late Colonial and Early National Periods," *The Historian* 65, no. 3 (Spring 2003): 563–86.

63. Aquinas, *Summa Theologica*, Pt. II-II, Q154, Art. 9 (2:1823–24).

64. Libro V, Título X: "Del concubinato y de las penas de los concubinatos y rufianes," in Peñafort (ed.), *El Cardenal Lorenzana y el IV Concilio Provincial Mexicano*, 269.

65. AGNM, Criminal, vol. 670, exp. 2, fols. 28–29.

66. For additional information on midwives, their role as experts in criminal cases, and the development of midwifery and obstetrics in Mexico, see Lee M. Penyak, "Midwives and Legal Medicine in Mexico, 1740–1846," *Journal of Hispanic Higher Education* 1, no. 3 (July 2002): 251–66; and Lee M. Penyak, "Obstetrics and the Emergence of Women in Mexico's Medical Establishment," *The Americas* 60, no. 1 (July 2003): 59–85.

67. AGNM, Criminal, vol. 585, exp. 9, fols. 321–31.

68. AJTSJ, Penales, leg. 12, exp. 28, fols. 17–24.

69. AGNM, Criminal, vol. 141, exp. 25, fols. 540–43.

70. Francisco de Paula de Arrangoiz, *México desde 1808 hasta 1867* (Mexico City: Editorial Porrúa S.A., 1968), 211–12.

71. AJTSJ, Penales, leg. 12, exp. 29, fols. 47, 49.

72. Ibid., exp. 27, fols. 1, 4. Pacheco and Vargas were sentenced to one year in prison and Rivera to two years in prison.

73. Ibid., exp. 30, fol. 4.

74. Ruth Behar, "Sex and Sin, Witchcraft and the Devil in Late-Colonial Mexico," *American Ethnologist* 14, no. 1 (February 1987): 34–54; Lisa Sousa, "The Devil and Deviance in Native Criminal Narratives from Early Mexico," *The Americas* 59, no. 2 (October 2002): 162; AGNM, Criminal, vol. 98, exp. 11, fol. 354; AGNM, Criminal, vol. 585, exp. 9, fol. 325.

75. Fernando Cervantes, *The Devil in the New World: The Impact of Diabolism in New Spain* (New Haven, Conn.: Yale University Press, 1994), 138, 151, 153.

76. Alexander von Humboldt, "Tablas geográficas políticas del reino de Nueva España, que manifiestan la superficie, población, agricultura, fábricas, comercio, minas, rentas y fuerza militar (enero 1804)," in *Descripciones económicas generales de Nueva España*, ed. Enrique Florescano and Isabel Gil (Mexico City: Instituto Nacional de Antropología e Historia, 1973), 142. Age statistics in documents are notoriously unreliable. Many people did not know the date of their birth and scribes sometimes took educated guesses, using phrases such as "more than twenty-five" or "appears more or less forty." Only eight cases studied here provided the ages of both the victim and the accused; the average difference was 20.6 years.

77. Frederick John Shaw, "Poverty and Politics in Mexico City, 1824–1854," Ph.D. diss., University of Florida, 1975, 391.

78. *Siete Partidas*, Part III, Title XXIV, in Scott (ed.), *Siete Partidas*, 811; Part VII, Title XXXII, Law I, ibid., 1469. For further information on clemency cases and important exclusions, see Lee Michael Penyak, "Criminal Sexuality in Central Mexico," Ph.D. diss., University of Connecticut, 1993, 310–21.

79. AGNM, Criminal, vol. 608, exp. 1, fols. 3, 9.

80. AJTSJ, Penales, leg. 12, exp. 29, fols. 47, 49.

81. AGNM, Justicia, vol. 416, exp. 76, fols. 275–77.

82. Hunefeldt, *Liberalism in the Bedroom*, 181.

83. AGNM, Justicia, vol. 416, exp. 76, fols. 275–77. The judge sentenced the father to six years in prison and the daughter to three years of seclusion.

84. Jaffary, "Incest, Sexual Virtue, and Social Mobility in Late Colonial Mexico," 107. For a further discussion of how endogamous marriages buttressed societal divisions based on race and class, see Muriel Nazzari, "Sex/Gender Arrangements and the Reproduction of Class in the Latin American Past," in Dore (ed.), *Gender Politics in Latin America*, 137.

85. *Siete Partidas*, Part IV, "Here Begins the Fourth Partida Which Treats of Betrothals and Marriages," in Scott (trans.), *Siete Partidas*, 877.

9

Bestiality

The Nefarious Crime in Mexico, 1800–1856

Mílada Bazant

Translated by Beatriz Álvarez and Zeb Tortorici

Together with sodomy, bestiality was the worst of all sexual crimes because it was, by definition, "against nature," and the penalty for it, at least in theory, was death. This essay demonstrates that just as notions of the unnatural were flexible, criminal courts in late colonial and early national Mexico maintained a high degree of flexibility vis-à-vis the law in determining the punishments for males convicted of the "sin against nature" of bestiality. In late colonial and early national Mexico, the most common extenuating circumstances resorted to by the defenders in their efforts to save those accused of bestiality were ignorance and inebriation. The following microhistorical analysis of fourteen penal causes discusses the administration of justice and the attitudes toward this practice, which supposedly filled good consciences with horror. A summary of one of the most complete files from 1809, expanded on below, is illustrative of the rural environment where such crimes were committed and of how the parties became involved.

In a letter dated April 10, 1809, Mario José Solano, the Indian governor of the central Mexican village of San Antonio de las Huertas, wrote to don Antonio Columna, judge and captain of the Acordada: "Sir, I am submitting to Your Honor a prisoner who had intercourse with a jenny *[burra]*. . . . He has confessed that this is true, that he was engaged with the jenny in this sin."[1] On that same day, the witness Cornelio Acamapichi—a forty-three-year-old single *castizo*[2] bricklayer, a native of the village of Tacuba and resident of San Cosme on the outskirts of Mexico City—in the house then known as El Elefante, declared by "God our Lord and the sign of the Holy Cross" that he had gone hunting, as he was accustomed to, together with a Spaniard who was founder of the Casa Real de Moneda (the Royal

Mint), on Easter Sunday. The two had spent the morning firing their shotguns at the hacienda Santa María, in the jurisdiction of Tacuba, until noon, when they went to eat at a *tlachiquería*—a saloon that sold the fermented alcoholic beverage *pulque*, derived from the agave plant—after which the Spaniard retired for a nap. Not wishing to do likewise, Acamapichi continued to amuse himself by hunting, when he saw the accused, whose name was unknown to him, but whom he recognized by sight because every Sunday he saw him at the said tlachiquería drinking pulque. José de los Reyes was driving a brownish-gray jenny with its foal, and Acamapichi thought that the animal was being used for carrying fermented agave juice. He urged the man to hurry on his way, for otherwise he "might lose his job." Acamapichi walked on until the end of the pasture but deemed that it was late, "an untimely hour for finding game." He then walked back along the same path, and to his surprise, on a small slope where no agaves grew, he saw:

> the abovementioned prisoner standing on top, and the animal at the bottom, with its buttocks against the thighs and groins of the accused, and the accused moved in such a manner that the utterer of these words [Acamapichi] was left with no doubt as to the bestial access that was being perpetrated, so that, because of these indecent demonstrations that have been explained and because the tail of the female donkey was lying on her right side, on the thigh of the accused, who, through his eagerness and clumsiness, did not see the deponent until he was at a distance of merely eight or nine yards[3] and, walking away from the animal, he turned to the side and covered himself like every man does after having finished pissing, for, as the deponent could see, his breeches had such a large fly that he had had no need to remove them to carry out his sin.

This fact was so "loathsome" that the witness, vexed, said to the accused, "Damn it, man! What are you doing? Are you not a Christian?" But the accused said nothing and merely smiled, "as though he cared little." When Acamapichi threatened him, saying that he would "blow the whistle," José de los Reyes, driving the jenny, "begged him to remain silent and not turn him in, while offering him pulque, which he refused." Soon after, Acamapichi arrived at the tlachiquería and denounced the deed before "the dispatcher of the beverage, named Joaquín Sánchez," who arrested José and took him before the authorities. The jenny, "brown-gray with a white muzzle . . . branded as follows on the neck" (the signs are drawn on the document), was deposited with Ramón de la Rosa, as was customary in criminal cases of bestiality.

On April 13, another witness, José Joaquín Sánchez de la Barquera, testified. He declared that he was Spanish, forty-one years of age, a native of the valley of Toluca and from the village of Santiago Temoaya; he was also married to María Aura López and an overseer of the hacienda Santa María. He pointed out that on the day of the report, the accused had left the room of the *tlachiquero* Anselmo, where he had been "put up and was given a drink and food" in exchange for helping the tlachiquero scrape and collect the juice of the agaves.[4] Sánchez de la Barquera, upon seeing "the pleasure that this lad exhibited," said to him, "Come, if you are to stay ten months in jail, you shall stay eleven, and if I have not confessed today, I shall confess tomorrow . . . suggesting with this that I would denounce him." Acamapichi also told the facts to the authorities, and they both took the accused to the hacienda; from there they brought him to the house of the governor, Mario José Solano, where he admitted his sin.

On the 14th of the same month, the accused stated that he was indigenous, "had sufficient knowledge of the Spanish language, for which reason he did not require an interpreter"; that he was a native of the village of Zinguilica and lived in the house of the governor; and that he was single and a tlachiquero. He was ignorant of his age but, according to the royal scribe, appeared to be more or less twenty years old. Having been explained the "effects worked by the legal guardianship," he appointed don Mariano de Ulibarri as his defense lawyer *(curador)*.[5] The accused said that it was true that he had been helping to scrape agave for hacienda La Teja, and that he earned one peso a month, plus meals.[6] He was also "charged with the duty of driving a brown-gray jenny to the fields and having her back loaded with two leather bottles filled with agave juice . . . that never had the devil tempted him until that Palm Sunday . . . that this disgrace had befallen him as a result of drunkenness . . . that he had drunk only one half, which at El Cuernito is twice the amount that is served in Mexico City, but although he was befuddled, he did not fall to the ground."[7] He confessed that he had "harnessed" *(empepextló)* the jenny "because the devil had put into his mind the evil thought of sinning with her, and bringing her close to a little mound . . . he had climbed it in order to be level with the hind of the jenny, whereby he had relieved himself." From there he went to harvest agave, and on his way back, after having poured the fermented agave juice into the vats, was tricked by Anselmo, whom he calls his "brother," into the hacienda La Teja, and from there, into the house of the Indian governor, who sent him to jail. José de los Reyes was unable to sign his statement because he could not write, so the judge and the lawyer signed in his stead.

The prisoner was summoned again on May 2, 1809, to appear before the counselor, the lawyer Pasqua, and don Antonio Columna, lieutenant colonel of the royal army, a professed knight of the Order of Saint James, provincial mayor of the Holy Brotherhood, interim judge of the Royal Court in the three kingdoms of New Spain, Galicia, and Bizcay, in charge exclusively of forbidden drinks. The authorities read out his statement to him, which was ratified by José de los Reyes. Subsequently, they laid down the law on him: "Having accused him of the execrable and shameful crime that he has committed, because of its intrinsic repugnance to what Nature herself inspires, it is abominated by her, and the legislators, in justice and as a manner of chastening him, have ordained the atrocious punishment of death by fire, to which the deponent and the jenny must be delivered in order to attain proper atonement of their hideous crime."

The prisoner replied that he had committed "such an ugly crime possessed by pulque," after which the judge made a series of statements to the effect that the crime, being "so against the natural," could not be committed even in a state of inebriation, just as an inebriated man does not deal himself death; that the amount of pulque that he had drunk was not sufficient to inebriate him; that the "people of his class" were accustomed to drink "hour after hour"; and that, furthermore, it was unknown whether he had been drunk at the time of the beastly action. The accused was urged to confess if his actions had been premeditated. The culprit declared that he had drunk much more than he was served in Mexico City and that "he had only recently used that liquor, for he had never tasted it in his hometown." However, the judge commented on the fact that he "had not been encumbered to perform all the motions required to set the jenny in place and to position himself in the best manner to consummate the action . . . which evidently proved that he was not drunk but in full command of his senses." He was asked at what time he had drunk the pulque and at what time he had committed the crime. The prisoner confessed that he had become inebriated at 11 A.M., and so it was indeed true that the effect of the beverage "had worn off by the time he sinned with the jenny."

In order to defend José de los Reyes, after three days the defense lawyer proposed carrying out the following procedures, which were standard legal practice:

1. To request from the parish priest of Zinguilica the baptismal certificate of the accused and information regarding his parents and godparents.
2. To request that Juan Rocha (brother of Anselmo), who was married to the sister of Reyes, María Marcela, bring witnesses that might confirm whether the prisoner had left Zinguilica in October, whether they could attest to his being indigenous, and whether "only once he had fulfilled the annual precept of the Church, for his coarseness, lack of understanding and most limited talents exceed even those that are typical of his station, and whether for the same reason they understand that he is unable to fathom or know the seriousness of crimes or their punishments."[8]
3. To request that Cornelio Acamapichi and José Joaquín Sánchez declare whether on the afternoon of the day of the incident José de los Reyes "was somewhat befuddled [perturbado de potencias] . . . and whether they had perceived this through the sense of smell."
4. To ask José Joaquín Sánchez, who had been at the pulque tavern El Cuernito that Sunday, whether a man named Esteban and another named Ignacio had been there. If so, these would testify as to the amount of pulque that it was customary to serve for half a real.

5. To ask the priest "who currently teaches the Christian doctrine" in prison "what is his concept of the knowledge and the malice of José de los Reyes"; the mayor would state the reason for which he had sent the prisoner to school, and the priest in charge of the doctrine would say "what proof he has given of his intelligence of the precepts of our holy religion."[9]

6. To request that the authorities of the prison or those who "deserve the trust of this Tribunal" state what was the disease suffered by Reyes, the symptoms thereof manifested by him, how long he had been suffering from it, and whether it was customary *(si era de naturaleza)* that he was agitated and moved "with vehemence the feelings of the flesh."

On June 5, José de los Reyes appeared in court and declared that he did not know who his father was, and that his mother, deceased, had been named María Josefa and had abandoned him at the parish of Tulancingo, where he had been baptized; his godparents were an indigenous man by the name of Félix and his wife, María Josefa. On the 7th, José Joaquín Sánchez ratified his statement, and the judge, Don Antonio Columna, ordered the lawyer José Ignacio Sotomayor—provincial lieutenant governor of Tulancingo—to carry out the said procedures. By June 12, the indigenous couple consisting of Juan Rocha and his wife appeared before Sotomayor, and the former declared that the prisoner had been at his service and had run away, nobody knew where to. Another witness from Tulancingo, named Nicolás de San Juan, an indigenous farmer and a tributary of the county seat, declared that José de los Reyes had stayed at his home for some five years, and that he had seen him subsequently at the ranch of Texcatitla; that he knew that he was indigenous because he, San Juan, had known his parents; that Reyes had run away when he had attempted to teach him the doctrine; and that he had such "limited faculties that even those of his class considered him to be dimwitted *[aún entre los de su clase lo tenían por insensato],*" and therefore he "understands that he is not capable of being aware of the seriousness of crimes or their punishments." Two other witnesses of the same village confirmed Nicolás de San Juan's opinion of how "simple and foolish" *(asimplado y atontado)* José de los Reyes was.

Two people confirmed, on June 22, the amount of pulque that José de los Reyes had drunk at El Cuernito: Ignacio Martínez, aged over fifty years, a Spanish native of Sonora and resident of the hacienda La Teja, where he served in the mines and the fields; and Esteban de la Natividad, twenty-seven, an indigenous native of Tepeapulco in the jurisdiction of Tacuba and a worker in the mine of the said hacienda. Ignacio Martínez declared that on that day Reyes had drunk "one *real* of pulque, which is approximately two quarts," a fact that was also confirmed by Esteban de la Natividad.

Also on June 22, Silvestre Rosete, surgeon of the royal prison, appeared and declared that the accused "was at the onset of elephantiasis, a disease that the responder does not judge capable of stirring the lascivious movements." Also, the defense lawyer of prisoners of the court, López, recalled that there had been a similar case at the beginning of the year 1806, and the viceroy had ordained not to proceed with the trial. López proposed that, because the disease of Reyes was contagious, he should be moved to the hospital.

A year and a half later, in November 1810, the civil prosecutor in charge of criminal affairs, Robledo, asked the prisoner to reply once again to the charges, and he asked a physician to examine José de los Reyes in order to determine whether he "could suffer the work of prison." The physician certified that Reyes was "healthy and able to walk in any direction." Yet Juan Francisco Río Frío, defense lawyer of Indians *(procurador de Indios)*, argued that all the witnesses had confirmed that the prisoner had "limited capabilities," and that although there was no doubt that the crime was typified as most execrable and therefore the penalty was to "deliver the corpse to the flames," the punishment of death by fire had been "abolished because of disuse." Although it had been stated that Reyes was accused of being "insane or an idiot" *(loco o mentecado)*, he should, according to his defense, be "worthy of pity rather than punishment," especially given that he was "incapable of correction and his impunity could not set a bad example or cause anyone else to be evil." Furthermore, since no one "was ignorant that a lack of knowledge mitigated the punishment," it should have been clear that such crimes committed through "ignorance, error, and rusticity are punished with a lesser punishment than those committed with full awareness and deliberation." As Reyes was inebriated and ill when he committed the crime, the procurador de Indios pled that, in case a punishment was to be imposed, it should be "quite moderate."

On December 10, the prosecutor Robledo, quoting law VII, title II, book VIII of the *Novísima Recopilación* of Castile, confirmed that capital punishment was the penalty ordained for the nefarious crime but that, since Reyes was indigenous and of scarce intelligence, and therefore ignorant of the seriousness of his crime, he proposed to acquit him from death at the stake and instead impose on him a sentence of ten years in prison, which he was to begin to serve by working in the square ditch—a moat then under construction around Mexico City to protect it against insurgents. Finally, on December 14, the assistant governor Rivero Torres Clavijo mandated Reyes's sentence: two years of labor digging the ditch, "previously instructing him in the Christian doctrine . . . and that the burra should be killed without making a scene, and the prisoner should pay its worth if he had the money to do so."

WHAT WAS THE NEFARIOUS CRIME?

The Spanish term for "nefarious," *nefando,* comes from the Latin *nefandus,* "the unnamable," and was used in reference to the "nefarious sin" *(pecado nefando)* or the "nefarious crime" *(delito nefando)* of sodomy and bestiality.[10] According to the *Siete Partidas,* a medieval compilation of the Spanish legislation carried out by Alfonso X of Castile in 1256, sodomy and bestiality were *pecados nefandos,* "nefarious sins" that offended God and "defame[d] the land." They were judged as *crimen laesae majestatis,* or crimes committed against the natural order,[11] the penalty for which was death at the stake: "That the offender be burnt in the flames of fire at the place [usually the central plaza], and by [secular] Justice to whom the knowledge and punishment of such crime may correspond; and that he, by that same deed and law, and without further statement, lose all his properties, whether movable or real estate, which from this very moment we confiscate and take . . . as applied to our Chamber and Treasury."[12] The law established that whoever attempted the crime, even if he did not succeed in carrying it out, should be punished in the same manner. Furthermore, a church burial was denied to the offender's ashes.[13]

Significantly, a major portion of the colonial legislation remained in use after Mexican independence in 1821, demonstrating continuities in legal tradition between the colonial and postcolonial eras. The newly national government made efforts to pass new codes to regulate justice in the early decades of the nineteenth century, but the prevailing political anarchy meant that results were scarce. It was not until the 1880s that Mexican legal codification was consolidated (the first comprehensive post-independence code was issued in 1870) and the "law became, as had been intended since long before, the sovereign of the modern times, and the judges began to behave as mere appliers of the text of the law."[14]

Until then, judges had had the possibility of passing sentences according to their own criteria. Discretional trials, according to the scholar Mario Téllez González, who contributes a different interpretation from the usual one of the abuse of this important aspect of the judiciary system, constituted the key piece "to mitigate the rigor of a penal law that was to a great extent antiquated, rigid, and inhuman."[15] According to Téllez González, such discretional trials "humanized the law." It might be said that the process of discretionary trials constituted a weapon that allowed sentences to be adapted to the circumstances, especially because the legislation regarding criminal justice was impracticable at that time. The sixteenth-century laws of New Spain could not effectively rule over an independent Mexican society three centuries later. In court, the judges quoted the laws verbatim, but when the moment came to pass sentence, they regularly mitigated the penalties. Lay judges (those without instruction, advised by a learned judge) and the learned judges (*letrados* who in time substituted for the lay ones after independence) played a major role in the establishment of justice, for they were in charge of passing sentences. They could similarly hold high positions in the royal councils or more modest positions in the municipal town halls, as advisors, auditing judges, mayors of criminal justice, chief magistrates, city mayors, or ordinary mayors. They all exercised, in their respective instances, the faculty of judging.

THE ADMINISTRATION OF SECULAR JUSTICE

The High Court of Mexico *(Audiencia de México)* was the superior tribunal in charge of both civil and criminal affairs and was located at the royal palace. Through the *Sala del Crimen,* the highest-ranking criminal judicial institution in Mexico, it exercised justice in the first instance. It was supposed to approve the most severe penalties imposed by provincial judges, public servants who worked for the Audiencia of Mexico.[16] The agents of the Sala del Crimen traversed the streets and apprehended delinquents. The last word in judiciary matters in New Spain was that of the viceroy, through his counselor or attorney.

The Royal Court *(Real Tribunal)* came into existence as an auxiliary body of justice in order to put an end to the growing crime that devastated towns and villages. In 1710, the former Holy Brotherhood *(Santa Hermandad),* subject to the Sala del Crimen, was reinstated and had the duty of informing about its sentences before executing them. However, as banditry was on the rise, it became necessary to penalize crimes as quickly as possible, so in 1719 the viceroy marquis of Valero rendered the Holy Brotherhood independent from the Sala del Crimen and founded the Tribunal of the Royal Acordada *(Tribunal de la Real Acordada),* to which he granted ample faculties. The judge held the highest authority of the Acordada, depending only on the viceroy. Initially, the Acordada was restricted to the rural areas, but in 1756 the Crown extended its purview to urban centers; its jurisdiction encompassed not only New Spain but also the kingdoms of Nueva Galicia, Nueva Vizcaya, Nuevo León, and since 1758, the Marquesado del Valle of Oaxaca (until then, the Crown had granted Hernán Cortés and his descendants the prerogative of administering justice in the territory of Oaxaca).[17] Its agents provided their services voluntarily, which rendered its functioning very cheap. Most lieutenants were local merchants and landowners, and the commissioners were their employees. This fact allowed them to solve issues according to their personal interests. Above all, they wished to maintain peace and safety in their districts, and as they despised the members of the lower classes, they had no "great concern for justice."[18]

Possibly because the judge of the Acordada exceeded his functions, in 1789 the Review Board *(Junta de Revisión)* was created with the purpose of reviewing, reforming, or revoking the sentences of the Acordada. By then, the court had spread considerably; nevertheless, crime continued to increase at an alarming rate.[19] In matters of justice, according to the second count of Revillagigedo, the Acordada functioned more efficiently than the Sala del Crimen and imposed more severe penalties.[20] The court was abolished by the liberal constitution of 1812, which reorganized the judiciary structure of the empire and created the Supreme Court of Justice *(Supremo Tribunal de Justicia),* to which the higher courts were subordinate.

The Tribunal of the Royal Acordada tended above all to cases involving infringe-ment of private property, such as theft and fraud, and rarely dealt with sexual crimes. According to the historian Colin M. MacLachlan, this fact shows the reluctance of the Acordada to engage in actions that might repress social conduct. The application of laws that concerned sexual crimes thus remained almost entirely at the discretion of the local authorities. Nevertheless, a certain number of cases did reach the Audiencia Royal, with the final sentence being passed at the Sala del Crimen. Among these were incest, sodomy, and bestiality, which shows that the authorities regarded them as serious crimes.[21]

THE PHASES OF THE CRIMINAL PROCESS

Most of the files in the criminal cases of bestiality—or the *delito nefando* (nefarious crime), as it was interchangeably called—between 1803 and 1856 are succinct and incomplete: either they contain no mention of the sentences meted out, or else they lack certain phases of the criminal process (table 6). The three trials that are complete (one of which was analyzed at the beginning of this chapter) consist, as did every criminal trial, of two parts. The first is the initial investigation, known as the summary trial, or *sumaria*, and it includes several phases, namely:

1. The writ known as "head of the process" *(cabeza de proceso),* which contains the initial accusation that originated the investigations. Already at this stage, the suspect had been imprisoned.
2. The statements of the different witnesses, who never were more than two or three individuals because the crimes were committed in the countryside and it was really only by chance that they were seen by anyone.
3. The investigatory declaration under oath, in which, in addition to general information about the suspect, the accused was asked about the specific circumstances of the crime. Sometimes the suspect—who was always male, at least in the corpus of cases I examine here—denied the charges. Some-times an interpreter, fluent in Nahuatl or another indigenous language of Mexico, was required because the accused did not speak Spanish.
4. Finally, there was the confession with the criminal charges. Based on the statement of the accused (which was, in theory, read back to him), the judge asked him certain questions and urged him to confess his crimes.

The second part was the full criminal trial, or *juicio plenario,* when the writs were delivered to the accused or to the attorney in order to formalize the lawsuit. It fol-lowed these phases:

1. The appointment of a *curador ad litem,* or attorney of the poor in charge of defending the accused.

TABLE 6 Crimes of bestiality 1800–1856

Year	Name	Place	Age	Marital status	Race	Occupation	Animal involved	Sentence
1800	Marcelo Antonio	Xonacantepec (Morelos)	15	Single	Indian	Farmhand	Jenny	Nine months in prison; ultimately acquitted.
1801	Isidro Bonifacio Peña	Tulancingo (Hidalgo)	15–18	Single	Mestizo	Servant	Jenny	Prison for 3 years following the 3 served initially. Death to the animal so as to "deaden the memory of the fact."
1803	José Antonio Rodríguez	Zimapán (Hidalgo)	23	Single	Mestizo	Mule driver	Mare	Fined 25 pesos. The mare died of feebleness.
1803	José Mariano	Izúcar de Matamoros (Puebla)	14–17	Single	Indian	Shepherd	Mare	Freed after spending 30 years in prison.
1804	José Vicente Sierra	Zacualtipán de la Sierra (Hidalgo)	23	Single	Spanish	Shepherd	Cow	One year of service at the parish. Death to the animal.
1804	Miguel Anastasio	Huichapan (Hidalgo)	—	Single	Indian	—	Jenny	Freed after 2 years of prison for lack of proof, with the request made to arrest witness for slander.
1807	Agustín Martín	Huichapan (Hidalgo)	17	Single	Indian	Shepherd	She-goat	Public shaming: put in the pillory for 2 hours on the day of highest public attendance, proclaiming his crime from time to time; a year of service in the village. Death to the goat.
1808	Venancio Martín	Zacualpan (State of Mexico)	60	Married	Indian	—	2 jennies	One year and a half in prison (no sentence).
1809	José de los Reyes	Tacuba (Mexico City)	~20	Single	Indian	*Tlachiquero*	Jenny	Two years of work in the square ditch of Mexico City. Death to the animal.
1821	José Chávez	Tula (Hidalgo)	—	Single	Indian	—	Jenny	Six years of work (doubled from 3 when he appealed).
1837	Juan Francisco	Tepeaca (Puebla)	<25	Married	Indian	—	Jenny	
1837	Tomás Victoriano	Izicatlán (Puebla)	15	Single	Indian	Farmhand	Jenny	Freed after 8 years in prison for lack of proof.
1838	José Silverio	Acatlán (Puebla)	—	Single	Indian	—	Beast	Freed after 1½ years in prison for lack of proof.
1856	Francisco Morales	Huejotzingo (Puebla)	18	Single	Mestizo	—	Beast	Three years of forced labor at a bakery. He appealed; resolution unknown.

SOURCES: AGN, Ramo Criminal (Criminal Branch), vol. 89, file 6, years 1809–10; vol. 3, file 13, years 1808–9; vol. 278, file 2, year 1800; vol. 467, file 7, year 1804; vol. 256, file 2, year 1803; vol. 62, file 20, year 1801. C., INAH, P, A.J, year 1803, No. 541; year 1837, No. 628; Tepeaca, year 1837; Huejotzingo, year 1856.

2. Procedures requested by the curador ad litem (such as obtaining the baptismal certificate, asking those who knew the accused to talk about him, and preparing very precise questions for the witnesses).
3. The statements of the eyewitnesses (who had seen the crime firsthand) and of others who knew the accused.
4. The legal defense presented by the curador ad litem.
5. The sentence, which was based on the law and explained the facts of the case.
6. Occasionally, other criminal authorities were called upon to confirm the sentence.[22]

In cases of appeal, new testimonies were presented, for example, that of the procurador ad litem and the sentence of the judge of the Audiencia. In cases of bestiality, when the accused "seeks reprieve," this was denied, since this crime "is excepted from pardon."[23] In general, criminal cases (obviously not only those related to bestiality) could last for years. There was no time limit for the verification of the charges, so the prisoner could remain in jail for several years without being sentenced.[24] According to the Castilian legislation, prisons at that time served to take custody of criminals, not necessarily to punish or rehabilitate them. This may be explained by the fact that there were very few prisons, and those that did exist consisted of two rooms, one for men and another for women, with a patio. The prisoners' diet could be complemented by the families of the prisoners. Generally, the penalties were served by performing forced tasks because there was need for labor, but also by death, flogging, banishment, fines, and the payment of the court costs (expenses derived from the civil or criminal lawsuit).[25]

Often, by the time the sentence was pronounced the accused had already been in prison longer than the period that he was condemned to serve.[26] The life conditions in the prisons of Acordada were so inhumane that the Audiencia asserted that it had become a "grave for the living."[27] When the Tribunal of the Acordada was abolished in 1812, the building remained in use as a prison until 1862, at which time the inmates were transferred to the new Belén prison.[28] The prisoners slept in a "filthy pigsty" *(pocilga asquerosa)*, the bodies heaped against each other, the walls filled with *chinches*—bedbugs that descended upon the inmates and sucked their blood—for which reason the townspeople dubbed the Acordada "La Chinche."[29] Making matters worse, the smell of sweat and feces was nauseating. The food consisted of *atole* (a traditional Mexican maize-based hot beverage), *pambazos* (a soft, oval nonsweet roll, bathed in hot chili sauce, then fried and stuffed with potatoes fried with Spanish sausage), and beans that tasted so bad the prisoners often resorted to rinsing them with water from the fountain.[30] According to the researcher Lozano Armendares, the justice that was practiced in New Spain concealed "a deep social and human spirit," for, as one lawyer argued in the 1806 defense of a miller accused of theft, "justice tries never to destroy but to edify."[31] Capital punishment was used only very occasionally, for the judiciary practice consisted, as mentioned above, in mitigating the punishments.[32]

BRIEF STORIES OF A MAJOR CRIME

Criminal lawsuits for bestiality have existed since at least 1611 for central Mexico (according to the database of Mexico's national archive).[33] In order to analyze this subject in depth, I have selected other cases from Mexico's national archive, including ones discovered in the judicial archives of Puebla. The cases analyzed occurred in the countryside and were carried out by young men who worked mostly as farmhands or shepherds. Ten of the fourteen infractions examined here were committed by Indians, three by mestizos, and one by a Spaniard (see table 6). It is important here to emphasize that, generally, native peoples in colonial Mexico had two given names, while the mestizos, Spaniards, and indigenous noblemen had given name(s) and a surname.[34] As for distinctions by race, it is noteworthy that in 1822 it was forbidden to classify citizens "in any record or public or private document" by their ethnic or racial origin; however, as we may observe from this and other research, Mexicans continued to be classified by race.[35]

In the corpus of criminal cases discussed here, the animals with which the crime was committed included jennies, mares, a cow, and a she-goat. Even when the accused denied the charges, the manner in which the witnesses described the crime appeared to prove that the crime had been committed; the merit of the defense lay in finding those details that allowed for the possibility that the accused might be innocent, even in those cases when he was known to be guilty, as may be seen in the documents themselves.

In May 1800, the attorney and the *topiles* (bailiffs who served in the villages and lower courts) of the republic had the tributary Indian Marcelo Antonio, approximately fifteen years old, "secured in their pillory" and placed in custody of the mayor Feliciano Antonio for having committed bestiality with a burra.[36] Antonio had perpetrated the crime in a "small ravine named El Zacate" near the village of Xonacatepec, in the jurisdiction of Cuernavaca, in the marquisate of the valley of Oaxaca. According to a statement by Juan Estevan, a former indigenous governor of that village, made through the interpreter and chief constable Rufino Rifo, the tributary Indian Marcelo Antonio was "standing on a large stone . . . with both hands he held the jenny, whose feet were tied with a belt . . . he had his breeches on." Marcelo Antonio was first appointed a curador, who swore in the name of God our Lord "to take advice from people of science and conscience," after which the accused proceeded to confess. He said that on that day he had gone to his orchard to harvest tomatoes, when he tried to mount the animal in order to "drive away the oxen that were causing her harm," and that he had indeed seized her, but from the neck. As the accused denied the charges, the local court attorney, don Raymundo Cervantes, said that for "further proof of this course" the two witnesses and the accused "should come face to face," in a procedure known as the *careo*. However, "after severe persuasions and counterclaims passed among them all," neither the accused nor the witnesses yielded in their respective and previous statements.

Several testimonies were given about the accused before the judge, the interpreter, and the attorney, which disagreed on the following points: whether Antonio had tied the jenny's front or hind legs; whether he had placed the stone behind the animal's haunches or at her side in order to climb and mount her—or whether no stone was required to mount the jenny (especially given that the accused always used a stone as a step when he climbed a horse or a donkey); whether, when he was caught in the act, he had pulled down his hat over his eyes in shame, or whether he had kept it "in the regular position"; and whether the suspect had contradicted himself "because of his poor memory."

In his defense, the attorney asked that several points be investigated, including whether the former governor Juan Estevan "has the vice of habitual inebriation," a fact that was confirmed by three witnesses: a forty-five-year-old mestizo "dealer," a twenty-eight-year-old Indian bricklayer, and a sixty-six-year-old mulatto. It was also confirmed that Juan Estevan felt a "deadly hatred" for the father of the accused, as well as for "all his poor family," for there were "bad feelings between them because of a horse" that had likely been sold or otherwise exchanged between the two families. Alcohol and allegations of drunkenness, as seen in the 1856 case quoted in sidebar 1, often played central roles in confirming or negating accusations of sexual misconduct within the court of law.

The extensive allegation of the attorney stated that "experience shows that we always judge according to the scales of passion; rare or absent is the work that is rated as good and correct . . . enmity and constant inebriation are two most powerful contrary forces that destroy it. . . . Because whoever is always dominated by this vice is capable of plotting against me . . . for the vice of drunkenness is one of the worst, and if hatred is added to it, it causes it to be a source of the ugliest of slanders." The law regarding the nefarious crime specified that this act must be proven by three witnesses (in this case there was only one drunk witness); it also required that the accused be at least seventeen years of age in order to be tried.[37] The specifics of this case show that the defense attorney analyzed, point by point, the impossibility that Marcelo Antonio might have committed the crime and requested his acquittal, quoting the "words of that law which establishes: *sanctius esse inosentem impunitum relinquere quam innocentem condemnare* [it is more saintly to leave the guilty man unpunished than to condemn the innocent]."

Since no resolution was reached, the procedures were referred to José Rafael Márquez, lawyer of the Real Audiencia, the Royal High Court of Mexico, and he,

SIDEBAR 1   INVALID WITNESSES DUE TO DRUNKENNESS

He was charged with the crime of bestiality, of which he appears to be responsible, and he replied that the witnesses who have declared against him were drunk, and for this reason declared falsely against him, for he has not committed the crime that is ascribed to him. He was reprimanded, being told that his reply did not invalidate the previous charge, because the crime, according to the records, was committed at two-thirty in the afternoon, and half an hour later, that is, at three o'clock in the afternoon that very day, when the said witnesses made their statements, they showed no signs of being even slightly drunk; and I, clerk of the court, certify that he replied that he had not seen them drink but that he had observed, when they had come into the pen and he approached them, that they reeked of liquor.

—*Juzgado de Letras (Civil Court), Huejotzingo, 1856, CINAH, P, A.J.*

with full knowledge of the laws on the subject, concluded that "there is no proper proof as that which the law demands in order to impose the ordinary penalty for the crime, and much less if it is a serious crime, for in such case the law states that it is indispensable that the proof be as clear as daylight."[38] After having remained in prison for a period of five months, Marcelo Antonio was freed, thanks to the favorable opinion of the royal attorney, and the court recommended that the governor watch the boy's behavior and that he be instructed in the Christian doctrine.

AN ATTEMPT THAT COST HIM THIRTY
YEARS IN PRISON

In July 1803, the *ladino* Indian Pedro Pablo Hinojosa saw an indigenous commoner *(macehual),* José Mariano, "squatting" *(en cuclillas;* underlined in the original) and lifting the tail of a mare that was lying on the ground with her hind legs tied to one mesquite tree and the front legs tied to another. The deponent, thinking "that he might be fornicating with the beast," approached slowly and realized that indeed the "young Indian boy" *(indisuelo)* was engaged in that very "brutish operation" *(torpe operación).* He immediately struck the boy, who "covered his shameful parts with his long cotton shirt," in the face. The witness then tied him with the rope that had previously been used to tie the beast, and brought him before the authorities of the Holy Brotherhood.

With the aid of an interpreter, it became known that José Mariano was the legitimate child of Pascual Antonio and Magdalena María, both deceased, and that he had been baptized at the parish of Santiago Tecali, Puebla. He knew "by heart the main mysteries of our Holy Faith, but he could not read or write." He lived in the house of the Indian José Zoyatitlán (his uncle had previously tried to find him accommodation with his *comadre*, but she had refused), who gave him one *real* for every workday, but gave him food only when he "drove the oxen to the pasture." Zoyatitlán declared that the boy had no malice, and therefore he "had not taken care to follow him." When José Mariano was arrested, Zoyatitlán supplicated to the judge to "return the beast to him," but "his Honor said that he could in no way give it back," given that it was customary for the beast in question to be "deposited" with authorities. From the file transcripts, nothing more is known about the animal. The criminal investigations were interrupted after a few months, and José Mariano remained in prison for the shocking duration of thirty years—a fact that highlights the unjust and unsystematic nature of the criminal process in late colonial and early national Mexico. Only in 1834 was Mariano granted his freedom, for the time that had passed, according to the court, "was sufficient to make the penal action expire."[39]

THE WORD OF ISABEL PRESENTACIÓN AGAINST THAT OF TOMÁS VICTORIANO

A criminal case of bestiality from 1837 also highlights the highly gendered personal and communal politics that complicated the court's job of determining innocence or guilt. The sole witness in this case was Isabel Presentación, who was married to the Indian Cirilo and lived with him in the village of Izicatlán, Puebla. One day the wife went to search for a brownish-gray jenny and her two foals but found only the foals by the river. She continued searching and, to her surprise, found Tomás Victoriano standing against an *amate* tree committing the unnatural act of bestiality with the jenny. He "covered his parts," and Isabel ran to denounce him before the local judge. Upon being apprehended, Tomás argued, with the aid of an interpreter, that initially he "had the intention to win the love of Isabel," and that he had waited for her beside the river at three o'clock in the afternoon because he knew at this time she typically went to look for her animals. According to his testimony, when he told Isabel of his intentions, she had been "quite vexed, to the point of threatening him with a stick." Subsequent statements reveal contradictory versions of this encounter. Tomás swore that he had merely used the animal as an "excuse" to cause Isabel to come near him so that he might "enjoy her body as she had offered when he [Tomás] had spoken to her near the clay vat *[cuexcomate]* at her house three days prior, because, as there were people around, they had been unable to carry out the act at that time." But that day Isabel was "far from willing to grant Tomás the favor that he hoped to receive from her; instead she showed him resentment, to the point of taking a stick and intending to hit him with it; she wanted to cause him harm, and in order to libel him she accused him of sinning with the burra." In her subsequent statement, Isabel reaffirmed her accusation and added that she had rebuked Tomás, asking him "if there was no old woman or girl with whom he could do that." To add a certain veracity to his defense, Tomás argued that "if his clothes were on the ground, why had she [Isabel] not taken them to add strength to her accusation?" The case of Tomás remains inconclusive; two years later it was argued that there was not sufficient proof to condemn him. However, once again highlighting the problematic and moralizing nature of the criminal justice system in Mexico, Tomás Victoriano remained in prison for another six years until he was granted his freedom.[40] This case and others like it demonstrate that allegations of the "unnatural crime" of bestiality, whether true or not, could be used to tarnish one's reputation and could have far-reaching implications for the accused, even when the accusations could not be proven in a court of law.

MARRIAGE, CULPABILITY, AND THE BESTIAL ACT

Marital status also performed a significant role in the ways in which allegations of the unnatural played themselves out. This corpus of bestiality cases shows that being married and committing an act of bestiality was even more detrimental to the accused than if he had been single and unmarried. In the 1808 case of a sixty-year-old Indian from Zacualpan, Venancio Martín, the defense argued: "It is impossible to understand how an old man who is sixty years old and married could have committed the crime of having [carnal] access with two burras within a very short while." A second testimony, which apparently played a key role in his acquittal, showed that there was "no body of the crime," as no examination was made of his "virile member to determine whether there was semen in the foreskin or on the shirt or clothing, and the vulvas of the jennies might also be examined to see whether they were wet or aroused, and that although these operations are filthy, they should not have been omitted, as they are not omitted in the case of rape of a maiden."[41] In the reviewed cases, it was only by exception that a physical examination of the accused and of the animals was carried out. After Venancio Martín had remained in prison for a period of one and a half years, his defense attorney requested a reprieve, which was refused. The criminal case is, however, incomplete, and we know nothing else about the fate of the accused.

In another case, from 1837, the Indian Juan Francisco, aged twenty-five years and a native of Tepeaca, Puebla, was given a double penalty for the sole reason that he was married: "He had at hand very plentiful means by which to satisfy his carnal appetites . . . because coition or copulation with a beast is one of the crimes most revolting to nature . . . it is the most serious and heinous . . . he who commits it manifests enormous perversity and a limitless prostitution . . . because [he insists] he had very plentiful means by which to attain his pleasures."[42]

In this case, the third attorney revoked the sentence, for he disagreed with the penalty imposed by the judge of first instance, who had only condemned Juan Francisco to three years of prison. He proposed to the *Tribunal Superior* of the third instance in Puebla that the boy's penalty be increased to eight years, arguing "that the excessive severity of these laws has been tempered by the practice of the courts, but not to the extreme to which it has been done in the present case. . . . The ministry cannot agree with that penalty, because the nature of the crime itself and its rarity demand a more severe punishment in order to prevent that, upon learning of it, and not fearing it due to the mildness of the penalty, the unwary youth may corrupt the populations." The attorney thought that rather than impos-ing the ordinary punishment, a different penalty should be applied, one that "might satisfy the very serious offense made to society." If not, he argued, the con-sequences might include the evils expounded in the first law of the *Novísima Recopilación:* "[The nefarious crime is] destructive of the natural order *[destruidor de la orden natural],* punished by the divine judgment, causing the nobility to be lost and the heart to become cowardly, and breeds weakness of the Faith and is abhorrent in the observance of God, and, being demeaning, it causes pestilence and other sufferings to befall upon humankind and on the earth, and is born of much shame and insult to the people and land where it is consented."[43]

The law, of course, had biblical origins: it was a reminder that God had sent famine, the plague, torments, and other sufferings to the cities of Sodom and Gomorrah because they were supposedly inhabited by men who committed the sin against nature (particularly in this section, the law mentions the sins commit-ted by men together, hence the terms *sodomía* and *sodomítico,* "sodomy" and "sod-omitical"), and it was thus that "Our Lord God caused both cities to sink, with all the people who lived in them." Only Lot was saved, along with his followers who had not committed "that wrong."[44]

Since he was familiar with this law, the attorney sought to "teach a lesson to"*(escarmentar)* the sinner and his village, and he succeeded in augmenting the penalty for Juan Francisco by at least six years of prison. To no avail did the procura-dor of the poor defend him with the usual arguments regarding his ignorance and rusticity: "if he had had principles and education . . . he would have reflected in such a manner that he would have abstained from committing the crime." The behavior of Juan Francisco in the past—the defense attorney insisted—was not evil, so "it is to be expected that he will never again incur such a crime." However, the attorney repeated that the village where Juan Francisco lived was not "a place so deprived of dealings and commerce that brings together its idiotic dwellers, nor is the criminal himself so ignorant or stupid as to deserve an extreme indulgence."

"RUSTICITY," IGNORANCE, AND INEBRIATION: EXTENUATING CIRCUMSTANCES

Rusticidad was a word commonly utilized by the legal defense to explain that the accused was incapable and ignorant, a sufficient reason to mitigate "the aggravating nature of his crime." Lack of knowledge of Christian doctrine also proved that the accused was ignorant of the moral precepts and therefore of the fact that the crime he had committed was a sin. Whether Indians or mestizos, those accused typically did not know their exact age because virtually none possessed their baptismal certificate (which was always sought out by the court but rarely ever found).

In this corpus of fourteen cases, the only culprit who was able to present his birth certificate was the eighteen-year-old Spanish shepherd José Vicente Sierra, the legitimate child of Pedro Sierra and Antonia Torres, both Spanish residents of the village of Santa María Zozoquipa, in the state of Hidalgo. Like the others, however, he could neither read nor write. His mother had been widowed at a very young age, "loaded with children," so that he was "quite wild" *(muy silvestre)*. As his defense attorney put it, he was "brought up on the mountains, and among brutes, with no religion or rudiments of Christianity, from the earliest age." Thus, his lawyer argued, "Can it be sensible to deem that Sierra committed his crime willfully? If he did not, nor was he instructed of these crimes or of the punishments to which he was subject as a Catholic and as a citizen, can it be said that he fell into that shameful excess? . . . For, although in the court of his conscience he may have been a criminal, because of his ignorance he was not."[45]

The witness who chanced upon Sierra when he was looking for an ox on the mountain found the accused "lying on his belly on the cow until having cohabited with her." The first thing that came to his mind was to ask him "if there were no women," but the lad became "embarrassed" and replied nothing. Then he begged him in the name of God not to accuse him, for tomorrow he would have children and these "would do likewise." This comment appears to imply that bestiality was an established custom in the rural setting. The witness, however, took the boy's unnatural proximity to the cow as proof of the crime.

According to the defense lawyer of one of the accused men in these court cases, rusticity was "incompatible with a wrongful intent," and furthermore, one should not "believe the confession of Indians in matters of debts or crimes."[46] In short, the word of an Indian was disqualified.

In the 1803 case of José Antonio Rodríguez, a twenty-three-year-old mestizo mule driver at the mine of Zimapan, Hidalgo, who committed the crime with a mare, the priest of the mining town was asked whether the accused was familiar with Christian doctrine. The procurador argued that:

> This is an extremely idiotic boy and a simpleton, and having been brought up, since he made use of reason, as a young shepherd among the animals *[de pastorcillo entre los animales]*, and having been incited to brutal concupiscence, he was ignorant of and certainly did not reflect on the seriousness of this sin. . . . Shepherds who grow up in the forest are by rule so savage *[son tan salvajes]* that they can be distinguished from the beasts only by their ability to speak, for among these people, even at an adult age, much ignorance can be perceived.[47]

SIDEBAR 2   BESTIALITY COMMITTED BY A MINOR

Regarding the minority of age stated in his baptismal certificate, which I duly enclose herein, and considering his education, his ignorance, and his unhappiness, as well as the fact that there is no proof on which to rely that might warrant a more severe punishment, and that, being an orphan, he may improve himself only through a light penalty, I entreat you to take all this into consideration when passing his sentence, which I request he may serve at a bakery, and which he hopes will be the lightest, as is befitting.

—*Court of First Instance, Huasipungo, 1856, Public Prosecutor's Office No. 2, CINAH, P, A.J.*

Such arguments contributed to colonial discourse about native peoples and were utilized to obtain freedom for the accused. It was argued that the "poor Indians" lived very much like animals, as they lived outside "civilization"; that their brutishness led them to commit excesses that were condemned by general morals and by society. The lack of "instruction in the good customs" was critical for committing crimes, all the more so in the case of young men, for the laws "do not assume they have the same judgment, ability to reflect, or experience as those over twenty-five."[48]

The defense lawyer of the mestizo Francisco Morales, who was humbly dressed in calico drawers, black corduroy pants, a straw hat, and a green kerchief, attempted to protect his client by arguing that his "ignorance and his unhappiness" were the result of his being an orphan. The defense lawyer's logic—touching on the suspect's age, education, and parentless status—behind why Morales deserved a mitigated sentence is reproduced in sidebar 2. He requested the court to give him "a light penalty," for only thus would he be able to "improve himself." The fact that the witnesses "smelled of liquor" also proved helpful in this case; indeed, alcohol often functioned as an important mitigating factor in such crimes.[49]

Inebriation on the part of the accused, too, could be a significant extenuating circumstance to which the defenders resorted in order to argue down the sentence. The excessive consumption of alcohol caused a dimming of the senses, and the subject was then susceptible of being "tempted or moved by the devil." Of Francisco Morales, for example, his lawyer explained: "It is true that he took a rigged black and white cow in order to milk it and drink the milk, and that the devil tempted him so that he sinned with the cow on a single occasion, and that he had never before done this with the said cow or with any other animal, that it was the first time that, to his disgrace and moved by the devil, he committed this excess."[50]

In another late colonial case, from 1801, the mestizo Isidro Bonifacio Peña, a servant at the Xalapilla Ranch, confessed that one day, "possessed by the ardors of concupiscence, and not having the means to relieve himself of these, [he] took a brown-gray jenny, property of his father, and had carnal intercourse with her"; it was the first time that he had "fornicated with a jenny . . . he committed the sin because the devil introduced himself in his body . . . and because he was miserable and frail."[51] A similar case was that of the mule driver José Antonio Rodríguez, who argued that he was drunk when he committed the crime in 1803. The witnesses declared that they had seen him virtually in the act on the street: that "the accused was without his breeches, and the mare lay on the ground in front of him . . . that she was against the wall . . . that they saw signs of moisture [señal de humedad] on the ground . . . that the mare was on the floor with her legs tied with a piece of rope." The scene also included a stool that Rodríguez had utilized "for his comfort in the act."[52]

According to a specialist on this topic, Spanish officers believed inebriation to be the main cause for the commission of crimes by Indians and by those of mixed race. Alcohol consumption increased considerably during the colonial period of the Viceroyalty of New Spain, as new alcoholic beverages like distilled cane alcohol were introduced, as the numerous festivities of the Catholic calendar increased drinking, and as pulque was introduced into the market as a commodity to be widely bought and sold.[53] The "legal advantage" of being drunk reached such extremes that the Indians' lawyers, in their legal defense, regularly employed such standard colonial tropes and stereotypes in their arguments as: "He was so drunk and so out of his senses that he acted like a madman [demente], like an automaton, or like an irrational machine whose movements were totally devoid of reason and free will." Furthermore, since Indians were acquainted with the legal ramifications of alcohol to mitigate a sentence, they sometimes willfully drank before they committed the crime, thereby ensuring that they would not be punished to the full extent of the law. In the sample of cases examined here, more than one judge stated that inebriation was actually a pretext for committing premeditated criminal acts.[54]

What, however, was the genealogy of this permissiveness toward inebriation? According to Téllez González, drunkenness as an extenuating circumstance for crime is stated in section VII, title VIII, law V of the medieval Siete Partidas, which deals with homicide: "as he who kills another by a chance born through his own fault deserves therefore to be punished." Téllez González writes, "The text of the law . . . deals with what today would be known as involuntary manslaughter," and quotes several examples, including that of a man who kills while inebriated.[55] It is similarly written: "Or if a man gets drunk in such a manner that he kills another due to his drunkenness . . ."[56] In legal practice, regardless of the "unnatural" nature of the crime, drunkenness was interpreted as an extenuating circumstance in determining one's culpability, and the abuse was such that "the homicide files where it is not invoked are scarce."[57] In my opinion, it is paradoxical that this legal practice has been maintained for centuries, thus promoting a higher consumption of alcohol from the colonial period to the present day. The criterion of the courts was a reflection of the everyday life of those villages where drunkenness was not socially condemned.[58]

SENTENCING AND THE NATURE OF BESTIALITY

According to the *Siete Partidas,* he who committed the crime of bestiality deserved the death penalty, though in practice the death sentence was rarely meted out. Zeb Tortorici, for example, has found that from 1563 to 1821 only three men (out of a corpus of 108 cases) were put to death in colonial Mexico for the crime of bestiality—coincidentally, all of them in the eighteenth century.[59] In the cases that I have reviewed in this essay, the penalties were reduced to several years of prison, forced labor in public works, fines of 25 pesos, "public shaming, put in the pillory for two hours on the day of highest attendance, proclaiming his crime from time to time," and service in the village. As for the animal, it was almost always killed (see table 6), a finding that has been confirmed by both Lee Penyak and Zeb Tortorici. Other sexual crimes like sodomy or rape with physical violence, which also deserved the death penalty in theory, were punished with forced labor, prison, and in the latter case more commonly, with a dowry arrangement and acquittal.[60] In the cases of bestiality reviewed here, we perceive few changes in the administration of justice, especially regarding the penalties meted out on the accused. The penal processes were carried out in a similar style, and the defenders utilized almost identical arguments to save the accused, whether or not they had admitted to the crime. Likewise, there was no difference in the legal practice in relation to Indians, mestizos, or Spaniards, although other, more complete studies assert the opposite.[61] What is evident, and unequivocally so, is the simultaneity of sympathy and contempt shown by the witnesses, judges, curators, and other social agents of the courts toward Indians.

We see in these cases of bestiality that both the lay and learned judges of New Spain and, after 1821, of independent Mexico reduced the penalties prescribed by law and responded to the huge social and economic differences manifested by the inhabitants in various spheres of life. According to other research on crime— not only of a sexual kind—the convicted, whether they were Indians, of mixed race, blacks, or Spaniards, tended to be engaged in the most marginal trades.[62] Justice did not necessarily favor a certain race, but generally it did favor the social elite and those who had the financial capital and "honor" that could help their plight.

There is room for yet another consideration: Were acts of bestiality provoked by an unsatisfied body, by an "unnatural" desire for a nonhuman animal, by the physical proximity of male youths to the sexuality and fornication of farm animals, or by the games and experiments of male adolescents? The fact that in most cases the accused were single young men who lived in the countryside seems to point to all these phenomena. During the trials the accused were incriminated for not having relationships with women, but what sexually available women were there in and around the fields and rural spaces where these young men worked? Acceptable sexual behavior was derived from standards known through the law, family tradition, Christian doctrine, and the sacrament of confession; essentially, the discourse was based on the concepts of chastity and honor, which were opposed to unbridled passions or to any ahistorical notion of "sexual freedom."[63] Most likely, few women in the largely rural communities were willing to have sexual intercourse with men who were not their husbands, so the crime of bestiality committed by peasant boys and adolescents may have stemmed from a sexual desire that could not be easily satisfied with the opposite sex. On the other hand, the cases of the Indians Venancio Martín, age sixty, and Juan Francisco, age twenty-five, both of whom were married, appear to demonstrate a more overt predilection for sex with animals, perhaps independent of sexual relations with their female partners.

This essay, with its microhistorical focus on the late colonial and early national periods of Mexican history, has demonstrated that when Mexico gained its independence from Spain in 1821, as in other newly independent states throughout Latin America, the definition of the "natural" and the "unnatural" remained largely fixed, a situation that changed only when updates to the legal code were enacted during the twentieth century. The nature of a crime such as bestiality is, in essence, always a reflection of particular legal codes and contexts—many of which, as this essay has shown, were unsystematic, mutually contradictory, and construed by criminal courts in ways that allowed human perpetrators of the crime to escape the death sentence. The animals, however, which were regularly killed for having been polluted by human bodies and desires, were not so lucky.

NOTES

1. Archivo General de la Nación, México [hereafter AGN], Ramo Criminal (Criminal Branch), vol. 89, exp. 6, years 1809–10. The following quotes and details are from this case.

2. The term *castizo*—also *cuarterón*—refers to a person born of the union between a mestizo and a Spaniard in the Americas.

3. A yard *(vara)* measures 0.84 meter.

4. A *tlachiquero* is in charge of collecting the juice of the magüey agave, which, when fermented, becomes the alcoholic drink known as *pulque*.

5. The *curador ad litem* (as is written in certain documents) comes from the Latin "for the litigation." He was the person appointed by the judge to follow the litigations and defend the rights of the accused. See Joaquín Escriche, *Diccionario razonado de la legislación civil, penal, comercial y forense. Con citas del derecho, notas y adiciones por el licenciado Juan Rodríguez de San Miguel* (Mexico City: Universidad Nacional Autónoma de México, 1993), 169.

6. A peso was equivalent to 8 *reales;* a *real* was 12.5 cents.

7. A quart is equivalent to 1.156 liters. At El Cuernito, half a quart was equivalent to a full quart in Mexico City. AGN, Ramo Criminal, vol. 89, exp. 6.

8. According to all these documents, the Indians were "ignorant" by nature (or more likely because they were denied the opportunity for education), but José de los Reyes was represented as being far more brutish and dim-witted than any member of his community.

9. The law ordained that prisons be overseen by an inspector once a week. The latter inquired about the inner workings and about the treatment given to the inmates; the chief officer of the police informed about the conditions of each of these. However, according to Hipólito de Villarroel, a witness of that time, the visits were "merely a matter of form." Teresa Lozano Armendares, *La criminalidad en la ciudad de México, 1800–1821* (Mexico City: Universidad Nacional Autónoma de México 1987), 167–68. The prisons usually had schools where the inmates were taught to read, write, and count and were instructed in the Christian doctrine.

10. Serge Grunzinski, "Las cenizas del deseo: Homosexuales novohispanos a mediados del siglo XVII," in *De la santidad a la perversión o de por qué no se cumplía la ley de Dios en la sociedad novohispana*, ed. Sergio Ortega (Mexico City: Grijalbo, 1985), 261; Marcela Suárez Escobar, "Sexualidad y norma sobre lo prohibido: La ciudad de México y las postrimerías del virreinato," Ph.D. diss., Universidad Nacional Autónoma de México, 1994.

11. Law signed by Fernando and Isabel in Medina del Campo on August 2, 1497: *Novísima recopilación*, part VII, book XII, title XXX, law I, in Juan N. Rodríguez San Miguel, *Pandectas hispano-mejicanas*, 3 vols. (facsimile of 1852 ed.; Mexico City: Universidad Nacional Autónoma de México, 1991), 3:489. This code attempted to homogenize all the legislation of the territory of Castile-León and sought a harmony between the civil and the ecclesiastic, the earthly and the spiritual dimensions. See Suárez Escobar, "Sexualidad y norma sobre lo prohibido."

12. Rodríguez de San Miguel, *Pandectas hispano-mejicanas*, 3:489.

13. Suárez Escobar, "Sexualidad y norma sobre lo prohibido."

14. María González del Refugio, "Estudio introductorio," in Rodríguez San Miguel, *Pandectas hispano-mejicanas*, 1:XXV–XXXVI.

15. Mario Téllez González, *La justicia criminal en el valle de Toluca, 1800–1829* (Zinacantepec: El Colegio Mexiquense, Universidad Autónoma del Estado de México, Instituto de Investigaciones Legislativas, Tribunal Superior de Justicia, 2001), 184, 262.

16. Court officials (mayors and chief magistrates) of the provinces of Yucatán, Tabasco, Nuevo León, Tamaulipas, and the Internal Provinces of the East, which depended on the Audiencia (High Court) of Mexico; the second Audiencia was that of Guadalajara. See Lozano Armendares, *La criminalidad en la ciudad de México*, 122, 158.

17. Ibid., 160.

18. According to Colin M. MacLachlan, *La justicia criminal del siglo XVIII en México. Un estudio sobre el Tribunal de la Acordada* (Mexico City: Secretaría de Educación Pública, 1976), 60, 90, 100, and 122.

19. See the tables in Alicia Bazán Alarcón, "El Real Tribunal de la Acordada y la delincuencia en la Nueva España," *Historia Mexicana* 13, no. 3 (1964): 317–45.

20. Ibid., 329; Lozano Armendares, *La criminalidad en ciudad de México*, 176.

21. MacLachan, *La justicia criminal del siglo XVIII*, 129; Lozano Armendares, *La criminalidad en la ciudad de México*, 176.

22. Téllez González, *La justicia criminal en el valle de Toluca*, 190–93; François Giraud, "La reacción social ante la violación: Del discurso a la práctica. Nueva España, siglo XVIII," in *El placer de pecar y el afán de normar. Seminario de Historia de las mentalidades y la religión en el México colonial* (Mexico City: Joaquín Mortiz–Instituto Nacional de Antropología e Historia, 1987), 323–24; Beatriz Urías Horcasitas, *Indígena y criminal. Interpretaciones del derecho y la antropología en México, 1871–1921* (Mexico City: Universidad Iberoamericana, 2000); Jorge Hernández Díaz, *Orden y desorden en Michoacán. El derecho penal en la república federal, 1824–1835* (Morelia: Escuela de Historia, Instituto de Investigaciones Históricas, Universidad Michoacana de San Nicolás Hidalgo / Morevallado Editores, 1999).

23. AGN, Ramo Criminal, vol. 3, file 14, years 1808–9. This file contains the case of Venancio.

24. MacLachlan, *La justicia criminal del siglo XVIII*, 123.

25. González del Refugio, "Estudio introductorio," 102–3; Téllez González, *La justicia criminal en el valle de Toluca*, 176.

26. Lozano Armendares, *La criminalidad en la ciudad de México*, 186.

27. MacLachlan, *La justicia criminal del siglo XVIII*, 123.

28. Gustavo Malo Camacho, *Historia de las cárceles en México* (Mexico City: Instituto Nacional de Ciencias Penales, Procuraduría General de la República, 1979), 77–78.

29. Manuel Payno, *Los bandidos de Río Frío* (Mexico City: Editorial Porrúa, 2001), 136.

30. Report of 1841 by Ignacio Cumplido, "La cárcel de la Acordada," in Manuel Orozco y Berra, *Diccionario universal de historia y geografía* (Mexico City: Imprenta de J. M. Andrada y Escalante, 1855), 42–44. Cumplido was superintendent of prisons; he proposed that the system should be based on three principles taken from the prisons of the United States: inviolable silence, common work, and isolation during the night. See Urías Horcasitas, *Indígena y criminal*; and Nydia E. Cruz Barrera, *Las ciencias del hombre en el México decimonónico. La expansión el confinamiento* (Puebla: Benemérita–Universidad Autónoma de Puebla, 1999) 42–64.

31. Lozano Armendares, *La criminalidad en la ciudad de México*, 172–76.

32. Out of 474 cases of criminals analyzed by Teresa Lozano for the years 1800 to 1812, 25 were for homicide, and only one death penalty was applied. See Lozano Armendares, *La criminalidad en la ciudad de México*, 186, app. 1. Out of 128 homicides analyzed in the valley of Toluca from between 1800 and 1829, not a single death penalty was applied. See Téllez González, *La justicia criminal en el valle de Toluca*, 289–290, tables 9 and 11.

33. According to the ARGENA II database of the Archivo General de la Nación, there was one case in the seventeenth century, nineteen cases in the eighteenth, and fourteen in the nineteenth (including those reviewed in this paper).

34. Those of the most humble station, devoted to the lowest trades, farmhands, servants, etc. Francisco J. Santamaría, *Diccionario de mejicanismos* (Mexico City: Editorial Porrúa, 1978), 673.

35. Decree dated September 17, 1822. Manuel Dublán y José María Lozano, *Legislación mexicana o colección completa de las disposiciones legislativas expedidas desde la Independencia de la república ordenada por los licenciados Manuel Dublán y José M. Lozano*, vol. 1 (Mexico City: Imprenta del Comercio 1876), 628–29.

36. AGN, Ramo Criminal, vol. 278, file 2, year 1800.

37. "Before the age of 17 years, the penalty established by the law is not imposed on the criminal, but a lesser penalty, due to his experience and to his limited capacity for malice compared to those of age." Escriche, *Diccionario razonado de la legislación civil, penal.*

38. He quotes parts 3 and 7 of AGN, Ramo Criminal, vol. 278, file 2, year 1800.

39. Centro del Instituto Nacional de Antropología e Historia, Puebla [hereafter CINAH, P], A.J. year 1803, No. 541.

40. CINAH, P, A.J. year 1837, No. 628.

41. The defender argued, besides, that the accused was drunk. AGN, Ramo Criminal, vol. 3, file 14, years 1808–9 (incomplete file).

42. The following account is from CINAH, P, A.J. year 1837.

43. *Novísima recopilación*, part VII, book XII, title XXX, in Rodríguez de San Miguel, *Pandectas hispano-mejicanas*, 3:489.

44. Lot and his followers were allowed to escape under the condition that they should not look back; Lot's wife disobeyed and was turned into a pillar of salt. The patriarch had fleshly intercourse with his two daughters, an act of incest that led to the birth of Moab and Ammon. As for why Jehovah brought a rain of sulphur and fire down upon Sodom and Gomorrah, see Genesis 18–19. According to Exodus 22:19, "Anyone who has sexual relations with an animal must certainly be put to death."

45. AGN, Ramo Criminal, vol. 467, file 7, year 1804.

46. AGN, Ramo Criminal, vol. 278, file 2, year 1800, fols. 96–137.

47. AGN, Ramo Criminal, vol. 256, file 2, year 1803.

48. CINAH, P, A.J., Tepeaca, year 1837. Coming of age was attained at 25. See Escriche, *Diccionario razonado*, 220.

49. CINAH, P, A.J., Huejotzingo, year 1856 (incomplete file).

50. AGN, Ramo Criminal, vol. 467, exp. 7, year 1804.

51. AGN, Ramo Criminal, vol. 62, file 20, year 1801.

52. AGN, Ramo Criminal, vol. 256, file 2, year 1803.

53. According to William B. Taylor, with time "the sacred and ritual signification of *pulque* lost strength." In certain places like Hidalgo, *pulque* was drunk instead of water during the dry season. See William B. Taylor, *Embriaguez, homicidio y rebelión en las poblaciones coloniales mexicanas* (Mexico City: Fondo de Cultura Económica, 1987), 86–87, 93, and 110–15.

54. Ibid., 104–5.

55. Téllez González, *La justicia criminal en el valle de Toluca,* 208.

56. Rodríguez de San Miguel, *Pandectas hispano-mejicanas,* 3:384.

57. Alamiro de Ávila, in Téllez González, *La justicia criminal en el valle de Toluca,* 208.

58. Taylor, *Embriaguez, homicidio y rebelión,* 96.

59. Zeb Tortorici, "Contra Natura: Sin, Crime, and 'Unnatural' Sexuality in Colonial Mexico, 1530–1821," Ph.D. diss., University of California, Los Angeles, 2010.

60. The exception makes the rule: in a study of 123 reports of sodomy committed in 1657–58, 14 died at the stake, one was condemned to forced labor, 9 were under trial, and 99 were sought by the authorities. Grunzinski, "Las cenizas del deseo."

61. See, for example, Giraud, "La reacción social ante la violación," 337; María González del Refugio, "La administración de justicia," in *El gobierno provincial en la Nueva España, 1570–1787* (Mexico City: Universidad Nacional Autónoma de México, 1985), 101–2.

62. There were farmers, mule drivers, shoemakers, bakers, etc. See Lozano Armendares, *Criminalidad en la ciudad de México,* 352–60.

63. Carmen Castañeda, "Historia de la sexualidad: Investigaciones del periodo colonial," in *Sexualidades en México. Algunas aproximaciones desde la perspectiva de las ciencias sociales,* ed. Ivonne Szasz and Susana Lerner (Mexico City: El Colegio de México, 1998), 277.

Epilogue

Unnatural Sex?

Pete Sigal

Twenty-five years ago, when I first decided to work on colonial Latin America, I took a trip to the local Church of Latter Day Saints in Los Angeles to see if I could engage in some genealogical work related to the Maya of Yucatán. I found some microfilm that had birth and marriage records of the Maya from one parish. Among the first things that I noticed was the term *hijo natural*, meaning a child born out of wedlock. At first glance it appeared that there were more *hijos* and *hijas naturales* than *hijos* and *hijas legítimas*, or "legitimate" sons and daughters. Immediately recognizing that this must mean something about the ubiquity of "illegitimate" children, I dutifully ignored the discursive and performative work the term for nature accomplished.

Within the next few months I had read Asunción Lavrin's 1989 collection *Sexuality and Marriage in Colonial Latin America*, along with another collection produced by a group of scholars in Mexico City, *El placer de pecar y el afán de normar.*[1] From these works I discovered that a large number of colonial Latin American children were born from parents outside the bonds of Christian marriage, and that indeed throughout Latin America and Spain baptismal records coded these children as *hijos naturales.*[2] Inspired by these works and by scholars who had begun studying sexuality in a rigorously theoretical manner that would soon come to be termed queer theory, I began a quest to analyze sexuality in colonial Latin America in a way that would not limit me to the quantitative studies then produced by demographers and social historians.

The following summer I went to Mérida and Mexico City, where I found a few documents that discussed something called the *pecado contra natura*, the "sin against nature," alternatively called the *pecado nefando*, "nefarious sin." As these documents seemed to refer to anal intercourse among men, I assumed that I had discovered what the term *nature* meant here, and that it fit quite well into Thomas Aquinas's notion of natural law. Only years later would I think about how those documents that I had seen in Los Angeles (and similar documents I found in the church archives in Mérida) related to the concept of nature in the discursive framework of sin. Why would illegitimate children be deemed *natural?* Weren't these children born through the sins of the parents—engaging in sexual activity outside the bonds of marriage? Was this some perverse conceptualization in which legitimate children, born to parents who were married in the eyes of the Catholic Church, were unnatural? How would Aquinas's conception of natural law fit into this? Because these rather odd (some would even say absurd) questions still resonate with me, when I was asked to contribute an epilogue to a volume on unnatural sexuality in colonial Latin America, I jumped at the chance to see how others came to terms with the struggles that colonial Latin Americans had developed around the ever changing notions of the natural and the unnatural.

The puzzling notion of nature is paired in this volume with another term fraught with conceptual difficulties: sexuality. How could one define these two terms in tandem, nature and its converse, the unnatural, along with sexuality? What is sexuality in this context? What is natural sex? And how can sexuality, something so linked with desire—seen in most contexts as very natural (even by those linking sexuality with original sin)—be deemed unnatural? In order to deal with these concepts, the authors here have focused, with incest the one exception, on sexual acts beyond procreation.[3] Yet even incest had the potential to be "unnatural," especially when enacted between individuals with a close degree of consanguinity or when a family member sexually assaulted a prepubescent girl who was biologically unable to become pregnant. Thus we find those sexual acts between individuals of the same sex, between people and supernatural beings, and between humans and animals, in addition to masturbation and other forms of autoeroticism and anal sex between men and women. Theoretically, to link unnatural sex with nonprocreative sex suggests a connection between sex for the sake of pleasure (or desire) and the unnatural. As Tortorici notes, such a linkage is too simplistic and does not allow for the significant debate around nature that took place during the colonial years—a debate encouraged both by Aquinas's conception of natural law (largely accepted and implemented by the clergy and other educated elites, but itself contradictory and up for extensive debate) and by the commonsense logic applied to the natural and to sexual activity by all of the non-elite individuals who came from a variety of ethnic, national, familial, and socioeconomic backgrounds. I further argue that the case of the *hijos* and *hijas naturales* suggests a link between natural sex and the unsanctified female body, a body laced with multiple levels of interpretation despite significant ignorance on the part of men (and all of the jurists, theologians, and judicial authorities discussed are men) as to the nature of women's corporeal practices.[4]

DEBATING NATURAL LAW IN COLONIAL
LATIN AMERICA

Aquinas conceived of natural law as a logical application of theological principles. He argued that humans have the ability to engage in reason, and that they should follow such reason in order to develop good in the world, as opposed to evil. People will follow human nature and God's will only by acting for the betterment of humanity and avoiding selfish acts.[5] By focusing on the rationality of humans, Aquinas makes certain arguments regarding sexual behaviors: It is rational for people to want humanity to continue, and thus they should desire to reproduce. It is selfish to want to engage in acts solely for the pleasure of the individual, and thus nonprocreative sexual acts defy human nature. Hence sodomy, bestiality, and masturbation, within this logic, become unnatural. Other sexual acts, including incest and rape, also become unnatural to some extent because they violate the order of charity and the ability for the human community to survive without excessive conflict.[6]

While on one level such natural philosophy is self-evident, Aquinas's conceptualization of nature also led to significant debate in the medieval and early modern Catholic worlds. After all, if human reason led to natural law and individuals could justify their reasons for engaging in a wide variety of acts in ways that were not selfish, wouldn't those humans then be following natural law? In colonial Latin America clerics debated these concepts, particularly focusing on the manner in which the indigenous populations engaged in acts deemed natural or unnatural.[7] Motolinia (Toribio de Benavente) and Andrés de Olmos, both Franciscan friars writing in the sixteenth century, developed close analyses of the Nahua population of central Mexico. Both authors deemed the Nahuas in need of correction and instruction, but they differed on their conclusions regarding the indigenous population's relationship with nature. Motolinia determined that while demonic forces had tricked the Nahuas into performing sacrificial acts, as a whole the population followed natural law.[8] Olmos, in contrast, argued that the Nahuas' failure to understand natural law had led to a series of crises in their history. Further, to Olmos, the Spanish conquest gave the Franciscans an opportunity to guide the Nahuas in the appropriate version of human nature to serve the Christian God.[9]

In the introduction to the present volume, Zeb Tortorici, admitting the importance of Aquinas, shows the complexity of conceptualizing nature. Tortorici shows that colonial Latin Americans struggled with the concept of "nature," pointing to an early medical treatise, published in 1595, in which Alonso López de Hinojosos states that "Nature is an *artifice*—cunning, clever, and occasionally insincere and deceptive, insofar as that which is natural gives rise to that which is unnatural, using Nature's materials and sustained by Nature's processes."[10] Nature as an artifice sounds like a postmodern concept, but Tortorici is correct in asserting that this notion was present in sixteenth-century Christian thought on the topic. The devil could trick an individual into deeming that the unnatural is natural. Take, for example, a 1775 Inquisition case that Tortorici notes elsewhere, in which Manuel Arroyo convinces José Antonio de la Peña that Arroyo must suck the semen out of de la Peña's penis in order to cure that man of a disease that had caused pustules around his genitals. Arroyo further argues that the act is not sinful.[11] In asserting the performance of the cure, Arroyo develops a logic about charity and natural law. This logic flows from Thomist thoughts about reason, but of course is deemed incorrect and unnatural by the inquisitors. The artifice of nature had made something unnatural seem momentarily natural.

This concept of artifice links closely with the idea that only an educated intermediary can determine natural law. Such a conceptualization thus invested clerics, inquisitors, and magistrates with authority and power. Only religious discourse could determine the distinction between the natural and the unnatural. Ronaldo Vainfas and Tortorici in particular make this point—the Portuguese Inquisition, in their view, closely linked sodomy, including sexual activity between women, with heresy. Vainfas and Tortorici argue that the Inquisition assimilated sodomy with heresy, rather than identifying it directly with heretical acts.[12] In other words, sodomy was not defined as heresy, but in practice, because of its association with the unnatural, sodomy came to be treated like heresy and was adjudicated by a tribunal of faith in Portugal and its colonies, including Brazil. This association between sodomy and heresy of course is complicated by the fact that in much of the Spanish kingdom and its colonies (though not all), it was secular authorities, not the Inquisition, who primarily punished individuals for sodomy.

However, the essays in this volume provide evidence that in colonial Spanish America, Spaniards most often prosecuted sodomy as an act that stemmed from a violation of nature. Fernanda Molina shows that, in Andean cases, magistrates and witnesses categorized emotions between men as unnatural and as evidence of sodomy. Both officials and the public at large found unmarried men of an age where they should be married suspicious—the fact that they remained unmarried raised questions about their adherence to the laws of nature. The unnatural here also extends to men who dressed in women's clothes and to men who engaged in cross-class, cross-ethnic relationships with other men. Molina finds evidence of a sodomitical subculture in colonial Peru, one in which men, with the self-identity of *putos*, could find one another in order to engage in emotionally important sexual relationships—which were seen by society and by the judicial authorities as unnatural.[13]

In the discursive frame of natural law, bestiality and sodomy were placed side by side as the two key *contra natura* acts. Mílada Bazant, however, in agreement with Zeb Tortorici's earlier work, shows that bestiality was largely a rural crime committed most often by people who labeled themselves as ignorant or intoxicated (obviously a defense strategy, but one that must be taken seriously). These individuals claimed to be inflamed with desire and without other options to meet their desires.

In other words, nature had inflamed them. Hence, the individuals accused of bestiality participated in a lively debate about nature: they presumed their acts natural, at least within their states of ignorance and intoxication. And it appears that judicial authorities agreed to a certain extent. While they termed bestiality a violation of nature, few cases in the late colonial and early national periods warranted significant punishment, although Tortorici has documented a few rare eighteenth-century cases of men being executed for the crime of bestiality in New Spain.[14]

Further complicating the religious notion of natural sex was the place of the devil within Catholic theology. Jacqueline Holler, for example, shows that sex with the devil was in certain ways one of the most unnatural acts known to humans, but it also could present for women the opportunity for a better sexual relationship than the natural relations they engaged in with their boyfriends and husbands. In fact, in many of Holler's cases, the unnatural (sex with the devil, a supernatural being) became natural (as the devil transformed himself into a human male, often some male to whom the woman had expressed—in her discussions with the devil—an attraction). Indeed, in Christian notions of the devil popular in colonial Spanish America, he could transform himself into an animal, a human, or a supernatural being.[15] If the women engaged in sexual activity with the devil in supernatural or animal form, their sex would be unnatural, but having sex with him when he was a human male meant that they engaged in natural (if sinful) sexual activity. As we shall see, the inquisitors thought differently, though not in the way we might imagine.

Adding to the conceptual questions regarding nature is the position of the female body. After all, *hijos naturales* come from a conception of natural sex as vaginal intercourse. Vainfas and Tortorici note that inquisitors had great difficulty determining whether a woman could engage in sodomy with another woman. The key question has to do with the woman's body: if her body does not have a penis, then, unless one woman uses a dildo, she cannot penetrate either the vagina or the "posterior vessel" of other women. And even then, if she does not penetrate the anus, she has not committed sodomy. Still, inquisitors arbitrarily asserted this rule, sometimes prosecuting women for sodomy when no evidence of anal penetration existed. Similarly, in late colonial Quito, Chad Black shows that there was significant discursive confusion regarding women's sexual acts with each other. Manuela Palis and Josefa Lara were initially charged with sodomy, but the case never again mentions this concept. The cover page of the case file refers to *incestuoso concubinato*, "incestuous concubinage," while the case narrative refers to *amistad ilícita*, an "illicit friendship." A friendship bent toward the illicit is about as far as the magistrates can get in their understanding of the female body and its relationship to sexuality without men. However, the archivist, in compiling the cover page, finds that he can somehow determine that the two were engaged in incestuous concubinage. Penetrational ambiguity, as these and other cases show, abounds in the colonial archive! In the testimony regarding both this case and another cited by Black, the evidence given against the women involves them engaging in activity that was not considered properly feminine: drinking together, engaging in jealous fits of violence, and supporting each other economically. The magistrates cannot, however, come to a determination because they cannot comprehend the role of the female body in sexual activity with other women.[16]

Incest cases provide further evidence of confusion regarding the notion of nature. Lee Penyak's chapter on incest is in certain senses a provocative outlier in this volume. After all, this is the one case where we have acts that not only can lead to procreation, but also in which pregnancy is often a defining marker—for that is the way many incestuous couples get caught. Penyak shows, however, that some conceptualizations of natural law in late colonial and early national Mexico considered incest unnatural, partly because of the possibility of monstrous birth and partly because sex with a prepubescent girl was typically nonprocreative, but also because the Church had forbidden these acts as specifically unnatural. Saint Augustine argued that marriage and sex should solidify friendships beyond the incestuous grouping, while Aquinas said that incest by persons related by blood violates natural reason. We can follow the Thomist argument quite easily: if one is to think about the human community as some sort of collective, incestuous relations, particularly if the participants are too closely related (e.g. father/daughter), will result in offspring that do not foment connections between a variety of different families and instead will make the individual family more insular. Thus incest can be an example of selfish behavior, not unlike the other "selfish" behaviors and sexual acts that were pleasurable but did not result in procreation.

However, Penyak argues that for individuals in late colonial and early national Mexico, marrying your social inferior was somehow much more unnatural than marrying your cousin. Socioeconomic (and ethnic) status here comes into the discussion of the relationship between nature and sex: the unnatural sexual behavior could be deemed secondary to unnatural social mixing. Similarly, regarding rape, Penyak notes some acceptance of such violence. In the case of incest-rape, the authorities and the community appear to have been inconsistent, sometimes treating these events as unnatural and at other times arguing that fathers need to have absolute authority in the household.[17]

We see, then, an intensive debate during the colonial period, and this volume represents the different arguments regarding the natural and the unnatural. While Christian religious authorities clearly defined sodomy, bestiality, and masturbation as unnatural, various individuals contested that definition through their actions. This performative argumentation found enough reception that communities appear to have tolerated some acts deemed unnatural by the Church and secular authorities. Further, when individuals engaged in sexual acts with supernatural beings (or fantasized about them in autoerotic ways), they determined manners of naturalizing those sexual acts. This naturalization of sexual behavior could have stemmed partly from a misreading of the female body and partly from debates regarding social mixture. Most pertinently, early modern notions of desire developed into certain commonsense notions of nature, and it is to this desire that I now turn.

THE NATURE OF DESIRE

Desire in the post-Freudian universe is a topic fraught with concepts of repression and libido, but many authors in this volume have used the concept in a different manner.[18] Indeed, the writings of clerics, the cases placed in front of the Inquisition, and the information we have about everyday life in colonial Latin America all point to the idea that desire played a major role. Franciscan friar Bernardino de Sahagún, in one of his Nahuatl sermons, expresses his concept of desire: "You black one, you dirty one: you please your body with filthy happiness. Because of your filthy happiness you harm the heart of our lord. And with your spouse you do that which should not be done. You make him black and dirty. You touch things for him and you make him touch things for you. Thus you sin and you cast him into sin, you malign God, who prohibits you from filthy happiness because of its wickedness."[19] For Sahagún, Nahua individuals, despite prohibitions, desire sexual activity that exceeds what is permissible for married partners: their desires appear in this example to overwhelm them, and they then engage in sinful activity that Sahagún elsewhere declares unnatural. Sahagún's preaching was not unique here: excess desire partly determined the very contours of the historical record—individuals accused of many acts that we would deem sexual often gave desire, through its excess, as the reason that the archived acts took place.

Excess desire also forms the backbone of the case against Esteban Sobrino, the friar from Cartagena who is the subject of Nicole von Germeten's chapter. He, too, is overcome with his desires—desires that unwittingly thrust him into the files of the colonial archive. For Sobrino, sexual desires were natural, and he could not repress them. Sobrino suggested to inquisitors that his desire for both women and men conformed with his understanding of nature. The inquisitor who questioned him and drove Sobrino to suicide was perplexed by Sobrino's conception of natural and unnatural desires. For Sobrino, however, the fact that he wanted to engage in vaginal intercourse with women suggested that he had natural desires. When his superiors found that he had violated the confessional with women, they restricted him to confessing men and boys. When he later admitted to touching boys, he claimed nature as an excuse—deprived of access to women, he had natural desires that he needed to express, but he did not go so far as to commit sodomy (a claim contradicted by witnesses).[20] Sobrino conceived of desire as something internal to his body, something that he needed to express: he could not contain this desire, despite his efforts to do so. Instead, deprived of women, he needed to have human contact, so he touched other men.

María Getrudis Arévalo in eighteenth-century Mexico also had significant bodily desires that she expressed through her use of sacred objects to satisfy her bodily needs. Here we need to take her expression of desire at face value. As Nora Jaffary shows, Arévalo desires proof of the existence of God in the presence of the poverty she sees around her. She thus puts God to the test by placing various sanctified items inside her vagina, which she terms her "filthy vessel." In a modern world influenced by psychoanalytic theory, we might envision Arévalo as a woman who has repressed her sexual needs and has become instead an insane masturbator. Yet, we would base such a conclusion on an ethnopornographic logic in which we assert the presence of the hysterical woman—the one who cannot become sexually satisfied through "normal" sex, but instead masturbates to what she knows: sacred objects. Such a logic envisions Arévalo, within our own framework, as sexually "repressed." We place this framework upon Arévalo's body, through the gaze of post-Freudian Western eyes, without paying enough attention to her local circumstances and her religious leanings.[21]

While we cannot be sure, Arévalo appears to conceive of herself as one who desires a closer embodied connection to her deity. For the inquisitors, however, she is a poor woman in need of pity and charity, who perhaps is a bit simple and sickly: she does not understand the distinction between the natural and the unnatural any more than she understands the distinction between religious observation and heresy. The inquisitors themselves fail to comprehend the female body, using the concept of religious error to veil what they do not understand. And here her sexual acts (we may, perhaps, call these acts masturbation, though they remain unnamed in the text) are not the key component—rather, these acts signify a desire to question religious authority and to put an end to poverty. And the inquisitors simply do not know what to do with her, except to suggest that her desires stem from some medicalized mental defect.[22]

Returning to Holler's cases of women who engaged in sexual activity with the devil, the inquisitors tended to naturalize the women's copulation with the devil by suggesting medical explanations for the acts confessed to them—in particular, these inquisitors focused on these women's melancholy.[23] Holler points most prominently to the contested boundary between the natural and the unnatural. In seventeenth-century Mexico, inquisitors and those accused had different concepts of this boundary-making process. The accused tended to argue that the devil could take the form of a very natural lover—a man—while the inquisitors argued that the women were using this conceptualization to deal with medical and social problems. Hence their life situations were natural, even if their imaginations tended to the unnatural. This concept of mental illness as tied to excesses of desire appears to have loomed large in the minds of the inquisitors, who did not want to suggest that these women had engaged in any powerful demonic pacts.

The mental illnesses mentioned here in some ways fit into psychoanalytic theory. Freudian psychoanalysis speaks extensively about the suppression of one's desires causing mental anguish, even melancholy.[24] Sobrino's inability to suppress his desires would make sense to an analyst, who might also diagnose Arévalo's use of sacred objects in masturbation as a case of hysteria and/or fetishism. However, within psychoanalysis human nature stems from sexual repression, while these cases suggest much more about the relationship between nature and religious ritual—with sexual acts becoming a way to express suppressed desires that are fundamentally religious.[25]

The Enlightenment will change this notion of desire. Pre-Enlightenment thinkers had already, in the seventeenth-century cases, begun to influence the inquisitorial concepts of desire and mentality. These changing conceptions of desire would become more profound during the Enlightenment. In Martín Bowen Silva's essay, the early-nineteenth-century confession of José Ignacio Eyzaguirre in Chile points to the centrality of desire and repression—concepts that would become key for Freud a hundred years later.[26] Eyzaguirre, an elite and politically connected Chilean man, wants to stress the importance of his childhood sexual development. He does this through the confessional genre as an attempt to make sense of his unnatural youthful desires. In this, we see Eyzaguirre narrating his adolescence from the perspective of a man in his early twenties. He narrates a story of guilt and shame, along with a particular understanding of the way his body relates to the unnatural. Adolescent sexuality becomes a quest to deal with same-sex attraction and desire. Eyzaguirre's confession in many senses challenges the distinction between the natural and the unnatural. For example, when he places a lit cigar on his penis or when he watches his penis becoming more erect to see how it pulls back the foreskin by itself, he suggests a natural youthful experimentation with his own body. He explores that body to try to understand the nature and enactment of desire.

Yet in the very act of confession, he acknowledges this bodily exploration as something that the Church would have deemed *contra natura*. And this extends to what we would perhaps understand as sexual acts: the child wants to find out what it is like for a woman to have sex, so he inserts his finger into his own rectum—which excites him. He then extends this knowledge by asking slave children more about sex and, through experimentation, by touching his brother's penis. Finally, going to a seminary school, a seminarian shows him how to ejaculate.

In his confession, Eyzaguirre shows that his adolescent self had unquenchable desires expressed through his body. One wonders if we could not use Freudian techniques to psychoanalyze Eyzaguirre. This very notion suggests that we need to engage in more research on early modern concepts of desire and pleasure. For I cannot imagine providing a Freudian analysis for Sahagún's sixteenth-century

Nahua parishioners, invested though they were (perhaps) in "filthy happiness." Nor can I conceive of a Freudian analysis of María Getrudis Arévalo. After all, she did not appear to repress her sexual desires; instead she expressed her sexual desires in order to repress her questioning of religious authority. Desire changed from the sixteenth century to the nineteenth.

Similarly, what we in the modern Western world express as sexuality had appeared by the nineteenth century, at least in the world of the wealthy. We no longer envision sex with devils turning into human form, but we delve into a confessional genre where sexuality becomes equated with notions of the self. This is indeed the change that Michel Foucault argued took place: pre-Enlightenment notions of sex relate to sin, nature, and other elements of spirituality, while post-Enlightenment sex becomes an internalized notion of the self and the subject.[27]

Returning to the *hijo natural*, we find that nature is linked with a particular sexual act (vaginal intercourse) connected with parts of the female body—parts that become sanctified only through marriage. This formulation, however, becomes extremely complex when linked with ignorance as to the nature of female sexuality. Unnatural sex will of course face greater challenges as the Enlightenment prevails and modern notions of desire become the driving forces. I see this volume as an excellent foray in which the authors challenge the terms by which we understand sexuality. Tortorici and the other contributors obliterate the binary of natural versus unnatural sex by representing religious discourse and showing the ways in which such discourse has a particular contested historical narrative. Others now must take this volume and move forward to develop a historically specific and rigorously theoretical analysis of sexual pleasure in the colonial past.

NOTES

1. Asunción Lavrin, ed., *Sexuality and Marriage in Colonial Latin America* (Lincoln: University of Nebraska Press, 1989); Seminario de Historia de las Mentalidades, *El placer de pecar y el afán de normar* (Mexico City: Instituto Nacional de Antropología e Historia, 1988).

2. See particularly Asunción Lavrin, "Sexuality in Colonial Mexico: A Church Dilemma," in Lavrin (ed.), *Sexuality and Marriage*.

3. Incest seems to be the exception in the volume: an act that could and often did lead to procreation. Of course, in cases that involved prepubescent girls, this act could not lead to procreation. See Penyak, "Incestuous Naures: Consensual and Forced Relations in Mexico, 1740–1854," this volume.

4. This ignorance existed despite an intense interest in late medieval and early modern times in the dead female body, dissected and examined to the minute detail for scientific and religious purposes. See Katharine Park, *Secrets of Women: Gender, Generation, and the Origins of Human Dissection* (New York: Zone Books, 2010).

5. See *Summa Theologica*, Pt. I-II, Q94.

6. Ibid., Pt. II-II, Q154.

7. Nahua notions of nature were significantly different from Spanish notions. See Alfredo López Austin, *Cuerpo humano e ideología: Las concepciones de los antiguos Nahuas* (Mexico City: Universidad

Nacional Autónoma de México, 1980); James Maffie, *Aztec Philosophy: Understanding a World in Motion* (Boulder: University Press of Colorado, 2014).

8. Motolinia, *Memoriales, o libro de las cosas de Nueva España y de los naturals de ella*, ed. Edmundo O'Gorman (Mexico City: Universidad Autónoma de México, 1971).

9. Andrés de Olmos, *Tratado de hechicerias y sortilegios*, ed. Georges Baudot (Mexico City: Universidad Nacional Autónoma de México, 1990).

10. Tortorici, "Unnatural Bodies, Desires, and Devotions," this volume.

11. Tortorici, "Visceral Archives of the Body: Consuming the Dead, Digesting the Divine," *GLQ: A Journal of Lesbian and Gay Studies* 20, no. 4 (2014): 407–37.

12. Vainfas and Tortorici, "Female Homoeroticism, Heresy, and the Holy Office in Colonial Brazil," this volume. See also Vainfas, *Trópico dos pecados: Moral, sexualidade e Inquisição no Brasil* (Rio de Janeiro: Editora Nova Fronteira, 1997).

13. Molina, "Sodomy, Gender, and Identity in the Viceroyalty of Peru," this volume. One can note certain methodological problems in the assertion of *puto* self-identity here. Molina only has access to juridical documents, and thus to juridical identities. One could argue, for example, that the assertion of a *puto* identity was an effort among certain men to make their lives legible to a court and not to assert an internalized notion of self. For more information on sodomitical subcultures in colonial Latin America, see Zeb Tortorici, "'Heran todos putos': Sodomitical Subcultures and Disordered Desire in Early Colonial Mexico," *Ethnohistory* 54, no. 1 (2007): 35–67.

14. Bazant, "Bestiality: The Nefarious Crime in Mexico, 1800–1856," this volume. See Zeb Tortorici, "Contra Natura: Sin, Crime, and 'Unnatural' Sexuality in Colonial Mexico, 1530–1821," Ph.D. diss., University of California, Los Angeles, 2010.

15. See Fernando Cervantes, *The Devil in the New World: The Impact of Diabolism in New Spain* (New Haven, Conn.: Yale University Press, 1994).

16. Black, "Prosecuting Female-Female Sex in Bourbon Quito," this volume. We should also note Black's important argument that the cases do not appear to assert a gender binary. In other words, we would expect from some historical sources that the only way for these women to understand their sexual activity would be for one to play the masculine role and the other to play the feminine role. Yet we see none of this type of gender binarism presented in the case files.

17. Penyak, "Incestuous Natures: Consensual and Forced Relations in Mexico, 1740–1854," this volume..

18. See Sigmund Freud, *Introductory Lectures on Psychoanalysis* (New York: Norton, 1966), particularly "Resistance and Repression" and the "Sexual Lives of Human Beings."

19. "Auh in tevatl in titliltic y ticatzavac in tlaelpaquiliztica ticpaquiltia monacayo, ipamapa y motlaelpaquiliz ticmoyolitlacalhuia in t° auh y monamic ytech ticchiva in achivaloni yva ticchivaltia in tliltic, i catzavac, tictlamatoq'lia yva ticcuitlaviltia inic mitztlamatoq'liz, etc. ic titlatlacoa yva tlatllacolli ypan titlaça, ticmotelchivilia in dios y mitzcavaltia tlaelpaquiliztli in ipampa ca tlavelilocayotl." Newberry Library, Ayer MS 1485, fol. 18–18v.

20. Von Germeten, "Archival Narratives of Clerical Sodomy and Suicide from Eighteenth-Century Cartagena," this volume.

21. On the possibilities and limitations of Freudian notions of hysteria, see particularly Jacques Lacan, *The Seminar of Jacques Lacan, Book XVII: The Other Side of Psychoanalysis* (New York: Norton, 2007). On the application of Freud to Mexican examples, see Rubén Gallo, *Freud's Mexico: Into the Wilds of Psychoanalysis* (Cambridge, Mass.: MIT Press, 2010).

22. Jaffary, "Sacred Defiance and Sexual Desecration: María Getrudis Arévalo and the Holy Office in Eighteenth-Century Mexico," this volume.

23. Holler, "The Devil or Nature Itself? Desire, Doubt, and Diabolical Sex among Colonial Mexican Women," this volume.

24. See Sigmund Freud, *Psychopathology of Everyday Life* (New York: New American Library, 1951).

25. I argue that we cannot psychoanalyze individuals or social groups from colonial Latin America (at least not until the eighteenth century). However, I also argue that we can use psychoanalysis as a theory to understand significant elements in textual production. We can, for example, use Jacques Lacan's theories to discuss the phallic investitures of particular images in the colonial past. This does not mean that we can psychoanalyze those who produced the images. See Pete Sigal, *The Flower and the Scorpion: Sexuality and Ritual in Early Nahua Culture* (Durham: Duke University Press, 2011).

26. Bowen Silva, "Experimenting with Nature: José Ignacio Eyzaguirre's *General Confession* and the Knowledge of the Body (1799–1804)," this volume.

27. Michel Foucault, *The History of Sexuality*, Vol. 1: *An Introduction* (New York: Vintage Books, 1978).

CONTRIBUTORS

MÍLADA BAZANT is Professor of History and researcher at El Colegio Mexiquense. Her main areas of interest are the history of education in Porfirian Mexico, everyday life in the nineteenth century, and biographies. She has published several books on these topics, the most recent of which is *Laura Méndez de Cuenca: Mujer indómita y moderna, 1853–1928*.

CHAD THOMAS BLACK is Associate Professor of History at the University of Tennesse. His scholarly focus is on the connections between law, governance, and gendered social authority. He is the author of *The Limits of Gender Domination: Women, the Law, and Political Crisis in Quito, 1765–1830*, and is currently working on a project on sex and criminality in Quito under the Bourbons.

MARTÍN BOWEN SILVA is Assistant Professor of History at New York University–Abu Dhabi. He is the author of *Experimentar el cuerpo y escribir los pecados: La confesión general de José Ignacio Eyzaguirre (1799–1804)*. His current book project explores the relationship between communication and politics in Chile during the Age of Revolution.

NICOLE VON GERMETEN is Professor of History at Oregon State University. She has published three books and numerous articles on race, religion, honor, sexuality, and violence. Her most recent book is *Violent Delights, Violent Ends: Sex, Honor, and Witchcraft in Colonial Colombia*, and she is currently investigating transactional sex, gender, and the law in the Spanish viceroyalties.

JACQUELINE HOLLER is Associate Professor of History and Women's and Gender Studies at the University of Northern British Columbia. She is author of *Escogidas Plantas: Nuns and Beatas in Mexico City, 1531–1601* and articles and chapters on early colonial New Spain; she has also co-authored texts in Latin American history and gender studies.

NORA E. JAFFARY is Associate Professor of History at Concordia University. She is the author of *False Mystics: Deviant Orthodoxy in Colonial Mexico* and recently published

"Reconceiving Motherhood: Infanticide and Abortion in Colonial Mexico" in *the Journal of Family History*. She is completing a book manuscript entitled *Reproduction and Its Discontents: A History of Childbirth and Contraception in Mexico, 1750–1905*.

ASUNCIÓN LAVRIN, Professor Emerita at Arizona State University, writes on colonial women, gender, and sexuality, as well as on early-twentieth-century women and feminism. She has published numerous articles and book chapters on these topics. Among her publications are *Brides of Christ: Conventual Life in Colonial Mexico; Women, Feminism, and Social Change: Argentina, Chile, and Uruguay, 1890–1940*; and *Diálogos espirituales: Letras femeninas Hispanoamericanas, Siglos XVI–XIX*, coedited with Rosalva Loreto.

FERNANDA MOLINA is Assistant Professor at the Universidad de Buenos Aires and a researcher at Argentina's Consejo Nacional de Investigaciones Científicas y Técnicas (CONICET). She has published numerous articles on marriage, gender, and sexual transgression in the Viceroyalty of Peru. Her current research focuses on the social representations, medical discourse, judicial practice, and construction of identity around sodomy, transvestism, and hermaphroditism in the sixteenth- and seventeenth-century Iberian Atlantic world.

LEE M. PENYAK, Professor of History and member of Latin American Studies and Women's Studies at the University of Scranton, has published articles on female confinement (*Hispanic American Historical Review*), the professionalization of obstetric medicine (*The Americas*), spousal abuse (*The Historian*), male same-sex attraction (*Colonial Latin American Historical Review*), and prohibited artworks in Mexico (*Colonial Latin American Review*), among other subjects. Additional research interests include the church and state and the hacienda complex, culminating in three edited books on these topics.

PETE SIGAL is Professor of History at Duke University, with specializations in Latin American history and the history of sexuality. His books include *From Moon Goddesses to Virgins: The Colonization of Yucatecan Maya Sexual Desire* and the anthology *Infamous Desire: Male Homosexuality in Colonial Latin America*. He recently published a study on the interaction of writing and sexual representation in sixteenth- and seventeenth-century indigenous Nahua societies of Mexico, *The Flower and the Scorpion: Sexuality and Ritual in Early Nahua Culture*.

ZEB TORTORICI is Assistant Professor in the Department of Spanish and Portuguese Language and Literatures at New York University. With Martha Few he recently coedited *Centering Animals in Latin American History*, and with Daniel Marshall and Kevin P. Murphy he coedited two special issues of *Radical History Review* on the topic of "Queering Archives." He is completing a book project titled *Sins against Nature: Sex and Archives in Colonial New Spain, 1530–1821*.

RONALDO VAINFAS is Professor of History at the Universidade Federal Fluminense, Brazil. He is author of several books and articles on colonial Brazil, Indian riots, the Portuguese Inquisition, and historical methodologies. His most recent books include *Jerusalém colonial: Judeus portugueses no Brasil holandês* and *Antônio Vieira: Jesuíta do rei*. Vainfas's now classic *Trópico dos pecados* (1989) analyzes patriarchy, misogyny, sexuality, and mentalities in colonial Brazil.

INDEX

Italic page numbers indicate figures and tables.